The Antifederalists

THE AMERICAN HERITAGE SERIES

THE

American Heritage

Series

UNDER THE GENERAL EDITORSHIP OF

LEONARD W. LEVY AND ALFRED YOUNG

The Antifederalists

EDITED BY

CECELIA M. KENYON

Smith College

THE BOBBS - MERRILL COMPANY, INC.

INDIANAPOLIS

The Bobbs-Merrill Company, Inc.
4300 West 62nd Street
Indianapolis, Indiana 46268

First Edition
Fifth Printing—1976

Designed by Stefan Salter Associates

Library of Congress Catalog Card Number: 65-23008
ISBN 0-672-60052-8 (pbk.)

The Antifederalists

FOREWORD

The Antifederalists, sufficiently popular in 1787–88 to come close to defeating the Constitution in the conflict over ratification, have had a poor reputation among later generations. One reason for this is the fact that they were the losers. Another is because their "states' rights" philosophy—actually only one strand of their thought—became identified in the nineteenth century with slavery and in the twentieth century with the defense of vested property interests. And a third is, no doubt, because they produced no single work to match *The Federalist* essays: as critics of the Constitution, the thrust of their thought was largely negative.

Yet surely they deserve better of posterity. Because so large a proportion of the American people were Antifederalists, as Professor Kenyon has pointed out, "a knowledge of their ideas and attitudes is essential to an understanding of American political thought in the formative years of the republic."

Antifederalist writings have been available only in libraries owning either the contemporary pamphlets and newspapers, the two volumes of pamphlets published by Paul Leicester Ford in 1888, or the five volumes of Jonathan Elliot's rendering of the debates in the state ratifying conventions. Professor Kenyon's anthology reprints generous excerpts from these rare pamphlets, debates, and newspaper articles, many of the latter for the first time. Until the National Historical Manuscripts Commission, under the direction of Robert Cushman, brings out the complete documentary record of the ratification controversy, this volume can serve as a rich, representative sampling of Antifederalist thought, selected by a political scientist long immersed in the study of eighteenth-century political thought.

In the introduction, Professor Kenyon develops at greater length her thesis about the Antifederalists as "Men of Little Faith" which attracted such attention among scholars. Her selections in this volume will enable readers to test this thesis. Here are the writings of the well known Antifederalists and of the anonymous scribblers. Here are spokesmen for the several wings of the movement—north and south, "aristocratic" and "democratic."

This book is one of a series the aim of which is to provide the essential primary sources of the American experience, especially of American thought. The series, when completed, will constitute a documentary library of American history, filling a need long felt among scholars, students, libraries, and general readers for authoritative collections of original materials. Some volumes will illuminate the thought of significant individuals; some will deal with movements, and others will be organized around special themes. Many volumes will deal with the large number of subjects traditionally studied in American history and for which, surprisingly, there are no documentary anthologies. Others will introduce contemporary subjects of increasing importance to scholars. The series aspires to maintain the high standards demanded of contemporary editing, providing authentic texts, intelligently and unobtrusively edited. It will have also the distinction of presenting pieces of substantial length that give the full character and flavor of the original. The series will be the most comprehensive and authoritative of its kind.

Alfred Young
Leonard W. Levy

CONTENTS

DOCUMENTS

1. The Letters of "Centinel"

1

I. Concerning the influence of great men; criticism of John Adams and defense of unicameralism; the national government will swallow up the state governments; republican government not possible for large territories; freedom of the press and other liberties not secured under the proposed Constitution.

III. The Constitution the work of the well-born, and will destroy equal liberty; the advocates of the constitution engage in improper methods to secure ratification; criticism of Article I, Sections 4, 8, 9.

2. The Address and Reasons of Dissent of the Minority of the Convention of Pennsylvania to their Constituents

27

Review of the general circumstances leading to the Convention that drafted the Constitution; the secrecy and illegality of the latter; criticism of the tactics used by the Pennsylvania Federalists in securing ratification; summary of the minority's views on the Constitution: republican government not possible over an extended area; the proposed national government will be a consolidated one and will destroy the states; representation will not be adequate; the judicial system criticized; relationship of President and Senate violates separation of powers; House of Representatives will tend to be filled by aristocrats; the national government will rest on force, the Constitution providing for a standing army and for Congressional control of state militia.

3. The Letter of "Montezuma"

61

The federal government designed to be an aristocratic tyranny, to destroy the states and subdue the common people to the well-born few.

4. The Letters of "Philadelphiensis"

69

IX. The Constitution the result of an aristocratic conspiracy to establish a despotic monarchy, in which the president will be a king commanding a standing army, supported by the well-born few.

X. The monarchical conspirators who betrayed the hopes and prayers of the people in drafting the Constitution have received a setback; their small margin of victory in Massachusetts may preface civil war, for the people there will never submit to the loss of their liberties.

XI. The people of Pennsylvania, having faithfully paid their share of the public debt, will suffer under the new government by having to assume part of the shares of states which have been delinquent; the new Constitution cannot be supported except by a standing army, which may lead to civil war.

XII. The president an elective king, the most dangerous kind; a new convention should be called, to draft a constitution in accordance with the spirit of the Revolution.

5. The Letters of "John De Witt"

89

I. The American people have managed their public affairs excellently, the present difficulties being a temporary exception caused by extravagances. The proposed Constitution should be examined with great care and in great detail, for it is not perfect, being admittedly the product of compromise.

II. The Constitution should be examined carefully, because once adopted, it will be difficult to amend; the omission of a Bill of Rights; adoption of the Constitution will effect great changes, including the reduction of the state governments to the status of city corporations, and a total dereliction from the sentiments of the Revolution.

III. Some of the advocates of the Constitution are opposed to republican government; the proposed system will become an aristocracy, fatal to the liberty of the people; the Senate, because of the long tenure combined with man's natural lust for power, will be aristocratic, and will be joined by the House, which will be too small to be truly representative, and which will not be subject to annual elections.

6. The Letters of "A Republican Federalist"

111

II. The delegates to the Federal Convention having exceeded their instructions which were to revise the Articles of Confederation, acted without public authority and therefore unconstitutionally; the Constitution, furthermore, should have been submitted to and debated in Congress and the state legislatures before being set before the people.

III. Adoption of the Constitution will mean a dissolution of the government of Massachusetts, or at the very least, an amendment of the state constitution contrary to the procedure provided in that constitution. Therefore, ratification cannot be binding on the citizens of Massachusetts, because it would be unconstitutional.

V. The arguments of previous letters summarized. Inclusion of slaves for the purpose of apportioning representation will eventually, when the states have ceased to exist, mean that a man's vote will be determined by the amount of his property: thus a man worth £ 50,000 will have as many votes as one thousand men worth £ 50 each.

7. *James Winthrop* [?] *The Letters of "Agrippa"*

131

IV. No extensive empire, such as that embraced by the American states, can be governed upon republican principles.

IX. The Articles of Confederation should be amended to give Congress a limited power over foreign affairs, including commerce but not naturalization, the benefits of foreign immigration being doubtful. Giving the central government an unlimited power of taxation, as the proposed Constitution does, will probably check the growth of the country.

XIII. The examples of Carthage and Rome show the stability of republics; the relationship between commerce and liberty; the proposed Constitution is one of unlimited powers: Article III, Section 2, together with the last clause of Article I, Section 8, and Article VI, give the national government power to legislate regarding all causes respecting property. Also the power to regulate internal commerce includes the power to establish monopolies. Rather than adopt the proposed Constitution, the Articles of Confederation should be amended.

XVII. There should have been a Bill of Rights, for according to the general principles of government, the people delegate all powers and rights to their rulers except those explicitly reserved. Thus the federal government will have many more powers than those of the states which, like Massachusetts, do have a Bill of Rights.

XVIII. Concerning the desirability of separation of powers and a Bill of Rights; proposals for amending the Constitution; Massachusetts, a commercial state, would be endangered under the proposed system by the planting states.

8. *A Letter of Luther Martin*

161

An explanation of the author's position at various times during the Federal Convention on the supreme law clause, the federal judiciary, the number of states required for ratification, and a bill of rights; his general posture was one of consistent and sustained opposition to the establishment of a national, consolidated system of government.

9. *Debates in the Legislature and Convention of South Carolina*

177

RAWLINS LOWNDES: Success of the Articles of Confederation; criticism of the great powers of the proposed government, of the method of electing the Senate and the President; fear of the majority of Eastern states; criticism of the tax power; paper money defended; a call for a new convention to consider all the objections expressed to the proposed Constitution, and to take appropriate action.

circumstances leading up to the Federal Convention, which contained too few men of republican sentiments; principal defects of the proposed system stem from its tendency toward complete consolidation and from provision for equal representation of states regardless of size in the Senate.

II. Essential to a free government are a full and equal representation, and trial by jury in the vicinage of the administration of justice, neither of which is feasible under the proposed system. Because of the vast extent of the country, the very great powers delegated to the central government cannot be effectively exercised in the normal way; the laws will either be neglected, or they will be executed by military force, and the result in either event will be revolution and the loss of freedom.

III. The system of representation in the House will operate to produce an aristocratic predominance, and the differences among Eastern, Middle, and Southern states will probably make it unwieldy. The compromises adopted by the Federal Convention in order to reconcile the many different interests and opinions represented there prove the impossibility of constructing a general government on proper principles. The inadvisability of giving such a government the power of internal taxation; the problems and dangers involved in providing for military power; jurisdictional problems between state and federal courts, the uncertainty surrounding trial by jury, and other problems pertaining to the judicial system.

PATRICK HENRY: A discursive, oratorical attack on the Constitution, in which many features are said to jeopardize the liberty of the people.

GEORGE MASON: That the judicial power of the proposed Constitution was probably intended to, and certainly will, destroy the state governments, for it is without any limitations; problems and dangers of federal appellate jurisdictions; effect of federal judicial powers on certain land titles.

WILLIAM GRAYSON: The difficulties and dangers cited by advocates of the Constitution as reasons for ratification grossly exaggerated; delay further experiments in government until the American character is more definite; criticism of the structure of the proposed government; fear of dominance in the federal legislature by a faction of seven states; opposition to the power of taxation given to the national government; impossibility of national taxes that will be both uniform and equitable; problem of the public debt; opposition to commerce and to a navy; potential dangers arising from federal jurisdiction over the ten-mile-square area; difference of interest among the several states with respect to the right of navigation on the Mississippi.

13. *George Clinton, The Letters of "Cato"*

301

IV. The method of election and the great powers of the office render the President exceedingly dangerous; the system will probably tend toward a vile and arbitrary aristocracy or monarchy.

V. The inexplicitness of the Constitution ill-calculated to prevent abuses and usurpations of power; the House of Representatives too small for adequate representations, and the two-year term violative of the principle of annual elections.

VI. Slaves should not be counted in the apportionment of representatives; heavy taxes will result if the Constitution is adopted; the Senate, an aristocratic body, will corrupt or overwhelm the lower House.

VII. The improper connection between the President and Senate; the dangers involved in the Congressional power to regulate the time, manner, and places of federal elections.

14. *Robert Yates, The Letters of "Brutus"*

VI. The state governments will be destroyed, as can be seen by examining the ramifications of the concurrent jurisdiction over taxation to be possessed by the central and state governments. The former's power to tax is unlimited, such terms as general welfare and common defense being too imprecise to afford any genuine restrictions.

XI, XII, XV. Under the Constitution, the Supreme Court will have the power to interpret the Constitution, and therefore it will have the power to decide whether the laws of Congress are in accord with it. The result, among others, will probably be an expansion of the powers of the central government. Because the members of the Court will be independent, serving during good behavior and impeachable only for gross crimes, this great authority of the Court will be exercised in a way that will make it superior to both the Executive and the Legislature. The latter, being accountable to the people, should have the final authority within the government to interpret the fundamental political compact.

15. *A Manifesto of a Number of Gentlemen from Albany County, New York*

Presentation of a slate of candidates for election to the state convention, together with a summary of reasons for opposing the ratification of the proposed Constitution.

of President and Senate too long; the President's veto objected to; dangers related to the appellate jurisdiction of the Supreme Court; power of raising armies criticized; prohibition of religious qualifications for officeholding in the federal government objected to.

INTRODUCTION

The Political Thought of The Antifederalists[1]

I. THE CONTEXT OF
THE DEBATE OVER RATIFICATION

Three days after a copy of the proposed Federal Constitution had arrived and been published in Boston, a thoughtful historian sat down and described its initial reception to a friend in England.

It is now only three days since the publication of the recommendations of this respectable body has appeared in our papers; almost everyone whom I have yet seen reads with attention, folds the paper with solemnity, and silently wraps up his opinions within his own breast, as if afraid of interrupting the calm expectation that has prevailed all ranks for several months past.[2]

It would be pleasant to think that the reaction of sober contemplation recorded by Mercy Otis Warren was typical,

---

[1] Parts of this essay were originally published by *The William and Mary Quarterly*, Third Series, Vol. XII, No. 1, (1955), pp. 3–46, under the title, "Men of Little Faith: The Anti-Federalists on the Nature of Representative Government."

[2] Mercy Otis Warren to Mrs. Catharine Macauley, September 28, 1787. Quoted in Charles Warren, "Elbridge Gerry, James Warren, Mercy Warren and the Ratification of the Federal Constitution in Massachusetts," *Proceedings*, Massachusetts Historical Society, LXIV (March 1931) 143–164, at p. 162. Reprinted with the permission of the Massachusetts Historical Society.

and to visualize all America as caught in a sudden hush of solemn deliberation, the prelude to months of vigorous discussion and rational analysis of the merits of the proposed new system of government. But another image intrudes, for at almost the same time that Mrs. Warren was writing to Mrs. Macauley, Philadelphia was producing a scene of mob action singularly lacking in dignity and decorum. Philadelphia, being the seat of the federal Convention, had received the Constitution a week earlier, and there the lines of opposition had already been drawn. Advocates of the Constitution had a majority within the Pennsylvania legislature, then in the last days of its regular session, and attempted to rush through an action calling for a convention to consider the Constitution. Opponents responded by absenting themselves from the Assembly in order to prevent a quorum and thus block the majority from prevailing. Friends of the Constitution then seized two members of the recalcitrant minority, brought them forcibly onto the floor of the house, and kept them there in order to establish a quorum until the vote had been taken and the call for a convention issued. It was an episode that did little credit to either side in the controversy.

Both reactions, that of the solemn and proper Bostonians and that of the riotous and factious Philadelphians, may be taken as characteristic of the great debate over the Constitution after its submission to the public in September of 1787. For many people, thoughtful like Mercy Warren, it was a solemn occasion. They thought of themselves as involved in a decision that would affect the destiny of this country for unknown generations to come – the phrase, "for millions yet unborn," was a favorite rhetorical flourish, and not necessarily insincere or inaccurate. An awesome responsibility, one that called for – and sometimes called forth – the most resolute exercise of disinterested and rational behavior. But men in politics rarely act without passion or with no motivation other than the considered welfare of their country and their posterity. Neither do they very often effect radical changes in the style and patterns of their politics, nor lightly and easily abandon fixed ideas. The ratification debate was not Chapter One in the book of American politics, and the behavior of both contestants in the Philadelphia incident, though doubtless deplorable, was not unprecedented. Americans were as familiar with backroom politics as with the principles of natural law, and although the Revolution was the very model of a moderate revolution, it had indubitably been preceded and accompanied by a considerable amount of quite unparliamentary politics. Similarly in the course of the ratification debate, one can find evidence of reason and riot, patriotism and propaganda, the most exquisitely sophisticated politics of the cloakroom side by side with the crudest politics of the mob in the street. All this is perhaps as it should be, for this was the first great national debate under an established and operating system of republican governments.[3] It is at least comfortable for posterity's ego to reflect that its illustrious ancestors, for all their great achievements, were not perfectly pure in politics, and that the Constitution was established after a struggle in the course of which both sides engaged in tactics that were not altogether above reproach, though a great deal better than they might have been.

---

[3]It is tempting to speculate on the extent to which *The Federalist Papers* set, not the spirit and style of the controversy, but the way in which the latter has been viewed by later historians. *The Federalist* is frequently the first source read, and because it maintains a high level of rational discourse, it seems to lead to an unconscious assumption that it typifies the behavior of both sides, and this in turn produces a sense of shock when it is subsequently discovered that the debate was not always fought on such a lofty level. The Federalists have usually borne the brunt of the resultant criticism, perhaps because the techniques of the losers have not been examined with the same scrutiny directed at the victors.

Consideration of the institutional and ideological setting of the ratification debate, as well as a survey of immediate social, political, and economic factors, is essential to an understanding of the ideas and attitudes of those who opposed the Constitution of 1787.

1)

The most important element in the situation, and the one so obvious as sometimes to be overlooked, was the recent achievement of independence and the establishment of republican governments. Although neither involved an absolute and total break with the past, both brought important changes in the function, operation, and structure of government, and in fundamental attitudes toward politics. Under their colonial charters, the Americans had enjoyed a very considerable degree of autonomy in intracolonial affairs, and this had equipped them with experience and political know-how of enormous importance for the success of their venture as independent and republican states. As members of the British Empire, however, they had not had much control over foreign policy (except, perhaps, in the area of Indian relations), and their formal and institutional relations with each other had been minimal. The decision for independence of course involved the assumption of responsibility for interstate and foreign relations, and therefore added a new and important function of government to those with which the Americans had long been familiar. The institutional response to this new situation had been a brilliant one, first a Congress representing all of the new states, and then the Articles of Confederation. It is easy to take this great achievement for granted, but a comparative glance at peoples more recently emerged from colonial status may suggest that the simultaneous confederation of thirteen states, whose inhabitants believed themselves to be a heterogeneous lot, was not inevitable. A defensive alliance might have been the alternative, with concerted rather than united action used as the method for conducting the war and concluding the peace. The decision to fight in a union rather than as an alliance was doubtless due partly to the exigencies of the immediate situation, but this decision itself, together with the Declaration of Independence and the Articles of Confederation, clearly suggested <u>an emerging conception of nationhood rather than a merely expedient confederation.</u> Thus the fight for and the attainment of independence had these results: <u>the assumption by the former colonies of the conduct of their foreign policy;</u> the decision to vest this <u>crucial element of statehood in a union of all the new states rather than in each separately;</u> the creation of a new and formal institutional structure to implement this function. The extent to which other governmental functions, particularly financial and commercial, might be transferred to this new union, and the corollary problems of its form and structure, were fundamental questions considered and debated in the period after 1776.

[margin: Results of independence]

[margin: other gov functions]

One basic question of politics, however, was answered with almost no debate at all: The new American states would be republican in their form of government. Hereditary monarchy, of course, was virtually unthinkable: Independence from Great Britain meant independence from King George III; and although the colonists, before the end of 1775, would perhaps have been content with something similar to commonwealth status within the Empire, once that alternative was foreclosed, so also was hereditary monarchy. The only real alternatives were a republic, an aristocracy, or some combination of the two. In fact, if one accepts the strictly classical definition of aristocracy—a government completely controlled by a legally privileged minority of citizens, usually an hereditary class—that form was also out of the question. <u>The lower houses of the colonial legislature, broadly representative of "the people,"</u> had long been a major if not the dominant element in all of the colonies, and it was unthinkable that these houses would abdicate their position of power. Indeed, their struggle to maintain that power was one of the most important causes of the Revolution.[4]

Range of choice

Both the historical evolution of the colonial political system, and the immediate circumstances of the fight for independence, really narrowed the practical range of alternatives to some form of republican government, perhaps with an admixture of modified aristocratic ingredients. This was, in fact, the range within which most of the debate over the first state constitutions took place.[5] It is therefore not surprising that all of the new constitutions were predominantly republican in character.

Consensus for republicanism as political right

A switch

What is more puzzling, and equally significant, is the very rapid and almost universal shift to an ideological commitment to republicanism as the fundamental principle of political right. Throughout all of their colonial experience, and until very late in the controversy which preceded the Revolution, Americans had believed that the ends of government—liberty, justice, happiness, the protection of property—could be secured through the means of a constitutional monarchy, or a mixed government, as the British system was sometimes called. They had thus been rather flexible with respect to means. But after the decision for independence had been taken, a substantial proportion of them seem to have acquired a greater rigidity concerning means, and especially with respect to republicanism: either it was good in itself, or it was the *only*

---

[4]See Jack P. Greene, *The Quest for Power; the Lower Houses of Assembly in the Southern Royal Colonies, 1689–1776* (Chapel Hill: University of North Carolina Press, 1963).

[5]There were a few proposals, like that of Carter Braxton in Virginia, for a mixed government composed of an elected lower house with limited tenure, and an elective upper house and executive serving for life, but these seemed to have reflected the views of a minority too small to be seriously considered.

means to the desired ends of government. This element of rigidity, once established in relation to the major principle of republicanism, seems to have spread into a generally pervasive tendency of thought among many Americans, and to have become a major factor in the debate over the Constitution of 1787.

As the Americans were generally agreed on two new principles of government, that there should be some institutional union among the separate states, and that the form of government within each state should be republican, so were they agreed on certain old principles. There was no rigorous and precise definition of the proper ends of government during the Revolutionary period, and perhaps because of this, there was widespread agreement on certain general and sometimes rather vague concepts. Liberty was one of these. Men were not agreed as to precisely what it meant. For example, with respect to freedom of the press they were not agreed as to where to draw the line between liberty and license. Or they might differ as to whether freedom of religion did or did not preclude religious qualifications for officeholding, or imply the right of Quakers to purchase exemption from military service. But they were generally agreed that liberty was a natural right of man, and that government existed to secure it. With liberty as a natural right were associated the three other familiar ones — life, property, and the pursuit of happiness. Again, there might be some disagreement as to what these meant in precise terms, but there was enough consensus as to their nature to say that Americans took it for granted that government existed to protect and promote the rights and interests of individual men. The more sophisticated were very much aware of the theoretical and practical difficulties inherent in this position: Individual interests and rights may conflict with each other, and/or with the general welfare or the public interest. It was a problem left over from

General concepts LIBERTY

colonial times, and one that clearly caused considerable perplexity and uneasiness among thoughtful men of the period. Still, most Americans seemed thoroughly committed to this position, awkward though it might be. To be sure, they also talked about justice as an end of government, but it was liberty to which their thinking was oriented more habitually, and with which they seemed most constantly preoccupied.

CONSENT

A second principle upon which there was general agreement was that government should rest on the consent of the governed, or at least on a substantial proportion of the governed. They did not believe that the consent of women, children, and slaves was necessary, and they were not agreed as to what group or groups of free adult males might justly be excluded from the franchise, or be given special protection through institutional safeguards or through apportionment of representation on some principle other than the strictly numerical. As in the case of liberty, the idea of consent was accepted in general terms, but disputed in precise definition and implementation.

LIMITED GOVERNMENT

A third principle, and one concerning which there was perhaps less disagreement than any other, was that good government must be limited government. This was the finest fruit of the English heritage, its seeds implanted before the Magna Carta in times exceeding the memory of man, and accepted by almost all Americans as beyond question. A corollary of this principle, evolved under the special circumstances of colonial charters and the even more special exigencies of Revolutionary legitimatization

(WRITTEN CONSTITUTIONS)

of new governments, was the necessity of written constitutions. The idea of a written constitution, creating the structure of the government and defining its limitations, was also a natural means of giving formal expression to the idea of consent—especially initial consent—as the proper foundation of government. It also was an appropriate sym-

bol and instrument of the idea that governments can be
created by the deliberation and choice of the people.

The optimism of this belief in the capacity of men to
shape their political institutions was tempered by an almost universally shared conviction of man's ineradicable
selfishness. It was assumed that self-interest was the dominant motive of man's political behavior, and though there
were constant appeals to altruism and patriotism in the
political language of the day, there was little tendency to
rely on the success of such appeals in the ordinary conduct
of politics. Self-interest, and its most extreme manifesta-
tion, a lust for power, were anticipated and had to be provided for in the structure and operation of governments, if
these were to secure to men the enjoyment of their natural
rights and of justice.

VIEW OF MAN (SELF-INTEREST ANTICIPATED)

Finally, as already indicated, there was widespread
agreement that republican government was the form most
likely to accomplish this purpose. As one would expect in
a revolutionary situation, there was both disagreement and
confusion as to the exact design of such a government. A
number of the constitutions were framed and adopted
rather hastily—one is reported to have been written over-
night in a tavern without the aid of a single book—and
some of these seem to reflect contradictory ideas, which
may have been the result of compromise, or which may
reflect simply the lack of experience or of systematic plan-
ning inherent in a sudden and novel situation. The principle of separation of powers was generally accepted in
theory, with Montesquieu frequently cited as an authority,
but men differed as to the meaning of the term and as to
the method of translating it into practice. For example,
some constitutions contain clear statements of the principle of separation of powers, but do not fully embody this
principle in the actual structure of the government. Some
proposals, such as one contained in a well-known pam-

REPUBLICAN GOVERNMENT

S of P

phlet originating in New Hampshire, speak of the desirability of establishing a simple form of government, but then proceed to outline one that involves separation of powers. Did the author contradict himself, or did he regard the two as compatible, whereas Tom Paine, for example, did not? There were also differences about such matters as the function of representation and of the representative: Should the latter merely transmit the instructions of his constituents to the representative assembly and consider himself as bound by them, or was he free to vote according to his conscience, informed perhaps by knowledge not available to his constituents when they expressed their will? What should be the role of the executive, and how should it be constituted and selected? Should there be one or two houses in the state legislatures, and if two (as was agreed in most of the states), how should each be constituted? On these and many other points, there was disagreement and sometimes uncertainty.

Modern scholars are not agreed in their interpretations and evaluations of these first republican constitutions. Some emphasize the similarity of most of them, and regard that similarity as a remarkable characteristic of a revolutionary situation. Others emphasize their differences, and see them as emerging from a sharp conflict between democratic and antidemocratic forces, with the constitutions of Pennsylvania and Massachusetts representing respectively the victories of the two sides. The reasons for differences in interpretation stem partly from the fragmentary nature of source material reflecting the contemporary debate, partly from the vantage point chosen by the critic, and partly from the use of the word *democratic*. It did not have a precise, fixed, universally agreed upon meaning then, nor does it now. Apart from the usual difficulties of precise definition of any word in the social sciences, there are rather special reasons for the difficulty respecting *democ-*

racy and its cognates. The operating system with which it
has been associated in this country is not a monolithic
structure. It has been a system that, while usually implying
the rule of the majority, has also usually involved some
limitations on the exercise of that rule. The reasons for
these limitations have varied. One reason has been the
protection of individuals and minorities against the will of
the majority, as in a bill of rights. Another has been the
belief that, paradoxically, the will of the majority must be
limited in order for it to continue to operate. An example
would be the belief in compulsory rotation in office, widespread during the Revolutionary period and embodied later
in both state and federal constitutions limiting the tenure
of governors and the President. Another has been the
desire to give some more or less permanent minority protection and thus achieve a concurrent or consensus majority rather than a mere numerical one. A separate house in
the legislature for an upper class or for small states, and
more recently, disproportionate representation in state
legislatures as well as in Congress, have been examples of
deviations from a system of strict and absolute majority
rule. Disagreements, or diversity, in the use of the term
democratic have frequently involved attitudes about the
legitimacy of these various limitations. And of course the
problem has been enormously complicated by the association of democracy with political right, and by the tendency
of almost all men to use the word without giving it a precise definition. Thus James Monroe's characterization in
the Virginia ratifying convention of all the state constitutions as "perfectly democratic"[6] would presumably con-
found anyone, contemporary or not, who saw great differ-

---

[6]Jonathan Elliot, *The Debates in the Several State Conventions on the
Adoption of the Federal Constitution as Recommended by the General
Convention at Philadelphia, in 1787*, Second Edition, 5, vols. (Philadel-
phia: J. B. Lippincott, 1896), III, 211. Hereinafter cited as *Elliot*.

ences between the constitutions of Pennsylvania and Massachusetts on this score, as would John Marshall's favorable appraisal of the Federal Constitution as also "democratic."[7] I rather doubt that the term was used with a high degree of consistency during the period under review, but until a careful study of this subject has been made, I am inclined to be somewhat wary in categorizing various contemporary groups as democratic or nondemocratic without making very clear what particular contemporary or other meaning I am attaching to the word at a given time. For one thing, one of the frequent contemporary uses appears to have been very close to the original meaning of the Greek word, i.e., rule of the poor or lower classes. Naturally, insofar as the term was associated with class dominance, democracy would not be regarded with favor by men who did not think of themselves as members of that class. This was obviously not the sense in which either Monroe or Marshall was using the word, however. Their usage, though not identical with ours, was closer to it in that it was associated with an *institutional system* rather than a *socioeconomic class*.

The term *democracy*, as well as the institutions that were then or were later to become associated with it, appears to have been in a state of transition during the period, and until we have more thorough research and precise analysis as to its contemporary usage, we cannot arrive at reliable evaluations of the degree and kind of "democracy" in either the institutions or the thought of Revolutionary America. In the meantime, it seems reasonably accurate to summarize the ideological and institutional setting of the ratification debate in the following manner.

Two underlying and opposing intellectual tendencies were operating, both characteristic of a revolutionary situ-

---

[7] *Ibid.*, p. 222.

Ideologes Doctrinaire + Empirical
1) Fixed ideas as ideo. security
2) open mindedness/ experimentation

ation. One was an inclination toward fixed ideas, a kind of *i)*
ideological security in unstable times. Thus the maxim:
"Where annual elections end, there tyranny begins." Or
the frequent references to the principle of separation of
powers and to the doctrine of natural rights. Or perhaps
even the commitment to republicanism. A quest for certainty seems natural to man, and in politics this may take
the form of ideology or at least of ideologically oriented
thought or opinion, and especially in the course of a revolution. Indeed, one may suggest that the presence of such
an element is one of the characteristics distinguishing a
revolution from a mere rebellion or *coup d'état*. Be that as
it may, this tendency was certainly present during and
after the American Revolution. But it was countered by a *2)*
willingness if not a will to experiment, an openminded-
ness, a sense of America as a great political laboratory.
Basically this attitude of flexibility stemmed from the
Aristotelian tradition of politics, with its emphasis on the
necessity of tailoring the form of government to fit the
people and their circumstances. It was a variety of political *Pol*
relativism that came over with the early settlers, and it was *relativism*
popularized in the eighteenth century by Montesquieu.
Implicit in this theory was a certain emphasis on empiri-
cism, and it was this that tempered and sometimes
checked the opposing tendency toward the doctrinaire.
The conflict in the American political mind of these two
tendencies, the empirical or pragmatic, and the doctrinaire
or ideological, is responsible for much of the contradiction
and contrast within the American political tradition, and it
contributed to the complexity of the situation during and
after the Revolution. For that situation was characterized
by both rigidity and flexibility of political ideas, and this
was especially apparent during the ratification debate.

In spite of the tendency toward rigidity, the situation in
1787–1788 was very favorable for the creation and adop-

Empirical/pragmatic
vs
Doctrinaire/ideological

tion of a new constitution, though not necessarily of a new *national* constitution. The experience gained from the Revolutionary state constitutions and from the Articles of Confederation was doubly salutary. It had accustomed people to the idea of framing a new government by choice and deliberation, blending old ingredients from the colonial period with new elements of republicanism, and finding that the results worked reasonably well in practice. Second, the experience of about a decade under these new governments had nevertheless revealed their defects or weaknesses, and induced among many Americans an inclination toward change. Indeed, one of the principal Antifederalists was to bemoan the fact that the Revolution had undermined the people's customary suspicion of innovation. It would seem that this factor was an important one in securing the ratification of the Constitution. Third, although there was already apparent a tendency toward doctrinaire thinking or attitudinizing among sizable portions of the population, among others there existed a remarkable flexibility and receptivity to new political ideas and institutions. A self-conscious and confident but sober will toward experimentation in politics was one of the leading characteristics in the American political mind of the period. But this will was both directed and restrained by almost universal agreement upon certain fundamental principles of politics.

Important as was the institutional and ideological context of the Constitution, there were geographical, economic, social, and cultural factors that were equally so.

The present size of the United States and the rapid means of both communication and transportation require an imaginative effort to perceive the country as it was in 1787 and as it appeared to its inhabitants. To them, the distance from Maine to Georgia was very long indeed. Differences in climate, soil, and terrain had produced differences in the economy, and these in combination with other factors, such as religion, had produced significant differences in culture as well as in interests. New England with its small farms was a society quite unlike that of tidewater Virginia. The settled areas of the seaboard were very different from the frontier regions of Georgia or Kentucky or Ohio, whose inhabitants were still threatened by Indians, and whose contacts with the outside world might be minimal. Such factors, and the contemporary awareness and interpretation of their significance, played an important role in the controversy over the Constitution as is to be observed in the documents included in the text.

Economic factors were also important, but as to *how* important, and in precisely what way, our knowledge is as yet imperfect. For one thing, there is the question of the relative health of the economy in 1787. It was disputed by the contestants of that period, and it still is. Federalists emphasized its weaknesses, especially in the commercial sector, and Antifederalists countered with charges of exaggeration, and sometimes a defense of the fundamental soundness of the economy. Certainly there were problems of adjustment after the peace treaty of 1783, especially involving the various currencies in existence, interstate and foreign commerce, and state and continental debts. But it was an expanding economy, and honest George Washington noted that it was on its way to recovery even before the Constitution was adopted and observed shrewdly that the Constitution would nevertheless be given some of the credit for this recovery.

Even more difficult to pin down than the exact state of the economy in the mid-1780's is the relationship between various economic interests and attitudes toward the Constitution. For nearly a half century Charles Beard's interpretation of this relationship was widely accepted, and it was believed that the Constitution was framed and supported by commercial and especially personal property interest groups, while its opposition came from debtors and groups whose interests were agrarian. This thesis has now been severely challenged, and in turn the challengers criticized.[8]

The debate continues, but the results are inconclusive. Before achieving a new interpretation with which we can all be reasonably comfortable, we need a more complete knowledge of the facts, and a rigorous analysis of the facts and of their interrelationships. The present evidence, tentative as it is, would seem to point toward a multicausational interpretation of the Constitution and its advocates and opponents, according to which economic factors played an important role but by no means an exclusive one, and certainly not so simple a one as Beard asserted. There appear to have been many and diverse influences at work, and it is obviously difficult to fit them all into a consistent pattern. Professor Main presents convincing evidence that a main line of division between advocates and opponents of the Constitution was the distinction between a subsistence agricultural economy and a commercial economy. In his opinion, urban areas were heavily Federalist, as were agricultural areas producing for a market, while areas inhabited predominantly by small farmers producing for subsistence only or primarily were (in the absence of some other factor such as Indians or British) heavily Antifederalist. But Main himself notes important exceptions to this generalization, and until more facts are available we must regard the conclusion as tentative.[9] Economic considerations seem to have influenced large numbers of men in their attitude toward the Constitution,

JTM

---

[8]For the relevant works see the titles listed in the Selected Bibliography.

[9]See Jackson T. Main, *The Anti-Federalists: Critics of the Constitution, 1781–1788* (Chapel Hill: University of North Carolina Press, 1961), Chap. 11.

but they did not always give a clear push either for or against it, and in some places there were other factors of apparently equal or overriding importance. Georgians seem to have supported the Constitution because it promised greater security from the Indians; Philadelphia workingmen apparently were for it because, among other things, they thought it would provide jobs by reviving the shipbuilding industry in the city; some western settlers supported it because they thought it would result in an expulsion of the British from posts held in violation of the Treaty of 1783, but others opposed it because they feared adoption would jeopardize American rights of navigation on the Mississippi. In New York and Pennsylvania one element involved in the opposition was pretty obviously partisan politics. In each state, two political parties or [*PARTIES* handwritten] factions were already organized and operating effectively, and in each state, opposition to the Constitution was reported as being planned before the document was released to the public and the proposed plan of government known. Although the prior political divisions were not completely irrelevant to the instant issue, opposition for opposition's sake was almost certainly a factor.

Thus, the conclusion seems inevitable that diverse causes were at work in determining men's opinions of and votes on the Constitution. And this means that we shall probably never know with absolute certainty what factors were the crucial ones.

What we can do, however, is to examine the expressed political thought of the Federalists and the Antifederalists. Both groups contained articulate spokesmen for their respective sides, and both wrote or spoke extensively and exhaustively during the months between the signing of the Constitution on September 17, 1787, and its ratification by New York in July of 1788. This volume is concerned only with the Antifederalists, and it is to their thought that I now turn.

As indicated by the name given to them, the Antifederalists were on the defensive during the ratification debates,
and this fact strongly influenced the expression of their
general theoretical position. Theirs was a negative case,
and they devoted much time and space to the listing of
specific objections to the Constitution. They therefore had
a tactical advantage in the contemporary controversy, for it
is always easier to criticize than to construct, and the Constitution was admittedly the product of compromise among
many varied and conflicting interests and opinions. It
made an easy target, and the Antifederalists attacked with
vigor. Whatever their primary or initial reason for opposition may have been, they probed the proposed new government for every conceivable weakness or defect. This
was doubtless an effective technique at the time, but it
robbed their thought of that timeless quality which *The
Federalist Papers* have, and lowered its intellectual cal-
iber. All too often, the Antifederalist speeches and essays
listed predicted dangers that have not materialized, or
dragged on with lengthy rhetoric that may have inspired
the contemporary audience, but that now seems outdated.
Nevertheless, the Antifederalist complex of ideas is worth
serious attention. Their influence was not cut off with the
defeat of 1788. Their criticism of the lack of a bill of rights
led to the adoption of the first ten amendments soon after
the new Constitution went into effect, and their general
opposition to centralized federal power has been passed
on from generation to generation until the present time.
Thus their ideas are an essential part of the American
tradition. But their thought is also of more general interest,
because it represents and reflects a significant stage in the
evolution of republican government. The Antifederalists
and their opponents were first-generation republicans, a
fact which we may take for granted, but which they did
not. What they thought about a new experiment with an

old form of government is interesting and significant. They believed that adoption of the proposed new frame of government would jeopardize if not certainly doom that experiment, and they had a logical and coherent argument to back up their case. To reconstruct that argument is the primary purpose of this introductory essay. No effort will be made to itemize every single objection to the Constitution. Rather, the intent is to answer two questions: (1) what the Antifederalists believed to be the nature of representative, republican government; and (2) why they thought adoption of the Constitution would threaten its continued existence in America.

II. THE IMPOSSIBILITY OF A NATIONAL GOVERNMENT OVER A LARGE AREA AND A HETEROGENEOUS POPULATION

At the center of the theoretical expression of Antifederalist opposition to increased centralization of power in the national government was the belief that republican government was possible only for a relatively small territory and a relatively small and homogeneous population. James Winthrop of Massachusetts expressed a common belief when he said, "The idea of an uncompounded republick, on an average one thousand miles in length, and eight hundred in breadth, and containing six millions of white inhabitants all reduced to the same standard of morals, of habits, and of laws, is in itself an absurdity, and contrary to the whole experience of mankind."[10] The last part of this statement, at least, was true; history was on the side of the Antifederalists. So was the authority of contemporary po-

---

[10]The *Agrippa* Letters in Paul Leicester Ford, *Essays on the Constitution of the United States* (Brooklyn: Historical Printing Club, 1892), p. 65. See also pp. 91–92.

litical thought. The name of Montesquieu carried great weight, and he had taught that republican governments were appropriate for small territories only. He was cited frequently, but his opinion would probably not have been accepted had it not reflected their own experience and inclinations. As colonials they had enjoyed self-government in colony-size packages only and had not sought to extend its operation empire-wise. This association of self-government with relatively small geographical units reinforced Montesquieu's doctrine and led to further generalizations. A large republic was impossible, it was argued, because the center of government must necessarily be distant from the people. Their interest would then naturally decrease; and when this happened, "it would not suit the genius of the people to assist in the government," and, "Nothing would support the government, in such a case as that, but military coercion."[11] Patrick Henry argued that republican government for a continent was impossible because it was "a work too great for human wisdom."[12] "An Old Whig," the author of a series of essays published in *The Independent Gazetteer* of Philadelphia, expressed a very common fear when he wrote, "From the moment we become one great Republic, either in form or substance, the period is very shortly removed, when we shall sink first into monarchy, and then into despotism."[13]

Associated with the argument regarding size was the

---

[11]Elliot, IV, 52.

[12]Elliot, III, 164; cf. III, 607 ff.; II, 69, 335; the *Centinel* Letters in John Bach McMaster and Frederick D. Stone, editors, *Pennsylvania and the Federal Constitution, 1787–1788* (Historical Society of Pennsylvania, 1888), p. 572; R. H. Lee, "Letters of a Federal Farmer," in Paul Leicester Ford, *Pamphlets on the Constitution of the United States* (Brooklyn: Historical Printing Club, 1888), p. 288; George Clinton, *Cato,* in Ford, *Essays,* p. 256 ff.

[13]*The Independent Gazetteer* (Philadelphia), October 27, 1787.

Necessity of Homogeneity –

assumption that any people who were to govern themselves must be relatively homogeneous in interest, opinion, habits, and mores. The theme was not systematically
explored, but it apparently stemmed from the political
relativism prevalent at the time,[14] and from the recent
experience of conflicts of interest between the colonies
and Great Britain, and later between various states and
sections of the new confederation.

It is not easy to measure the relative strength of national
and state sentiment in either individuals or groups,[15] but it
is clear that the Antifederalists were conscious of, and
emphasized, the cultural diversity of the peoples in the
thirteen states. They argued that no one set of laws could
operate over such diversity. Said a Southerner, "We see
plainly that men who come from New England are different from us."[16] He did not wish to be governed either with
or by such men. Neither did the New Englanders wish to
share a political roof with Southerners. "The inhabitants of
warmer climates are more dissolute in their manners, and
less industrious, than in colder countries. A degree of
severity is, therefore, necessary with one which would

---

[14]Political relativism had long been a part of the colonial heritage.
Seventeenth-century Puritans, who were sure that God had regulated
many aspects of life with remarkable precision, believed that He had left
each people considerable freedom in the choice of their form of government. The secularized legacy of this belief prevailed throughout the era
of framing state and national constitutions. Fundamental principles
derived from natural law were of course universally valid, and certain
"political maxims" regarding the structure of the government very nearly
so, but the embodiment of these general truths in concrete political forms
was necessarily determined by the nature and circumstances of the
people involved.

[15]On this subject see John C. Ranney, "The Bases of American Federalism," *William and Mary Quarterly,* Series 3, Vol. III, No. 1 (January,
1946), 139–156.

[16]Elliot, IV, 24.

cramp the spirit of the other. . . . It is impossible for one code of laws to suit Georgia and Massachusetts."[17] To place both types of men under the same government would be abhorrent and quite incompatible with the retention of liberty. Either the new government would collapse, or it would endeavor to stamp out diversity and level all citizens to a new uniformity in order to survive. Such reasoning was common among the Antifederalists. Their indebtedness to Montesquieu is obvious. Their failure to grasp the principles of the new federalism is also clear; for the purposes of this argument, and indeed for almost all of their arguments, they refused to consider the proposed government as one of limited, enumerated powers. They spoke and wrote constantly as if the scope and extent of its powers would be the same as those of the respective state governments, or of a unified national government.

Indeed, the belief that the proposed constitution would establish a "consolidated" government was central to the Antifederalist argument. In terms of pure logic, the argument was unanswerable. First, and perhaps most important of all, was the power to tax. Under Article I, Section 8, Congress was empowered to levy taxes directly upon individuals, whereas the Congress under the Articles of Confederation had had only the authority to make requisitions upon the states and had lacked any real power to compel payment. John Marshall had yet to issue his famous dictum that the power to tax involves the power to destroy, but the Antifederalists had no need of his tutelage. To give the central government the power to tax was to give it the power of the purse, and that, they argued, meant to give it an independence of the people that was thoroughly dangerous. It made it a *national, consoli-*

---

[17]From the *Agrippa* Letters, Ford, *Essays*, p. 64.

dated government, no longer a federal or confederated one as it had been before. Not only would the new government have the power of the purse, it would also have the power of the sword. Article I, Section 8, and Article II, Section 2 conferred on Congress and the President the powers to raise and maintain an army and navy, to command the same, and to call forth and command the militia of the several states in the service of the nation. These provisions not only made possible the existence of a standing army—an issue naturally sensitive to a people less than a generation removed from the Boston Massacre and all that it symbolized—but threatened to undermine the means of each state to defend itself by subjecting the citizen militia to national control. National taxes and a national standing army clearly implied consolidation. In terms of strict logic, the Antifederalists might have added to the list the nationalizing or consolidating implications of empowering Congress to regulate interstate and foreign commerce, but in practice most of them did not object to this power, though some wanted it exercised only by a majority of two-thirds.

Although there were other specific substantive powers to which the Antifederalists objected, the third great pillar of consolidation was the one we now call the "elastic" clause, and which they called the "sweeping" one, the last clause in Article I, Section 8: "To make all Laws which shall be necessary and proper for carrying into Execution the foregoing Powers, and all other Powers vested by this Constitution in the Government of the United States, or in any Department or Officer thereof." This was a clause so sweeping in its possible implications—and it is to be remembered that the Constitution did not at this time include a Bill of Rights—that the Antifederalists could see no logical limit to the powers of the central government. In vain did the Federalists argue that it was to be a government of delegated, enumerated powers only; in vain did Madison analyze the various "federal" and "national" elements of the new Constitution in *Federalist 39*. Alexander Hamilton himself could not have bettered the Antifederalists in seeing this clause as a great and inexhaustible reservoir of national power. To the Antifederalists, it meant, and was intended to mean, that the new government was to be a consolidated one, and that its authority was to be boundless.

Article VI   The fourth pillar of consolidation was equally formidable; it was to be found in Article VI: "This Constitution, and the Laws of the United States which shall be made in Pursuance thereof; and all Treaties made, or which shall be made, under the Authority of the United States, shall be the supreme Law of the Land; and the Judges in every State shall be bound thereby, any Thing in the Constitution or Laws of any State to the Contrary notwithstanding." This provision seemed clearly and explicitly to define the location of sovereign power: in the new central government, not in the states. The last clause sounded particularly ominous, for it seemed to reduce the states to little more than administrative provinces or local corporations. State legislatures would have little to do except provide for such matters as the mending of fences, and reduced to such insignificance, they might even be abolished by a people weary of the crushing burden of double taxation.

This edifice of constructive prediction may not seem entirely fanciful. The Presidential candidate of the Republican Party in 1964 appeared to entertain views rather similar, but the proper starting place for understanding the logic and the fears of the Antifederalists is not the political scene in 1964, but the Declaratory Act of 1766 and two fundamental characteristics of colonial and Revolutionary thought. One of the latter was the profound distrust of political power and its effects on men who possessed it.

The Americans of 1787, and their colonial forebears, believed that the natural and virtually irresistible tendency of men who held political power was to seek to increase it and to abuse it. It was almost inconceivable to them that men would be content to use less power than they were authorized to use. Their love of the legend of Cincinnatus, and their pleasure in associating George Washington with it, indicate what their normal expectations were. Hence their reaction to the Declaratory Act with its assertion of Parliament's complete authority over the colonies: the power that Great Britain claimed, that power it would eventually use. The other political trait that helps to explain the attitude of the Antifederalists toward the potentially consolidating elements in the Constitution was their habit of thinking and arguing in terms of principle and implication. Professor Greene, in his monumental study of Southern colonial legislatures, shows that over and over again the Americans, rather than settle gracefully and comfortably for an immediate policy that was in substance satisfactory, would think instead of the principle of the action and the possibly dangerous precedent it might establish for the future. They were constantly and habitually thinking in terms of what might be, not simply of what was. So it was with the Antifederalists, who had the added incentive of deciding on a constitution that might determine the future of America (and of each of the separate states) for generations to come. The Constitution did not make so bold an assertion of power as the Declaratory Act had done, but to a people accustomed to thinking carefully and prudently about the logical implications of every principle and policy, the cumulative effect of the provisions cited above spelled a consolidation of power no less great than that formerly claimed by the British government. There is a special irony in the fact that in this first encounter with the Constitution, the Antifederalists anticipated and indeed exaggerated the theory of broad construction later used by Alexander Hamilton and his supporters.

If, after ratification, the new government had proceeded to exercise the vast powers that the Antifederalists said the Constitution vested in it, the results might well have been similar to those predicted – dissolution of the Union, perhaps preceded by an abortive attempt at forcible and tyrannical coercion. That nothing of so drastic a nature occurred was of course due to the fact that Congress was reasonably responsive and responsible to public opinion, which in turn was effectively channeled by the emergence of organized national parties. But in 1787–1788, the Antifederalists did not believe in the likelihood of the former, perhaps because they did not anticipate the possibility of the latter.[18] Thus they refused to see the proposed new government as one of limited and enumerated powers, in structure and in operation a mixture of national and federal elements as portrayed by Madison in the 39th *Federalist*. They saw it as a national, consolidated government which would almost certainly swallow up the state governments, and which would attempt to impose uniform laws upon a people who were diverse and heterogeneous. This could only mean tyranny and the end of republicanism.

Although the Antifederalists emphasized this general and logical argument of the incompatibility of republican government with consolidated rule over a large area and a

Parties

---

[18]The Federalists did not anticipate the development of national parties either, and of course did not desire them. Perhaps they would have had more success in persuading the Antifederalists that Congress would, by and large, act in accordance with public opinion if they had recognized the potentially positive functions that political parties could perform as well as their potential dangers. But this was probably impossible without some practical experience with republican politics of national scope.

heterogeneous population, they also cited the clash of specific economic and political interests. These were primarily sectional,[19] and were of more acute concern in the South than in the North. In Virginia, for example, George Mason expressed the fear that the power of Congress to regulate commerce might be the South's downfall. In Philadelphia he had argued that this power be exercised by a two-thirds majority, and he now feared that by requiring only a simple majority "to make all commercial and navigation laws, the five southern states (whose produce and circumstances are totally different from those of the eight northern and eastern states) will be ruined. . . ."[20] It was also argued in several of the Southern conventions that a majority of the Eastern states might conspire to close the Mississippi,[21] and that they might eventually interfere with the institution of slavery.[22] In New England and the Middle States, there was less feeling that the interests of the entire section were in jeopardy, and therefore less discussion of these concrete issues and their divisive effect. One writer did strike out at the Federalist plea for a transcendent nationalism and repudiated the notion of sacrificing local interests to a presumed general interest as unrealistic and prejudicial to freedom. "It is vain to tell us that we ought to overlook local interests. It is only by protecting local concerns that the interest of the whole is preserved." He went on to say that men entered into society for egoistic rather than altruistic motives, that having once done so, all were bound to contri-

---

[19]Curiously enough, the Big-Little State fight, which almost broke up the Convention, played very little part in the ratification debates. And ironically one of the evidences of ideological unity which made the "more perfect union" possible was the similarity of arguments put forth by the Antifederalists in their respective states.

[20]"Objections," Ford, *Pamphlets*, p. 331.

[21]Elliot, III, 326.

[22]Elliot, IV, 272–273.

bute equally to the common welfare, and that to call for sacrifices of local interest was to violate this principle of equality and to subvert "the foundation of free government."[23]

There was much to be said for Winthrop's argument. It was an unequivocal statement of the principle that self-interest is the primary bond of political union. It was also an expression of an attitude that has always played a large part in our national politics: a refusal to sacrifice—sometimes even to subordinate—the welfare of a part to that of the whole. Pursuit of an abstract national interest has sometimes proved dangerous, and there was a healthy toughness in the Antifederalist insistence on the importance of local interests. But Winthrop skirted around the really difficult questions raised by his argument, which were also inherent in the Antifederalist position that the size of the United States and the diversity that existed among them were too great to be consistent with one republican government operating over the whole. No one would deny that a certain amount of unity or consensus is required for the foundation of popular, constitutional government; not very many people—now or in 1787—would go as far as Rousseau and insist on virtually absolute identity of interest and opinion. The Antifederalists were surprisingly close to Rousseau and to the notions of republicanism which influenced him, but they were sensible, practical men and did not attempt to define their position precisely. Consequently they left untouched two difficult questions: How much, and what kind of unity is required for the foundation of any republican government, large or small? And how, in the absence of perfect uniformity, are differences of opinion and interest to be resolved?

---

[23]*Agrippa* Letters, Ford, *Essays,* p. 73.

III. THE INADEQUACY OF REPRESENTATION AND THE PROBABLE ARISTOCRATIC EFFECT THEREOF

Associated with the prediction that the new Constitution would establish a consolidated government was the Antifederalist charge that it would establish an aristocratic government, or, less frequently, a monarchical one. Mercy Warren said that it was "dangerously adapted to the purposes of an immediate *aristocratic tyranny*," and that it "must soon terminate in the most *"uncontrouled despotism."*[24] The author of the "Philadelphiensis" letters asserted that "Our thirteen free commonwealths are to be consolidated into one *despotic monarchy*," that the new government, "were it possible to establish it, would be a compound of *monarchy* and *aristocracy*," that the members of Congress would be of "the *well born*," and the President a *"military king."*[25] A contributor to the same journal charged that "the whole of the new plan was entirely the work of an *aristocratic majority."*[26]

Two kinds of reasoning lay back of such charges. One was judgment of the Constitution on the basis of the class origin of its authors and advocates; the other was analysis of the Constitution itself. Suspicion of and hostility to the new government because of the alleged aristocratic status and bias of its supporters was quite common and was

---

[24]*Observations on the new Constitution, and on the Federal and State Conventions*, by a Columbian Patriot. Reprinted in Ford, *Pamphlets*, pp. 1–23. Quotation on p. 6. This essay was attributed by Ford to Elbridge Gerry. Charles Warren attributed it to Mercy Warren; on the basis of a letter from the latter referring to it on her own. See Charles Warren, "Elbridge Gerry, James Warren, Mercy Warren and the Ratification of the Federal Constitution in Massachusetts," Proceedings, Massachusetts Historical Society, Vol. 64 (March 1931).

[25]Philadelphiensis, Number IX, *The Independent Gazetteer,* February 7, 1788.

[26]"An Officer of the Late Continental Army," *The Independent Gazetteer,* November 6, 1787.

probably one of the most effective arguments of the opposition. The remarks of old Amos Singletary in the Massachusetts ratifying convention express the defiant insecurity of the embattled commoner:

These lawyers, and men of learning and moneyed men, that talk so finely, and gloss over matters so smoothly, to make us poor illiterate people swallow down the pill, expect to get into Congress themselves; they expect to be managers of this Constitution, and get all the power and all the money into their own hands, and then they will swallow all us little folks like the great *Leviathan;* yes, just as the whale swallowed up Jonah![27]

Something of this same class antagonism and overt anti-intellectualism was expressed by a group of Pennsylvanians:

It is, gentlemen, with the most agreeable surprise that we behold a very few country farmers and mechanics nonplus the great rabbies [*sic*] and doctors of the schools, who no doubt summoned in all the rhetoric, logic, and sophistry they were capable of on this occasion—We rejoice to see scholastic learning and erudition fly before simple reason, plain truth and common sense. But though you defeated them in argument, they exceeded you in numbers. . . .[28]

Consideration of such attitudes is essential for an understanding of Antifederalist psychology and tactics, for they appear to reflect a major cause for opposition to the Constitution. They do not represent much of value in the way

---

[27]Elliot, II, 102. See also reference to this attitude in a letter from Rufus King to James Madison, January 27, 1888, in *Documentary History of the Constitution of the United States of America, 1786–1870* (Washington, D.C.; Department of State, 1894–1905), 5 vols., IV, 459. A similar feeling was reported to exist in the New Hampshire convention. See John Langdon to George Washington, February 28, 1788, *ibid.,* p. 524.

[28]From "An Address of Thanks from a number of the Inhabitants of the Borough of Carlisle, to the Minority of the late State Convention, in general, and the representatives of Cumberland County, in particular," *The Freeman's Journal* (Philadelphia), February 13, 1788.

of rational criticism of the document itself. The reasoning that underlay the Antifederalist belief that the new government would be aristocratic and/or monarchic in practice was a combination of their fear of consolidation with their ideal of representation and their conception of the representative process as it was likely to operate under the proposed system.

The Antifederalist theory of representation was closely allied to the belief that republican government could operate only over a small area. The proposed Constitution provided that the first House of Representatives should consist of sixty-five members, and that thereafter the ratio of representation should not exceed one representative for thirty thousand people. This provision was vigorously criticized and was the chief component of the charge that the Constitution was not sufficiently democratic. The argument was twofold: first, that sixty-five men could not possibly represent the multiplicity of interests spread throughout so great a country; secondly, that those most likely to be left out would be of the more democratic or "middling" elements in society. The minority who voted against ratification in the Pennsylvania convention calculated that the combined quorums of the House and Senate was only twenty-five, and concluded that this number plus the President could not possibly represent "the sense and views of three or four millions of people, diffused over so extensive a territory, comprising such various climates, products, habits, interests, and opinions. . . ."[29] This argument, accompanied with the same calculus, was repeated many times during the ratification debate.

Almost all of the leaders of the opposition laid down what they believed to be the requisites of adequate repre-

---

[29]"Address and Reasons of Dissent of the Minority of the Convention of Pennsylvania to their Constituents," reprinted in McMaster and Stone, *Pennsylvania and the Constitution*, p. 472.

sentation, and there is a remarkable similarity in their definitions. George Mason, speaking in the Virginia convention against giving the central government the power of taxation, based his argument on the inadequacy of representation as measured by his criteria: "To make representation real and actual, the number of representatives ought to be adequate; they ought to mix with the people, think as they think, feel as they feel,—ought to be perfectly amenable to them, and thoroughly acquainted with their interest and condition."[30] In his *Letters of a Federal Farmer*, Richard Henry Lee developed the same idea further:

Reps as microcosm of society

. . . a full and equal representation is that which possesses the same interests, feelings, opinions, and views the people themselves would were they all assembled—a fair representation, therefore, should be so regulated, that every order of men in the community, according to the common course of elections, can have a share in it—in order to allow professional men, merchants, traders, farmers, mechanics, etc. to bring a just proportion of their best informed men respectively into the legislature, the representation must be considerably numerous.[31]

It was the contention of the antifederalists that because of the small size of the House of Representatives, the middle and lower orders in society would not be elected to that body, and that consequently this, the only popular organ of the government, would not be democratic at all. It would, instead, be filled by aristocrats, possibly by military heroes and demagogues.[32] Why should this be? Lee asserted simply that it would be "in the nature of things."

---

[30]Elliot, III, 32.

[31]Ford, *Pamphlets*, pp. 288–289.

[32]This idea appeared frequently in Antifederalist arguments. See, for example, the "Address and Dissent of the Minority. . . ," McMaster and Stone, *Pennsylvania and the Constitution*, pp. 472, 479; Lee, "Letters of a Federal Farmer," Ford, *Pamphlets*, p. 295; Elliot, III, 266–267, 426 (George Mason).

Mason seems to have assumed it without any comment or argument. Patrick Henry reasoned that since the candidates would be chosen from large electoral districts rather than from counties, they would not all be known by the electors, and "A common man must ask a man of influence how he is to proceed, and for whom he must vote. The elected, therefore, will be careless of the interest of the electors. It will be a common job to extort the suffrages of the common people for the most influential characters."[33] This argument reflects one of the basic fears of the Antifederalists: loss of personal, direct contact with and knowledge of their representatives. They sensed quite accurately that an enlargement of the area of republican government would lead to a more impersonal system, and that the immediate, individual influence of each voter over his reresentative would be lessened.

The most elaborate explanation of the anticipated results of the electoral process was given by the moderate Antifederalist in New York, Melancton Smith. He argued that very few men of the "middling" class would choose to run for Congress because the office would be "highly elevated and distinguished," the style of living probably "high." Such circumstances would "render the place of a representative not a desirable one to sensible, substantial men, who have been used to walking in the plain and frugal paths of life." Even if such should choose to run for election, they would almost certainly be defeated. In a large electoral district it would be difficult for any but a person of "conspicuous military, popular, civil, or legal talents" to win. The common people were more likely to be divided among themselves than the great, and "There will be scarcely a chance of their uniting in any other but some great man, unless in some popular demagogue, who will probably be destitute of principle. A substantial yeoman,

---

[33]Elliot, III, 322.

of sense and discernment, will hardly ever be chosen."[34] Consequently, the government would be controlled by the great, would not truly reflect the interests of all groups in the community, and would almost certainly become oppressive.

Antifederalists in Massachusetts were also uneasy about the capacity of the people to elect a legislature which would reflect their opinions and interests. The arguments emphasized geographical as well as class divisions, and expressed the fear and suspicion felt by the western part of the state toward Boston and the other coastal towns. It was predicted that the latter would enjoy a great advantage under the new system, and this prediction was supported by a shrewd analysis in the *Cornelius* Letter:

The citizens in the seaport towns are numerous; they live compact; their interests are one; there is a constant connection and intercourse between them; they can, on any occasion, centre their votes where they please. This is not the case with those who are in the landed interest; they are scattered far and wide; they have but little intercourse and connection with each other. To concert uniform plans for carrying elections of this kind is entirely out of their way. Hence, their votes if given at all, will be no less scattered than are the local situations of the voters themselves. Wherever the seaport towns agree to centre their votes, there will, of course, be the greatest number. A gentleman in the country therefore, who may aspire after a seat in Congress, or who may wish for a post of profit under the federal government, must form his connections, and unite his interest with those towns. Thus, I conceive, a foundation is laid for throwing the whole power of the federal government into the hands of those who are in the mercantile interest; and for the landed, which is the great interest of this country to lie unrepresented, forlorn and without hope.[35]

---

[34]Elliot, II, 246.

[35]The *Cornelius* Letter is reprinted in Samuel Bannister Harding, *The Contest over the Ratification of the Federal Constitution in the State of Massachusetts* (New York: Longman, Green, and Co., 1896). See pp. 123–124.

What the Antifederalists feared, in other words, were the superior opportunities for organized voting that they felt to be inherent in the more thickly populated areas. They shared with the authors of *The Federalist* the fear of party and faction in the eighteenth-century American sense of those words. But they also feared, as the preceding analyses show, the essence of party in its modern meaning, i.e., organizing the vote, and they wanted constituencies sufficiently small to render such organization unnecessary.

This belief that larger electoral districts would inevitably be to the advantage of the well-to-do partially explains the relative scarcity of criticism of the indirect election of the Senate and the President.[36] If the "middling" class could not be expected to compete successfully with the upper class in congressional elections, still less could they do so in statewide or nationwide elections. It was a matter where size was of the essence. True representation—undistorted by party organization—could be achieved only where electoral districts were small.

According to this reasoning, there would be no truly representative organ in the central government, not even a recently elected House of Representatives. The belief that this government would therefore be alien to them, unresponsive to public opinion and dominated by an aristocracy, contributed to the apparent expectation that it would

---

[36]There were a few such criticisms. See the "Montezuma" letter already referred to (*The Independent Gazetteer*, October 17, 1787); also see *The New York Journal*, April 26, 1788, the instructions to the Albany delegation to the ratifying convention; "Cincinnatus" in *Ibid*, November 22, 1787. These criticisms are among those of the Antifederalists which are most difficult to evaluate, because they do not usually lead to an explicit demand for direct election. It is therefore difficult to know whether the few who made them would have actually preferred a popularly elected Senate. Such would have made the government more "national," and therefore presumably less congenial to men already fearful of the rights of the states. It is another instance of the tactical advantage of the opposition: They had merely to criticize; they did not have to reconcile possibly contradictory criticisms.

immediately embark upon a program of coercive consolidation and deliberate tyranny. And there would be no way to stop it.

One aspect of Antifederalist thought that is both intriguing and puzzling is the rapidity with which the Antifederalists imagined wholesale political corruption might occur, and their duly elected representatives might embark on a deliberate regime of oppression. Two measures commonly accepted as calculated to prevent the corruption of public officials were frequent elections and compulsory rotation in office. To some men of the age, a year was enough for any man to be entrusted with power, and to them the practice of annual elections was very nearly sacred. Compulsory rotation in office was an added check on the potential emergence of a latent lust for power. Even if a man were the choice of a majority of the electorate, his and their will should both be blocked, and he should be returned to the people, to live as they lived, feel as they felt, and become one of them once again. Without these checks, it was feared that the government would become oppressive.

Since the Constitution ignored the principle of compulsory rotation completely, and provided for a six-year term for the Senate, a four-year term for the President, and a two-year term for the House of Representatives, it ran counter to this kind of opinion. Criticism concerning the lack of a provision requiring rotation was most common; there were also criticisms about the comparatively long terms of office, but on this point there seemed to be a greater willingness to concede the legitimacy of the Federalist argument that the different circumstances of a central government and the sheer length of time required for representatives to travel from their home districts to the seat of the government justified the longer terms of office in that government. Annual elections in these circumstances were really not feasible, and only the more extreme Antifederalists continued to press for them.

In order to get at the theory of representation that was associated with this view, it is worth probing a little further. It obviously reflected a profound distrust of the representative officials, whether elected directly or indirectly by the people, and embodied an attempt to insure that the former did not develop an interest separate from that of the latter. Two separate but related principles seemed to be involved: first, to prevent corruption; and second, to insure that at any given moment, the representatives reflected the immediate will of the electors. Consider the statement in the "Montezuma" letter, written by an Antifederalist to caricature the views of his opponents:

. . . nor have we allowed the *populace* the right to elect their representatives annually, as usual, lest this body should be too much under the influence and controul of their constituents, and thereby prove the "weatherboard of our grand edifice [*sic*], to shew the shiftings of every fashionable gale," for we have not yet to learn that little else is wanting, to aristocratize the most democratical representative than to make him somewhat independent of his *political creators*—We have taken away that rotation of appointment which has no long perplexed us—that *grand engine* of popular influence; every man is eligible into our government, from time to time for live [*sic*]—this will have a two-fold good effect; first, it prevents the representatives from mixing with the *lower class*, and imbibing their foolish sentiments, with which they have come charged on re-election.

2d. They will from the perpetuity of office be under *our* eye, and in a short time will think and act like us, independently of popular whims and prejudices. . . .[37]

This is an exceedingly interesting passage, because in allegedly exposing the supposed motives and wiles of the opposition, the writer seems unwittingly to reveal the fearful expectations of his own class. There is of course the

[37]"Montezuma," *The Independent Gazetteer*, October 17, 1787.

assumption that men's ideas and opinions are very much
influenced if not determined by their associates, and there
is a further assumption of great instability in these ideas.
Perhaps what was really involved here was plainly indicated in a letter from a disgruntled citizen of Bucks County,
Pennsylvania, complaining about some of his representatives who had gone to the Pennsylvania ratifying convention and voted for the Constitution. He explained why:
"Our members of convention, I am told, neither dined nor
supped at their own lodgings, the whole time they were in
town; if so, no wonder they voted for the proposed constitution."[38] There it is—rural America, proud but insecure,
fearful of the glamorous seductions of the city and of skillful
city politicians like James Wilson and Benjamin Rush
assiduously exercising the social graces upon the plain and
poor country cousin. And the country cousin was seduced
—he voted for the Constitution. If Bucks County representatives could not be trusted for even the few weeks of
the Pennsylvania convention, how could one possibly trust
men who would not be returned to their constituents for
two, four, or six years? Especially when they would be
associating with and apparently even welcomed by the so-
called aristocracy. I would emphasize the "so-called," because "Montezuma," for all his use of that word and its
frequent alternative "well-born," lets slip an important
assumption: Whatever aristocracy there was in America in
those years, it was not a closed group to which admission
was by birth alone. If this had been the case, "Montezuma"
and others like him would not have feared its influence
over their representatives so much. The aristocrats were
believed to corrupt such men not by *buying* them but by
associating with and *absorbing* them. In short, America
was an open society, and one of the means of social mobility

---

[38]"One of the People," *The Independent Gazetteer*, February 26, 1788.

was a career in politics. The Antifederalists, or a part of them, apparently wanted to make such a career impossible.[39] Rotation would seem to insure that politics remained an occasional, if not a completely amateur occupation, at least for elective officials. The Antifederalists do not seem to have thought much about the implications of this with respect to the economic problems of the ordinary small farmer, who would surely find it more difficult to absent himself for the long period required of a federal representative than would a planter or wealthy merchant. Or perhaps they did see the difficulties implicit in the situation, and for that reason were opposed to any national government whose officers would be independent of immediate control by state legislatures, whose sessions were usually short and therefore more easily amenable to the amateur politician without independent means.[40]

In addition to this class-conscious element in the thinking of the Antifederalists, there was also an institutional consideration involved in the preference for annual elections and compulsory rotation. These seemed to constitute either a substitute for or a reinforcement of the practice of instructed representatives. We do not have an adequate knowledge of either theories or practices of representation for the colonial and early republican periods, but it seems that the practice of constituent instruction of delegates sent to the state legislatures was fairly common in certain areas, though not universal and not consistently followed

[39]An interesting development, because it corresponded in an odd sort of way with the "aristocratic" notion of accomplishing the same thing by refusing to make political office financially attractive.

[40]Melancton Smith, in the debates previously cited, did comment on the uncongenial "high style" of life that would confront the independent yeoman at the seat of the national government, but Smith in the end voted for ratification.

in the areas where it was popular. For example, some delegates to the New Hampshire ratifying convention, who had been instructed to vote against the Constitution, changed their minds after attending debates and discussion, and then sought an adjournment in order to return home and try to persuade their electors to change their instructions also. Their experience reflects the inherent awkwardness of this kind of representation, for the delegate obligated to obey instructions that new information or deliberation and discussion leads him to regard as erroneous or misguided is confronted with a hard choice: betray his instructions, or betray his reason. In either case, his conscience takes a beating. Annual elections gave him a little more leeway, for at least he could violate his instructions and take the consequences of defeat at the next election. At the same time, that next election was so close that *every* year was an election year, and no representative who got far out of line could last very long. As a system, of course, representation by instructed delegates leaves much to be desired, because it leaves little or no place for the operation of reason, discussion, and compromise. It is merely a mechanical substitute for direct democracy, but without the give-and-take which that system provides for. It could not and did not work for any sustained period of time in any of the American states, and it most assuredly could not work in a genuine national government. It does seem, nevertheless, to have influenced some of the Anti-federalists in their criticism of the Constitution.

The fear that the small number of representatives and the large size of electoral districts would combine to make the lower house of Congress inadequately representative of the many diverse interests and opinions throughout the vast extent of the country, and that it would in fact be biased in favor of the presumed aristocracy, thus led the

Antifederalists to distrust the only directly elected department of the new government. There were a few criticisms
of the Senate and the President because these were not
also directly elected. The instructions for Albany County's
delegates to the ratifying convention included this statement: "The members of the senate are not to be chosen by
the people, but appointed by the legislature of each state
for the term of six years. This will destroy their responsibility, and induce them to act like the masters and not the
servants of the people."[41] The author of the "Cincinnatus"
Letters explicitly spoke of the dangers of aristocracy in
connection with the Senate:

1st. It is removed from the people, being chosen by the legislatures—and exactly in the ratio of their removal from the people,
do aristocratic principles constantly infect the minds of man.
2d. They endure, two thirds for four, and one third for six years,
and in proportion to the duration of power, the aristocratic exercise of it, and attempts to extend it, are invariably observed to
increase.[42]

Some Antifederalists also objected to the length of tenure
of all three departments but the major criticism was the
lack of compulsory rotation. The total picture was one of a
government that would be alien and irresponsible. At best,
the voters of any one state could control only their own
representatives, and these would necessarily constitute a
minority of the total number in both houses of Congress.
At worst—and the Antifederalists insisted on emphasizing
the worst—it would be a government not responsive to the
wishes of the people, aristocratically biased, and bent on oppression. In short, it would be a government of strangers.

---

[41]*The New York Journal*, April 26, 1788.
[42]*The New York Journal*, November 22, 1787.

IV. ABUSES OF POWER PREDICTED UNDER VARIOUS CLAUSES IN THE CONSTITUTION

The newness of the proposed system, the anticipation that it would be staffed by men totally unknown, and the ordinary eighteenth-century distrust of government and of human nature—these factors combined to inspire in the Antifederalists a spirit of extreme criticism. An author writing in a Boston newspaper made explicit a revealing element in this spirit: "In considering the present Government before us, we therefore certainly ought to look upon those who are to put it into motion, as our enemies—to be careful what we give—to see what use it is to be put to —and where to resort for a remedy, if it is abused. —Every door unguardedly left open, they will take care we never shall thereafter shut—every link in the chain unrivetted, they will provide shall always remain so."[43]

This advice was doubtless gratuitous, but it described with perfect accuracy one of the favorite tactics of the Antifederalists. They built up an extraordinary picture of anticipated treachery on the part of the representatives to be elected under the proposed government. No distinction was made on the basis of their method of election, whether directly or indirectly by the people. All were regarded as potential tyrants.

The picture of tyranny thus constructed stemmed directly from the Antifederalist conception of human nature. They shared with their opponents many of the assumptions regarding the nature of man characteristic of American thought in the late eighteenth century. They took for granted that the dominant motive of human behavior was

---

[43]"John De Witt," in *The American Herald*, November 19, 1787.

self-interest, and that this drive found its most extreme
political expression in an insatiable lust for power. These
were precisely the characteristics with which the authors
of *The Federalist Papers* were preoccupied.[44] Yet the Antifederalists chided the Federalists for their excessive
confidence in the future virtue of elected officials, and
criticized the Constitution for its failure to provide adequate protection against the operation of these tyrannical
drives. There is surely an amusing irony to find the
Founding Fathers, who prided themselves on their real-
ism, and who enjoy an enviable reputation for that quality
today, taken to task for excessive optimism. But they had to
meet this charge again and again. Thus Caldwell in the
North Carolina convention found it "remarkable,—that
gentlemen, as an answer to every improper part of it [the
Constitution], tell us that every thing is to be done by our
own representatives, who are to be good men. There is no
security that they will be so, or continue to be so."[45] In
New York Lansing expressed the same feeling in a passage
strikingly reminiscent of the famous paragraph in Madison's *Federalist 51*:

Scruples would be impertinent, arguments would be in vain,
checks would be useless, if we were certain our rulers would be
good men; but for the virtuous government is not instituted: its
object is to restrain and punish vice; and all free constitutions are

---

[44]See Benjamin F. Wright, *"The Federalist* on the Nature of Political
Man," *Ethics Vol. LIX, No.* 2 (January 1949), and Introduction to *The
Federalist,* John Harvard Library edition (Cambridge, Massachusetts:
Harvard University Press, 1961).

[45]Elliot, IV, 187; cf. 203–204, and III, 494. Caldwell's statement is very
similar to Madison's comment in *Federalist 10:* "It is in vain to say that
enlightened statesmen will be able to adjust these clashing interests, and
render them all subservient to the public good. Enlightened statesmen
will not always be at the helm."

formed with two views—to deter the governed from crime, and the governors from tyranny.[46]

This and many other similar statements might have been used interchangeably by either side in the debate, for they symbolized an attitude deeply embedded and widely dispersed in the political consciousness of the age. There were frequent references to "the natural lust of power so inherent in man";[47] to "the predominant thirst of dominion which has invariably and uniformly prompted rulers to abuse their power";[48] to "the ambition of man, and his lust for domination";[49] to rulers who would be "men of like passions," having "the same spontaneous inherent thirst for power with ourselves."[50] In Massachusetts, a delegate said, "we ought to be jealous of rulers. All the godly men we read of have failed; nay, he would not trust a 'flock of Moseses.'"[51]

It is to be noted that this dreadful lust for power was regarded as a universal characteristic of the nature of man, which could be controlled but not eradicated. The Anti-federalists charged that the authors of the Constitution had failed to put up strong enough barriers to block this inevitably corrupting and tyrannical force. They painted a very black picture indeed of what the national representatives

---

[46]Elliot, II, 295–296. Madison's declaration was this: "But what is government itself, but the greatest of all reflections on human nature? If men were angels, no government would be necessary. If angels were to govern men, neither external nor internal controls on government would be necessary. In framing a government which is to be administered by men over men, the great difficulty lies in this: you must first enable the government to control the governed; and in the next place oblige it to control itself."

[47]Mason in Virginia, Elliot, III, 32.

[48]Henry in Virginia, *ibid.*, p. 436.

[49]"Letters of Luther Martin," Ford, *Essays*, p. 379.

[50]Barrell in Massachusetts, Elliot, II, 159.

[51] White in Massachusetts, Elliot, II, 28.

might and probably would do with the unchecked power conferred upon them under the provisions of the new Constitution. The "parade of imaginary horribles" has become an honorable and dependable technique of political debate, but the marvelous inventiveness of the Antifederalists has rarely been matched. Certainly the best achievements of their contemporary opponents were conspicuously inferior in dramatic quality, as well as incredibly unimaginative in dull adherence to at least a semblance of reality. The anticipated abuses of power, some real, some undoubtedly conjured as ammunition for debate, composed a substantial part of the case against the Constitution, and they must be examined in order to get at the temper and quality of Antifederalist thought as well as at its content. Their source was ordinarily a distorted interpretation of some particular clause.

One clause that was believed to lay down a constitutional road to legislative tyranny was Article I, Section 4: "The times, places, and manner of holding elections for senators and representatives, shall be prescribed in each state by the legislature thereof; but the Congress may, at any time, by law, make or alter such regulations, except as to the places of choosing senators." Here was the death clause of republican government. "This clause may destroy representation entirely," said Timothy Bloodworth of North Carolina.[52] If Congress had power to alter the times of elections, Congress might extend its tenure of office from two years to four, six, eight, ten, twenty, "or even for their natural lives."[53] Bloodworth and his colleagues feared the worst. In Massachusetts, where debate over this clause occupied a day and a half, the primary fear was that Congress, by altering the places of election, might rig them so

---

[52]Elliot, IV, 55.
[53]Elliot, IV, 51–52, 55–56, 62–63, 87–88.

as to interfere with a full and free expression of the people's choice. Pierce suggested that Congress could "direct that the election for Massachusetts shall be held in Boston," and then by preelection caucus, Boston and the surrounding towns could agree on a ticket "and carry their list by a major vote."[54] In the same state the delegate who would not trust "a flock of Moseses" argued thus: "Suppose the Congress should say that none should be electors but those worth 50 or a 100 sterling; cannot they do it? Yes, said he, they can; and if any lawyer . . . can beat me out of it, I will give him ten guineas."[55] In Virginia, George Mason suggested that Congress might provide that the election in Virginia should be held only in Norfolk County, or even "go farther, and say that the election for all the states might be had in New York. . . ."[56] Patrick Henry warned, "According to the mode prescribed, Congress may tell you that they have a right to make the vote of one gentleman go as far as the votes of a hundred poor men."[57]

Any of these acts would have been a flagrant abuse of power, but no more so than that which Mason and others predicted under Article II, Section 2, which gave to the President the power to make treaties with the advice and consent of two-thirds of the senators present. This power was believed to be fraught with danger, particularly among Southerners, who feared that the majority of Northern states might use it to give up American rights of navigation on the Mississippi. The North would not have a two-thirds majority of the entire Senate, of course, but Mason suggested that when a "partial" treaty was involved, the Pres-

---

[54]Elliot, II, 22.

[55]Elliot, II, 28.

[56]Elliot, III, 403–404.

[57]Elliot, III, 175. Cf. *Centinel,* McMaster and Stone, *Pennsylvania and the Constitution,* p. 598, and James Winthrop in the *Agrippa* Letters, Ford, *Essays,* p. 105.

ident would not call into session senators from distant
states, or those whose interests would be affected adverse-
ly, but only those he knew to be in favor of it.[58] His colleague, William Grayson, suggested the similarly treacherous prospect of such a treaty's being rushed through
while members from the Southern states were momentarily absent from the floor of the Senate: "If the senators of
the Southern States be gone but one hour, a treaty may be
made by the rest. . . ."[59]

This fear at least had some foundation in fact—there *was*
a conflict of interest between North and South over the
Mississippi. It would seem that the fear expressed in
North Carolina by Abbott on behalf of "the religious part
of the society" was pure fantasy: "It is feared by some
people, that, by the power of making treaties, they might
make a treaty engaging with foreign powers to adopt the
Roman Catholic religion in the United States. . . ."[60]

This was not the only provision objected to by "the
religious part of the society." Some were greatly dis-
pleased with the last clause of Article VI, Section 3: "but
no religious test shall ever be required as a qualification
to any office or public trust under the United States." In
the same speech quoted above, Abbott reported, presumably on behalf of his constituents, "The exclusion of religious tests is by many thought dangerous and impolitic."
For without such, "They suppose . . . pagans, deists, and
Mahometans might obtain offices among us, and that the
senators and representatives might all be pagans."[61] David
Caldwell thought that the lack of a religious qualification

---

[58]Elliot, III, 499.

[59]Elliot, III, 502.

[60]Elliot, IV, 191–192. Abbott was not an Antifederalist, but was, according to L. I. Trenholme, in *The Ratification of the Federal Constitution in North Carolina* (New York: Columbia University Press, 1932),
something of an independent. See p. 178. Abbott voted for ratification.

[61]Elliot, IV, 192.

constituted "an invitation for Jews and pagans of every kind to come among us," and that since the Christian religion was acknowledged to be the best for making "good members of society . . . those gentlemen who formed this Constitution should not have given this invitation to Jews and heathens."[62] Federalist James Iredell reported a pamphlet in circulation "in which the author states, as a very serious danger, that the pope of Rome might be elected President."[63] This unwittingly placed fresh ammunition at the disposal of the opposition. An Antifederalist admitted that he had not at first perceived this danger and conceded that it was not an immediate one: "But," said he, "let us remember that we form a government for millions not yet in existence. I have not the art of divination. In the course of four or five hundred years, I do not know how it will work. This is most certain, that Papists may occupy that chair, and Mahometans may take it. I see nothing against it. There is a disqualification, I believe, in every state in the Union—it ought to be so in this system."[64]

It is to be noted that these fears were fears of the majority of electors as well as of their elected representatives, and that these statements can hardly be said to glow with the spirit of liberty and tolerance. These beliefs were

---

[62]*Ibid.*, p. 199.

[63]*Ibid.*, p. 195.

[64]*Ibid.*, p. 215. This quotation transmits a sense of the method of Antifederalist debate admirably. A similar statement by Amos Singletary of Massachusetts gives something of the flavor of the thinking done by the honest and pious patriots of the back country, in which opposition to the Constitution was strong: "The Hon. Mr. Singletary thought we were giving up all our privileges, as there was no provision that men in power should have any *religion,* and though he hoped to see Christians, yet by the Constitution, a Papist, or an Infidel, was as eligible as they. It had been said that men had not degenerated; he did not think that men were better now than when men after God's own heart did wickedly. He thought, in this instance, we were giving great power to we know not whom." Elliot, II, 44.

undoubtedly not shared by all Antifederalists, but they would not have been expressed so vigorously in the convention debates had they not represented a sizable segment of constituent opinion.

Another provision severely and dramatically criticized was that which gave to Congress exclusive jurisdiction over the future site of the national capital and other property to be purchased for forts, arsenals, dockyards, and the like.[65] It was predicted that the ten-mile-square area would become an enormous den of tyranny and iniquity. In New York George Clinton warned "that the ten miles square . . . would be the asylum of the base, idle, avaricious and ambitious. . . ."[66] In Virginia Patrick Henry pointed out that this provision, combined with the necessary and proper clause, gave Congress a right to pass "any law that may facilitate the execution of their acts," and within the specified area to hang "any man who shall act contrary to their commands . . . without benefit of clergy."[67] George Mason argued that the place would make a perfect lair for hit-and-run tyrants. For if any of the government's "officers, or creatures, should attempt to oppress the people, or should actually perpetrate the blackest deed, he has nothing to do but get into the ten miles square. Why was this dangerous power given?"[68] One man observed that the Constitution did not specify the location of this site, and that therefore Congress was perfectly free to seat itself and the other offices of government in Peking. All in all, a terrible prospect: the Pope as President, operating from a base in Peking, superintending a series of hangings without benefit of clergy! Or worse.

---

[65]Article I, Section 8.
[66]The *Cato* Letters; reprinted in Ford, *Essays*, p. 265.
[67]Elliot, III, 436.
[68]*Ibid.*, p. 431.

Although one may regard some of the fears expressed by the Antifederalists as somewhat fanciful and possibly exaggerated for propaganda purposes, there is no mistaking their genuine shock at the lack of a Bill of Rights in the Constitution, or the force and validity of their arguments in demand for one. On this point the Federalists showed a puzzling obtuseness, and their attempt to defend the omission was as unconvincing then as it is now. If George Washington's word is to be trusted, the actions of the Founding Fathers with respect to trial by jury and a Bill of Rights did not stem from any sinister motives. In a letter to Lafayette on April 28, 1788, he gave this explanation: ". . . There was not a member of the convention, I believe, who had the least objection to what is contended for by the Advocates for a *Bill of Rights* and *Tryal by Jury*. The first, where the people evidently retained everything which they did not in express terms give up, was considered nugatory. . . . And as to the second, it was only the difficulty of establishing a mode which should not interfere with the fixed modes of any of the States, that induced the Convention to leave it, as a matter of future adjustment."[69] To the argument that no Bill of Rights was necessary because the Constitution was one of enumerated powers only, and that since Congress and the Executive would have only those powers specifically delegated to them, the Antifederalists replied by pointing out the broad generality of some of the specific powers, such as that to make war. And they pointed out the implications of the "necessary and proper" clause in combination with these broadly defined powers. If Congress had the power to make war, and decided that curtailment of freedom of the press was a necessary and proper means to this end, what was to prevent Congress from passing a law to this effect? The Antifederalists also

---

[69]*Documentary History of the Constitution*, IV, 601–602.

hit on the inconsistency of this particular Federalist argument with the fact that Article I, Section 9 did contain some provisions usually associated with a Bill of Rights—especially those relating to habeas corpus, bills of attainder, and *ex post facto* laws. If it was thought necessary to include these, then by implication it was also necessary to protect other rights against infringement by any of the departments of the central government. To the Federalist argument that the rights of the people would be secured by the bills of rights in the state constitutions, the Antifederalists replied first, that not all the state constitutions had them, and secondly (and more devastatingly), that the "supreme law" clause of the national constitution would render these state bills of rights nugatory in the case of a conflict with that constitution. This logic was irrefutable. To the Federalist argument that bills of rights were the historical product of conflict between the people and a monarch, and that they were unnecessary in a republic where the people governed themselves, the Antifederalists replied with withering scorn, reiterating their constant remarks concerning the universal perfidy of all men intrusted with power.

The victory in this argument clearly lay with the Antifederalists, for the reasoning of their opponents was muddled, inconsistent, contradictory, and thoroughly unpersuasive. It is significant that this was the one major area in which the Federalists conceded the legitimacy of the Antifederalist position and, led by Madison, helped to supply the defect by agreeing to what we now call the Bill of Rights in the first Congress. The great vulnerability of the Constitution because of the absence of such a bill in its original form was made obvious over and over again in essays and in the state ratifying conventions. One example will suffice.

The Constitution guaranteed the right of trial by jury in

all criminal cases[70] except impeachment, but it did not list
the procedural safeguards associated with that right. There
was no specification that the trial should be not merely in
the state but in the vicinity where the crime was committed (which was habitually identified with the neighborhood of the accused); there were no provisions made for
the selection of the jury or of the procedure to be followed;
there were no guarantees of the right to counsel, of the
right not to incriminate oneself; there was no prohibition
against cruel and unusual punishments. In short, there
were few safeguards upon which the citizen accused of
crime could rely. Apprehension concerning the latitude
left to Congress in this matter was expressed in several conventions;[71] it was Holmes of Massachusetts who painted
the most vivid and fearful picture of the possible fate of
the unfortunate citizen who ran afoul of federal law. Such
an individual might be taken away and tried by strangers
far from home; his jury might be hand-picked by the
sheriff, or hold office for life; there was no guarantee that
indictment should be by grand jury only, hence it might
be by information of the attorney-general, "in consequence of which the most innocent person in the commonwealth may be . . . dragged from his home, his
friends, his acquaintance, and confined in prison. . . ."
"On the whole," said Holmes, ". . . we shall find Congress possessed of powers enabling them to institute

---

[70]Article III, Section 2. The Constitution made no provision for jury
trial in civil cases, because different procedures in the several states had
made the formulation of a general method difficult. The Antifederalists
leaped to the conclusion that the lack of a written guarantee of this right
meant certain deprivation of it, and they professed to be thoroughly
alarmed. But their primary fear centered around what they regarded as
the inadequate guarantees of the right of trial by jury in criminal cases.

[71]In New York; see Elliott, II, 400; Virginia, III, 523 ff.; North Carolina, IV, 143, 150, 154–155.

judicatories little less inauspicious than a certain tribunal in Spain, which has long been the disgrace of Christendom: I mean that diabolical institution, the *Inquisition*. . . . They are nowhere restrained from inventing the most cruel and unheard-of punishments and annexing them to crimes; and there is no constitutional check on them, but that *racks* and *gibbets* may be amongst the most mild instruments of their discipline."[72]

Should Congress have attempted any of these actions, it would have amounted to a virtual coup d'état and a repudiation of republicanism.[73] The advocates of the Constitution argued that such abuse of power could not reasonably be expected on the part of representatives elected by the people themselves. This argument was not satisfactory to the Antifederalists. They charged that the authors and advocates of the Constitution were about to risk their liberties and those of all of the people on the slim possibility that the men to be elected to office in the new government would be, and would always be, good men.

The Federalists also argued that election would serve as a check, since the people could remove unfaithful or unsatisfactory representatives, and since knowledge of this would make the latter refrain from incurring the dis-

---

[72]Elliot, II, 109–111.

[73]This method of arguing drove the Federalists to exasperation more than once, as when one delegate in the Virginia Convention, an infrequent speaker, lost patience with Patrick Henry's "bugbears of hobgoblins" and suggested that "If the gentleman does not like this government, let him go and live among the Indians." Elliot, III, 580; cf. 632, 644. Also note the reporter's tongue-in-cheek note on Henry's opposition to the President's power of Commander-in-Chief: "Here Mr. Henry strongly and pathetically expatiated on the probability of the President's enslaving America, and the horrid consequences that must result." *Ibid.*, p. 60. But Henry, who was so good at this technique himself, attacked it in his opponents. See *Ibid.*, p. 140.

pleasure of their constituents. This argument was flatly rejected. Patrick Henry stated his position emphatically during the course of his objection to Congressional power of taxation:

I shall be told in this place, that those who are to tax us are our representatives. To this I answer, that there is no real check to prevent their ruining us. There is no actual responsibility. The only semblance of a check is the negative power of not re-electing them. This sir, is but a feeble barrier, when their personal interest, their ambition and avarice, come to be put in contrast with the happiness of the people. All checks founded on anything but self-love, will not avail.[74]

In North Carolina the same opinion was expressed in a rather remarkable interchange. Taylor objected to the method of impeachment on the ground that since the House of Representatives drew up the bill of indictment, and the Senate acted upon it, the members of Congress themselves would be virtually immune to this procedure. Governor Johnston answered that impeachment was not an appropriate remedy for legislative misrule, and that "A representative is answerable to no power but his constituents. He is accountable to no being under heaven but the people who appointed him." To this, Taylor responded simply, "that it now appeared to him in a still worse light than before."[75] Johnston stated one of the great principles of representative government; it merely deepened Taylor's fear of Congress. He and his fellow Antifederalists strongly wished for what Madison had referred to as "auxiliary precautions" against possible acts of legislative tyranny.

---

[74]Elliot, III, 167; cf. 327.
[75]Elliot, IV, 32–34.

V. PROPOSED CHANGES

Additional safeguards were of two kinds: more explicit limitations written into the Constitution, and more institutional checks to enforce these limitations.

In recent years the Constitution has been much admired for its brevity, its generality, its freedom from the minutiae which characterized nineteenth-century constitutions. These qualities were feared and not admired by the Antifederalists. They wanted explicitness that would confine the discretion of congressional majorities within narrow boundaries. One critic complained of "a certain darkness, duplicity and studied ambiguity of expression running through the whole Constitution. . . ."[76] Another said that "he did not believe there existed a social compact on the face of the earth so vague and so indefinite as the one now on the table."[77] A North Carolinian demanded to know, "Why not use expressions that were clear and unequivocal?"[78] Later, the same critic warned, "Without the most express restrictions, Congress may trample on your rights."[79] Williams of New York expressed the general feeling when he said in that state's convention, "I am sir, for certainty in the establishment of a constitution which is not only to operate upon us, but upon millions yet unborn."[80] These men wanted everything down in black and white, with no latitude of discretion or interpretation left to their representatives in Congress. It was an attitude that

---

[76]Thomas B. Wait to George Thatcher, January 8, 1788, in "The Thatcher Papers," selected from the papers of Hon. George Thatcher, and communicated by Captain Goodwin, U.S.A., *The Historical Magazine* (November and December 1869, Second Series, Vols. 15–16), No. V, p. 262.

[77]Elliott, III, 583.

[78]Elliot, IV, 68; cf. 70, 153, 154–155, 168.

[79]*Ibid.*, p. 167.

[80]Elliot, II, 339.

anticipated the later trend toward constitutions filled with innumerable and minute restrictions on the legislatures.

To no avail did the Federalists argue that if future representatives should indeed prove to be so treacherous and tyrannical as to commit the horrible deeds suggested, then mere guarantees on paper would not stop them for a minute. It is easy to call the Antifederalist attitude unrealistic, but to do so is to miss a large part of its significance. Like the Founding Fathers, like all men of their age, they were great constitutionalists. They were also first-generation republicans, still self-consciously so, and aware that their precious form of government was as yet an experiment that had not proved its capacity for endurance. Its greatest enemy was man's lust for power, and the only thing that could hold this in check, they were convinced, was a carefully written and properly constructed constitution. They placed even greater emphasis on the structure of government than did the Founding Fathers, and refused to take for granted, as the latter did, that the "genius" of the country was republican, and that the behavior of the men to be placed in office would in general be republican also.

The Antifederalists wanted a more rigid system of separation of powers, more numerous and more effective checks and balances, than the Founding Fathers had provided.[81] They thought this elementary principle of good government, this "political maxim," had been violated, and that corruption leading to tyranny would be the inevitable result. That the doctrine celebrated by Montesquieu did enjoy the status of "maxim" seems unquestionable.

---

[81]Thus in *The Federalist 47*, Madison felt obliged to defend the Constitution against this charge. This was first pointed out to me by B. F. Wright and was the origin of the present essay. See the discussion in his article *"The Federalist* on the Nature of Political Man," *Ethics* (January 1949), especially pp. 7 ff.

Violation of separation of powers was one of George Mason's major objections to the Constitution.[82] Richard Henry Lee made the same protest,[83] and further lamented that there were no "checks in the formation of the government, to secure the rights of the people against the usurpations of those they appoint to govern. . . ."[84] James Monroe said that he could "see no real checks in it."[85] It is no wonder that an obscure member of the Virginia convention, when he rose with great diffidence to make his only speech, chose safe and familiar ground to cover:

That the legislative, executive, and judicial powers should be separate and distinct, in all free governments, is a political fact so well established, that I presume I shall not be thought arrogant, when I affirm that no country ever did, or ever can, long remain free, where they are blended. All the states have been in this sentiment when they formed their state constitutions, and therefore have guarded against the danger; and every schoolboy in politics must be convinced of the propriety of the observation; and yet, by the proposed plan, the legislative and executive powers are closely united. . . .[86]

In Pennsylvania, whose Revolutionary state constitution had embodied very little of separation of powers, an apparent return to Montesquieu's doctrine led to criticism of the Constitution. In the ratifying convention, one of the amendments submitted had for its purpose, "That the legislative, executive, and judicial powers be kept sepa-

---

[82]"Objections of the Hon. George Mason, to the proposed Federal Constitution. Addressed to the Citizens of Virginia." Ford, *Pamphlets,* p. 330.
[83]"Letters of a Federal Farmer," Ford, *Pamphlets,* p. 299.
[84]*Ibid.,* p. 318.
[85]Elliot, III, 219.
[86]*Ibid.,* p. 608.

rate. . . ."[87] In that same state, the leading Antifederalist pamphleteer "Centinel," who is believed to have been either George Bryan, a probable co-author of the 1776 Constitution and formerly in sympathy with the ideas of Tom Paine on this subject, or his son Samuel, now expressed himself in the usual manner:

This mixture of the legislative and executive moreover highly tends to corruption. The chief improvement in government, in modern times, has been the complete separation of the great distinctions of power; placing the *legislative* in different hands from those which hold the *executive*; and again severing the *judicial* part from the ordinary *administrative*. "When the legislative and executive powers (says Montesquieu) are united in the same person, or in the same body of magistrates, there can be no liberty."[88]

The Antifederalists were just as unequivocal about the inadequacy of the Constitution's system of checks and balances. Patrick Henry hit his top form when he took up the matter in Virginia: "There will be no checks, no real balances, in this government. What can avail your specious, imaginary balances, your rope-dancing, chain-rattling, ridiculous ideal checks and contrivances?"[89] Later in the Convention he argued that what checks there were had no practical value at all—for reasons that must cloud his reputation as a spokesman for the masses imbued with the radical spirit of Revolutionary democracy: "To me it appears that there is no check in that government. The President, senators, and representatives, all, immediately or

---

[87]McMaster and Stone, *Pennsylvania and the Constitution*, p. 423. See also pp. 475–477 for discussion back of this.
[88]McMaster and Stone, *Pennsylvania and the Constitution*, p. 587.
[89]Elliot, III, 54.

mediately, are the choice of the people."[90] His views were echoed by his colleague, William Grayson.[91]

In New York, Melancton Smith returned to the subject several times, arguing that because there would eventually be corruption in Congress, "It is wise to multiply checks to a greater degree than the present state of things requires."[92] In Massachusetts James Winthrop tied up the concept of separation of powers with checks and balances very neatly. "It is now generally understood that it is for the security of the people that the powers of the government should be lodged in different branches. By this means publick business will go on when they all agree, and stop when they disagree. The advantage of checks in government is thus manifested where the concurrence of different branches is necessary to the same act. . . ."[93]

There can be little doubt that the Antifederalists were

[90]*Ibid.*, p. 164. He then went on to point out that the British House of Lords constituted a check against both the King and the Commons, and that this check was founded on "self-love," i.e., the desire of the Lords to protect their interests against attack from either of the other two branches of the government. This consideration, he said, prevailed upon him "to pronounce the British government superior, in this respect, to any government that ever was in any country. Compare this with your Congressional checks. . . . Have you a resting-place like the British government? Where is the rock of your salvation? . . . Where are your checks? You have no hereditary nobility—an order of men to whom human eyes can be cast up for relief; for, says the Constitution, there is no title of nobility to be granted. . . . In the British government there are real balances and checks: in this system there are only ideal balances." *Ibid.*, pp. 164–165.

[91]*Ibid.*, pp. 421, 563. Grayson also expressed his preference for a form of government—if there was to be a national government at all—far less popular than the one proposed. He favored one strikingly similar to the plan Hamilton had suggested in Philadelphia, a president and senate elected for life, and a lower house elected for a three-year term. See Elliot, III, 279.

[92]Elliot, II, 259, 315.

[93]*Agrippa* Letters in Ford, *Essays*, p. 116.

united in their desire to put more checks on the new government. This was natural, since they greatly feared it. Expressions of the opposite opinion were extremely rare. Rawlins Lowndes in South Carolina remarked casually and without elaboration that it was possible to have too many checks on a government.[94] George Clinton and the Pennsylvanian "Centinel" both warned that a government might become so complex that the people could not understand it,[95] but both men expressed the usual fear of abuse of power,[96] and "Centinel" paid his respects to Montesquieu and explicitly criticized the inadequacy of checks by the President or the House of Representatives on the Senate.[97]

Thus no one, so far as I have been able to discover, attacked the general validity of the system of separation of powers and checks and balances. The Antifederalists were staunch disciples of Montesquieu on this subject, and they would have found quite unacceptable J. Allen Smith's dictum that "The system of checks and balances must not be confused with democracy; it is opposed to and cannot be reconciled with the theory of popular government."[98]

Although there was much oratory about the Founding Fathers' deviation from Montesquieu's doctrine, there were surprisingly few proposals for specific alterations in the structure of the new government. Of these, one of the most important was a change in the relationship between Pres-

---

[94]Elliot, IV, 308–309.

[95]Clinton's *Cato* Letters in Ford, *Essays,* p. 257; *Centinel* in McMaster and Stone, *Pennsylvania and the Constitution,* p. 569. "Centinel" expressed a desire for a unicameral legislature.

[96]Clinton in Ford, *Essays,* pp. 261, 266; *Centinel* in McMaster and Stone, *Pennsylvania and Constitution,* p. 617.

[97]McMaster and Stone, *Pennsylvania and the Constitution,* pp. 586–587, 475–477.

[98]*The Spirit of American Government* (New York: The Macmillan Company, 1907), p. 9.

ident and Senate. The latter's share in the treaty-making and appointing powers was believed to be a dangerous blending of executive and legislative power which ought to have been avoided. Possibly because of their recent memory of the role of the colonial governor's council, possibly because there was no clear provision in the Constitution for an executive cabinet or council, the Antifederalists saw the Senate very much in the latter's role and expected it to play a very active and continuous part in giving advice to the President. This was clearly contrary to the doctrine of the celebrated Montesquieu—at least it seemed so to them.

The result would certainly be some form of joint Presidential-Senatorial tyranny, it was argued, but as to which of the two departments would be the stronger of the "partners in crime," the Antifederalists were not agreed. Patrick Henry said that the President, with respect to the treaty-making power, "as distinguished from the Senate, is nothing."[99] Grayson, with the North-South division in mind, predicted a *quid pro quo* alliance between the President and "the seven Eastern states." "He will accommodate himself to their interests in forming treaties, and they will continue him perpetually in office."[100] Mason predicted a "marriage" between the President and Senate: "They will be continually supporting and aiding each other: they will always consider their interest as united. . . . The executive and legislative powers, thus connected, will destroy all balances. . . ."[101] "Centinel" of Pennsylvania also feared that the President would not be strong enough to resist pressure from the Senate, and that he would join with them as "the head of the aristocratic

---

[99]Elliot, III, 353.
[100]*Ibid.*, p. 492.
[101]*Ibid.*, pp. 493–494.

junto."[102] Spencer of North Carolina, in support of a remedy in which all of the above men concurred, argued that with an advisory council entirely separate from the legislature, and chosen from the separate states, the President "would have that independence which is necessary to form the intended check upon the acts passed by the legislature before they obtain the sanction of laws."[103]

Although the prevailing opinion thus seemed to be that the President was not strong enough, there were some who believed that he was *too* strong. George Clinton argued that the extensive powers given to him, combined with his long tenure of office, gave him both "power and time sufficient to ruin his country." Furthermore, since he had no proper council to assist him while the Senate was recessed, he would be without advice, or get it from "minions and favorites"—or "a great council of state will grow out of the principal officers of the great departments, the most dangerous council in a free country."[104]

One man in North Carolina departed from the ordinary Antifederalist line of attack and criticized the executive veto from a clear majoritarian position. It was Lancaster, who projected the hypothetical case of a bill that passed the House of Representatives unanimously, the Senate by a large majority, was vetoed by the President and returned to the Senate, where it failed to get a two-thirds vote. The House would never see it again, said Mr. Lancaster, and thus, "This is giving a power to the President to overrule fifteen members of the Senate and every member of the House of Representatives."[105]

Except for Lancaster, most Antifederalists feared the

---

[102]McMaster and Stone, *Pennsylvania and the Constitution*, p. 586.
[103]Elliot, IV, 117–118.
[104]*Cato* Letters, Ford, *Essays*, pp. 261–262.
[105]Elliot, IV, 214.

Senate more than the President, but all feared the two in combination and wanted some checks against them. The separate advisory council for the President was one, and shorter terms and/or compulsory rotation for Senators and President, plus the power of state recall of the former, were others. Direct, popular election of either was *not* proposed.

Since most of the state executives and legislators held office for annual or biennial terms, one would naturally expect the substantially longer tenure of the President and Senate to be severely criticized. There were numerous objections to the six-year term of Senators, some to the four-year term of the President, and a few to the two-year term of members of the House of Representatives. It is to be noted, however, that there was no serious attempt to shorten the length of term of any of these officers, nor was there any attempt to make the tenure of either the President or the Senate correspond with that of the House. It was agreed that the two houses should "afford a mutual check" on each other,[106] and some believed that the "stability" provided by the Senate "was essential to good government."[107]

The most insistent and repeated criticism, as indicated above, was the failure of the Constitution to provide for the compulsory rotation of office for Senators and the President. "Nothing is so essential to the preservation of a republican government as a periodical rotation," said George Mason [108] and Melancton Smith pronounced it "a very important and truly republican institution."[109] They greatly feared that President and Senators would be per-

---

[106]Elliot, II, 308 (Lansing).
[107]*Ibid.*, p. 309 (Smith).
[108]Elliot, III, 485.
[109]Elliot, II, 310.

petually reelected, and in effect hold office for life. Mason, for example, was quite content for the Senate to serve six years, and the President even eight, but he believed that without rotation, the new government would become "an elective monarchy."[110] The President would be able to perpetuate himself forever, it was assumed, because his election would always be thrown into the House of Representatives. In that body, corruption, intrigue, foreign influence, and above all else, the incumbent's use of his patronage, would make it possible for every man, once elected, to hold office for life. Senators would "hold their office perpetually,"[111] by corrupting their electors, the state legislatures. In New York, where the subject was debated very thoroughly, the Antifederalists were challenged to show how such corruption could take place, and continue for life, among a group which was continuously subject to popular election, and which would presumably not be permanent. To this challenge Lansing replied, "It is unnecessary to particularize the numerous ways in which public bodies are accessible to corruption. The poison always finds a channel, and never wants an object."[112] No distinction as to comparative corruptibility was made between national and state representatives.

To Federalist objections that compulsory rotation constituted an abridgment of the people's right to elect whomsoever they wished, Melancton Smith replied impatiently, "What is government itself but a restraint upon the natural rights of the people? What constitution was ever devised that did not operate as a restraint on their natural liberties?"[113] Lansing conceded that rotation placed a restric-

---

[110]Elliot, III, 485.
[111]Elliot, II, 309 (Smith).
[112]Elliot, II, 295.
[113]*Ibid.*, p. 311.

tion on the people's free choice of rulers, but he thought this beneficial: "The rights of the people will be best supported by checking, at a certain point, the current of popular favor, and preventing the establishment of an influence which may leave to elections little more than the form of freedom."[114]

The power of recall by state legislatures was associated with compulsory rotation as a means of preventing senatorial abuse of power. Not only would it enforce strict responsibility of senators to their electors, but in so doing it would protect the interests and preserve the sovereignty of the separate states. For these reasons, its adoption was strongly pressed in several of the ratifying conventions. Beyond these reasons, which were primary, recall combined with rotation would have a secondary beneficent result. It would serve to prevent the perpetuation of intralegislative parties and factions—something which the Antifederalists feared quite as much as their opponents. Even if the power of recall should not actually be used, said Lansing, it would "destroy party spirit."[115] When his opponents turned this argument against him, and suggested that factions within the state legislatures might use the power to remove good, honorable, and faithful men from the Senate, the answer was that the legislatures had not abused the power under the Articles of Confederation and would almost certainly not do so in the future, and that even if they did, ample opportunity would be provided for the displaced senator to defend himself. The influence of "ambitious and designing men" would be detected and exposed, and the error easily corrected.[116] A curious "Trust

---

[114]*Ibid.*, p. 295. It was in this debate that Lansing made the Madisonian statement quoted on p. lxiii–lxiv.

[115]Elliot, II, 290.

[116]*Ibid.*, p. 299.

them, trust them not" attitude toward the state legislatures is thus revealed. They could not be trusted to refuse reelection to unfaithful or ambitious senators, though they could be trusted to remove the same and to leave in office all those who deserved well of them and of their constituents.

From this it is clear that the Antifederalists were not willing to trust either upper or lower house of the proposed national Congress; neither were they willing to trust their own state legislatures completely, though they had less fear of the latter because these could be kept under closer observation.

The same attitude is indicated by Antifederalist reaction to the restrictions placed on state legislatures by Article I, Section 10 of the Constitution, and to the then potential review of both state and national legislation by the Supreme Court.

Of the latter prospect, frequently said to have been one of the great bulwarks erected aginst the democratic majority, very little was said during the ratification debate. There was no explicit provision for judicial review in the Constitution, and it is probably not possible to prove conclusively whether or not its authors intended the Supreme Court to exercise this power. The evidence suggests that they probably assumed it would. Hamilton's *Federalist 78* supports this view. The issue was never debated in the state conventions, and there were few references to it in any of the Antifederalist arguments. Since *Federalist 78* was published before the Virginia, New York, and North Carolina conventions met, this lack of discussion is significant and would seem to reflect lack of concern. There was severe criticism of Article III, particularly in Virginia, but it centered around the jurisdiction of the lower federal courts to be established by Congress, not around the Supreme Court. The issue was entirely one of state courts versus federal courts, not of courts versus legislatures.

The single direct reference to judicial review made in the Virginia convention suggests that this institution was, or would have been, thoroughly congenial to the Antifederalists. The statement was made by Patrick Henry:

Yes, sir, our judges opposed the acts of the legislature. We have this landmark to guide us. They had fortitude to declare that they were the judiciary, and would oppose unconstitutional acts. Are you sure that your federal judiciary will act thus? Is that judiciary as well constructed, and as independent of the other branches, as our state judiciary? Where are your landmarks in this government? I will be bold to say you cannot find any in it. I take it as the highest encomium on this country, that the acts of the legislature, if unconstitutional, are liable to be opposed by the judiciary.[117]

There was nothing equivocal about Henry's attitude. It elicited no comment. Possibly neither side wished to commit itself; more likely the statement was lost and forgotten after brighter flames had issued from the great orator's fire. What is really significant, however, is the almost complete absence of debate over judicial review. One major exception is to be found in the "Brutus" letters of Robert Yates. Yates had an excellent legal mind and was particularly adept at analyzing the Constitution for implied as well as explicit meaning. He inferred, before Hamilton wrote *Federalist 78*, that the Supreme Court would have and would exercise the power of judicial review. "The supreme court then have a right, independent of the legislature, to give a construction to the constitution and every part of it, and there is no power provided in this system to correct their construction or do it away. If, therefore, the legislature pass any laws, inconsistent with the sense the judges put upon the constitution, they will de-

---

[117]Elliot, III, 325.

clare it void; and therefore in this respect their power is superior to that of the legislature." Yates also expressed the opinion that it would be preferable to leave to the legislature the final power of interpreting the Constitution, for the members of the legislature were subject to removal by the people, who could therefore remedy the evil through the electoral process. But to leave the power of final construction with an independent judiciary meant to leave the people with no remedy save *"a high hand and an outstretched arm."*[118] Thus one Antifederalist anticipated and opposed the power of judicial review of legislation. That others did not follow his lead is puzzling and perhaps significant. The Antifederalists probed the Constitution for every conceivable threat, explicit or implicit, to their conception of free and popular government. If they had considered judicial review such a threat, they would surely have made the most of it, and particularly after *Federalist 78* was published.

There was also comparatively little attention given to the restrictions that Article I, Section 10 of the Constitution placed on the state legislatures. Among other things, the states were forbidden to coin money, emit bills of credit, make anything but gold or silver legal tender for the payment of debts, or pass any law impairing the obligation of contracts. These are the provisions that recent historians have emphasized as designed to protect the property of the conservative class against the onslaughts of the radical democratic majority. The Antifederalists had very little to say about these provisions. The notation of the New York Convention's action is significant: "The committee then proceded through sections 8, 9, and 10, of this article [I], and the whole of the next, with little or no de-

---

[118]"Brutus", Letter XV, *The New York Journal and Weekly Register* (New York City), March 20, 1788.

bate."[119] In Virginia and the Carolinas there was more discussion, but nothing like a full-dress debate, and very little indication of any strong or widespread opposition. In fact, Patrick Henry said that the restrictions were "founded in good principles,"[120] and William Grayson said of the prohibition against paper money, "it is unanimously wished by every one that it should not be objected to."[121] Richard Henry Lee expressed his preference for paper money to be issued by Congress only.[122] Of the few objections or doubts expressed, these were typical. Henry in Virginia and Galloway in North Carolina both expressed a fear that the contract clause might be interpreted to force the states to redeem their respective shares of the depreciated Continental currency and of state securities at face value.[123] Henry was also angry because of the necessary implication that the states were too "depraved" to be trusted with the contracts of their own citizens.[124] With regard to the prohibition of paper money, two men in North Carolina defended the previous state issue as having been a necessary expedient in troublesome times, but did not seem to object to the prohibition of future issues.[125] One man argued against this clause and the supreme law clause on the ground that the effect might be to destroy the paper money already in circulation and thereby create great confusion.[126] His contention was denied.[127] These remarks, none of which expressed direct opposition, were

---

[119]Elliot, II, 406.
[120]Elliot, III, 471.
[121]*Ibid.*, p. 566.
[122]J. C. Ballagh, editor, *The Letters of Richard Henry Lee*, 2 vols. (New York: The Macmillan Company, 1911–1914), pp. 421–422.
[123]Elliot, III, 318–319; IV, 190.
[124]Elliot, III, 156.
[125]*Ibid.*, IV, 88, 169–170.
[126]*Ibid.*, pp. 180, 184–185.
[127]*Ibid.*, pp. 181–185.

typical. In South Carolina, however, Rawlins Lowndes came out flatly against this restriction, and defended the previous issue of paper money and the right of the state to make further issues in the future.[128] His position appears to have been the exception at least of those that were expressed openly and publicly on the various convention floors.[129]

The response of the Antifederalists to these important limitations on the power of the states can accurately be described, I think, as one of over-all approbation tempered by some doubts caused by fear that they would be applied retroactively. This attitude is in rather curious contrast with the extremely jealous reaction to other changes in federal-state relations for which the Constitution provided. There were violent objections to federal control over state militia, to congressional power to tax and to regulate commerce, to the creation of an inferior system of federal courts. All these things brought forth loud cries that the states would be swallowed up by the national government. These important restrictions on the economic powers of the states were received with relative silence.

[128]*Ibid.*, pp. 289–290.

[129]There appears to have been more opposition to the provisions of Article I, Section 10 expressed outside of the Convention than inside. See Trenholme, *Ratification in North Carolina*, p. 42, and Clarence E. Miner, *The Ratification of the Federal Constitution in New York*, Studies in History, Economics and Public Law, Vol. XCIV, No. 3, Whole No. 214 (New York: Columbia University Press, 1921), for the extra-Convention debate in New York. It may be that this was one of the subjects the Antifederalists preferred not to debate for the official record. See Trenholme, pp. 166–167, for a discussion of the refusal of North Carolina Antifederalists to state in the Convention objections to the Constitution being made outside. There was also apparently a similar situation during the Virginia convention, where the Federalists objected to what was happening "outdoors." See Elliot, III, 237. See also the remarks of Alexander C. Hanson, a member of the Maryland convention. In discussing these provisions, of which he strongly approved, he wrote, "I have here perhaps touched a string, which secretly draws together many of the foes to the plan." In *Aristides*, "Remarks on the Proposed Plan of a Federal Government," Ford, *Pamphlets*, p. 243.

There was apparently very little objection to these limitations on the power of state legislative majorities.

The Antifederalist demand for more limitations upon and checks within the national government, and their relative quiescence concerning the restrictions imposed on state legislatures by Article I, Section 10, reflected an attitude of distrust toward the representatives of the people, whether directly or indirectly elected. These and other arguments also involved rather serious reservations about the competence of the people to make wise and just decisions with respect to both men and issues.

One of the issues was, of course, the rejection or ratification of the Constitution. Antifederalist leaders expressed fear that the people might not see in the proposed new government all of the dangers and defects that they themselves saw. "Centinel," the author or the son of the author of Pennsylvania's Revolutionary constitution, was particularly dubious on this count, and expounded a kind of Burkeian conservatism as the best guarantor of the people's liberties. In a passage apparently aimed at the prestige given to the proposed Constitution by the support of men like Washington and Franklin, "Centinel" wrote that "the science of government is so abstruse, that few are able to judge for themselves." Without the assistance of those "who are competent to the task of developing the principles of government," the people were "too apt to yield an implicit assent to the opinions of those characters whose abilities are held in the highest esteem, and to those in whose integrity and patriotism they can confide. . . ." This was dangerous, because such men might easily be dupes, "the instruments of despotism in the hands of the *artful and designing*." "Centinel" then continued:

If it were not for the stability and attachment which time and habit gives to forms of government, it would be in the power of the enlightened and aspiring few, if they should combine, at any time to destroy the best establishments, and even make the people the instruments of their own subjugation.

The late revolution having effaced in a great measure all former habits, and the present institutions are so recent, that there exists not that great reluctance to innovation, so remarkable in old communities, and which accords with reason, for the most comprehensive mind cannot foresee the full operation of material changes on civil polity; it is the genius of the common law to resist innovation.[130]

In the New York convention, there were similar fears expressed about the instability of public opinion. Said George Clinton, "The people, when wearied with their distresses, will in the moment of frenzy, be guilty of the most imprudent and desperate measures. . . . I know the people are too apt to vibrate from one extreme to another. The effects of this disposition are what I wish to guard against."[131] His colleague, Melancton Smith, spoke in a similar vein:

Fickleness and inconstancy, he said, were characteristic of a free people; and, in framing a constitution for them, it was, perhaps, the most difficult thing to correct this spirit, and guard against the evil effects of it. He was persuaded it could not be altogether prevented without destroying their freedom. . . . This fickle and inconstant spirit was the more dangerous in bringing about changes in the government.[132]

These doubts about the people's judgment of issues were matched by skepticism about their capacity as electors implicit in several of the arguments noted above. The ad-

---

[130]McMaster and Stone, *Pennsylvania and the Constitution*, pp. 566–567.

[131]Elliot, II, 359.

[132]*Ibid.*, p. 225.

vocacy of religious qualifications for officeholding indicated a desire to restrict the choice of the electorate to certified Protestants, and the demand for compulsory rotation of Senators and President rested on the fear that corruption of both state and national legislatures by the incumbents of those offices could not be prevented by the feeble check of popular election. Perhaps most important was the belief that the people, voting in the large constituencies provided for by the Constitution, would either lose elections to their presumed aristocratic opponents because of the latter's superior capacity for organization, or would themselves let their choice fall on such aristocrats, or be deceived by ambitious and unscrupulous demagogues.

There was also fear that the decisions of the majority would not always be just. That a Bill of Rights was needed not only to protect the people from their government but also to protect individuals and minorities from the will of the majority was stated explicitly by James Winthrop. In refuting the Federalist argument that bills of rights were not necessary in republican governments, he replied:

that the sober and industrious part of the community should be defended from the rapacity and violence of the vicious and idle. A bill of rights, therefore, ought to set forth the purposes for which the compact is made, and serves to secure the minority against the usurpation and tyranny of the majority. . . . The experience of mankind has proved the prevalence of a disposition to use power wantonly. It is therefore as necessary to defend an individual against the majority in a republick as against the king in a monarchy.[133]

Distrust of majority factions in much the same sense as Madison's was emphatically expressed by the one sector of

---

[133]*Agrippa* Letters, Ford, *Essays*, p. 117. See also Elliot, III, 499, for a similar statement from William Grayson.

Antifederalism which constituted the most self-conscious minority. Southerners felt keenly the conflict of interest between North and South and were vehemently opposed to surrendering themselves to the majority of the seven Eastern states. One of the reasons for George Mason's refusal to sign the Constitution had been his failure to get adopted a two-thirds majority vote for all laws affecting commerce and navigation. His fears for the South's interests were shared by his fellow Southerners and were frequently expressed in the Convention debates. "It will be a government of a faction," said William Grayson, "and this observation will apply to every part of it; for having a majority, they may do what they please."[134] Other colleagues in Virginia joined in this distrust of the anticipated Northern majority uniting to oppress the South.[135] In North and South Carolina it was much the same. Bloodworth lamented, "To the north of the Susquehanna there are thirty-six representatives, and to the south of it only twenty-nine. They will always outvote us."[136] In South Carolina, Rawlins Lowndes predicted that "when this new Constitution should be adopted, the sun of the Southern States would set, never to rise again." Why? Because the Eastern states would have a majority in the legislature and would not hesitate to use it—probably to interfere with the slave trade, "because they have none themselves, and therefore want to exclude us from this great advantage."[137]

There was, then, no doctrinaire devotion to majoritarianism. It was assumed that oppression of individuals or of groups might come from majorities of the people themselves as well as from kings or aristocrats.

---

[134]Elliot, III, 492.
[135]*Ibid.*, pp. 152, 221–222.
[136]Elliot, IV, 185.
[137]*Ibid.*, p. 272.

VI. CONCLUDING OBSERVATIONS

It should not be forgotten, in attempting to piece together the lineaments of Antifederalist thought, that the situation in which these were produced was a polemical one. The opponents of the Constitution held no convention that could serve as a counterpart to that in which the Constitution was framed, and there is therefore no record of the ideas of men expressed during the process of attempting to solve a problem, in an atmosphere conducive to candor, mutual good will, and dispassionate discussion. What an Antifederalist convention might have been like, it is difficult to say. One can visualize a group dominated by the sober moderation of a Melancton Smith or a George Mason (as he was in Philadelphia rather than in Richmond), or one can visualize a convention paralyzed by oratorical duels between the likes of Patrick Henry and Luther Martin, with the aristocratic views of a William Grayson and the more democratic views of a "Centinel" waiting on the sidelines for their chance of expression, and a Rawlins Lowndes fighting out the related issues of slavery and taxation with a Rhode Island Quaker. It is difficult, as an historian of political ideas, not to wish for such a convention in order to see the Antifederalists operating in a less polemical situation. That the situation does make a difference is suggested by the very different performances given by George Mason and Alexander Hamilton while they were members of the Philadelphia convention and while they were attacking and defending the Constitution afterward.

The Antifederalist essays and speeches that we have were produced at a late stage in the debate over the Constitution. They were not like the Virginia Plan or the Paterson Plan, introduced early in the session at Philadelphia as initial starting points for discussion among men who had accepted as one of their working rules a willingness to change their minds and their votes as they moved along toward a solution. The Antifederalists were presented with a finished document, and the strategy first adopted by its authors and advocates was, "Take it or leave it." With the challenge made in this way, the Antifederalists naturally were tempted to respond in kind: a plague on your *entire* house. With the outstanding exception of the commerce power, which many Southerners wanted exercised only by a two-thirds majority in Congress, they tended to strike out in all directions and hit the Constitution on many points which, if they had themselves been in a situation to frame instead of to accept or reject in toto, they might have accepted. As a result, their bark was sometimes worse than their bite. The scholar is therefore faced with a problem of interpretation and evaluation which, though familiar and indeed characteristic of American politics, is everlastingly difficult. Whereas the delegates to the Philadelphia convention had deliberately sought to minimize the differences among them, the Antifederalists, caught in a campaign situation, deliberately sought to maximize the differences between themselves and their opponents. This makes it possible for the scholar to do the same, and indeed almost obligatory on the basis of the evidence presented by the combatants. Yet some allowance should be made for the exigencies of the controversy and the passions of the moment. The civil war predicted by some Antifederalists if the Constitution were adopted did not in fact materialize. The incompatibility of republican government with a national government, which almost all of them asserted during the debate, was not so strongly felt as to prevent them from submitting to and participating in the new government when it was once established. To read the repeated charges of "aristocracy" and "tyranny" and "conspiracy" issued during the campaign by the Anti-federalists can easily give the impression that America was on the verge of, if not actually engaged in, a class war in 1787–1788, and that the issue was in truth one of democracy versus aristocracy, or liberty versus tyranny. But one should not forget that these charges were made as part of a political campaign, and an American one at that. It has been typical of us as a people to engage in political hyperbole. Perhaps it is necessary as a means of articulating differences which to us are quite real and easily discernible, but which are not always gross enough to fit a political vocabulary derived to a very great extent from European systems. The campaign of 1787–1788 was a hard-fought one, and apparently in some places and with respect to some participants, bitterly fought. Yet I think it would be a mistake to accept all of the charges and counter-charges at face value. This campaign, like many subsequent ones, had that peculiar quality of sparring so violent that both participants and spectators may momentarily forget that it *is* only sparring, and intramural sparring too. In this, our first great national campaign, a genuinely radical change was at issue, and according to the evidence we now have, the sides were about evenly divided. Yet the campaign ended, like all but one of its successors, not with bitter estrangement but with relatively equable relations among the previous contestants. This result, which we take so much for granted now, was truly remarkable.

In an essay restricted to the political ideas of one party to the controversy, it is obvious that only a partial and tentative explanation can be suggested. It would seem to be very clear, nevertheless, that the factors that united the Federalists and Anti-federalists were stronger than those that divided them. Among these were the fundamental principles mentioned earlier in this introduction. There was a general agreement that liberty and certain other related rights and interests of the individual were the proper ends of government; that consent was the only legitimate source of political authority; that the only form of government proper and feasible for Americans was republican; that republican governments, like monarchical governments, should be limited in the excercise of their powers, and by written fundamental laws or constitutions; that there should be some kind and degree of union among the separate states. The Antifederalist method of debate was such as to question the attachment of their opponents to some of these principles, especially republicanism and liberty, and no doubt some of the more ardent spokesmen may have become convinced by their own hyperbole. (It may have been the first, but it was certainly not the last time that this has happened in American politics.) But in view of the final result, one suspects that in spite of all the dreadful possibilities portrayed by the Antifederalists, in spite of all their charges of aristocratic conspiracy, their fundamental attitude toward the Federalists was one of considerable though not unlimited trust. They apparently believed that the Federalists, at least when properly watched by themselves, would operate under the Constitution as republicans *and as constitutionalists.* (Indeed, one of the curiosities of the Antifederalist debate had been the constant assumption that the various anticipated treacheries of the "aristocrats" would be conducted under cover of law.) Furthermore, their sense of what was proper behavior for themselves involved a profound if largely inarticulate commitment to republicanism and constitutionalism. Although there was a good bit of loose talk about civil war and other means of resistance, there does not, at that time, appear to have been any serious movement in that direction. The losing side accepted its defeat,

Accepting the verdict

at the polls or on the convention floors, sometimes gracefully and sometimes grumblingly, but it accepted it. There was already an American political comity in existence, republican and constitutionalist, and it involved a set of unwritten rules about what was, and what was not, "done." How enormously significant and sophisticated this political comity was can perhaps only now be appreciated.

To emphasize the essential unity of the Federalists and Antifederalists is not to deny that important differences divided them. American politics may seem dull or even incomprehensible to foreigners, because the great principles of systematic political philosophy are rarely at issue and the differences between contending parties seem to be minute. To which James Madison might have replied, that they are the only differences we have, and that we make the most of them.

The Antifederalists differed from the Federalists, in the first place, in being more ideologically oriented, more inflexible, more doctrinaire in their political thinking. This may have been due partly to the exigencies of the immediate situation. Since the Federalists had produced and were defending an acknowledged compromise, it was less easy for them to fall back on either old or new doctrines. But the Antifederalists could and did easily appeal to familiar maxims, established practices, and popular prejudices and fears. The proposed change involved a truly new political form; it abandoned such cherished practices as annual elections, and undermined equally cherished concepts such as the sovereignty of the states; it had, moreover, been framed by men who had worked in secret, and who were well above the average in wealth and education. Indeed the Constitution was extremely vulnerable, and the forensic position of the Antifederalists enviably strong. They did not even have to present a united front.

Federalists were forced to defend provisions in the Constitution of which they did not personally approve, or which were adverse to the interests or opinions of their particular state or section—such as those relating to slavery. Antifederalists in New England could and did disagree sharply with Antifederalists in the South on these issues, and it did not hurt their case locally at all.

The temptation to argue from doctrinal maxims could be combined with the advantages of arguing from a purely negative position. Thus the Constitution could be criticized for its abandonment of annual elections without the necessity of explaining how, if there were to be a national government at all, it could operate effectively without extending the terms of office beyond a year's duration. It is significant that the tendency to rely on such arguments was somewhat less in the convention debates than in the newspapers. In conventions, where immediate confrontation was possible, the Federalists were likely to probe the doctrinaire position and expose its weakness, as they did in New York with reference to the rationale of compulsory rotation (See pp. lxxxiii – lxxxvi). In the newspapers, it was easy enough to raise the cry of aristocracy, with or without explanation. In the conventions, the presence of the opposition helped to encourage responsible and rational substantiation of such charges, based on consideration of the actual structure of the proposed government rather than on insinuations and assumptions about the sinister intentions of the framers. The unwillingness of the Antifederalists to express some of their ideas in the conventions, where they might be met and countered by the opposition, is reflected in the occasional Federalist complaint that "gentlemen" were saying things "out-of-doors" which they would not repeat in open debate on the floor of the house.

The tendency of the Antifederalists to rely on certain

doctrinal positions, combined with their essentially negative strategy of attacking the proposed frame. of government on many different counts without always expounding each thoroughly or weaving them all into a systematic pattern, makes the task of interpreting their thought a difficult one. For although their polemical position was highly advantageous, it was not conducive to the creation of a disciplined and coherent production comparable in intellectual quality to *The Federalist*. The problem is not merely one of bringing together and putting into order ideas and attitudes expressed in the numerous essays and speeches of many men—though that is certainly part of it. It is rather that there were internal contradictions in the Antifederalist case, and that certain major topics were not fully treated. Of these defects, the latter is the more serious one for the scholar. Contradictions can be dealt with rather easily, but an unfinished product may not reveal its original design, or even whether it had one.

Thus it is difficult to derive from Antifederalist criticisms of the Presidency a clear picture of their conception of the proper nature and function of the executive in a republican government. They feared the proposed presidency because they thought it combined great power without adequate responsibility, and that the relationship between the President and the Senate violated the principle of separation of powers. They proposed to modify the office by introducing compulsory rotation and by instituting a separate council (not a cabinet) that would perform the advice and consent functions assigned to the Senate by the Constitution. The method of selecting this additional council was not always clearly specified, but there was apparently no intent to make it directly representative of the people. It was desired as a check on the executive power, but not necessarily one designed to make the President more immediately responsive to a national popular will.[138] The fear of the President, and the tendency to regard the office as tinged with monarchy and thus destructive of republicanism seemed to spring not from a belief that it was unrepresentative of the people, but from doubts about the accountability of the occupant. To my knowledge, none of the Antifederalists ever visualized the President ordinarily as the "President of all the people," a symbol and focus of national sentiment. They would almost certainly have been frightened of such a prospect, at least for any man except George Washington. In the Federal Convention, Governeur Morris did have this conception, and proposed the direct election of the President in order to achieve what he thought of as a potent institution for an increase in the spirit of nationalism. This, of course, would not have been congenial to the Antifederalists, just as it was not to the majority of Morris's colleagues in Philadelphia. With respect to the presidency, the intent of the Antifederalists was to prevent an abuse of power, not to make it a great and responsive instrument of the national will. This was natural, because they did not believe in the possibility of a single republican government operating over the entire nation.

The criticism of the relationship established by the Constitution between the President and the Senate also makes reasonably clear another point, because that criticism involved the fear of too great interdependence between the two organs. The implication would seem to be the Antifederalists wanted the executive to have some degree of independence from the legislature, rather than

---

[138]This proposed council bore a strong resemblance to the Governor's Council provided for in the 1780 Massachusetts constitution, an interesting fact in view of the tendency among some historians to associate the Antifederalist position with a conception of Revolutionary democracy somewhat opposed to the principles of that constitution.

be merely the agency for executing the latter's will. But there is far too little exposition of this or of any other aspect of the office (except for the various elaborations on the theme of potential presidential tyranny)[139] to enable us to know precisely what the Antifederalist conception of the executive was. What does emerge rather clearly is a tendency to identify a strong executive with monarchy. This was of course very natural, their English and colonial heritage being what it was, and the corpus of European political theory being so scanty on the structure and operation of the executive power in a republic. The Antifederalists were quite simply unable to conceive of a strong *republican* executive. Their conception of republicanism was more narrow and rigid than that of their opponents. Indeed, in a curious way, they were still much more dominated by the intellectual habits of monarchy than were the Federalists. The latter were sufficiently liberated as to be able to think in terms of different forms of republicanism, while many of the Antifederalists were inclined to identify republican government with their own variety of it and to regard other versions as necessarily deviationist.

The unfinished, amorphous quality of their thought is also reflected in the frequent proposal to grant the central government only a conditional or contingent power to levy taxes directly upon individuals. The Antifederalists wanted to continue with the existing system of requisitions laid upon the states as states, and to permit individual taxation only when a state refused to comply with the original

---

[139]It is possible, just barely possible, that the constantly reiterated fears of the Antifederalists, their habitual emphasis on the negative, may have inhibited their own constructive powers and even have cost them votes —especially in the conventions. It was, after all, a revolutionary generation to whom they were appealing, and even a revolutionary spirit as sober and pessimistic as our own was not untempered by the more characteristically revolutionary traits of hope and self-confidence.

requisition. At the same time, they were strongly opposed to a standing army, or to national control over state militias, and they made gloomy predictions about the militia of Maine being sent to Georgia, or vice versa, in order to compel a state or its citizens to submit to federal laws. How, then, if the central government was to have no means of coercion over either states or citizens, would their proposal have guaranteed the national revenue which they admitted to be desirable if not necessary? Yet there was certainly something to be said for the Antifederalist contention that the diversities to be found in the economies of the separate states would make it difficult to establish a system of uniform taxation that would be both efficacious and just. And for polemical purposes, the proposal was ideal: it not only struck a moderate, middle-of-the-roadish note, it also promised an escape from the terrible prospect of double taxation.

In addition to the defect of incompleteness, the polemical tactics of the Antifederalists were also conducive to inconsistency. Their intellectual position was compromised in a manner quite different from that of their opponents. The latter were defending a proposed system of government that was admittedly and avowedly the product of compromise. Still, it *was a system,* and it was possible to defend it by the development of a systematic body of thought.[140] The Antifederalists chose to fight their battle with shotguns. There was thus a contradiction between the requirements of an intellectually systematic position and the demands of their polemical method. If, for example, they had stopped with the assertion and exposition of their central tenet that republican government could not be instituted and maintained over the entire nation from

---

[140]The one serious lapse of the Federalists was their muddled defense of the lack of a Bill of Rights.

Maine to Georgia and from the Atlantic to the Mississippi, their case would have had a beautiful clarity and consistency. They could have concluded simply: This government cannot possibly be republican; therefore it is totally unacceptable and there is no point in further discussion. But they did not stop, with the result that their theoretical position was full of weaknesses and characterized by internal contradictions that may or may not have been apparent to them at the time.

For example, consider the House of Representatives and the Senate. If the Antifederalists had maintained their fundamental principle about the impossibility of a national republic, and argued from it consistently, they should have repudiated the House completely on the grounds that it would not and could not be truly representative, and accepted the Senate as the legitimate representative body of the separate states. They could then have made their demands for shorter terms of office, compulsory rotation, and recall by state legislatures. But the Antifederalists could not have done this without appearing to be less republican than the Federalists, for the House was directly elected by the people, and proportionately representative of them. If they wanted to appear more republican than the Federalists, they should have severely attacked the indirect election of both the President and the Senate and vigorously advocated direct election. But this would have been inconsistent with their central tenet about the incompatibility of republicanism and nationalism (if the nation were large and populous), and only rarely was this inconsistency committed.[141]

Or consider how much more consistent the Antifederalists could have been with respect to the argument about a

---

[141]The criticism of indirect election was sometimes made, but almost never accompanied by a positive demand for direct election.

Bill of Rights. If they had stuck to their fundamental principle, they could have then argued: This government will *not* be republican, and *therefore* a Bill of Rights is absolutely essential. Happily for the posterity about whom both sides spoke so often, the Antifederalists argued that a Bill of Rights was necessary in a republican government, but this of course was implicitly to contradict their argument that the proposed government could not be republican because it was to be a national government operating over a large territory with a diverse population.

In spite of these weaknesses, inconsistencies, and sometimes inchoate qualities in the political theory of the Antifederalists, its major outlines are reasonably clear and certain. The Antifederalists reflected a relatively early stage in the evolution of modern republican thought, and their ideas, though less advanced than those of the Federalists, are not uninteresting.

Their fundamental principle was the belief that republican government could not be extended over a large geographical area with a numerous and heterogeneous population. In this belief they appeared to be sustained by the lessons of history and by the authority of reputable political theorists. Like James Madison, these first-generation republicans had a strong sense of the fragility of the system they had only recently adopted, but they differed from him as to the conditions most appropriate for its nurture. On this point they were profoundly conservative. They frequently referred to the opinion of Montesquieu, drawing together that theorist's specific dictum on the incompatibility of republicanism with largeness and his more general principle that a people's form of government must be adapted to their physical circumstances, their customs, laws, habits, mores, and general character. The Antifederalists believed that the American people were too diverse in these respects to operate and be subject to a single, national, and to use their favorite term, *consolidated* government. They also believed that the sheer physical size of the United States would make impossible that willing obedience to law which they rightly associated with a free and republican government. Believing this, and seizing on the Constitution's allowance for that *bête noire* of Anglo-American liberalism, a standing army, they saw the proposed new system as a direct and sinister threat to the continued existence of republicanism.

When one considers the prevailing opinion of the age, and the newness of this recent experiment with republican governments, it is easy to understand and sympathize with the reaction of shock, fear, and suspicion with which the Antifederalists met the Constitution. It would be a radical innovation, not only in relation to the United States at that time, but in the entire history of political theory and institutions as then known. Its ramifications were far more revolutionary in the literal sense of that word than was their recent break with Great Britain, for the Constitution proposed to establish not merely a new nation, but a new kind of nation with an unheard of form of government. It is therefore not remarkable that it met with vigorous and extreme opposition. It is remarkable that a project so truly radical was adopted, and with so little departure from the normal and ordinary politics of the day.

The Antifederalist belief that republican government could not be extended nationwide was integrally related to their theory of representation. They regarded representation primarily as an institutional substitute for direct democracy and endeavored to restrict its operation to the performance of that function; hence their plea that the legislature should be an exact miniature of the people, containing spokesman for all classes, all groups, all interests, all opinions, in the community; hence, too, their preference for short legislative terms of office and their inclination, especially in the sphere of state government, to regard representatives as delegates bound by the instructions of constituents rather than as men expected and trusted to exercise independent judgment. This was a natural stage in the development of representative government, but it contained several weaknesses and was already obsolete in late eighteenth-century America.

Its major weaknesses were closely akin to those of direct democracy itself, for representation of this kind makes difficult the process of genuine deliberation, as well as the reconciliation of diverse interests and opinions. Indeed, it is notable, and I think not accidental, that the body of Antifederalist thought as a whole showed little consideration of the necessity for compromise. The Founding Fathers were not democrats, but in their recognition of the role which compromise must play in the process of popular government, they were far more advanced than their opponents.

It is clear, too, that the same factors limiting the size and extent of direct democracies would also be operative in republics where representation is regarded only as a substitute for political participation by the whole people. Within their own frame of reference, the Antifederalists were quite right in insisting that republican government would work only in relatively small states, where the population was also small and relatively homogeneous. If there is great diversity among the people, with many interests and many opinions, then all cannot be represented without making the legislature as large and unwieldy as the citizen assemblies of ancient Athens. And if the system does not lend itself readily to compromise and conciliation, then the basis for a working consensus must be considerable homogeneity in the people themselves. In the opinion of the Antifederalists, the American people lacked that homogeneity.[142] This Rousseauistic vision of a small, simple, and homogeneous democracy may have been a fine ideal, but it *was* an ideal even then. It was not to be found even in the small states, and none of the Antifederalists produced a satisfactory answer to Madison's analysis of the weaknesses inherent in republicanism operating on the small scale preferred by his opponents.

Associated with this theory of representation and its necessary limitation to small-scale republics was the Antifederalists' profound distrust of the electoral and representative processes provided for and implied in the proposed Constitution. Their ideal of the legislature as an "exact miniature" of the people envisaged something not unlike the result hoped for by modern proponents of proportional representation. This was impossible to achieve in the national Congress.[143] There would not and could not be enough seats to go around. The constituencies were to be large—the ratio of representatives to population was not to exceed one per thirty thousand—and each representative must therefore represent not one, but many groups among his electors. And whereas Madison saw in this process of "filtering" or consolidating public opinion a virtue, the Antifederalists saw in it only danger. They did not think that a Congress thus elected could truly represent the will of the people, and they particularly feared

---

[142]I do not mean to suggest that the Antifederalist attitude concerning homogeneity and what modern social scientists refer to as *consensus* was hopelessly wrong. A degree of both is necessary for the successful operation of democracy, and the concept itself is an extremely valuable one. I would merely contend that the Federalist estimate of the degree required was both more liberal and more realistic. On the subject of the extent to which the American people were united in tradition, institutions, and ideas in 1787–1788, see Ranney, *op. cit.*, note 15.

[143]Nor for that matter, has it been the pattern of representation in state legislatures.

that they themselves, the "middling class," to use Melancton Smith's term, would be left out.

They feared this because they saw clearly that enlarged
constituencies would require more preelection political
organization than they believed to be either wise or safe.
Much has been written about the Founding Fathers' hostility to political parties. It is said that they designed the
Constitution, especially separation of powers, in order to
counteract the effectiveness of parties.[144] This is partly
true, but I think it worth noting that the contemporary
opponents of the Constitution feared parties or factions in
the Madisonian sense just as much as did Madison, and
that they feared parties in the modern sense even more
than Madison did. They feared and distrusted concerted
group action for the purpose of "centering votes" in order
to obtain a plurality, because they believed this would
distort the automatic or natural expression of the people's
will. The necessity of such action in large electoral districts would work to the advantage of the upper classes,
who, because of their superior capacity and opportunity for
organization of this kind, would elect a disproportionate
share of represenatives to the Congress. In other words,
the Antifederalists were acutely aware of the role that
organization played in the winning of elections, and they
were not willing to accept the "organized" for the "real"
majority. Instead they wanted to retain the existing system,
where the electoral constituencies were small, and where
organization of this kind was relatively unnecessary. Only
then could a man vote as he saw fit, confident that the
result of the election would reflect the real will of the
people as exactly as possible.

---

[144]See, e.g., E. E. Schattschneider, *Party Government* (New York:
Farrar and Rinehart, Inc., 1942), pp. 4 ff.

These fears that the electoral system would operate to produce an aristocratically biased Congress suggest that the Antifederalist theory of representation may have been in an awkwardly transitional state. Although the usual statement of the ideal implied the existence of numerous groups, all of whose interests and opinions should be reflected in the legislature, the prediction about aristocratic bias clearly emphasized a horizontal division of society between two classes, the people and the upper class or the aristocrats. The prediction was based on the assumption that the ordinary voter, confronted with the choice of representative in a district so large that he could not personally know the candidates, would vote for someone who was outstanding—perhaps a demagogue or perhaps an aristocrat—or else seek advice from a leader, probably an aristocrat, in his own community. The expressed fear of demagogues needs no comment, except perhaps to note again the sophistication it implied, but the fear relating to the reliance on members of the upper class is worth exploring further. It seems to reflect an odd ambivalence in the relationship between the two classes presumed to exist. On the one hand, the two are assumed to have different interests, and the aristocrats are assumed to be oppressively inclined toward the people. But on the other hand, it seems to be accepted that as a matter of custom and practice, the people will either seek advice from the aristocrats, or elect them as their representatives.

In addition to the fear relating to large electoral districts, the Antifederalists were also afraid of the greater independence of the representatives that would result from the longer terms of office provided for by the Constitution. Some of them associated this independence with aristocracy, their assumption apparently being that even a man who was not an aristocrat when elected would, if not returned to the voters annually, begin to behave like an aristocrat. Some of the reasons for this assumption are fairly obvious: There was the familiarity with the long struggle in Britain for regular, periodic elections, and all that that struggle had involved; and there was the fact that independence was, so to speak, an intrinsic ingredient of aristocracy, though to be sure, not the mere independence of a two- or six-year term of office. To these factors associated with a traditional class structure with which the Americans were familiar and which they feared, there seemed to be added an uneasiness derived from the social mobility of their own society. A man chosen *by* the people from among themselves, might, by this very act, cease to be *of* the people. Especially in a system of representation whose longer terms of office rendered the practice of instructed delegates no longer very practicable.

What the Antifederalists lacked was a theory of leadership. Their expressed fear about the probable behavior of voters in large districts was a recognition of the empirical fact that men do seek leadership. Many of their essayists recognized the same fact when they tried to fight the influence upon the voters of George Washington and Benjamin Franklin's adherence to the Constitution. But they did not incorporate this fact into the structure of their theory. Nor did they produce anything comparable to *The Federalist* on the function of leadership in a representative government. They did, of course, write and speak voluminously on the dangers of leadership, on the universal tendency of political leaders to abuse their power and position. But the lack of an adequate treatment of the necessary and positive role of leadership remains one of the gravest defects of Antifederalist thought. It was as if the Antifederalists had become entangled within their theory of representation. Their ideal of the legislature as an exact miniature of the people emphasized the necessity of personal like-for-like representatives of all groups within the political community. Yet they feared the tendency of the voters to choose outstanding and possibly aristocratic men to be their spokesmen. It was almost as if, with John Adams, they identified the capacity for leadership with aristocracy, and it was a two-way identification: Those who because of their birth, wealth, or position, could be called the "artificial" aristocracy constituted a reservoir of leadership to which the people turned; and those whose natural abilities fitted them for leadership, when chosen for such, then gravitated toward the "artificial" aristocrats. What the Antifederalists lacked was a theory of democratic leadership, and this lack was both a cause and an effect of their great fear of aristocrats combined with the obscurity of their conception of aristocracy [145]

The Antifederalist distrust of the electoral process, and their fear that it would produce an aristocratically biased legislature, was of course joined with localist fears of a legislature in which of necessity the representatives of any single state could always be outvoted by a majority from other states. The result was an attitude of profound fear and suspicion toward Congress. That body, it was felt, would be composed of aristocrats and of men elected from faraway places by the unknown peoples of distant states. It would meet at a yet undesignated site hundreds of miles from the homes of most of its constituents, outside the jurisdiction of any particular state, and protected by an army of its own making. When one sees Congress in this light, it is not surprising that the Antifederalists were

---

[145]It is possible that the Jacksonian generation's attitude that government is, after all, a very simple business, was an attempt to escape from the problems which the Antifederalists were unable to solve.

afraid, or that they had little faith in elections as a means of securing responsibility and preventing Congressional tyranny.[146]

In view of this very profound distrust of the representative process, especially and specifically as they expected it to operate in the new system, it was natural that the Antifederalists wanted more limitations and checks written into the Constitution. They saw much more clearly than did the Federalists that the power of the central government to act directly upon individuals, combined with the "necessary and proper" and "supreme law" clauses, rendered essential a Bill of Rights. More generally, their distrust of the broad language of the Constitution, and especially of the broad definition of powers, and their desire for more precise, detailed language reflected an attempt to guard against the abuse of power by limiting the discretion of Congress and the President. It reflected, too, the very strong strain of legalism in the American political mind.[147] As mentioned before, this legalistic attitude involved a curious assumption about the methods of would-be oppressors: The blackest kinds of treachery were anticipated from elected representatives lusting after power, but it would be treachery performed under cover of law. It was perhaps naïve to believe in the possibility of language so clear, precise, and unequivocal that it could

---

[146]It is worth noting again that the abuses of power dwelt upon by the Antifederalists were usually extreme ones, almost amounting to a complete subversion of republican government. They did not regard as of any value the Federalists' argument that a desire to be reelected would serve to keep the representatives in line. The Federalists had no clear idea of politics as a profession, but they were close to such a notion.

[147]This latter was perhaps related to the spirit of Protestantism, with its emphasis on the Word, and on the capacity of every man to read and interpret it. This is a subject that needs further exploration, because it appears to involve some oddly paradoxical relationship between democracy and a fundamental law and the institution of judicial review.

check the will toward oppression, but the Antifederalists thought that the language of the Constitution was simply an invitation to constitutional tyranny. Their distrust of the representative process and their desire to restrict the discretion of the legislature found later expression in the longer constitutions of the nineteenth century and the adoption of the techniques of the initiative and referendum.

As for additional institutional checks, the Antifederalists proposed a separate executive council, compulsory rotation in office for the President and the Senate, and the power of state recall for the latter. The first of these would have resulted in a purer, more rigid system of separation of powers. The second was aimed at preventing corruption and reflected the belief that election—in this case of the state legislatures, the electoral college, and the House of Representatives—was not an adequate check against the ambitious politician. The third would have increased the dependence of Senators upon the state legislatures and therefore presumably reduced the national character of the Senate. If, according to some proposals, the executive council were to be chosen by the separate states, it would have decreased the status and power of the President as a national figure. All three proposals would probably have increased the difficulty of securing executive and legislative agreement on a national policy. The Antifederalists would also have enlarged the House of Representatives, but, in spite of the preference expressed for annual elections, they did not make a serious proposal to reduce its term to one year.

Taken together, the desire for more limitations and for additional checks in the institutional structure of the central government added up to an attempt to reduce its powers and its ability to exercise power independently of the state governments. There was no attempt to make the national government more responsive and responsible to a national electorate. This was natural, because the Anti-federalists did not believe that a national electorate could operate to translate the real interests and opinions of a constituent majority into a legislative majority within the House of Representatives. The electoral districts would be too large to function without organization, and organization would work to the advantage of the upper classes, or of the more thickly populated sections. If this were true of Congressional districts, it would be even more true of statewide districts for the Senate, or for the Presidency. This, presumably, was one of the reasons the Antifederalists made no concerted demand for the direct, popular election of these officers, though their indirect election was occasionally mentioned as a criticism. Believing, as they did, that a single republican government could not successfully operate over the entire United States, they did not attempt to change the design of the one proposed to make it more immediately responsive to a national mandate—which they did not really imagine, or accountable only to a national majority, which many of them feared. Their concern was to prevent the government from doing harm, not enable it to operate smoothly as an instrument of the people's will. They did not really think the latter was possible, and the last thing in the world they wanted was a national democracy which would permit congressional majorities to operate freely and without restraint. It was the Federalists of 1787–1788 who created a national framework which would accommodate the later rise of democracy.

SELECTED BIBLIOGRAPHY

I. Original Materials

A. DOCUMENTARY COLLECTIONS

Documentary History of the Constitution of the United States of America, 1788–1870. 5 vols. Washington, D. C.: Department of State, 1894–1895.

Elliot, Jonathan [compiler]. *The Debates in the Several State Conventions on the Adoption of the Federal Constitution as Recommended by the General Convention at Philadelphia, in 1787.* 5 vols. Philadelphia: J. B. Lippincott, second ed., 1896.

Ford, Paul Leicester, ed. *Essays on the Constitution of the United States, 1787–1788.* Brooklyn, N. Y.: Historical Printing Club, 1892.

———, *Pamphlets on the Constitution of the United States* Brooklyn, N. Y.: Historical Printing Club, [?] 1888.

Harding, Samuel B. *The Contest over the Ratification of the Federal Constitution in the State of Massachusetts* New York: Longmans, Green, and Co. 1896 [contains documents].

McMaster, John Bach and Frederick Stone, eds. *Pennsylvania and the Federal Constitution, 1787–1788.* Lancaster, Pa.: Historical Society of Pennsylvania, 1888.

Mason, Alpheus Thomas. *The States Rights Debate: Antifederalists and the Constitution.* Englewood Cliffs, N. J.: Prentice Hall, 1964 ["with selected documents"].

B. NEWSPAPERS

Extensive reading in the newspapers of the time is essential. The following papers will afford a representative sampling of Antifederalist opinion.

The *American Herald* [Boston]

The *Massachusetts Centinel* [Boston]

The *New York Journal and Weekly Register* [New York City]

The *Independent Gazetteer* [Philadelphia]

The *Virginia Independent Chronicle* [Richmond]

II. Secondary Authorities

Beard, Charles. *An Economic Interpretation of the Constitution.* New York: The Macmillan Co., 1913.

Benson, Lee. *Turner and Beard: American Historical Writing Reconsidered.* Chicago: The Free Press, 1960.

Brown, Robert E. *Charles Beard and the Constitution: A Critical Analysis of "An Economic Interpretation of the Constitution."* Princeton, N. J.: Princeton University Press, 1956.

Jensen, Merrill. *The Making of the American Constitution.* Princeton, N. J.: D. Van Nostrand Co., Inc., 1964.

Kenyon, Cecelia M. "An Economic Interpretation of the Constitution After Fifty Years," *The Centennial Review,* VII: (Summer 1963) 327–352.

———— "Men of Little Faith: the anti-Federalists on the Nature of Representative Government," *William and Mary Quarterly,* 3rd series, XII:1 (1955) 3–46.

McDonald, Forest. *We the People: The Economic Origins of the Constitution.* Chicago: University of Chicago Press, 1958.

Main, Jackton T. *The Antifederalists: Critics of the Constitution.* Chapel Hill: University of North Carolina Press, 1961.

———— Charles Beard and the Constitution: A Critical Review of Forest McDonald's *We the People,"* *William and Mary Quarterly,* 3rd series, XVII (1960), 86–110, with a rejoinder by Forest McDonald.

EDITOR'S NOTE

Because the primary purpose of this anthology is to make easily accessible a sampling of Antifederalist ideas and attitudes, the primary principle of selectivity has been to make the sample a representative one. I have therefore attempted to include statements of all the major arguments of the Antifederalists, and of many of their minor ones. I have also tried to reflect the different attitudes, temperaments, and methods of argumentation that characterized Antifederalist debates in the newspapers and on the convention floors. Thus the keen and careful legal logic of "Brutus" and the wildly swinging demogoguery of "Philadelphiensis"; the sober, temperate Melancton Smith in the New York convention, and the rambling rhetoric of Patrick Henry in Virginia. Nevertheless, this primary principle of selectivity has been somewhat qualified by a second one. It has also been my purpose to present selections from serious and sustained critiques of the Constitution, and to present enough of each selection to enable the reader to observe the structure of the argument and the method of reasoning as well as the specific counts in the indictment. The emphasis has been on reasoned analysis rather than unreasoned assertion, and although some examples of the latter have been deliberately included, the intellectual quality of Antifederalism reflected in this volume is probably somewhat superior to that of the entire corpus of Antifederalist essays and speeches. Perhaps there is a rough justice in this; their opponents are know primarily by *The Federalist Papers*.

A few words of explanation about the form in which the selections are presented here seem in order. First, for the reasons given above, no single essay or speech has been cut: each is given in its entirety. Ordinarily, however, only a few of the separate numbers in a series of essays have been reprinted. Their original numbers are given in the Contents: thus the four essays from "Philadelphiensis" are numbered IX, X, XI, XII, as they were when they first appeared in the newspaper of publication, rather than I–IV, as might appear appropriate for their sequential appearance in this collection. This was done in order to indicate to the reader that these essays, though taken whole, are yet taken from a larger context of argumentation.

Second: with a few exceptions, the text given here reproduces the text of the source from which the document was reprinted. Thus Ford's text has been followed for those documents first reprinted in his *Essays* and *Pamphlets,* except that the bracketed page numbers of the original pamphlets, which he printed, have been omitted, and a uniform system of title and signature has been adopted in place of his exact following of the originals. The latter is also true for those selections reprinted directly from the newspapers — there seemed little point in following the original editor's vagaries of arranging title and signature. The original punctuation and spelling have been retained, again with minor exceptions. The long "s" has been reluctantly replaced by a modern one, and there has been some tempering of the eighteenth-century printer's penchant for lengthening the dash either for emphasis or to make the print come out even on the right-hand side of the column. Obvious typographical errors have been silently corrected without a "[sic]", and the latter has been used only sparingly after words that look peculiar to the twentieth-century eye, but probably looked all right to the eighteenth-century one. The beloved italics of the earlier period have been retained, but the occasional use of quotation marks at the beginning of each line of a quoted passage has been replaced with modern usage. A sustained effort has been made to remain faithful to the eighteenth century "&c.", but I fear that a few "etc." 's may have slipped through to mar the purity of this attempted fidelity. It is nevertheless hoped that enough of the original peculiarities of printing, punctuation, and spelling remain to remind the reader constantly that the documents he reads belong to another age, and that though they may indeed contain something of relevance for our own, yet they require an effort of imagination to be understood in that earlier context.

Cecelia M. Kenyon

Northampton, Massachusetts
October 1965

1. *The Letters of "Centinel"*

The two essays printed below are selected from twenty-four letters that appeared first in *The Independent Gazetteer* of Philadelphia between October 5, 1787, and November 24, 1788. They are believed to have been written by Samuel Bryan, son of George Bryan, who was one of the authors of the Pennsylvania constitution of 1776. A few may have been written by Eleazar Oswald, printer of the *Gazetteer*.[1] The internal evidence certainly suggests that the writer was an admirer of that constitution, for the first letter contains an attack on the recently published *Defence of the Constitutions of the American States* by John Adams, and a forthright defense of unicameralism, one of the distinguishing characteristics of the Pennsylvania constitution. Much of the fury of Pennsylvania politics after 1776 centered around this feature, and George Bryan was a leader of the "Constitutionalists," the party that supported it and other seemingly democratic policies. Opposed were the "Republicans," led by such men as James Wilson and Benjamin Rush, who advocated changing the constitution in order to provide a bicameral legislature, and whose republicanism was more moderate than that of Bryan. At the time of the Federal Convention, the "Republicans" had a majority in the state legislature; they led the fight and provided much of the organization for ratification of the national Constitution and subsequently amended the state constitution in 1790.

These essays were first published in *The Independent Gazetteer, or Chronicle of Freedom,* a daily newspaper in Philadelphia. They are reprinted here from the text in John Bach McMaster and Frederick D. Stone, *Pennsylvania and the Federal Constitution 1787–1788,* The Historical Society of Pennsylvania, 1888, pp. 565–576, 592–601.

[1] See McMaster and Stone, *op. cit.*, pp. 6–7, who cite Paul Leicester Ford.

Since these signal victories were won under a political system allegedly the most democratic of the Revolutionary period, but in opposition to the supporters of the system and with the intention of changing parts of it, the historian is necessarily confronted with the interesting questions: What is democracy? And who were then the democrats? However those questions are answered finally, one thing is clear. The "Constitutionalists" regarded their opponents as aristocratic, and suspected them of the most sinister motives. The third letter in the series (the second printed here) presents a good example of the Antifederalist attack on the "well-born few."

NO. I.

[October 5, 1787]

MR. OSWALD: *As the Independent Gazetteer seems free for the discussion of all public matters, I expect you will give the following a place in your next.*

To the FREEMEN of PENNSYLVANIA. *Friends, Countrymen and Fellow Citizens.*

Permit one of yourselves to put you in mind of certain *liberties* and *privileges* secured to you by the constitution of this commonwealth, and to beg your serious attention to his uninterested opinion upon the plan of federal government submitted to your consideration, before you surrender these great and valuable privileges up forever. Your present frame of government secures to you a right to hold yourselves, houses, papers and possessions free from search and seizure, and therefore warrants granted without oaths or affirmations first made, affording sufficient foundations for them, whereby any officer or messenger may be commanded or required to search your houses or seize your persons or property not particularly described in such warrant, shall not be granted. Your constitution further provides "that in controversies respecting property, and in suits between man and man, the parties have a right *to trial by jury, which ought to be held sacred.*" It also provides and declares, *"that the people have a right of* FREEDOM OF SPEECH, *and of* WRITING *and* PUBLISHING *their senti-* [handwritten: *Freedom of Press*] *ments,* therefore THE FREEDOM OF THE PRESS OUGHT NOT TO BE RESTRAINED." The constitution of Pennsylvania is *yet* in existence, *as yet* you have the right to *freedom of speech,* and of *publishing your sentiments.* How long those rights will appertain to you, you yourselves are called upon to say; whether your *houses* shall continue to be your *castles,* whether your *papers,* your *persons* and your *property,* are to be held sacred and free from *general warrants,* you are now to determine. Whether the *trial by jury* is to continue as your birth-right, the freemen of Pennsylvania, nay, of all America, are now called upon to declare.

Without presuming upon my own judgment, I cannot think it an unwarrantable presumption to offer my private opinion, and call upon others for theirs; and if I use my pen [handwritten: *TRIAL by JURY*] with the boldness of a freeman, it is because I know that *the liberty of the press yet remains unviolated and juries yet are judges.*

The late Convention have submitted to your consideration a plan of a new federal government. The subject is highly interesting to your future welfare. Whether it be calculated to promote the great ends of civil society, viz., the happiness and prosperity of the community, it behoves you well to consider, uninfluenced by the authority of names. Instead of that frenzy of enthusiasm, that has actuated the citizens of Philadelphia, in their approbation of the proposed plan, before it was possible that it could be the result of a rational investigation into its principles, it ought to be dispassionately and deliberately examined on its own intrinsic merit, the only criterion of your patronage. If ever free and unbiased discussion was proper or necessary, it is on such an occasion. All the blessings of liberty and the dearest privileges of freemen are now at stake and dependent on your present conduct. Those who are competent to the task of developing the principles of government, ought to be encouraged to come forward, and thereby the better enable the people to make a proper judgment; for the science of government is so abstruse, that few are able to judge for themselves. Without such assistance the people are too apt to yield an implicit assent to the opinions of those characters whose abilities are held in the highest esteem, and to those in whose integrity and patriotism they can confide; not considering that the love of domination is generally in proportion to talents, abilities and superior requirements, and that the men of the greatest purity of intention may be made instruments of despotism in the hands of the *artful and designing.* If it were not for the stability and attachment which time and habit gives to forms of government, it would be in the power of the enlightened and aspiring few, if they should combine, at any time to destroy the best establishments, and even make the people the instruments of their own subjugation.

The late revolution having effaced in a great measure all former habits, and the present institutions are so recent, that there exists not that great reluctance to innovation, so remarkable in old communities, and which accords with reason, for the most comprehensive mind cannot foresee the full operation of material changes on civil polity; it is the genius of the common law to resist innovation.

The wealthy and ambitious, who in every community think they have a right to lord it over their fellow creatures, have availed themselves very successfully of this

favorable disposition; for the people thus unsettled in their
sentiments, have been prepared to accede to any extreme
of government. All the distresses and difficulties they
experience, proceeding from various causes, have been
ascribed to the impotency of the present confederation,
and thence they have been led to expect full relief from
the adoption of the proposed system of government; and in
the other event, immediately ruin and annihilation as a
nation. These characters flatter themselves that they have
lulled all distrust and jealousy of their new plan, by gaining the concurrence of the two men in whom America has   *G-W*
the highest confidence, and now triumphantly exult in the   *B F*
completion of their long meditated schemes of power and
aggrandizement. I would be very far from insinuating that
the two illustrious personages alluded to, have not the
welfare of their country at heart; but that the unsuspecting
goodness and zeal of the one has been imposed on, in a
subject of which he must be necessarily inexperienced,
from his other arduous engagements; and that the weakness and indecision attendant on old age, has been prac-
ticed on in the other.

I am fearful that the principles of government inculcated
in Mr. Adams' treatise, and enforced in the numerous   *Adams*
essays and paragraphs in the newspapers, have misled
some well designing members of the late Convention. But
it will appear in the sequel, that the construction of the
proposed plan of government is infinitely more extravagant.

I have been anxiously expecting that some enlightened
patriot would, ere this, have taken up the pen to expose the
futility, and counteract the baneful tendency of such principles. Mr. Adams' *sine qua non* of a good government is
three balancing powers; whose repelling qualities are to
produce an equilibrium of interests, and thereby promote
the happiness of the whole community. He asserts that the
administrators of every government, will ever be actuated

by views of private interest and ambition, to the prejudice of the public good; that therefore the only effectual method to secure the rights of the people and promote their welfare, is to create an opposition of interests between the members of two distinct bodies, in the exercise of the powers of government, and balanced by those of a third. This hypothesis supposes human wisdom competent to the task of instituting three co-equal orders in government, and a corresponding weight in the community to enable them respectively to exercise their several parts, and whose views and interests should be so distinct as to prevent a coalition of any two of them for the destruction of the third. Mr. Adams, although he has traced the constitution of every form of government that ever existed, as far as history affords materials, has not been able to adduce a single instance of such a government; he indeed says that the British constitution is such in theory, but this is rather a confirmation that his principles are chimerical and not to be reduced to practice. If such an organization of power were practicable, how long would it continue? Not a day—for there is so great a disparity in the talents, wisdom and industry of mankind, that the scale would presently preponderate to one or the other body, and with every accession of power the means of further increase would be greatly extended. The state of society in England is much more favorable to such a scheme of government than that of America. There they have a powerful hereditary nobility, and real distinctions of rank and interests; but even there, for want of that perfect equality of power and distinction of interests in the three orders of government, they exist but in name; the only operative and efficient check upon the conduct of administration, is the sense of the people at large.

Suppose a government could be formed and supported on such principles, would it answer the great purposes of civil society? If the administrators of every government are actuated by views of private interest and ambition, how is the welfare and happiness of the community to be the result of such jarring adverse interests?

Therefore, as different orders in government will not produce the good of the whole, we must recur to other principles. I believe it will be found that the form of government, which holds those entrusted with power in the greatest responsibility to their constituents, the best calculated for freemen. A republican, or free government, can only exist where the body of the people are virtuous, and where property is pretty equally divided. In such a government the people are the sovereign and their sense or opinion is the criterion of every public measure; for when this ceases to be the case, the nature of the government is changed, and an aristocracy, monarchy or despotism will rise on its ruin. The highest responsibility is to be attained in a simple structure of government, for the great body of the people never steadily attend to the operations of government, and for want of due information are liable to be imposed on. If you complicate the plan by various orders, the people will be perplexed and divided in their sentiments about the source of abuses or misconduct; some will impute it to the senate, others to the house of representatives, and so on, that the interposition of the people may be rendered imperfect or perhaps wholly abortive. But if, imitating the constitution of Pennsylvania, you vest all the legislative power in one body of men (separating the executive and judicial) elected for a short period, and necessarily excluded by rotation from permanency, and guarded from precipitancy and surprise by delays imposed on its proceedings, you will create the most perfect responsibility; for then, whenever the people feel a grievance, they cannot mistake the authors, and will apply the remedy with certainty and effect, discarding them at the next election. This tie of responsibility will obviate all the dangers apprehended from a single legislature, and will the best secure the rights of the people.

Having premised this much, I shall now proceed to the examination of the proposed plan of government, and I trust, shall make it appear to the meanest capacity, that it has none of the essential requisites of a free government; that it is neither founded on those balancing restraining powers, recommended by Mr. Adams and attempted in the British constitution, or possessed of that responsibility to its constituents, which, in my opinion, is the only effectual security for the liberties and happiness of the people; but on the contrary, that it is a most daring attempt to establish a despotic aristocracy among freemen, that the world has ever witnessed.

I shall previously consider the extent of the powers intended to be vested in Congress, before I examine the construction of the general government.

It will not be controverted that the legislative is the highest delegated power in government, and that all others are subordinate to it. The celebrated *Montesquieu* establishes it as a maxim, that legislation necessarily follows the power of taxation. By sect. 8, of the first article of the proposed plan of government, "the Congress are to have power to lay and collect taxes, duties, imposts, and excises, to pay the debts and provide for the common defense and *general welfare* of the United States; but all duties, imposts and excises, shall be uniform throughout the United States." Now what can be more comprehensive than these words? Not content by other sections of this plan, to grant all the great executive powers of a confederation, and a STANDING ARMY IN TIME OF PEACE, that grand engine of oppression, and moreover the absolute control over the commerce of the United States and all external objects of revenue, such as unlimited imposts upon imports, etc., they are to be vested with every species of *internal* taxation; whatever taxes, duties and excises that they may deem requisite for the *general welfare*, may be imposed on the citizens of these states, levied by the officers of Congress, distributed through every district in America; and the collection would be enforced by the standing army, however grievous or improper they may be. The Congress may construe every purpose for which the State legislatures now lay taxes, to be for the *general welfare*, and thereby seize upon every object of revenue.

The judicial power by Article 3d sect. 1st shall extend to all cases, in law and equity, arising under this constitution, the laws of the United States, and treaties made or which shall be made under their authority; to all cases affecting ambassadors, other public ministers and consuls; to all cases of admiralty and maritime jurisdiction, to controversies to which the United States shall be a party, to controversies between two or more States, between a State and citizens of another State, between citizens of different States, between citizens of the same State claiming lands under grants of different States, and between a State, or the citizens thereof, and foreign States, citizens or subjects.

The judicial power to be vested in one Supreme Court, and in such inferior Courts as the Congress may from time to time ordain and establish.

The objects of jurisdiction recited above are so numerous, and the shades of distinction between civil causes are oftentimes so slight, that it is more than probable that the State judicatories would be wholly superseded; for in contests about jurisdiction, the federal court, as the most powerful, would ever prevail. Every person acquainted with the history of the courts in England, knows by what ingenious sophisms they have, at different periods, extended the sphere of their jurisdiction over objects out of the line of their institution, and contrary to their very nature; courts of a criminal jurisdiction obtaining cognizance in civil causes.

To put the omnipotency of Congress over the State government and judicatories out of all doubt, the 6th article ordains that "this constitution and the laws of the United States which shall be made in pursuance thereof, and all treaties made, or which shall be made under the authority of the United States, shall be the *supreme law of the land*, and the judges in every State shall be bound thereby, anything in the constitution or laws of any State to the contrary notwithstanding."

By these sections the all-prevailing power of taxation, and such extensive legislative and judicial powers are vested in the general government, as must in their operation necessarily absorb the State legislatures and judicatories; and that such was in the contemplation of the framers of it, will appear from the provision made for such event, in another part of it (but that, fearful of alarming the people by so great an innovation, they have suffered the forms of the separate governments to remain, as a blind). By Article 1st sect. 4th, "the times, places and manner of holding elections for senators and representatives, shall be prescribed in each State by the legislature thereof; *but the Congress may at any time, by law, make or alter such regulations, except as to the place of choosing senators.*" The plain construction of which is, that when the State legislatures drop out of sight, from the necessary operation of this government, then Congress are to provide for the election and appointment of representatives and senators.

If the foregoing be a just comment, if the United States are to be melted down into one empire, it becomes you to consider whether such a government, however constructed, would be eligible in so extended a territory; and whether it would be practicable, consistent with freedom? It is the opinion of the greatest writers, that a very extensive country cannot be governed on democratical principles, on any other plan than a confederation of a number of small republics, possessing all the powers of internal government, but united in the management of their foreign and general concerns.

It would not be difficult to prove, that anything short of despotism could not bind so great a country under one government; and that whatever plan you might, at the first setting out, establish, it would issue in a depotism.

If one general government could be instituted and maintained on principles of freedom, it would not be so competent to attend to the various local concerns and wants, of every particular district, as well as the peculiar governments, who are nearer the scene, and possessed of superior means of information; besides, if the business of the *whole* union is to be managed by one government, there would not be time. Do we not already see, that the inhabitants in a number of larger States, who are remote from the seat of government, are loudly complaining of the inconveniences and disadvantages they are subjected to on this account, and that, to enjoy the comforts of local government, they are separating into smaller divisions?

Having taken a review of the powers, I shall now examine the construction of the proposed general government.

Article 1st, sect. 1st. "All legislative powers herein granted shall be vested in a Congress of the United States, which shall consist of a senate and house of representatives." By another section, the President (the principal executive officer) has a conditional control over their proceedings.

Sect. 2d. "The house of representatives shall be composed of members chosen every second year, by the people of the several States. The number of representatives shall not exceed one for every 30,000 inhabitants."

The senate, the other constituent branch of the legislature, is formed by the legislature of each State appointing two senators, for the term of six years.

The executive power by Article 2d, sect. 1st, is to be vested in a President of the United States of America, elected for four years: Sec. 2 gives him "power, by and with the consent of the senate to make treaties, provided two-thirds of the senators present concur; and he shall nominate, and by and with the advice and consent of the senate, shall appoint ambassadors, other public ministers and consuls, judges of the Supreme Court, and all other officers of the United States, whose appointments are not herein otherwise provided for, and which shall be established by law, etc. And by another section he has the absolute power of granting reprieves and pardons for treason and all other high crimes and misdemeanors, except in case of impeachment.

The foregoing are the outlines of the plan.

Thus we see, the house of representatives are on the part of the people to balance the senate, who I suppose will be composed of the *better sort*, the *well born*, etc. The number of the representatives (being only one for every 30,000 inhabitants) appears to be too few, either to communicate the requisite information of the wants, local circumstances and sentiments of so extensive an empire, or to prevent corruption and undue influence, in the exercise of such great powers; the term for which they are to be chosen, too long to preserve a due dependence and accountability to their constituents; and the mode and places of their election not sufficiently ascertained, for as Congress have the control over both, they may govern the choice, by ordering the *representatives* of a *whole* State, to be *elected* in *one* place, and that too may be the most *inconvenient*.

The senate, the great efficient body in this plan of government, is constituted on the most unequal principles.

The smallest State in the Union has equal weight with the great States of Virginia, Massachusetts or Pennsylvania. The senate, besides its legislative functions, has a very considerable share in the executive; none of the principal appointments to office can be made without its advice and consent. The term and mode of its appointment will lead to permanency; the members are chosen for six years, the mode is under the control of Congress, and as there is no exclusion by rotation, they may be continued for life, which, from their extensive means of influence, would follow of course. The President, who would be a mere pageant of State, unless he coincides with the views of the senate, would either become the head of the aristocratic junto in that body, or its minion; besides, their influence being the most predominant, could the best secure his re-election to office. And from his power of granting pardons, he might screen from punishment the most treasonable attempts on the liberties of the people, when instigated by the senate.

From this investigation into the organization of this government, it appears that it is devoid of all responsibility or accountability to the great body of the people, and that so far from being a regular balanced government, it would be in practice a *permanent* ARISTOCRACY.

The framers of it, actuated by the true spirit of such a government, which ever abominates and suppresses all free inquiry and discussion, have made no provision for the *liberty of the press*, that grand *palladium of freedom*, and *scourge of tyrants;* but observed a total silence on that head. It is the opinion of some great writers, that if the liberty of the press, by an institution of religion or otherwise, could be rendered *sacred*, even in *Turkey*, that despotism would fly before it. And it is worthy of remark that there is no declaration of personal rights, premised in most free constitutions; and that trial by *jury* in *civil* cases is taken away; for what other construction can be put on the following, viz: Article 3d, sect. 2d, "In all cases affecting ambassadors, other public ministers and consuls, and those in which a State shall be party, the Supreme Court shall have *original* jurisdiction. In all the other cases above mentioned, the Supreme Court shall have *appellate* jurisdiction, both as to *law and fact!*" It would be a novelty in jurisprudence, as well as evidently improper, to allow an appeal from the verdict of a jury, on the matter of fact; therefore it implies and allows of a dismission of the jury in civil cases, and especially when it is considered, that jury trial in criminal cases is expressly stipulated for, but not in civil cases.

But our situation is represented to be so *critically* dreadful, that, however reprehensible and exceptionable the proposed plan of government may be, there is no alternative between the adoption of it and absolute ruin. My fellow citizens, things are not at that crisis; it is the argument of tyrants; the present distracted state of Europe secures us from injury on that quarter, and as to domestic dissensions, we have not so much to fear from them, as to precipitate us into this form of government, without it is a safe and a proper one. For remember, of all *possible* evils, that of *despotism* is the *worst* and the most to be dreaded.

Besides, it cannot be supposed that the first essay on so difficult a subject, is so well digested as it ought to be; if the proposed plan, after a mature deliberation, should meet the approbation of the respective States, the matter will end; but if it should be found to be fraught with dangers and inconveniences, a future general Convention, being in possession of the objections, will be the better enabled to plan a suitable government.

"WHO'S HERE SO BASE, THAT WOULD A BONDMAN BE?
IF ANY, SPEAK; FOR HIM HAVE I OFFENDED.
WHO'S HERE SO VILE, THAT WILL NOT LOVE HIS COUNTRY?
IF ANY, SPEAK; FOR HIM HAVE I OFFENDED."

NO. III

[November 8, 1787]

To the People of Pennsylvania

John 3d, verse 20th.—*"For everyone that doeth evil, hateth the light, neither cometh to the light, lest his deeds should be reproved." But "there is nothing covered that shall not be revealed; neither hid that shall not be known. Therefore whatever ye have spoken in darkness shall be heard in the light: and that which ye have spoken in the ear in closets, shall be proclaimed on the housetops."* — St. Luke, chap. xii, 2d and 3d verses.

Friends, Countrymen, and Fellow Citizens!

The formation of a good government is the greatest effort of human wisdom, actuated by disinterested patriotism; but such is the cursed nature of ambition, so prevalent among men, that it would sacrifice everything to its selfish gratification; hence the fairest opportunities of advancing the happiness of humanity, are so far from being properly improved, that they are too often converted by the votaries of power and domination, into the means of obtaining their nefarious ends. It will be the misfortune of America of adding to the number of examples of this kind, if the proposed plan of government should be adopted; but I trust, short as the time allowed you for consideration is, you will be so fully convinced of the truth of this, as to escape the impending danger; it is only necessary to strip the monster of its assumed garb, and to exhibit it in its native colours, to excite the universal abhorrence and rejection of every virtuous and patriotic mind.

For the sake of my dear country, for the honor of human nature, I hope and am persuaded that the good sense of the people will enable them to rise superior to the most formidable conspiracy against the liberties of a free and enlightened nation, that the world has ever witnessed. How glorious would be the triumph! How it would immortalize the present generation in the annals of freedom!

The establishment of a government, is a subject of such momentous and lasting concern, that it should not be gone into without the clearest conviction of its propriety, which can only be the result of the fullest discussion, the most thorough investigation and dispassionate consideration of its nature, principles and construction. You are now called upon to make this decision, which involves in it not only your fate, but that of your posterity for ages to come. Your determination will either ensure the possession of those blessings which render life desirable, or entail those evils which make existence a curse: that such are the consequences of a wise or improper organization of government, the history of mankind abundantly testifies. If you viewed the magnitude of the object in its true light, you would join with me in sentiment, that the new government ought not to be implicitly admitted. Consider then duly before you leap, for after the Rubicon is once passed, there will be no retreat.

If you were even well assured that the utmost purity of intention predominated in the production of the proposed government, such is the imperfection of human reason and knowledge, that it would not be wise in you to adopt it with precipitation in toto, for all former experience must teach you the propriety of a revision on such occasions, to correct the errors, and supply the deficiencies that may appear necessary. In every government whose object is the public welfare, the laws are subjected to repeated revisions, in some by different orders in the governments, in others by an appeal to the judgment of the people and deliberative forms of procedure. A knowledge of this, as well as of other states, will show that in every instance where a law has been passed without the usual precautions, it has been productive of great inconvenience and evils, and frequently has not answered the end in view, a supplement becoming necessary to supply its deficiencies.

What then are we to think of the motives and designs of those men who are arguing the implicit and immediate adoption of the proposed government; are they fearful, that if you exercise your good sense and discernment, you will discover the masqued aristocracy, that they are attempting to smuggle upon you under the suspicious garb of republicanism? When we find that the principal agents in this business are the very men who fabricated the form of government, it certainly ought to be conclusive evidence of their invidious design to deprive us of our liberties. The circumstances attending this matter, are such as should in a peculiar manner excite your suspicion; it might not be useless to take a review of some of them.

In many of the states, particularly in this and the northern states, there are aristocratic juntos of the *well-born few,* who had been zealousy endeavoring since the establishment of their constitutions, to humble that offensive *upstart, equal liberty;* but all their efforts were unavailing, the *ill-bred churl* obstinately kept his assumed station.

However, that which could not be accomplished in the several states, is now attempting through the medium of the future Congress. Experience having shown great defects in the present confederation, particularly in the regulation of commerce and maritime affairs; it became the universal wish of America to grant further powers, so as to make the federal government adequate to the ends of its institution. The anxiety on this head was greatly increased, from the impoverishment and distress occasioned by the excessive importations of foreign merchandise and luxuries and consequent drain of specie, since the peace: thus the people were in the disposition of a drowning man; eager to catch at anything that promised relief, however delusory. Such an opportunity for the acquisition of *undue* power has never been viewed with indifference by the ambitious and designing in any age or nation, and it has accordingly been too successfully improved by such men among us. The deputies from this state (with the exception of two) and most of those from the other states in the union, were unfortunately of this complexion, and many of them of such superior endowments, that in an *ex parte* discussion of the subject by specious glosses, they have gained the concurrence of some well disposed men, in whom their country has great confidence, which has given a great sanction to their scheme of power.

A comparison of the authority under which the convention acted, and their form of government, will show that they have despised their delegated power, and assumed sovereignty; that they have entirely annihilated the old confederaton, and the particular governments of the several States, and instead thereof have established one general government that is to pervade the union; constituted on the most *unequal* principles, destitute of accountability to its constituents, and as despotic in its nature, as the Venetian aristocracy; a government that will give full scope to the magnificent designs of the *well-born,* a government where tyranny may glut its vengeance on the *low-born,* unchecked by *an odious bill of rights,* as has been fully illustrated in my two preceding numbers; and yet as a blind upon the the understandings of the people, they have continued the forms of the particular governments, and termed the whole a confederation of the United States, pursuant to the sentiments of that profound, but corrupt politician Machiavel, who advises any one who would change the constitution of a State to keep as much as possible to the old forms; for then the people seeing the same officers, the same formalities, courts of justice and other outward appearances, are insensible of the alteration, and believe themselves in possession of their old government. Thus Caesar, when he seized the Roman liberties, caused

Form w/out reality of freedom

himself to be chosen dictator (which was an ancient office) continued to senate, the consuls, the tribunes, the censors, and all other offices and forms of the commonwealth; and yet changed Rome from the most free, to the most tyrannical government in the world.

The convention, after vesting all the great and efficient powers of sovereignty in the general government, insidiously declare by section 4th of article 4th, "that the United States shall guarantee to every State in this union, a republican *form* of government;" but of what avail will be the *form,* without the *reality* of freedom?

The late convention, in the majesty of its assumed omnipotence, have not even condescended to submit the plan of the new government to the confederation of the people, the true source of authority; but have called upon them by their several constitutions, to 'assent to and ratify'[*] in toto, what they have been pleased to decree; just as the grand monarque of France requires the parliament of Paris to register his edicts without revision or alteration, which is necessary previous to their execution.

The authors and advocates of the new plan, conscious that its establishment can only be obtained from the ignorance of the people of its true nature, and their unbounded confidence in some of the men concurring, have hurried on its adoption with a precipitation that betrays their design; before many had seen the new plan, and before any had time to examine it, they by their ready minions, attended by some well-disposed but mistaken persons, obtained the subscriptions of the people to papers expressing their entire approbation of, and their wish to have it established; thus precluding them from any consideration; but

---

[*]See resolution of Convention accompanying the instrument of the proposed government.

assembly, is one of the most extravagant instances of this kind; and even this was only prevented by the secession of nineteen virtuous and enlightened members. °

In order to put the matter beyond all recall, they have proceeded a step further; they have made the deputies nominated for the state convention for this city and elsewhere, pledge their sacred honor, previous to their election, that they would implicitly adopt the proposed government in toto. Thus, short as the period is before the final fiat is to be given, consideration is rendered nugatory, and conviction of its dangers or impropriety unavailable. A good cause does not stand in need of such means; it scorns all indirect advantages and borrowed helps, and trusts alone to its own native merit and intrinsic strength: the lion is never known to make use of cunning, nor can a good cause suffer by a free and thorough examination—it is knavery that seeks disguise. Actors do not care that any one

---

°The message of the President and Council, sent into the present General Assembly on the 27th of October last, discloses another imposition. The Board sent to the House the official transmission of the proposed constitution of the United States, inclosed in a letter from the President of Congress, which proves that the paper produced to the last House on the day before the final rising of the same, was a surreptitious copy of the vote of Congress, obtained for the purpose of deluding the Legislature into the extravagance of directing an election of Convention within *nine* days.

The provision made by the Convention of Pennsylvania, which sat in 1776 for amending the constitution, is guarded with admirable wisdom and caution. A Council of Censors is to be holden every seven years, which shall have power (two-thirds of the whole number elected agreeing) to propose amendments of the same government, and to call a Convention to adopt and establish these propositions; but the alterations must be "promulgated *at least* six months before the day appointed for the *election* of such Convention, for the *previous consideration* of the people, that they may have an opportunity of instructing their delegates on the subject." The present measures explain the conduct of a certain party of the Censors, who sat in 1784 (much fewer than two-thirds of the whole), that proposed to abolish the 47th article of the constitution, whereby the manner of amending the same was regulated.

should look into the tiring room, nor jugglers or sharpers into their hands or boxes.

Every exertion has been made to suppress discussion by shackling the press; but as this could not be effected in *this* state, the people were warned not to listen to the adversaries of the proposed plan, lest they should impose upon them, and thereby prevent the adoption of this blessed government. What figure would a lawyer make in a court of justice, if he should desire the judges not to hear the counsel of the other side, lest they should perplex the cause and mislead the court? Would not every bystander take it for granted, that he was conscious of the weakness of his client's cause, and that it could not otherwise be defended than by not being understood?

All who are friends to liberty are friends to reason, the champions of liberty; and none are foes to liberty but those who have truth and reason for their foes. He who has dark purposes to serve, must use dark means: light would discover him, and reason expose him: he must endeavor to shut out both, and make them look frightful by giving them ill names.

Liberty only flourishes where reason and knowledge are encouraged: and whenever the latter are stifled, the former is extinguished. In Turkey printing is forbid, enquiry is dangerous, and free speaking is capital; because they are all inconsistent with the nature of the government. Hence it is that the Turks are all stupidly ignorant and are all slaves.

I shall now proceed in the consideration of the construction of the proposed plan of government. By section 4th of article 1st of the proposed government it is declared, "that the times, places, and manner of holding elections for senators and representatives shall be prescribed in each State by the legislature thereof; *but the Congress may at any time by law make or alter such regulations except as to the place of choosing senators.*" Will not this section put it in the power of the future Congress to abolish the suffrage by ballot, so indispensable in a free government? Montesquieu in his Spirit of Laws, vol. 1, page 12, says "that in a democracy there can be no exercise of sovereignty, but by the suffrages of the people, which are their will; now the sovereign's will is the sovereign himself. The laws therefore which establish the right of suffrage, are fundamental to this government. In fact it is as important to regulate in a republic, in what manner, by whom, and concerning what, suffrages are to be given, as it is in a monarchy to know who is the Prince and after what manner he ought to govern." This valuable privilege of voting by ballot ought not to rest on the discretion of the government, but be irrevocably established in the constitution.

Will not the above quoted section also authorize the future Congress to lengthen the terms for which the senators and representatives are to be elected, from 6 and 2 years respectively, to any period, even for life?—as the parliament of England voted themselves from triennial to septinnial; and as the long parliament under Charles the 1st became perpetual?

Section 8th of article 1st, vests Congress with power "to provide for calling forth the militia to execute the laws of the union, suppress insurrections and repel invasions; to provide for organizing, arming, and disciplining the militia, and for governing such part of them as may be employed in the service of the United States, reserving to the States respectively, the appointment of the officers, and the authority of training the militia according to the discipline prescribed by Congress." This section will subject the citizens of these States to the most arbitrary military discipline: even death may be inflicted on the disobedient; in the character of militia, you may be dragged from your families and homes to any part of the continent and for any length of time, at the discretion of the future Congress; and as militia you may be made the unwilling in-instruments of oppression, under the direction of government; there is no exemption upon account of conscientious scruples of bearing arms, no equivalent to be received in lieu of personal services. The militia of Pennsylvania may be marched to Georgia or New Hampshire, however incompatible with their interests or consciences; in short, they may be made as mere machines as Prussian soldiers.

Section the 9th begins thus:—"The migration or importation of such persons as any of the states, now existing, shall think proper to admit, shall not be prohibited by Congress, prior to the year 1808, but a duty or tax may be imposed on such importation, not exceeding ten dollars for each person." And by the fifth article this restraint is not to be removed by any future convention. We are told that the objects of this article are slaves, and that it is inserted to secure to the southern states the right of introducing ne-groes for twenty-one years to come, against the declared sense of the other states to put an end to an odious traffic in the human species, which is especially scandalous and inconsistent in a people, who have asserted their own liberty by the sword, and which dangerously enfeebles the districts wherein the laborers are bondsmen. The words, dark and ambiguous, such as no plain man of common sense would have used, are evidently chosen to conceal from Europe, that in this enlightened country, the practice of slavery has its advocates among men in the highest stations. When it is recollected that no poll tax can be imposed on *five* negroes, above what *three* whites shall be charged; when it is considered, that the imposts on the consumption of Carolina field negroes must be trifling, and the excise nothing, it is plain that the proportion of contributions, which can be expected from the southern states under the new constitution, will be unequal, and yet they are to be allowed to enfeeble themselves by the further importation of negroes till the year 1808. Has not the con-currence of the five southern states (in the convention) to the new system, been purchased too dearly by the rest, who have undertaken to make good their deficiences of revenue, occasioned by their wilful incapacity, without an equivalent?

The general acquiescence of one description of citizens in the proposed government, surprises me much; if so many of the Quakers have become indifferent to the sacred rights of conscience, so amply secured by the constitution of this commonwealth; if they are satisfied to rest this inestimable privilege on the discretion of the future government; yet in a political light they are not acting wisely: in the state of Pennsylvania, they form so considerable a portion of the community, as must ensure them great weight in the government; but in the scale of general empire, they will be lost in the balance.

I intended in this number to have shown from the nature of things, from the opinions of the greatest writers and from the peculiar circumstances of the United States, the impracticability of establishing and maintaining one government on the principles of freedom in so extensive a territory; to have shown, if practicable, the inadequacy of such government to provide for its many and various concerns; and also to have shown that a confederation of small republics, possessing all the powers of internal government, and united in the management of their general and foreign concerns, is the only system of government by which so extensive a country can be governed consistent with freedom: but a writer under the signature of Brutus, in the New York paper, which has been re-published by Messrs. Dunlap and Claypoole, has done this in so masterly a manner, that it would be superfluous in me to add anything on this subject.

My fellow citizens, as a lover of my country, as the friend to mankind, whilst it is yet safe to write, and whilst

it is yet in your power to avoid it, I warn you of the impending danger. To this remote quarter of the world has liberty
fled. Other countries now subject to slavery, were once as
free as we yet are; therefore for your own sakes, for the
sake of your posterity, as well as for that of the oppressed
of all nations, cherish this remaining asylum of liberty.

2. The Address and Reasons of Dissent of the Minority of the Convention of the State of Pennsylvania to their Constituents

As the title indicates, this essay reflects the opinions of those delegates to the Pennsylvania ratifying convention who opposed the adoption of the Constitution. The final vote on ratification was 46 to 23, and would thus seem to indicate an easy victory for the Federalists. Their contemporary opponents, and some modern scholars, have argued that it was not a victory fairly won, and that the two-to-one majority in the convention did not reflect the real divison of opinion among Pennsylvania's voters. The principal charge against the Federalists was that they rushed through the entire procedure provided for ratification without giving the people of Pennsylvania adequate time for careful consideration and due deliberation. The Pennsylvania legislature issued the call for the convention and for election to it less than two weeks after the publication of the Constitution, and under somewhat indecorous circumstances. Although the friends of the Constitution had a majority in the legislature, they did not constitute a quorum. Realizing this, the minority absented itself in order to prevent the majority from taking action, whereupon two of them were forcibly seized, dragged into the legislative chamber, and kept there to establish a quorum so that the majority could call for the convention and for the election of delegates to it. The

---

The text of this essay, first printed in *The Pennsylvania Packet and Daily Advertiser* on December 18, 1787, is taken from John Bach McMaster and Frederick D. Stone, *Pennsylvania and the Federal Constitution 1787–1788*, The Historical Society of Pennsylvania, 1888, pp. 454–482.

elections were held on November 6, the convention sat on November 21, and the vote on the Constitution was taken December 12, 1787—less than three months after the signing of the Constitution on September 17, 1787. The resentment of the minority over this haste and over other tactics of the Federalists is expressed in this essay, as it was in much of the Antifederalist literature throughout the ratification period. In view of the previous record of the party the minority represented, however, one suspects that their protests are not without a note of self-righteousness. The politics of Pennsylvania from 1776 to 1790 were notably vigorous and hard-fought between two rather well-organized parties. That this prior partisan conflict was an element in the ratification debate is obvious from the newspapers and other commentaries of the day.

It was not until after the termination of the late glorious contest, which made the people of the United States an independent nation, that any defect was discovered in the present confederation. It was formed by some of the ablest patriots in America. It carried us successfully through the war, and the virtue and patriotism of the people, with their disposition to promote the common cause, supplied the want of power in Congress.

The requisition of Congress for the five *per cent.* impost was made before the peace, so early as the first of February, 1781, but was prevented taking effect by the refusal of one State; yet it is probable every State in the Union would have agreed to this measure at that period, had it not been for the extravagant terms in which it was demanded. The requisition was new moulded in the year 1783, and accompanied with an additional demand of certain supplementary funds for twenty-five years. Peace had now taken place, and the United States found themselves laboring under a considerable foreign and domestic debt, incurred during the war. The requisition of 1783 was commensurate with the interest of the debt, as it was then calculated; but it has been more accurately ascertained since that time. The domestic debt has been found to fall several millions of dollars short of the calculation, and it has lately been considerably diminished by large sales of the Western lands. The States have been called on by Congress annually for supplies until the general system of finance proposed in 1783 should take place.

It was at this time that the want of an efficient federal government was first complained of, and that the powers vested in Congress were found to be inadequate to the procuring of the benefits that should result from the union. The impost was granted by most of the States, but many refused the supplementary funds; the annual requisitions were set at naught by some of the States, while others complied with them by legislative acts, but were tardy in their payments, and Congress found themselves incapable of complying with their engagements and supporting the federal government. It was found that our national character was sinking in the opinion of foreign nations. The Congress could make treaties of commerce, but could not enforce the observance of them. We were suffering from the restrictions of foreign nations, who had suckled our commerce while we were unable to retaliate, and all now agreed that it would be advantageous to the union to enlarge the powers of Congress, that they should be enabled in the amplest manner to regulate commerce and to lay and collect duties on the imports throughout the United States. With this view, a convention was first proposed by Virginia, and finally recommended by Congress for the different States to appoint deputies to meet in convention, "for the purposes of revising and amending the present articles of confederation, so as to make them adequate to the exigencies of the union." This recommendation the legislatures of twelve States complied with so hastily as

not to consult their constituents on the subject; and though
the different legislatures had no authority from their constituents for the purpose, they probably apprehended the
necessity would justify the measure, and none of them
extended their ideas at that time further than "revising and
amending the present articles of confederation." Pennsylvania, by the act appointing deputies, expressly confined
their powers to this object, and though it is probable that
some of the members of the assembly of this State had at
that time in contemplation to annihilate the present confederation, as well as the constitution of Pennsylvania, yet
the plan was not sufficiently matured to communicate it to
the public.

The majority of the legislature of this commonwealth
were at that time under the influence of the members from
the city of Philadelphia. They agreed that the deputies
sent by them to convention should have no compensation
for their services, which determination was calculated to
prevent the election of any member who resided at a distance from the city. It was in vain for the minority to attempt electing delegates to the convention who understood the circumstances, and the feelings of the people,
and had a common interest with them. They found a disposition in the leaders of the majority of the house to
choose themselves and some of their dependents. The
minority attempted to prevent this by agreeing to vote for
some of the leading members, who they knew had influence enough to be appointed at any rate, in hopes of
carrying with them some respectable citizens of Philadelphia, in whose principles and integrity they could have
more confidence, but even in this they were disappointed,
except in one member: the eighth member was added at a
subsequent session of the assembly.

The Continental Convention met in the city of Philadelphia at the time appointed. It was composed of some

men of excellent character; of others who were more remarkable for their ambition and cunning than their patriotism, and of some who had been opponents to the independence of the United States. The delegates from
Pennsylvania were, six of them, uniform and decided
opponents to the Constitution of this commonwealth. The
convention sat upwards of four months. The doors were
kept shut, and the members brought under the most solemn engagements of secrecy.* Some of those who opposed
their going so far beyond their powers, retired hopeless,
from the convention; others had the firmness to refuse
signing the plan altogether; and many who did sign it, did
it not as a system they wholly approved, but as the best
that could be then obtained, and notwithstanding the time
spent on this subject, it is agreed on all hands to be a work
of haste and accommodation.

Whilst the gilded chains were forging in the secret conclave, the meaner instruments of the despotism without
were busily employed in alarming the fears of the people
with dangers which did not exist, and exciting their hopes
of greater advantages from the expected plan than even the
best government on earth could produce. The proposed
plan had not many hours issued forth from the womb of
suspicious secrecy, until such as were prepared for the
purpose, were carrying about petitions for people to sign,
signifying their approbation of the system, and requesting
the legislature to call a convention. While every measure
was taken to intimidate the people against opposing it, the
public papers teemed with the most violent threats against
those who should dare to think for themselves, and *tar and
feathers* were liberally promised to all those who would
not immediately join in supporting the proposed government, be it what it would. Under such circumstances peti-

---

*The Journals of the conclave are still concealed.

tions in favor of calling a Convention were signed by great numbers in and about the city, before they had leisure to read and examine the system, many of whom—now they are better acquainted with it, and have had time to investigate its principles—are heartily opposed to it. The petitions were speedily handed in to the legislature.

Affairs were in this situation, when on the 28th of September last, a resolution was proposed to the assembly by a member of the house, who had been also a member of the federal convention, for calling a State convention to be elected within *ten* days for the purpose of examining and adopting the proposed Constitution of the United States, though at this time the house had not received it from Congress. This attempt was opposed by a minority, who after offering every argument in their power to prevent the precipitate measure, without effect, absented themselves from the house as the only alternative left them, to prevent the measures taking place previous to their constituents being acquainted with the business. That violence and outrage which had been so often threatened was now practised; some of the members were seized the next day by a mob collected for the purpose, and forcibly dragged to the house, and there detained by force whilst the quorum of the legislature *so formed,* completed their resolution. We shall dwell no longer on this subject: the people of Pennsylvania have been already acquainted therewith. We would only further observe that every member of the legislature, previously to taking his seat, by solemn oath or affirmation, declares "that he will not do or consent to any act or thing whatever, that will have a tendency to lessen or abridge their rights and privileges, as declared in the constitution of this State." And that constitution which they are so solemnly sworn to support, cannot legally be altered but by a recommendation of the council of censors, who alone are authorized to propose alterations and amendments, and even these must be published at least

Riding roughshod over the state constitution —
Call to ratify was illegal

six months for the consideration of the people. The proposed system of government for the United States, if adopted, will alter and may annihilate the constitution of Pennsylvania; and therefore the legislature had no authority whatever to recommend the calling a convention for that purpose. This proceeding could not be considered as binding on the people of this commonwealth. The house was formed by violence, some of the members composing it were detained there by force, which alone would have vitiated any proceedings to which they were otherwise competent; but had the legislature been legally formed, this business was absolutely without their power.

In this situation of affairs were the subscribers elected members of the Convention of Pennsylvania—a Convention called by a legislature in direct violation of their duty, and composed in part of members who were compelled to attend for that purpose, to consider of a Constitution proposed by a Convention of the United States, who were not appointed for the purpose of framing a new form of government, but whose powers were expressly confined to altering and amending the present articles of confederation. Therefore the members of the continental Convention in proposing the plan acted as individuals, and not as deputies from Pennsylvania.* The assembly who called the State Convention acted as individuals, and not as the legislature of Pennsylvania; nor could they or the Convention chosen on their recommendation have authority to do

---

*The continental Convention, in direct violation of the 13th article of the confederation, have declared "that the ratification of nine States shall be sufficient for the establishment of this Constitution, between the States so ratifying the same." Thus has the plighted faith of the States been sported with! They had solemnly engaged that the confederation now subsisting should be inviolably preserved by each of them, and the Union thereby formed should be perpetual, unless the same should be altered by mutual consent.

any act or thing that can alter or annihilate the Constitution of Pennsylvania (both of which will be done by the new Constitution), nor are their proceedings, in our opinion, at all binding on the people.

The election for members of the Convention was held at so early a period, and the want of information was so great, that some of us did not know of it until after it was over, and we have reason to believe that great numbers of the people of Pennsylvania have not yet had an opportunity of sufficiently examining the proposed Constitution. We apprehend that no change can take place that will affect the internal government or Constitution of this commonwealth, unless a majority of the people should evidence a wish for such a change; but on examining the number of votes given for members of the present State Convention, we find that of upwards of *seventy thousand* freemen who are entitled to vote in Pennsylvania, the whole convention has been elected by about *thirteen thousand* voters, and though *two-thirds* of the members of the Convention have thought proper to ratify the proposed Constitution, yet those *two-thirds* were elected by the votes of only *six thousand and eight hundred* freemen.

In the city of Philadelphia and some of the eastern counties the junto that took the lead in the business agreed to vote for none but such as would solemnly promise to adopt the system *in toto*, without exercising their judgment. In many of the counties the people did not attend the elections, as they had not an opportunity of judging of the plan. Others did not consider themselves bound by the call of a set of men who assembled at the State-house in Philadelphia and assumed the name of the legislature of Pennsylvania; and some were prevented from voting by the violence of the party who were determined at all events to force down the measure. To such lengths did the tools of despotism carry their outrage, that on the night of the election for members of convention, in the city of Philadelphia, several of the subscribers (being then in the city to transact your business) were grossly abused, ill-treated and insulted while they were quiet in their lodgings, though they did not interfere nor had anything to do with the said election, but, as they apprehend, because they were supposed to be adverse to the proposed constitution, and would not tamely surrender those sacred rights which you had committed to their charge.

The convention met, and the same disposition was soon manifested in considering the proposed constitution, that had been exhibited in every other stage of the business. We were prohibited by an express vote of the convention from taking any questions on the separate articles of the plan, and reduced to the necessity of adopting or rejecting *in toto.* 'Tis true the majority permitted us to debate on each article, but restrained us from proposing amendments. They also determined not to permit us to enter on the minutes our reasons of dissent against any of the articles, nor even on the final question our reasons of dissent against the whole. Thus situated we entered on the examination of the proposed system of government, and found it to be such as we could not adopt, without, as we conceived, surrendering up your dearest rights. We offered our objections to the convention, and opposed those parts of the plan which, in our opinion, would be injurious to you, in the best manner we were able; and closed our arguments by offering the following propositions to the convention.

1. The right of conscience shall be held inviolable; and neither the legislative, executive nor judical powers of the United States shall have authority to alter, abrogate or infringe any part of the constitution of the several States, which provide for the preservation of liberty in matters of religion.

2. That in controversies respecting property, and in suits between man and man, trial by jury shall remain as heretofore, as well in the federal courts as in those of the several States.

3. That in all capital and criminal prosecutions, a man has a right to demand the cause and nature of his accusation, as well in the federal courts as in those of the several States; to be heard by himself and his counsel; to be confronted with the accusers and witnesses; to call for evidence in his favor, and a speedy trial by an impartial jury of his vicinage, without whose unanimous consent he cannot be found guilty, nor can he be compelled to give evidence against himself; and, that no man be deprived of his liberty, except by the law of the land or the judgment of his peers.

4. That excessive bail ought not to be required, nor excessive fines imposed, nor cruel nor unusual punishments inflicted.

5. That warrants unsupported by evidence, whereby any officer or messenger may be commanded or required to search suspected places; or to seize any person or persons, his or their property not particularly described, are grievous and oppressive, and shall not be granted either by the magistrates of the federal government or others.

6. That the people have a right to the freedom of speech, of writing and publishing their sentiments; therefore the freedom of the press shall not be restrained by any law of the United States.

7. That the people have a right to bear arms for the defence of themselves and their own State or the United States, or for the purpose of killing game; and no law shall be passed for disarming the people or any of them unless for crimes committed, or real danger of public injury from individuals; and as standing armies in the time of peace are dangerous to liberty, they ought not to be kept up; and that the military shall be kept under strict subordination to, and be governed by the civil powers.

8. The inhabitants of the several States shall have liberty to fowl and hunt in seasonable time on the lands they hold, and on all other lands in the United States not in-

closed, and in like manner to fish in all navigable waters, and othes not private property, without being restrained therein by any laws to be passed by the legislature of the United States.

9. That no law shall be passed to restrain the legislatures of the several States from enacting laws for imposing taxes, except imposts, and duties on goods imported or exported, and that no taxes, except imposts and duties upon goods imported and exported, and postage on letters, shall be levied by the authority of Congress.

10. That the house of representatives be properly increased in number; that elections shall remain free; that the several States shall have power to regulate the elections for senators and representatives, without being controlled either directly or indirectly by any interference on the part of Congress; and that the elections of representatives be annual.

11. That the power of organizing, arming and disciplining the militia (the manner of disciplining the militia to be prescribed by Congress), remain with the individual States, and that Congress shall not have authority to call or march any of the militia out of their own State, without the consent of such State, and for such length of time only as such State shall agree.

That the sovereignty, freedom and independency of the several States shall be retained, and every power, jurisdiction and right which is not by this Constitution expressly delegated to the United States in Congress assembled.

12. That the legislative, executive and judicial powers be kept separate; and to this end that a constitutional council be appointed to advise and assist the President, who shall be responsible for the advice they give—hereby the senators would be relieved from almost constant attendance; and also that the judges be made completely independent.

13. That no treaty which shall be directly opposed to the

existing laws of the United States in Congress assembled, shall be valid until such laws shall be repealed or made conformable to such treaty; neither shall any treaties be valid which are in contradiction to the Constitution of the United States, or the constitution of the several States.

14. That the judiciary power of the United States shall be confined to cases affecting ambassadors, other public ministers and consuls, to cases of admiralty and maritime jurisdiction; to controversies to which the United States shall be a party; to controversies between two or more States—between a State and citizens of different States—between citizens claiming lands under grants of different States, and between a State or the citizens thereof and foreign States; and in criminal cases to such only as are expressly enumerated in the constitution; and that the United States in Congress assembled shall not have power to enact laws which shall alter the laws of descent and distribution of the effects of deceased persons, the titles of lands or goods, or the regulation of contracts in the individual States.

After reading these propositions, we declared our willingness to agree to the plan, provided it was so amended as to meet those propositions or something similar to them, and finally moved the convention to adjourn, to give the people of Pennsylvania time to consider the subject and determine for themselves; but these were all rejected and the final vote taken, when our duty to you induces us to vote against the proposed plan and to decline signing the ratification of the same.

During the discussion we met with many insults and some personal abuse. We were not even treated with decency, during the sitting of the convention, by the persons in the gallery of the house. However, we flatter ouselves that in contending for the preservation of those invaluable rights you have thought proper to commit to our charge, we acted with a spirit becoming freemen; and being de-

The Dissent

sirous that you might know the principles which actuated our conduct, and being prohibited from inserting our reasons of dissent on the minutes of the convention, we have subjoined them for your consideration, as to you alone we are accountable. It remains with you whether you will think those inestimable privileges, which you have so ably contended for, should be sacrificed at the shrine of despotism, or whether you mean to contend for them with the same spirit that has so often baffled the attempts of an aristocratic faction to rivet the shackles of slavery on you and your unborn posterity.

Our objections are comprised under three general heads of dissent, viz.:

We dissent, first, because it is the opinion of the most celebrated writers on government, and confirmed by uniform experience, that a very extensive territory cannot be governed on the principles of freedom, otherwise than by a confederation of republics, possessing all the powers of internal government, but united in the management of their general and foreign concerns.

1)

If any doubt could have been entertained of the truth of the foregoing principle, it has been fully removed by the concession of *Mr. Wilson*, one of the majority on this question, and who was one of the deputies in the late general convention. In justice to him, we will give his own words; they are as follows, viz.: "The extent of country for which the new constitution was required, produced another difficulty in the business of the federal convention. It is the opinion of some celebrated writers, that to a small territory, the democratical; to a middling territory (as Montesquieu has termed it), the monarchical; and to an extensive territory, the despotic form of government is best adapted. Regarding then the wide and almost unbounded jurisdiction of the United States, at first view, the hand of despotism seemed necessary to control, connect and protect it; and hence the chief embarrassment rose. For we know that although our constituents would cheerfully submit to the legislative restraints of a free government, they would spurn at every attempt to shackle them with despotic power." And again, in another part of his speech, he continues: "Is it probable that the dissolution of the State governments, and the establishment of one *consolidated empire* would be eligible in its nature, and satisfactory to the people in its administration? I think not, as I have given reasons to show that so extensive a territory could not be governed, connected and preserved, but by the *supremacy of despotic power.* All the exertions of the most potent emperors of Rome were not capable of keeping that empire together, which in extent was far inferior to the dominion of America."

We dissent, secondly, because the powers vested in Congress by this constitution, must necessarily annihilate and absorb the legislative, executive, and judicial powers of the several States, and produce from their ruins one consolidated government, which from the nature of things will be *an iron handed despotism,* as nothing short of the supremacy of despotic sway could connect and govern these United States under one government.

As the truth of this position is of such decisive importance, it ought to be fully investigated, and if it is founded to be clearly ascertained; for, should it be demonstrated that the powers vested by this constitution in Congress will have such an effect as necessarily to produce one consolidated government, the question then will be reduced to this short issue, viz.: whether satiated with the blessings of liberty, whether repenting of the folly of so recently asserting their unalienable rights against foreign despots at the expense of so much blood and treasure, and such painful and arduous struggles, the people of America are now willing to resign every privilege of freemen, and submit to the dominion of an absolute government that

will embrace all America in one chain of despotism; or
whether they will, with virtuous indignation, spurn at the
shackles prepared for them, and confirm their liberties by
a conduct becoming freemen.

That the new government will not be a confederacy of
States, as it ought, but one consolidated government,
founded upon the destruction of the several governments
of the States, we shall now show.

The powers of Congress under the new constitution are
complete and unlimited over the *purse* and the *sword*, and
are perfectly independent of and supreme over the State
governments, whose intervention in these great points is
entirely destroyed. By virtue of their power of taxation,
Congress may command the whole or any part of the property of the people. They may impose what imposts upon
commerce, they may impose what land taxes, poll taxes,
excises, duties on all written instruments and duties on
every other article, that they may judge proper; in short,
every species of taxation, whether of an external or internal nature, is comprised in section the eighth of article the
first, viz.:

"The Congress shall have power to lay and collect taxes,
duties, imposts, and excises, to pay the debts, and provide
for the common defence and general welfare of the United
States."

As there is no one article of taxation reserved to the State
governments, the Congress may monopolize every source
of revenue, and thus indirectly demolish the State governments, for without funds they could not exist; the taxes,
duties and excises imposed by Congress may be so high as
to render it impracticable to levy farther sums on the same
articles; but whether this should be the case or not, if the
State governments should presume to impose taxes, duties
or excises on the same articles with Congress, the latter
may abrogate and repeal the laws whereby they are im-

posed, upon the allegation that they interfere with the due collection of their taxes, duties or excises, by virtue of the following clause, part of section eighth, article first, viz.:

"To make all laws which shall be necessary and proper for carrying into execution the foregoing powers, and all other powers vested by this constitution in the government of the United States, or in any department or officer thereof."

The Congress might gloss over this conduct by construing every purpose for which the State legislatures now lay taxes, to be for the "*general welfare*," and therefore as of their jurisdiction.

And the supremacy of the laws of the United States is established by article sixth, viz.: "That this constitution and the laws of the United States which shall be made in pursuance thereof, and *all treaties* made, or which shall be made under the authority of the United States, shall be the *supreme law* of the *land; and the judges in every State shall be bound thereby; anything in the constitution or laws of any State to the contrary notwithstanding.*" It has been alleged that the words "pursuant to the constitution," are a restriction upon the authority of Congress; but when it is considered that by other sections they are invested with every efficient power of government, and which may be exercised to the absolute destruction of the State governments, without any violation of even the forms of the constitution, this seeming restriction, as well as every other restriction in it, appears to us to be nugatory and delusive; and only introduced as a blind upon the real nature of the government. In our opinion, "pursuant to the constitution" will be co-extensive with the *will* and *pleasure* of Congress, which, indeed, will be the only limitation of their powers.

We apprehend that two co-ordinate sovereignties would

be a solecism in politics; that, therefore, as there is no line of distinction drawn between the general and State governments, as the sphere of their jurisdiction is undefined, it would be contrary to the nature of things that both should exist together—one or the other would necessarily triumph in the fulness of dominion. However, the contest could not be of long continuance, as the State governments are divested of every means of defence, and will be obliged by "the supreme law of the land" *to yield at discretion.*

It has been objected to this total destruction of the State governments that the existence of their legislatures is made essential to the organization of Congress; that they must assemble for the appointment of the senators and President-general of the United States. True, the State legislatures may be continued for some years, as boards of appointment merely, after they are divested of every other function; but the framers of the constitution, foreseeing that the people will soon become disgusted with this solemn mockery of a government without power and usefulness, have made a provision for relieving them from the imposition in section fourth of article first, viz.: "The times, places and manner of holding elections for senators and representatives shall be prescribed in each State by the legislature thereof; *but the Congress may at any time by law make or alter such regulations, except as to the place of choosing senators.*"

As Congress have the control over the time of the appointment of the President-general, of the senators and of the representatives of the United States, they may prolong their existence in office for life by postponing the time of their election and appointment from period to period under various pretences, such as an apprehension of invasion, the factious disposition of the people, or any other plausible pretence that the occasion may suggest; and having thus obtained life-estates in the government, they may fill up the vacancies themselves by their control over the mode of appointment; with this exception in regard to the senators that as the place of appointment for them must, by the constitution, be in the particular State, they may depute some body in the respective States, to fill up the vacancies in the senate, occasioned by death, until they can venture to assume it themselves. In this manner may the only restriction in this clause be evaded. By virtue of the foregoing section, when the spirit of the people shall be gradually broken, when the general government shall be firmly established, and when a numerous standing army shall render opposition vain, the Congress may complete the system of despotism, in renouncing all dependence on the people by continuing themselves and children in the government.

The celebrated *Montesquieu*, in his Spirit of Laws, vol. i., page 12, says, "That in a democracy there can be no exercise of sovereignty, but by the suffrages of the people, which are their will; now the sovereign's will is the sovereign himself—the laws, therefore, which establish the right of suffrage, are fundamental to this government. In fact, it is as important to regulate in a republic in what manner, by whom, and concerning what suffrages are to be given, as it is in a monarchy to know who is the prince, and after what manner he ought to govern." The *time, mode* and *place* of the election of representatives, senators and president-general of the United States, ought not to be under the control of Congress, but fundamentally ascertained and established.

The new Constitution, consistently with the plan of consolidation, contains no reservation of the rights and privileges of the State governments, which was made in the confederation of the year 1778, by article the 2d, viz.: "That each State retains its sovereignty, freedom and independence, and every power, jurisdiction and right which is not by this confederation expressly delegated to the United States in Congress assembled."

The legislative power vested in Congress by the foregoing recited sections, is so unlimited in its nature, may be so comprehensive and boundless in its exercise, that this alone would be amply sufficient to annihilate the State governments, and swallow them up in the grand vortex of general empire.

The judicial powers vested in Congress are also so various and extensive, that by legal ingenuity they may be extended to every case, and thus absorb the State judiciaries; and when we consider the decisive influence that a general judiciary would have over the civil polity of the several States, we do not hesitate to pronounce that this power, unaided by the legislative, would effect a consolidation of the States under one government.

The powers of a court of equity, vested by this constitution in the tribunals of Congress—powers which do not exist in Pennsylvania, unless so far as they can be incorporated with jury trial—would, in this State, greatly contribute to this event. The rich and wealthy suitors would eagerly lay hold of the infinite mazes, perplexities and delays, which a court of chancery, with the appellate powers of the Supreme Court in fact as well as law would furnish him with, and thus the poor man being plunged in the bottomless pit of legal discussion, would drop his demand in despair.

In short, consolidation pervades the whole constitution. It begins with an annunciation that such was the intention. The main pillars of the fabric correspond with it, and the concluding paragraph is a confirmation of it. The preamble begins with the words, "We the people of the United States," which is the style of a compact between individuals entering into a state of society, and not that of a confederation of States. The other features of consolidation we have before noticed.

Thus we have fully established the position, that the powers vested by this constitution in Congress will effect a consolidation of the States under one government, which even the advocates of this constitution admit could not be done without the sacrifice of all liberty.

3) 3. We dissent, thirdly, because if it were practicable to govern so extensive a territory as these United States include, on the plan of a consolidated government, consistent with the principles of liberty and the happiness of the people, yet the construction of this Constitution is not calculated to attain the object; for independent of the nature of the case, it would of itself necessarily produce a despotism, and that not by the usual gradations, but with the celerity that has hitherto only attended revolutions effected by the sword.

To establish the truth of this position, a cursory investigation of the principles and form of this constitution will suffice.

No Bill of Rights

The first consideration that this review suggests, is the omission of a BILL OF RIGHTS ascertaining and fundamentally establishing those unalienable and personal rights of men, without the full, free and secure enjoyment of which there can be no liberty, and over which it is not necessary for a good government to have the control—the principal of which are the rights of conscience, personal liberty by the clear and unequivocal establishment of the writ of *habeas corpus*, jury trial in criminal and civil cases, by an impartial jury of the vicinage or county, with the common law proceedings for the safety of the accused in criminal prosecutions; and the liberty of the press, that scourge of tyrants, and the grand bulwark of every other liberty and privilege. The stipulátions heretofore made in favor of them in the State constitutions, are entirely superseded by this Constitution.

The legislature of a free country should be so formed as to have a competent knowledge of its constitutents, and enjoy their confidence. To produce these essential requisites, the representation ought to be fair, equal and sufficiently numerous to possess the same interests, feelings, opinions and views which the people themselves would possess, were they all assembled; and so numerous as to prevent bribery and undue influence, and so responsible to the people, by frequent and fair elections, as to prevent their neglecting or sacrificing the views and interests of their constituents to their own pursuits.

We will now bring the legislature under this Constitution to the test of the foregoing principles, which will demonstrate that it is deficient in every essential quality of a just and safe representation.

The House of Representatives is to consist of sixty-five members; that is one for about every 50,000 inhabitants, to be chosen every two years. Thirty-three members will form a quorum for doing business, and seventeen of these, being the majority, determine the sense of the house.

The Senate, the other constituent branch of the legislature, consists of twenty-six members, being *two* from each State, appointed by their legislatures every six years; fourteen senators make a quorum—the majority of whom, eight, determines the sense of that body, except in judging on impeachments, or in making treaties, or in expelling a member, when two-thirds of the senators present must concur.

The president is to have the control over the enacting of laws, so far as to make the concurrence of two-thirds of the representatives and senators present necessary, if he should object to the laws.

Thus it appears that the liberties, happiness, interests, and great concerns of the whole United States, may be dependent upon the integrity, virtue, wisdom, and knowledge of twenty-five or twenty-six men. How inadequate and unsafe a representation! Inadequate, because the sense and views of three or four millions of people, diffused over so extensive a territory, comprising such various climates, products, habits, interests, and opinions, cannot be collected in so small a body; and besides, it is not a fair and equal representation of the people even in proportion to its number, for the smallest State has as much weight in the Senate as the largest; and from the smallness of the number to be chosen for both branches of the legislature, and from the mode of election and appointment, which is under the control of Congress, and from the nature of the thing, men of the most elevated rank in life will alone be chosen. The other orders in the society, such as farmers, traders, and mechanics, who all ought to have a competent number of their best informed men in the legislature, shall be totally unrepresented.

The representation is unsafe, because in the exercise of such great powers and trusts, it is so exposed to corruption and undue influence, by the gift of the numerous places of honor and emolument at the disposal of the executive, by the arts and address of the great and designing, and by direct bribery.

The representation is moreover inadequate and unsafe, because of the long terms for which it is appointed, and the mode of its appointment, by which Congress may not only control the choice of the people, but may so manage as to divest the people of this fundamental right, and become self-elected.

The number of members in the House of Representatives *may* be increased to one for every 30,000 inhabitants. But when we consider that this cannot be done without the consent of the Senate, who from their share in the legislative, in the executive, and judicial departments, and permanency of appointment, will be the great efficient body in this government, and whose weight and predominancy would be abridged by an increase of the representatives, we are persuaded that this is a circumstance that cannot be expected. On the contrary, the number of representatives will probably be continued at sixty-five, although the population of the country may swell to treble what is now is, unless a revolution should effect a change.

We have before noticed the judicial power as it would affect a consolidation of the States into one government; we will now examine it as it would affect the liberties and welfare of the people, supposing such a government were practicable and proper.

The judicial power, under the proposed constitution, is founded on well-known principles of the *civil law*, by which the judge determines both on law and fact, and appeals are allowed from the inferior tribunals to the superior, upon the whole question; so that *facts* as well as *law*, would be re-examined, and even new facts brought forward in the court of appeals; and to use the words of a very eminent civilian—"The cause is many times another thing before the court of appeals, than what it was at the time of the first sentence."

That this mode of proceeding is the one which must be adopted under this constitution, is evident from the following circumstances: 1st. That the trial by jury, which is the grand characteristic of the common law, is secured by the constitution only in criminal cases. 2d. That the appeal from both *law* and *fact* is expressly established, which is utterly inconsistent with the principles of the common law and trials by jury. The only mode in which an appeal from law and fact can be established, is by adopting the principles and practice of the civil law, unless the United States should be drawn into the absurdity of calling and swearing juries, merely for the purpose of contradicting their verdicts, which would render juries contemptible and worse than useless. 3d. That the courts to be established would decide on all cases *of law and equity,* which is a well-known characteristic of the civil law, and these courts would have conusance not only of the laws of the United States, and of treaties, and of cases affecting ambassadors, but of all cases of *admiralty and maritime jurisdiction,* which last are matters belonging exclusively to the civil law, in every nation in Christendom.

Not to enlarge upon the loss of the invaluable right of trial by an unbiased jury, so dear to every friend of liberty, the monstrous expense and inconveniences of the mode of proceeding to be adopted, are such as will prove intolerable to the people of this country. The lengthy proceedings of the civil law courts in the chancery of England, and in the courts of Scotland and France, are such that few men of moderate fortune can endure the expense of; the poor man must therefore submit to the wealthy. Length of purse will too often prevail against right and justice. For instance, we are told by the learned Judge *Blackstone,* that a question only on the property of an ox, of the value of three guineas, originating under the civil law proceedings in Scotland, after many interlocutory orders and sentences below, was carried at length from the court of sessions, the highest court in that part of Great Britain, by way of *appeal* to the House of Lords, where the question of law and fact was finally determined. He adds, that no pique or spirit could in the court of king's bench or common pleas at Westminister, have given continuance to such a cause for a tenth part of the time, nor have cost a twentieth part of the expense. Yet the costs in the courts of king's bench and common pleas in England, are infinitely greater than those which the people of this country have ever experienced.

We abhor the idea of losing the transcendent privilege of trial by jury, with the loss of which, it is remarked by the same learned author, that in Sweden, the liberties of the commons were extinguished by an aristocratic Senate; and that *trial by jury* and the liberty of the people went out together. At the same time we regret the intolerable delay, the enormous expense, and infinite vexation, to which the people of this country will be exposed from the voluminous proceedings of the courts of civil law, and especially from the appellate jurisdiction, by means of which a man may be drawn from the utmost boundaries of this extensive country to the seat of the Supreme Court of the nation to contend, perhaps, with a wealthy and powerful adversary. The consequence of this establishment will be an absolute confirmation of the power of aristocratical influence in the courts of justice; for the common people will not be able to contend or struggle against it.

Trial by jury in criminal cases may also be excluded by declaring that the libeller for instance shall be liable to an action of debt for a specified sum, thus evading the common law prosecution by indictment and trial by jury. And the common course of proceeding against a ship for breach of revenue laws by informa (which will be classed among civil causes) will at the civil law be within the resort of a court, where no jury intervenes. Besides, the benefit of jury trial, in cases of a criminal nature, which cannot be evaded, will be rendered of little value, by calling the accused to answer far from home; there being no provision that the trial be by a jury of the neighborhood or country. Thus an inhabitant of Pittsburgh, on a charge of crime committed on the banks of the Ohio, may be obliged to defend himself at the side of the Delaware, and so *vice versa*. To conclude this head: we observe that the judges of the courts of Congress would not be independent, as they are not debarred from holding other offices, during the pleasure of the President and Senate, and as they may derive their support in part from fees, alterable by the legislature.

The next consideration that the constitution presents, is the undue and dangerous mixture of the powers of government; the same body possessing legislative, executive and judicial powers. The Senate is a constituent branch of the legislature, it has judicial power in judging on impeachments, and in this case unites in some measure the characters of judge and party, as all the principal officers are appointed by the president-general, with the concurrence of the Senate, and therefore they derive their offices in part from the Senate. This may bias the judgments of the senators, and tend to screen great delinquents from punishment. And the Senate has, moreoever, various and great executive powers, viz., in concurrence with the president-general, they form treaties with foreign nations, that may control and abrogate the constitutions and laws of the several States. Indeed, there is no power, privilege or liberty of the State governments, or of the people, but what may be affected by virtue of this power. For all treaties, made by them, are to be the "supreme law of the land; anything in the constitution or laws of any State, to the contrary notwithstanding."

And this great power may be exercised by the President and ten senators (being two-thirds of fourteen, which is a quorum of that body). What an inducement would this offer to the ministers of foreign powers to compass by bribery *such concessions* as could not otherwise be obtained. It is the unvaried usage of all free States, whenever treaties interfere with the positive laws of the land, to make the intervention of the legislature necessary to give them operation. This became necessary, and was afforded by the parliament of Great Britain, in consequence of the late commercial treaty between that kingdom and France.

As the Senate judges on impeachments, who is to try the members of the Senate for the abuse of this power! And none of the great appointments to office can be made without the consent of the Senate.

Such various, extensive, and important powers combined in one body of men, are inconsistent with all freedom; the celebrated Montesquieu tells us, that "when the legislative and executive powers are united in the same person, or in the same body of magistrates, there can be no liberty, because apprehensions may arise, lest the same monarch or *senate* should enact tyrannical laws, to execute them in a tyrannical manner."

"Again, there is no liberty, if the power of judging be not separated from the legislative and executive powers. Were it joined with the legislative, the life and liberty of the subject would be exposed to arbitrary control; for the judge would then be legislator. Were it joined to the executive power, the judge might behave with all the violence of an oppressor. There would be an end of everything, were the same man, or the same body of the nobles, or of the people, to exercise those three powers; that of enacting laws, that of executing the public resolutions, and that of judging the crimes or differences of individuals."

The president general is dangerously connected with the senate; his coincidence with the views of the ruling junto in that body, is made essential to his weight and importance in the government, which will destroy all independency and purity in the executive department; and having the power of pardoning without the concurrence of a council, he may screen from punishment the most treasonable attempts that may be made on the liberities of the people, when instigated by his coadjutors in the senate. Instead of this dangerous and improper mixture of the executive with the legislative and judicial, the supreme executive powers ought to have been placed in the president, with a small independent council, made personally responsible for every appointment to office or other act, by having their opinions recorded; and that without the concurrence of the majority of the quorum of this council, the president should not be capable of taking any step.

We have before considered internal taxation as it would effect the destruction of the State governments, and produce one consolidated government. We will now consider that subject as it affects the personal concerns of the people.

The power of direct taxation applies to every individual, as Congress, under this government, is expressly vested with the authority of laying a capitation or poll tax upon every person to any amount. This is a tax that, however oppressive in its nature, and unequal in its operation, is certain as to its produce and simple in its collection; it cannot be evaded like the objects of imposts or excise, and will be paid, because all that a man hath will he give for his head. This tax is so congenial to the nature of despotism, that it has ever been a favorite under such governments. Some of those who were in the late general convention from this State, have labored to introduce a poll tax among us.

The power of direct taxation will further apply to every individual, as Congress may tax land, cattle, trades, occupations, etc., to any amount, and every object of internal taxation is of that nature that however oppressive, the people will have but this alternative, either to pay the tax or let their property be taken, for all resistance will be vain. The standing army and select militia would enforce the collection.

For the moderate exercise of this power, there is no control left in the State governments, whose intervention is destroyed. No relief, or redress of grievances, can be extended as heretofore by them. There is not even a declaration of RIGHTS to which the people may appeal for the vindication of their wrongs in the court of justice. They must therefore, implicitly obey the most arbitrary laws, as the most of them will be pursuant to the principles and form of the constitution, and that strongest of all checks upon the conduct of administration, *responsibility to the people,* will not exist in this government. The permanency of the appointments of senators and representatives, and the control the congress have over their election, will place them independent of the sentiments and resentment of the people, and the administration having a greater interest in the government than in the community, there will be no consideration to restrain them from oppression and tyranny. In the government of this State, under the old confederation, the members of the legislature are taken from among the people, and their interests and welfare are so inseparably connected with those of their constituents, that they can derive no advantage from oppressive laws and taxes; for they would suffer in common with their fellow-citizens, would participate in the burthens they impose on the community, as they must return to the common level, after a short period; and notwithstanding every exertion of influence, every means of corruption, a necessary rotation excludes them from permanency in the legislature.

This large State is to have but ten members in that Congress which is to have the liberty, property and dearest concerns of every individual in this vast country at absolute command, and even these ten persons, who are to be our only guardians, who are to supersede the legislature of Pennsylvania, will not be of the choice of the people, nor amenable to them. From the mode of their election and appointment they will consist of the lordly and high minded; of men who will have no congenial feelings with the people, but a perfect indifference for, and contempt of them; they will consist of those harpies of power that prey upon the very vitals, that riot on the miseries of the community. But we will suppose, although in all probability it may never be realized in fact, that our deputies in Congress have the welfare of their constituents at heart, and will exert themselves in their behalf, what security could even this afford? what relief could they extend to their oppressed constitutents? To attain this, the majority of the deputies of the twelve other States in Congress must be alike well disposed; must alike forego the sweets of power, and relinquish the pursuits of ambition, which, from the nature of things, is not to be expected. If the people part with a responsible representation in the legislature, founded upon fair, certain and frequent elections, they have nothing left they can call their own. Miserable is the lot of that people whose every concern depends on the *will* and *pleasure* of their rulers. Our soldiers will become Janissaries, and our officers of government Bashaws; in short, the system of despotism will soon be completed.

From the foregoing investigation, it appears that the Congress under this constitution will not possess the confidence of the people, which is an essential requisite in a good government; for unless the laws command the confidence and respect of the great body of the people, so as to induce them to support them when called on by the civil magistrate, they must be executed by the aid of a numerous standing army, which would be inconsistent with every idea of liberty; for the same force that may be employed to compel obedience to good laws, might and probably would be used to wrest from the people their constitutional liberties. The framers of this constitution appear to have been aware of this great deficiency—to have been sensible that no dependence could be placed on the people for their support: but on the contrary, that the government must be executed by force. They have therefore made a provision for this purpose in a permanent *standing army* and a *militia* that may be objected to as strict discipline and government.

A standing army in the hands of a government placed so independent of the people, may be made a fatal instrument to overturn the public liberties; it may be employed to enforce the collection of the most oppressive taxes, and to carry into execution the most arbitrary measures. An ambitious man who may have the army at his devotion, may step up into the throne, and seize upon absolute power.

The absolute unqualified command that Congress have over the militia may be made instrumental to the destruction of all liberty, both public and private; whether of a personal, civil or religious nature.

First, the personal liberty of every man, probably from sixteen to sixty years of age, may be destroyed by the power Congress have in organizing and governing of the militia. As militia they may be subjected to fines to any amount, levied in a military manner; they may be subjected to corporal punishments of the most disgraceful and humiliating kind; and to death itself, by the sentence of a court martial. To this our young men will be more immediately subjected, as a select militia, composed of them, will best answer the purposes of government.

Secondly, the rights of conscience may be violated, as there is no exemption of those persons who are conscientiously scrupulous of bearing arms. These compose a respectable proportion of the community in the State. This is the more remarkable, because even when the distresses of the late war, and the evident disaffection of many citizens of that description, inflamed our passions, and when every person who was obliged to risk his own life, must have been exasperated against such as on any account kept back from the common danger, yet even then, when outrage and violence might have been expected, the rights of conscience were held sacred.

At this momentous crisis, the framers of our State Constitution made the most express and decided declaration and stipulations in favor of the rights of conscience; but now, when no necessity exists, those dearest rights of men are left insecure.

Thirdly, the absolute command of Congress over the militia may be destructive of public liberty; for under the guidance of an arbitrary government, they may be made the unwilling instruments of tyranny. The militia of Pennsylvania may be marched to New England or Virginia to quell an insurrection occasioned by the most galling oppression, and aided by the standing army, they will no doubt be successful in subduing their liberty and independency; but in so doing, although the magnanimity of their minds will be extinguished, yet the meaner passions of resentment and revenge will be increased, and these in turn will be the ready and obedient instruments of despotism to enslave the others; and that with an irritated vengeance. Thus may the militia be made the instruments of crushing the last efforts of expiring liberty, of riveting the chains of despotism on their fellow-citizens, and on one another. This power can be exercised not only without violating the Constitution, but in strict conformity with it; it is calculated for this express purpose, and will doubtless be executed accordingly.

As this government will not enjoy the confidence of the people, but be executed by force, it will be a very expensive and burthensome government. The standing army must be numerous, and as a further support, it will be the policy of this government to multiply officers in every department; judges, collectors, tax-gatherers, excisemen and the whole host of revenue officers, will swarm over the land, devouring the hard earnings of the industrious—like the locusts of old, impoverishing and desolating all before them.

We have not noticed the smaller, nor many of the considerable blemishes, but have confined our objections to the great and essential defects, the main pillars of the constitution; which we have shown to be inconsistent with the liberty and happiness of the people, as its establishment will annihilate the State governments, and produce one consolidated government that will eventually and speedily issue in the supremacy of despotism.

In this investigation we have not confined our views to the interests or welfare of this State, in preference to the others. We have overlooked all local circumstances—we have considered this subject on the broad scale of the general good; we have asserted the cause of the present and future ages—the cause of liberty and mankind.

Nathaniel Breading,	John Ludwig,
John Smilie,	Abraham Lincoln,
Richard Bard,	John Bishop,
Adam Orth,	Joseph Hiester,
John A. Hannah,	Joseph Powell,
John Whitehill,	James Martin,
John Harris,	William Findley,
Robert Whitehill,	John Baiad,
John Reynolds,	James Edgar,
Jonathan Hoge,	William Todd.
Nicholas Lutz,	

The yeas and nays upon the final vote were as follows, viz.:

YEAS.	YEAS.
George Latimer,	John Barclay,
Benjamin Rush,	Thomas Yardley,
Hilary Baker,	Abraham Stout,
James Wilson,	Thomas Bull,
Thomas M'Kean,	Anthony Wayne,

William Macpherson,
John Hunn,
George Gray,
Samuel Ashmead,
Enoch Edwards,
Henry Wynkoop,
Sebastian Graff,
John Hubley,
Jasper Yeates,
Henry Slagle,
Thomas Campbell,
Thomas Hartley,
David Grier,
John Black,
Benjamin Pedan,
John Arndt,
Stephen Balliet,
Joseph Horsfield,

William Gibbons,
Richard Downing,
Thomas Cheyney,
John Hannum,
Stephen Chambers,
Robert Coleman,
David Deshler,
William Wilson,
John Boyd,
Thomas Scott,
John Neville,
John Allison,
Jonathan Roberts,
John Richards,
F. A. Muhlenberg,
James Morris,
Timothy Pickering,
Benjamin Elliott.

NAYS.
John Whitehill,
John Harris,
John Reynolds,
Robert Whitehill,
Jonathan Hoge,
Nicholas Lutz,
John Ludwig,
Abraham Lincoln,
John Bishop,
Joseph Hiester,
James Martin,
Joseph Powell,

NAYS.
William Findley,
John Baird,
William Todd,
James Marshel,
James Edgar,
Nathaniel Breading,
John Smilie,
Richard Bard,
William Brown,
Adam Orth,
John Andre Hannah.

Philadelphia December 12, 1787

3. The Letter of "Montezuma"

The identity of "Montezuma" is not known, but that he was a man of strong feelings and much talent for propaganda seems evident. The Pennsylvania Antifederalists were rather fond of the tactic employed in this letter. It purports to be written by an advocate of the Constitution and to give the "inside" story on the dark designs of aristocrats to establish themselves in power. Thus the letter reflects the relatively strong sense of class conflict with which some Antifederalists were imbued, as well as an intensely suspicious attitude toward the motives of their opponents. It is a good example of the more inflammatory propaganda produced during the ratification debate.

MR. OSWALD,
   That the enclosed defence may be laid open to the general scrutiny of my fellow citizens, I request a place for it in your paper.

                          LYCURGUS

   We the Aristicratic party of the United States, lamenting the many inconveniencies to which the late confederation subjected the *well-born*, the *better kind* of people bringing them down to the level of the *rabble*, and holding in utter detestation, that frontispiece to every bill of rights—"that all men are born equal," beg leave (for the purpose of drawing a line between such as we think were *ordained* to

---

Reprinted from *The Independent Gazetteer* (Philadelphia), October 17, 1787.

govern, and such as were *made* to bear the weight of government without having any share in its administration) to submit to *our friends* in the first class for their inspection, the following defence of *our monarchical, aristocratical democracy.*

1st. As a majority of all societies consist of men who (though totally incapable of thinking or acting in governmental matters) are more readily led than driven, we have thought meet to indulge them in something like a democracy in the new constitution, which part we have designated by the popular name of the House of Representatives; but to guard against every possible danger from this *lower house,* we have subjected every bill they bring forward, to the double negative of our *upper house* and president—nor have we allowed the *populace* the right to elect their representatives annually, as usual, lest this body should be too much under the influence and controul of their constituents, and thereby prove the "weatherboard of our grand edifice, to shew the shiftings of every fashionable gale," for we have not yet to learn that little else is wanting, to aristocratize the most democratical representative than to make him somewhat independent of his *political creators*—We have taken away that rotation of appointment which has so long perplexed us—that *grand engine* of popular influence; every man is eligible into our government, from time to time for live—this will have a two-fold good effect; first it prevents the representatives from mixing with the *lower class,* and imbibing their foolish sentiments, with which they would have come charged on re-election.

2d. They will from the perpetuality of office be under *our* eye, and in a short time will think and act like *us,* independently of popular whims and prejudices; for the assertions "that evil communications corrupt good manners," is not more true than its reverse. We have allowed this house the power to impeach, but we have tenaciously reserved the right to try. We hope gentlemen, you will see the policy of this clause—for what matters it who accuses, if the accused is tried by his friends—in time this *plebian house* will have little power, and that little be rightly shaped by our house of *gentlemen,* who will have a very extensive influence, from their being chosen out of the *genteeler class,* and their appointment being almost a life, one as seven years is the calculation on a man's life, and they are chosen for six: It is true, every third senatorial seat is to be vacated duennually, but two-thirds of this influential body will remain in office, and be ready to direct or (if necessary) bring over to the good old way, the young members, if the old ones should not be returned; and whereas many of our brethren, from a laudable desire to support their rank in life above the commonality, have not only deranged their finances, but subjected their persons to indecent treatment (as being arrested for debt, etc.) we have framed a privilege clause, by which they may laugh at the fools who trusted them; but we have given out, that this clause was provided, only that the members might be able without interruption, to deliberate on the important business of their country.

We have frequently endeavoured to effect in our respective states, the happy discrimination which pervades this system, but finding we could not bring the states into it individually, we have determined, and in this our general plan we have taken pains to leave the legislature of each *free and independent* state, as they now call themselves, in such a situatuon that they will eventually be absorbed by our *grand continental vortex,* or dwindle into petty corporations, and have power over little else than *yoaking hogs* of determining the width of *cart wheels*—but (aware that an intention to annihilate state legislatures, would be objected to our favorite scheme) we have made their existence (as a *board of electors*) necessary to ours; this furnishes us and our advocates with a fine answer to any clamours that may be raised on this subject, viz——We have so interwoven continental and state legislatures that they cannot exist separately; whereas we in truth, only leave them the power of electing us, for what can a provincial legislature do when we possess "the exclusive regulation of external and internal commerce, excise, duties, imports, post-offices and roads; when we and we alone, have the power to wage war, make peace, coin money (if we can get buillion) if not, borrow money, organize the militia and call them forth to execute our decrees, and crush insurrections assisted by a noble body of veterans subject to our nod, which we have the power of raising and keeping even in the time of peace. What have we to fear from state legislatures or even from states, when we are armed with such powers, with a president at our head? (a name we thought proper to adopt in conformity to the prejudices of a silly people who are so foolishly fond of a Republican government, that we were obliged to accommodate in names and forms to them, in order more effectually to secure the substance of our proposed plan, but we all know that Cromwell was a King, with the title of protector.) I repeat it, what have we to fear armed with such powers, with a president at our head who is captain-general of the army, navy and militia of the United States, who can make and unmake treaties, appoint and commission ambassadors and other ministers, who can grant or refuse reprieves or pardons, who can make judges of the supreme and other continental courts, in short who will be the source, the fountain of honor, profit and power, whose influence like the rays of the sun will diffuse itself far and wide, will exhale all *democratical vapours* and break the *clouds of popular insurrection*? But again gentlemen, our judicial power is a strong work, a masked battery, few people see the guns we can and will ere long play off from it; for the judicial power embraces every question which can arise in law or equity, under this constitution and under the laws of "the United States"—(which laws will be you know, the supreme laws of the land)—This power extends to all cases, affecting ambassadors or other public ministers, and "consuls to all cases of admiralty and maritime jurisdiction—to controversies to which the United States are a party, to controversies between two or more states, between a state and citizens of another state, between citizens of different states, between citizens of the same state claiming lands under grants of different states, and between a state or the citizens thereof and foreign states, citizens or subjects."

Now, can a question arise in the colonial courts, which the ingenuity or sophistry of an able lawyer may not bring within one or other of the above cases? Certainly not. Then our court will have original or appellate jurisdiction in all cases—and if so how fallen are state judicatures—and must not every provincial law yield to our supreme fiat? Our constitution answers yes—then how insignificant will the makers of these laws be—it is in the nature of power to create influence—and finally we shall entrench ourselves so as to laugh at the cabals of the commonalty—a few regiments will do at first, it must be spread abroad that they are absolutely necessary to defend the frontiers. Now a regiment and then a legion must be added quietly, by and bye a frigate or two must be built, still taking care to intimate that they are essential to the support of our revenue laws and to prevent smuggling. We have said nothing about a bill of rights, for we viewed it as an eternal clog upon our designs—as a lock chain to the wheels of government—though by the way as we have not insisted on rotation in our offices, the simile of a wheel is ill. We have for some time, considered the freedom of the press as a great evil—it spreads information, and begets a licentiousness in the people which needs the rein more than the spur; besides a daring printer may expose the plans of government and lessen the consequence of our president and senate; for these and many other reasons we have said nothing with respect to the "right of the people to speak and publish their sentiments," or about their "palladiums of liberty," and such stuff. We do not much like that sturdy privilege of the people—the right to demand the writ of *habeas corpus*—we have therefore reserved the power of refusing it in cases of rebellion, and you know we are the judges of what is rebellion. Things as yet are well—our friends we find have been assiduous in representing our federal calamities, until at length the people at large frightened by the gloomy picture on one side, and allured by the prophecies of some of our fanciful and visionary adherents on the other, are ready to accept and confirm our proposed government without the delay or forms of examination, which was the more to be wished as they are wholly unfit to investigate the principles or pronounce on the merit of so exquisite a system. Impressed with a conviction that this constitution is calculated to restrain the influence and power of the LOWER CLASS—to draw that *discrimination* we have so long sought after, to secure to our friends *privileges and offices,* which were not to be valued on under the former government, because they were in common—to take the burthen of *legislation and attendance on public business* off the commonalty, who will be much better able thereby to prosecute with effect their private business, to destroy that *political thirteen-headed monster* the state sovereignties, to check the *licentiousness* of the people by making it dangerous to *speak or publish* daring or tumulteary sentiments, to enforce obedience to laws by a *strong executive,* aided by *military pensioners,* and finally to promote the public and private interests of the *better kind* of people. We submit it to your judgement to take such measure for its adoption as you in your wisdom may think fit.

Signed by unanimous order of the lords
Spiritual and temporal
MONTEZUMA, President

4. The Letters of *"Philadelphiensis"*

These letters, the last of a series published in *The Independent Gazetteer* of Philadelphia, November 1787 to April 1788, represent some of the more flamboyant of the Antifederalist attacks on the Constitution. There is a strong appeal to class-consciousness, and a tendency to portray the authors and advocates of the proposed new government as engaged in a deliberate conspiracy to delude the people into a surrender of their liberties. The author predicts that the new constitution, if adopted, cannot be effectively established without a standing army, and that any attempt thus to establish it may well result in civil war. In addition to the very common fear of a standing army, "Philadelphiensis" expresses his preference for a navy, which would not be so grave a threat to liberty, and which would have the salutary effect of putting the Philadelphia shipwrights back to work. Although "Philadelphiensis" may strike the modern reader as possessed of rather extravagant notions, he may be remembered for at least one insight. He observed that parties and factions in England, together with their recurrent conflicts, were not dangerous because they were in agreement on the fundamentals of the constitution. This observation, applied to America (which he thought impossible) was worthy of consideration, both at the time he made it, and at the present time also.

"Philadelphiensis" was probably a tutor at the University of Pennsylvania named Benjamin Workman. He was identified as the

---

The Letters of Philadelphiensis, Numbers IX-XII. From the text in *The Independent Gazetteer* [Philadelphia], February 7, 21, March 8, April 11, 1788.

author of the letters at the time, and although in a series of comments[1] in *The Independent Gazetteer* he neither denied nor confirmed the identification, the tone and content of his replies leads me to believe that he was indeed the author of those letters. He had been in this country only three years.

[IX]

[February 7, 1788]

FOR THE INDEPENDENT GAZETTEER.

Instamus tamen immemores, caecique furore,
Et monstrum infelix sacrata sistimus arce.   Virg.

TRANSLATION
Thus we, by madness blinded and o'ercome,
Lodge the dire monster in the sacred dome.

My Fellow-Citizens,
Before *martial law* is declared to be the supreme law of the land, and your character of free citizens be changed to that of the subjects of a *military king*, which are necessary consequences of the adoption of the proposed constitution, let me admonish you in the name of *sacred liberty*, to make a solemn pause. Permit a freeman to address you, and to solicit your attention to a cause wherein yourselves and your posterity are concerned. The sun never shone upon a more important one: it is the cause of freedom—of a whole continent—of yourselves and of your fellow men.

Men who have so gloriously asserted the rights of human nature, and overcome tyranny, one ought reasonably to suppose could not have their spirits so much broken as

---

[1]See *The Independent Gazetteer*, March 11, 21, 26; April 1, 15, 24, 1788.

peaceably to submit to it a few years afterwards. By the declaration of peace, wherein Britain acknowledged the independence and sovereignty of the United States, the people of America became citizens of the freest country under heaven. But under the proposed plan of government the least fragment of liberty cannot exist.

The writers against the proposed constitution are denominated, by the *aristocratics, incendiaries,* and enemies to America, men whose writings tend to involve this devoted country in anarchy, and in all the horrors of a civil war. Now, in reply to this charge; let me ask the friends of this government, Is that man an *incendiary* who advocates the unalienable rights of the people? Is he an enemy to America who endeavors to protect the *oppressed* from the *oppressor*; who opposes a conspiracy against the liberties of his country, concerted by a few *tyrants,* whose views are to lord it over the rest of their fellow citizens, to trample the poorer part of the people under their feet, that they may be rendered their servants and slaves? If such a writer is an incendiary, and an enemy to America, then I glory in the character. A conspiracy against the freedom of America, both deep and dangerous, has been formed by an infernal junto of demagogues. Our thirteen free commonwealths are to be consolidated into one *despotic monarchy.* Is not this a position obvious? Its evidence is intuitive; and the address and dissent of the minority of the convention of Pennsylvania add such strength to its illustration, that no man of common sense can refuse his assent. But why need I attempt to prove a point, that that honest man and firm patriot, MR. MARTIN,[2] says the monarchy men of the federal convention declared was their intention.

---

[2]Luther Martin, delegate from Maryland to the Federal Convention [Ed.].

Who can deny but the *president general* will be a *king* to all intents and purposes, and one of the most dangerous kind too; a king elected to command a standing army? Thus our laws are to be administered by this *tyrant*; for the whole, or at least the most important part of the executive department is put in his hands.

A quorum of 65 representatives, and of 26 senators, with a king at their head, are to possess powers, that extend to the *lives*, the *liberties*, and *property* of every citizen of America. This novel system of government, were it possible to establish it, would be a compound of *monarchy* and *aristocracy*, the most accursed that ever the world witnessed. About 50 (these being a quorum) of the *well born*, and a *military king*, with a *standing army* devoted to his will, are to have an uncontrouled power over our lives, our liberties, and property, in all cases whatsoever. Is he an incendiary who abhors the thought of such a government, who declares it his opinion, that none but a sycophant or a slave could submit to it? I think not; and there is no power under heaven that could cause me to change my opinion; which has the joint evidences of reason and experience for its foundation.

There is not a tincture of democracy in the proposed constitution, except the nominal elections of the president general and the illustrious Congress be supposed to have some colour of that nature; but this is a mere deception, invented to gull the people into its adoption. Its framers were well aware that some appearance of election ought to be observed, especially in regard to the first Congress; for without such an appearance there was not the smallest probability of their having it organized and set in operation. But let the wheels of this government be once cleverly set in motion, and I'll answer for it, that the people shall not be much troubled with future elections, especially in choosing their *king*, the *standing army* will do that business for them.

The thoughts of a military officer possessing such powers, as the proposed constitution vests in the president general, are sufficient to excite in the mind of a freeman the most alarming apprehensions; and ought to rouse him to oppose it at *all events*. Every freeman of America ought to hold up this idea to himself, *that he has no superior but God and the laws*. But this tyrant will be so much his superior, that he can at any time he thinks proper, order him out in the militia to exercise, and to march when and where he pleases. His officers can wantonly inflict the most disgraceful punishment on a peaceable citizen, under pretense of disobedience, or the smallest neglect of militia duty.

Among the substantial objections to the great powers of the president, that of his *negative* upon the laws, is one of the most inconsiderable, indeed it is more a sound than any thing else; For, if he be a bold enterprising fellow, there is little fear of his ever having to exercise it. The two branches of the legislature, will be at his service; no law contrary to his sentiments, however salutary in its operations, dare be mentioned by them. As a body, and as individuals, they will be his sycophants and flatterers. But, if on the contrary he should not be a man of spirit, a thing very improbable, as none but an ambitious man, well versed in the ways of men, could have the address to be raised to that elevated station; if, however, I say, he should not be a man of an enterprising spirit, in that case he will be a *minion* of the aristocratics, doing according to their will and pleasure, and confirming every law they may think proper to make, without any regard to their public utility.

Every idea of such unlimited powers being lodged in so small a number of the *well born*, elevated so far above the rest of their fellow citizens, and supported by a *king* with a *standing army* at his disposal, ought to cause the blood of a free citizen to boil with indignation: the very mentioning of it shocks my whole frame. I abhor the thought from my soul: And I flatter myself that the people of this continent will not suffer such a government to be placed over them. Indeed it astonishes me, that the conspirators who framed it, had not the most dreadful apprehensions of their personal safety, from the just resentment of the freemen of an insulted country.

To such lengths have these bold conspirators carried their scheme of despotism, that your most sacred rights and privileges are surrendered at discretion. When government thinks proper, under the pretence of writing a libel, etc. it may imprison, inflict the most cruel and unusual punishment, seize property, carry on prosecutions, etc. and the unfortunate citizen has no *magna charta*, no *bill of rights*, to protect him; nay, the prosecution may be carried on in such a manner that even a *jury* will not be allowed him. Where is that *base slave* who would not appeal to the *ultima ratio*, before he submits to this government?

If the despots persist in pushing it on, let them answer the consequences; they may fall a sacrifice to their own obstinacy; for liberty will triumph over every obstacle, even were a *standing army* opposed to it.

To preserve the peace of the country, every patriot should exert himself at this awful crisis, and use his influence to have another federal convention called as soon as possible; either to amend the old articles of confederation, or to frame a constitution on revolution principles, that may secure the freedom of America to the remotest time.

If the State of Massachusetts should reject the proposed constitution, of which there is a strong probability, what a contemptible figure must its advocates make, who, after it made its appearance from the *dark conclave*, affirmed that there was but *five men* opposed to it in the United States.

The convention of that state was chosen in the moment of blind enthusiasm, and yet we find it so much divided that the issue is doubtful. The sentiments of the people are changing every day, and were that convention to be elected now, I doubt not but four fifths would be against it. In the back counties of Pennsylvania, where the *well born* have no influence, the opposition is said to have become so powerful that a person would be in danger of losing his life, if he ventured to speak a word in its favor.

The conspirators saw clearly, that such a system of government could never be established over freemen, except they were taken by surprize; and hence they hurried matters forward with that view; in short, the people were made to believe, that they were all *dead men*, if they did not adopt it immediately. Even still they were endeavoring to hold up the idea of anarchy being the consequence of rejection: But he must have very weak intellects indeed, and little acquainted with the spirit of freemen, to whom it is not obvious that adoption will produce anarchy and ruin.

No evil can result from calling another general convention, but much good would be the consequence. The distresses of America are not of that nature to be healed all of a sudden; some of them indeed have arisen from the defects in the general government; but there are others of a different kind, that must be removed by time, and by the prudence of the people at large.

Ye patriots! ye lovers of peace, of liberty, and of your fellow men! Ye are called upon at this solemn juncture, to stand forth and save your country; before the breach is too wide, and while the parties may still be reconciled to each other; before anarchy stalks through the land; and before the sword of civil discord is unsheathed. For the sake of every thing that is great and good, and as you shall answer for it at the great tribunal, use your influence to procure another general convention with all possible speed, as the only way left to preserve the union of America, and to save your fellow citizens from misery and destruction.

[x]

[February 21, 1788]

For the Independent Gazetteer.

My Fellow-Citizens,
If stupid irony, falsehood, scurrility, and abusive language, be sufficient to silence a writer in the cause of freedom, my sentiments must have been suppressed long ago; but that old saying, that *nothing cuts like the truth*, has encouraged me to address you once more. Probably this essay may be more obnoxious to the friends of the proposed plan of government than any of my former publications; and if so, the above saying is farther confirmed. A freeman must have a *little soul* indeed, whose attention can be diverted from its proper object, by the schemes practised by the friends of unlimited dominion. His own happiness, as being connected with the happiness of his fellow-men, ought to be his chiefest good. The *divine founder* of our religion and his beatified followers had no aim but this, and they pursued it with a zeal consistent with its excellence.

If the proposed plan be a good one upon the whole, why should its friends endeavour to prevent investigating its merits or defects? Why should they hurry it on us before we have even read it? Does not this look suspicious like? Is it not a proof that it is the works of darkness and cannot bear the light? Why should they summon a Convention in Pennsylvania, before the tenth part of the people had time to judge for themselves, or to know whether it was a free or a tyrannical system of government? Why employ bullies to drag some members of the Assembly per force to the House to make a quorum, in order to call a Convention? The answers of these interrogatives are obvious, and the conclusions deduced from them will in time have their proper effect.

The principles of its framers are now clearly understood; the proceedings of the *dark conclave* have undergone an *ordeal* in Maryland, that exhibits the monarchy-men in convention as a set of the basest conspirators that ever disgraced a free country. At the time that these men were plotting the ruin of their country, and forming a system of national cruelty unequalled in the annals of time, the unsuspecting freemen of America were blessing them, were praying for them in their private families, and in their public churches, and looking up to them for relief; they even called the federal convention an *august body, the most excellent assembly of men that ever appeared in the world.*

The *President-general*, who is to be our *king* after this government is established, is vested with powers exceeding those of the most *despotic monarch* we know of in modern times. What a handsome return have these men made to the people of America for their confidence! Through the misconduct of these bold conspirators we have lost the most glorious opportunity that any country ever had to establish a free system of government. America under one purely democratical, would be rendered the happiest and most powerful nation in the universe; but under the proposed one, composed of an *elective king* and a standing army, officered by his sycophants, the starvelings of the Cincinnati, and an aristocratical Congress of the *well-born*, an iota of happiness, freedom or national strength cannot exist. What a pitiful figure will these ungrateful men make in history; who, for the hopes of obtaining some lucrative employment, or of receiving a little more homage from the rest of their fellow creatures, framed a system of oppression that must involve in its consequences the misery of their own offspring? There is but one rational way remaining to prevent themselves from being eye witnesses of a dreadful scene, and that is for them to cease immediately every operation that respects the establishing of this plan of government; and then all parties will join heartily in calling another federal convention, and the peace of the country will be preserved.

One of the members of the virtuous minority of the convention of Massachusetts openly declared in that assembly, that pushing on this accursed system would produce a *civil war*: the freemen of New-England, the best soldiers on the continent, have had their eyes opened, and begin to see through the conspiracy; that sacred palladium of liberty, *the freedom of the press*, has dispelled the cloud, and cleared their understandings. In that state, through the influence of the tyrants of Boston, very little information has reached the people; the *press*, generally speaking, was devoted to the *well-born* and their tools; yet out of near 400 members, of which that convention consisted, only a majority of 19 could be procured, notwithstanding every possible method of over-awing, threatening, and *bribing* was practised.

I conceive that carrying it by so small a majority, is little better than a rejection; in fact it may prove worse, for the breach is only widened so much the more by it, and truly it was wide enough before. The freemen of Massachusetts will never cowardly surrender their sacred rights and liberties into the hands of one man, or any body of men whatever. They know what freedom is, and they will support it at the risque of their lives and fortunes. Their courage, fortitude, and achievements in the late war have rendered their character, as friends to liberty, immortal.

The amendments proposed by the president will be another source of mischief; the people cannot be so ignorant as to be deceived by so pitiful a manoeuvre. Here is a positive acknowledgement made by one of its advocates who hopes to be appointed the *little king* if not the *big one*, that it is objectionable; and his amendments are introduced as a blind; the weighty ones are untouched: not a whimper of the extraordinary powers of the *President-general*, the *standing army*, the *liberty of the press*, etc. No, no! if these *glorious parts* be lopped off, what would become of the monarchy-men? And respecting *internal taxation*, is not his amendment a disgrace to himself, and an insult to the understanding of the people? Mr. Hancock knows, or ought to know at least, that the liberties of the citizens of America are not to be trifled with: his schemes are too flimsey not to be seen through.

The allegiance of freemen to government will ever be a consequence of protection; the Congress of America withdrew their allegiance from the king of Great Britain when he changed his protection into acts of cruelty; and on the same account the citizens of these United States will not chearfully [*sic*] bear allegiance to the new government; which, instead of protecting them in their sacred rights and privileges,will be a system of tyranny and oppression. The unlimited powers of the new Congress in respect to taxation, are abundantly sufficient to alarm the people. While the state assemblies retained the right of *internal taxation*, the country farmers could not be burdened beyond their abilities; these men being the true representatives of the people, would never attempt to levy an oppressive tax; their own feelings and interests being congenial with those of their constituents, their consent must be withheld when a measure was proposed subversive of public good.

That the new Congress will not be the immediate representatives of the people, that their number is too small, their powers too great, their accountability to the people not properly secured, and above all the *executive* dangerously placed in the hands of one man who is really a *king*, have been fully illustrated by many able writers, and ably proved in the conventions of this state and Massachusetts by worthy patriots whose names will be revered as long as time shall remain. Upon the whole, my fellow citizens, if the great characters who are said to advocate this system of government, wish to act consistently, the greatest proof they can give of their love for their country, is to join the rest of their fellow citizens in endeavouring to call another federal convention.

[XI]

[March 8, 1788]

My Fellow Citizens,
Every day opens a new scene of the baseness of the conspirators, their intentions of screening themselves from rendering an account of the public money so fradulently detained, will rank them among the meanest traitors, that ever dishonoured the human character. How must their consciences condemn them, when avarice and lust of dominion are suffered for a moment to subside, and reason and reflection take their place? Let these men but cooly consider the misery that must inevitably befal millions of their countrymen, in consequence of their treachery in framing this system of fraud and oppression; and remorse and deep anguish of soul must await them! Humanity brings a tear of sympathetic pity from the eye of their fellow men, whose ruin they had secretly projected. As our holy religion expressly enjoins it as a duty, not to return

evil for evil, but to overcome evil with good; consequently our resentment against these ungrateful men should be moderated by christian charity: Yet as freemen and citizens, determined to hand down to posterity sacred liberty unimpaired, we are solemnly bound at the hazard of our fortunes and lives, to oppose this base attempt of theirs to enslave our country.

If on the broad basis of equity and justice, crimes and punishments have their proper proportion: What punishment then, on the scale of moderation, could counterpoise, or atone, for a crime so aggravated as that charged to the majority of the members of the late federal convention? I assert roundly, that another assembly of men never met in this or any other country, possessing so fully the confidence of so many freemen: and to their shame be it said, they abused this confidence; their own private interest, private emolument and hopes of dominion, overcame every consideration of duty, honor, and gratitude.

The citizens of Pennsylvania have nobly shown their love for liberty, and attachment to the true interests of the union by their generous exertions in favor of public credit. They have rigidly fulfilled their engagements in regard to the general debt; the requisitions of Congress have been swiftly attended to, and fully answered. Add to this, that we have sunk a considerable part of the domestic debt, *and in fact* assumed a larger portion of it than in justice belonged to us. These spirited exertions, while they contributed to the general welfare of the union, and raised the reputation of the state, did not fail however to distress our farmers and every other class and description of citizens, very sensibly indeed.

But what is the result of their unshaken loyalty to the cause of liberty, and the honor of their country? What recompence will the honest and industrious Pennsylvanians receive for their patriotism, if the new government be established? Such a return as perhaps history does not afford a single instance similar to. So base a violation of public justice and plighted faith, is certainly a novelty in politics, and begins a new epoch in history. Pennsylvania, instead of receiving credit for the immense sums she has paid into the general treasury, will be placed on a footing with the most delinquent state in the union; and which is highly probable she and all the other states will be taxed hereafter in an exact ratio of the sums they have hitherto raised. Consequently our former acts of generosity, in support of public faith, is to terminate in a two-fold loss to our citizens. In the first place we have nearly ruined ourselves already, through our punctuality in paying our quota of the public debt; and secondly, to complete the scene, our future quotas of continental revenue will be apportioned to the exertions we have heretofore made: That is in plain terms, Pennsylvania will be much worse under this cruel system of tyranny in consequence of her fidelity and honor, than she would have been had she never attempted to pay a shilling of public debt; or if she be not worse, the uniformity of internal taxation through the union, which is expressly stipulated by the constitution, necessarily places her citizens on a parallel with those of that state which has not paid a shilling of public debt since the peace.

The people of the delinquent states might inconsiderately be induced to triumph in the new system of government; for they may conclude, now our public debts are paid as far forward as those of any other state, but attentive consideration will soon convince them of their mistake. Although the new constitution advances them as high in the public scale as if they had strictly and honorably made good the requisitions of the old Congress; yet the unbounded powers of the new Congress in respect to internal taxation, must eventually fleece them of their all; and from their inability heretofore to pay their just quotas as levied by Congress, we may rationally conclude, that, even the states of Pennsylvania and New-York, which are in advance at present, will still be above them, supposing the extra payments of these two states not to be carried to the credit of their account, which they certainly will not, on the principles of this constitution.

The truth of this matter is simply this: the taxes will hereafter be uniform in all the states, and as oppressive as tyranny can make them. In every state the face of the poor must be ground to dust; and where any appearance of prosperity or wealth is observed, an additional tax will be devised; for so complicated and uncontrouled a government will find ways and means to apply all the revenue that America can raise; indeed the whole produce of the lands cultivated by three millions and an half of people, could not satiate the desires of such a government. If the *lesser* or rather *greater* states would moderate their precipitancy, in urging forward the constitution, by reason and the certainty of misery that stares them in the face, I imagine they would find their advantage in the measure. Lenity in the old Congress has in some degree screened them; and besides their fellow citizens in the other states befriend them; but the high hand of power, so completely vested in the new Congress, will exact the uttermost farthing, both from the states and individuals: No excuse will satisfy the demands of a cruel *excise-man*; we must instantly pay the federal tax, or have our property seized, and ourselves dragged to prison by a federal soldier.

That this government, should it be ratified by nine states, will not possess the confidence of the majority of the people, is a truth incontrovertible. I admit, that through fraud and surprise, many have inconsiderately joined themselves to its deceptive standard; but their number is diminishing rapidly; and I sincerely believe, that in a few months the *office-hunters*, the *well-born*, and their sycophants, will be left alone: The farmer, the mechanic, and even the merchant, would be ruined if it took effect; their interest is to oppose it, and to endeavor to have another convention called immediately.

Who is so dimsighted as to suppose that a constitution so essentially differing from the principles of the revolution, and from freedom, and opposed by so respectable a body of freemen, could be established in America; or if it were possible, by force or surprise to put it in motion, could it exist any space of time? Nay, the idea is futile, and common sense spurns at it. While it would exist, it must be by the power of a standing army alone; but its warmest advocates know, that all their credit, and influence could not support a standing army equal to the business, six months.

It is admitted, that in Great Britain they are scarce ever without violent factions and parties, and yet no injury is apprehended to the country on that account, but generally much good: But let us attend to this matter seriously, and we must see clearly that factions and parties in America in respect to the present important object, would eventually ruin this country. The parties, factions, and cabals, so frequent in Britain, are not from a dislike to the fundamentals of their constitution, but on account of maladministration: All parties glory in the constitution, and disagree only, when it is infringed, or violated.

To infer then, from the example of Britain, that the opposition to the new government would not terminate in our ruin, if it were adopted by a majority in nine states, would be a dangerous mistake; for there is no analogy between the premises, the conclusions are therefore different. The opposition in America is against the fundamentals of the constitution itself, but this is not so in England. No constitution that is not popular can possibly be established in America; or if for a short time it were established, we would have nothing but anarchy and civil war, while it was in existence.

Let us not be deceived by delusive tales, that it shall be amended after the meeting of the first Congress; since it is admitted almost universally that it wants amendments; now is the time to have them done, while we are at peace abroad, and among ourselves. A fragment of liberty cannot remain, if we once set it in motion in its imperfect state. How can we suppose, that the president general, being once in full possession of his unlimited powers, would deliver them back again to the people; the supposition is preposterous; he must be more than *man* if he would; a more dangerous king is not in the world than he will be; liberty will be lost in America the day on which he is proclaimed, and must be recovered by the *sword*, if ever we are to enjoy it again.

[XII]

[April 11, 1788]

For the Independent Gazetteer.

My Fellow Citizens,
The essays under the signature of Philadelphiensis are represented as without argument, and their prime object is said to be to involve this devoted country in a civil war. But *time*, the discoverer of future events, will certainly show that the calling of another Federal Convention is the only rational way to prevent it. Heaven grant that these eyes may never behold that dreadful scene. The writer of these essays was actuated by the purest motives, namely, to defend the liberty and advance the happiness of his fellow citizens. These he conceived insecure, or rather destroyed, if the proposed constitution should be estab-

lished, and hence he laboured to procure another Convention. The expediency of this measure was demonstrated by illustrating the principal defects in the proposed system;—defects did I say—the expression is too soft—the ruin that must follow its adoption.

If pointing out the unlimited powers of the new Congress over the lives and property of their fellow citizens, which may and certainly would be abused, be not an argument against it, there remains no fixed determinate idea to be annexed to the term argument; indeed, on such principles right and wrong, freedom and slavery have no essential difference, and the human mind is a mere chaos.

Some feeble attempts have been made by the advocates of this system of tyranny, to answer the objections made to the smallness of the number of representatives and senators, and the improper powers delegated to them; but, as far as I recollect, no one has been found bold enough to stand forth in defence of that dangerous and uncontrouled officer, the *President General*, or more properly, our new KING.

A few pieces under the signature of *An American Citizen* were published immediately after the Constitution broke the shell, and the hydra made its way from the *dark conclave* into the open light; in the first number of which the writer, in touching on the *President*, endeavored to conceal his immense powers, by representing the King of Great Britain as possessed of many hereditary prerogatives, rights and powers that he was not possessed of; that is, he shews what he is not, but neglects to shew what he really is; but so flimsey a palliative could scarcely escape the censure of the most ignorant advocate for such an officer; and since we hear of no further attempts to prove the necessity of a King being set over the freemen of America.

The writer of these essays has clearly proven, that the president is a King to all intents and purposes, and at the same time one of the most dangerous kind too—an *elective King,* the commander in chief of a standing army, etc. and to these add, that he has a negative over the proceedings of both branches of the legislature: and to complete his uncontrouled sway, he is neither restrained nor assisted by a *privy council,* which is a novelty in government. I challenge the politicians of the whole continent to find in any period of history a monarch more absolute.

Who is so base as not to burn with resentment against the conspirators, who have dared to establish such a tyrant over his life, his liberty and property? Is the flame of sacred liberty so entirely extinguished in the American breast as not to be kindled again? No; you mistaken despots, do not let such a preposterous thought madden you into perseverance, lest your persons fall sacrifices to the resentment of an injured country. Stop at once, and join the rest of your fellow citizens. Let another Convention be immediately called, and let a system of government fitted to the pure principles of the Revolution, be framed. Then a general amnesty among all ranks and degrees of your fellow citizens must succeed, and America become the seat of liberty, peace, friendship and happiness; and her government have ample *energy* and *respectability* among the nations of the earth; yes, she will thereby be rendered the great arbiter of the world.

5. The Letters of "John De Witt"

The identity of the man who wrote under the signature of "John De Witt" is not known, but that he was one of the best stylists of the Antifederalists is certain. The letters in this series are graced by sentences and phrases that are striking, appealing, or felicitous. "It is true, that many of us have but our liberties to loose [*sic*], but they are dearly bought, and are not the least precious in estimation." The author described the proposed new government as "a hasty stride to Universal Empire in this Western World," and predicted that the House of Representatives would become "an Assistant Aristocratical Branch." Of the proposed Congressional power of direct, internal taxation, he proclaimed, "A dry tax is at all times odious." And he warned the people of Massachusetts that if they acceded to the new Constitution, "your chains will be gradual, and gilded." One would like to have known a man with so powerful and skillful a pen. "John De Witt" criticized the great extent of powers conferred upon Congress by the Constitution, especially those of direct taxation and the maintenance of a standing army, which he believed to be closely related and inevitably destructive of liberty. He made the usual criticisms of the inadequate representation to be afforded by the size of the House of Representatives, and explained in explicit and precise terms why the Senate would be an aristocratic branch of the government. Its long tenure would make it independent of popular control, and its share in the appointive power would enable individual senators to use this source of patronage

---

These three letters were from a series of five addressed "To the *Free Citizens* of the *Commonwealth* of *Massachusetts*," published in *The American Herald* [Boston], October-December 1787. They are reprinted from the text in that newspaper.

to insure their re-election, perhaps even for life. The five letters constitute an extremely able contribution to the Antifederalist case against the Constitution.

I

[October 22, 1787]

To The Free Citizens of The Commonwealth of Massachusetts

Whoever attentively examines the history of America, and compares it with that of other nations, will find its commencement, its growth, and its present situation, without a precedent.

It must ever prove a source of pleasure to the Philosopher, who ranges the explored parts of this inhabitable globe, and takes a comparative view, as well of the rise and fall of those nations, which have been and are gone, as of the growth and present existence of those which are now in being, to close his prospect with this Western world. In proportion as he loves his fellow creatures, he must here admire and approve; for while they have severally laid their foundations in the blood and slaughter of three, four, and sometimes, ten successive generations, from their passions have experience, every misery to which human nature is subject, and at this day present striking features of usurped power, unequal justice, and despotic tyranny, America stands completely systemised without any of these misfortunes. —On the contrary, from the first settlement of the country, the necessity of civil associations, founded upon equality, consent, and proportionate justice have ever been universally acknowledged. —The means of education always attended to, and the fountains of science brought within the reach of poverty. —Hitherto we have commenced society, and advanced in all respects resembling a family, without partial affections, or even a domestic bickering: And if we consider her as an individual, instead of an undue proportion of violent passions and bad habits, we must set her down possessed of reason, genius, and virtue. —I premise these few observations because there are too many among us of narrow minds, who live in the practice of blasting the reputation of their own country. —They hold it as a maxim, that virtues cannot grow in their own soil. —They will appreciate those of a man they know nothing about, because he is an exotic; while they are sure to depreciate those much more brilliant in their neighbors, because they are really acquainted with them and know them.

Civil society is a blessing. —It is here universally known as such. —The education of every child in this country tends to promote it. —There is scarcely a citizen in America who does not wish to bring it, consistent with our situation and circumstances, to its highest state of improvement. —Nay, I may say further that the people in general aim to effect this point, in a peaceable, laudable, and rational way. These assertions are proved by stubborn facts, and I need only resort to that moment, when, in contest with a powerful enemy, they paid such an unprecedented attention to civilization, as to select from among themselves their different conventions, and form their several constitutions, which, for their beautiful theoretical structure, caught the admiration of our enemies, and secured to us the applause of the world. —We at this day feel the effects of this disposition, and now live under a government of our own choice, constructed by ourselves, upon unequivocal principles, and requires but to be well administred to make us as happy under it as generally falls to the lot of humanity. The disturbances in the course of the year past cannot be placed as an objection to the principle I advance. —They took their rise in idleness, extravagance

Shay's Rebellion

and misinformation, a want of knowledge of our several finances, a universal delusion at the close of the war, and in consequence thereof, a pressure of embarrassments, which checked, and in many cases, destroyed that disposition of forbearance, which ought to be exercised towards each other. These were added to the accursed practice of letting money at usury, and some few real difficulties and grievances, which our late situation unavoidably brought upon us. The issue of them, however, rather proves the position for, a very few irreclaimables excepted, we find even an anxiety to hearken to reason pervading all classes—industry and frugality increasing, and the advantages arising from good, wholesome laws, confessed by every one. —Let who will gain say it, I am confident we are in a much better situation, in all respects, than we were at this period the last year; and as fast as can be expected, consistent with the passions and habits of a free people, of men who will think for themselves, coalescing, as a correspondent observes in a late paper, under a firm, wise and efficient government. The powers vested in Congress have hitherto been found inadequate. —Who are those that have been against investing them? The people of this Commonwealth have very generally supposed it expedient, and the farmer equally with the merchant have taken steps to effect it. —A Convention from the different States for that sole purpose hath been appointed of their most respectable citizens—respectable indeed I may say for their equity, for their literature, and for their love of their country. —Their proceedings are now before us for our approbation. —The eagerness with which they have been received by certain classes of our fellow citizens, naturally forces upon us this question? Are we to adopt this Government, without an examination. —Some there are, who, literally speaking, are for pressing it upon us at all events. The name of the man who but lisps a sentiment in objection to it, is to be handed to the printer, by the printer to the publick, and by the publick he is to be led to execution. They are themselves stabbing its reputation. For my part, I am a stranger to the necessity for all this haste! Is it not a subject of some small importance? Certainly it is. —Are not your lives, your liberties and properties intimately involved in it? —Certainly they are. Is it a government for a moment, a day, or a year? By no means—but for ages. —Altered it may possibly be, but it is easier to correct before it is adopted. —Is it for a family, a state, or a small number of people? It is for a number no less respectable than three millions. Are the enemy at our gates, and have we not time to consider it? Certainly we have. Is it so simple in its form as to be comprehended instantly? —Every letter, if I may be allowed the expression, is an idea. Does it consist of but few additions to our present confederation, and those which have been from time to time described among us, and known to be necessary? —Far otherwise. —It is a compleat system of government and armed with every power, that a people in any circumstances ought to bestow. It is a path newly struck out, and a new set of ideas are introduced that have neither occurred or been digested. —A government for national purposes, preserving our constitution entire, hath been the only plan hitherto agitated. I do not pretend to say, but it is in theory the most unexceptionable, and in practice will be the most conducive to our happiness of any possible to be adopted: —But it ought to undergo a candid and strict examination. It is the duty of every one in the Commonwealth to communicate his sentiments to his neighbour, divested of passion, and equally so of prejudices. If they are honest and he is a real friend to his country, he will do it and embrace every opportunity to do it. If thoroughly looked into before it is adopted, the people will be more apt to approve of it in practice, and every man is a TRAITOR to

himself and his posterity, who shall ratify it with his signature, without first endeavouring to understand it. —We
are but yet in infancy; and we had better proceed slow
than too fast. —It is much easier to dispense powers, than
recall them. —The present generation will not be drawn
into any system; they are too enlightened; they have not
forfeited their right to a share in government, and they
ought to enjoy it.

Some are heard to say, "When we consider the men who
made it, we ought to take it for sterling, and without hesitation—that they were the collected wisdom of the States,
and had no object but the general good." —I do not doubt
all this, but facts ought not to be winked out of sight: —
They were delegated from different States, and nearly
equally represented, though vastly disproportionate both
in wealth and numbers. They had local prejudice to combat, and in many instances, totally opposite interests to
consult. Their situations, their habits, their extent, and
their particular interest, varied each from the other. The
gentlemen themselves acknowledge that they have been
less rigid upon some points, in consequence of those difficulties than they otherwise should have been. —Others
again tell you that the Convention is or will be dissolved;
that we must take their proceedings in whole or reject
them. —But this surely cannot be a reason for their speedy
adoption; it rather works the other way. If evils are acknowledged in the composition, we ought, at least, to see
whose shoulders are to bear the most; to compare ours with
those of other States, and take care that we are not saddled
with more than our proportion: That the citizens of Philadelphia are running mad after it, can be no argument for us
to do the like: —Their situation is almost contrasted with
ours; they suppose themselves a central State; they expect
the perpetual residence of Congress, which of itself alone
will ensure their aggrandizement: We, on the contrary, are

sure to be near one of the extremes; neither the loaves or fishes will be so plenty with us, or shall we be so handy to procure them.

We are told by some people, that upon the adopting this New Government we are to become every thing in a moment: —Our foreign and domestic debts will be as a feather; our ports will be crowded with the ships of all the world, soliciting our commerce and our produce: Our manufactures will increase and mulitply; and, in short, if we STAND STILL, our country, notwithstanding, will be like the blessed Canaan, a land flowing with milk and honey. Let us not deceive ourselves; the only excellency of any government is in exact proportion to the administration of it: —Idleness and luxury will be as much a bane as ever; our passions will be equally at war with us then as now; and if we have men among us trying with all their ability to undermine our present Constitution, these very persons will direct their force to sap the vitals of the new one.—

Upon the whole, my fellow countrymen, I am as much a federal man as any person: In a federal union lies our political salvation. —To preserve that union, and make it respectable to foreign opticks, the National Government ought to be armed with all necessary powers; but the subject I conceive of intimate delicacy, and requires both ability and reflection. In discussing points of such moment, America has nothing to do with passions or hard words; every citizen has an undoubted right to examine for himself, neither ought he to be ill treated and abused, because he does not think at the same moment exactly as we do. It is true, that many of us have but our liberties to loose, but they are dearly bought, and are not the least precious in estimation: —In the mean time, is it not of infinite consequence, that we pursue inflexibly that path, which I feel persuaded we are now approaching, wherein we shall discourage all foreign importations; shall see the necessity of greater economy and industry; shall smile upon the husbandman, and reward the industrious mechanick; shall promote the growth of our own country, and wear the produce of our own farms; and, finally, shall support measures in proportion to their honesty and wisdom, without any respect to men. Nothing more is wanted to make us happy at home, and respectable abroad.

II

[October 27, 1787]

To The Free Citizens of The Commonwealth of Massachusetts

In my last address upon the proceedings of the Federal Convention, I endeavored to convince you of the importance of the subject, that it required a cool, dispassionate examination, and a thorough investigation, previous to its adoption—that it was not a mere revision and amendment of our first Confederation, but a compleat System for the future government of the United States, and I may now add in preference to, and in exclusion of, all others heretofore adopted. —It is not temporary, but in its nature, PERPETUAL. —It is not designed that you shall be annually called, either to revise, correct, or renew it; but, that your posterity shall grow up under, and be governed by it, as well as ourselves. —It is not so capable of alterations as you would at the first reading suppose; and I venture to assert, it never can be, unless by force of arms. The fifth article in the porceedings, it is true, expressly provides for an alteration under certain conditions, whenever "it shall be ratified by the Legislatures of three fourths of the several States, or by Conventions in three fourths thereof, as the one or the other mode of ratification may be proposed by Congress." —Notwithstanding which, such are the *"heterogeneous materials from which this System was formed,"* such is the difference of interest, different manners, and different local prejudices, in the different parts of the United States, that to obtain that majority of three fourths to any one single alteration, essentially affecting this or any other State, amounts to an absolute impossibility. The conduct of the Delegates in dissolving the Convention, plainly speaks this language, and no other. — Their sentiments in their Letter to his Excellency the President of Congress are—That this Constitution was the result of a spirit of amity—that the parties came together disposed to concede as much as possible each to the other—that mutual concessions and compromises did, in fact, take place, and all those which could, consistent with the peculiarity of their political situation. Their dissolution enforces the same sentiment, by confining you to the alternative of taking or refusing their doings in the gross. In this view, who is there to be found among us, who can seriously assert, that this Constitution, after ratification and being practised upon, will be so easy of alteration? Where is there the probability that a future Convention, in any future day, will be found possessed of a greater spirit of amity and mutual concession than the present? Where is the probability that three fourths of the States in that Convention, or three fourths of the Legislatures of the different States, whose interests differ scarcely in nothing short of everything, will be so very ready or willing materially to change any part of this System, which shall be to the emolument of an individual State only? No, my fellow citizens, as you are now obliged to take it in the whole, so you must hereafter administer it in whole, without the prospect of change, unless by again reverting to a state of Nature, which will be ever opposed with success by those who approve of the Government in being.

That the want of a Bill of Rights to accompany this proposed System, is a solid objection to it, provided there is nothing exceptionable in the System itself, I do not assert. —If, however, there is at any time, a propriety in having one, it would not have been amiss here. A people, entering into society, surrender such a part of their natural rights, as shall be necessary for the existence of that society. They are so precious in themselves, that they would never be parted with, did not the preservation of the remainder require it. They are entrusted in the hands of those, who are very willing to receive them, who are naturally fond of exercising of them, and whose passions are always striving to make a bad use of them. —They are conveyed by a written compact, expressing those which are given up, and the mode in which those reserved shall be secured. Language is so easy of explanation, and so difficult is it by words to convey exact ideas that the party to be governed cannot be too explicit. The line cannot be drawn with too much precision and accuracy. The necessity of this accuracy and this precision encreases in proportion to the greatness of the sacrifice and the numbers who make it. —That a Constitution for the United States does not require a Bill of Rights, when it is considered, that a Constitution for an individual State would, I cannot conceive. —The difference between them is only in the numbers of the parties concerned: They are both a compact between the Governors and Governed, the letter of which must be adhered to in discussing their powers. That which is not expressly granted, is of course retained.

The Compact itself is a recital upon paper of that proportion of the subject's natural rights, intended to be parted with, for the benefit of adverting to it in case of dispute. Miserable indeed would be the situation of those individual States who have not prefixed to their Constitution a

Bill of Rights, if, as a very respectable, learned Gentleman at the Southward observes, "the People, when they established the powers of legislation under Representatives with every right and authority which they did not, in explicit terms, reserve; and therefore upon every question, respecting the justification of the House or Assembly, if the Frame of Government is silent, the jurisdiction is efficient and complete." In other words, those powers which the people by their Constitutions expressly give them, they enjoy by positive grant, and those remaining ones, which they never meant to give them, and which the Constitutions say nothing about, they enjoy by tacit implication, so that by one means and by the other, they become possessed of the whole. —This doctrine is but poorly calculated for the meridian of America, where the nature of compact, the mode of construing them, and the principles upon which society is founded, are so accurately known and universally diffused [?]. That insatiable thirst for unconditional controul over our fellow-creatures, and the facility of sounds to convey essentially different ideas, produced the first Bill of Rights ever prefixed to a Frame of Government. The people, altho' fully sensible that they reserved every tittle of power they did not expressly grant away, yet afraid that the words made use of, to express those rights so granted might convey more than they originally intended, they chose at the same moment to express in different language those rights which the agreement did not include, and which they never designed to part with, endavoring [*sic*] thereby to prevent any cause for future altercation and the intrusion into society of that doctrine of tacit implication which has been the favorite theme of every tyrant from the origin of all governments to the present day.

The proceedings of the Convention are now handed to you by your Legislature, and the second Wednesday in

January is appointed for your final answer. To enable you to give that with propriety; that your future reflections may produce peace, however opposed the present issue of your present conduct may be to your present expectations, you must determine, that, in order to support with dignity the Foederal Union, it is proper and fit, that the present Confederation shall be annihilated: —That the future Congress of the United States shall be armed with the powers of Legislation, Judgment and Execution: —That annual elections in this Congress shall not be known, and the most powerful body, the Senate, in which a due proportion of representation is not preserved, and in which the smallest State has equal weight with the largest, be the longest in duration: —That it is not necessary for the publick good, that persons habituated to the exercise of power should ever be reminded from whence they derive it, by a return to the station of private citizens, but that they shall at all times at the expiration of the term for which they were elected to an office, be capable of immediate re-election to that same office: —That you will hereafter risque the probability of having the Chief Executive Branch chosen from among you; and that it is wholly indifferent, both to you and your children after you, whether this future Government shall be administred within the territories of your own State, or at the difference of four thousand miles from them. You must also determine, that they shall have the exclusive power of imposts and the duties on imports and exports, the power of laying excise and other duties, and the additional power of laying internal taxes upon your lands, your goods, your chattels, as well as your persons at their sovereign pleasure: —That the produce of these several funds shall be appropriated to the use of the United States, and collected by their own officers, armed with a military force, if a civil aid should not prove sufficient: —That the power of organizing, arming and disci-

plining the militia shall be lodged in them, and this thro'
fear they shall not be sufficiently attentive to keeping so
respectable a body of men as the yeomanry of this Commonwealth, compleatly armed, organized and disciplined;
they shall also have the power of raising, supporting and
establishing a standing army in time of peace in your several towns, and I see not why in your several houses:
—That should an insurrection or an invasion, however
small, take place, in Georgia, the extremity of the Continent,
it is highly expedient they should have the power of suspending the writ of Habeas Corpus in Massachusetts, and
as long as they shall judge the public safety requires it:
—You must also say, that your present Supreme Judicial
Court shall be an Inferior Court to a Continental Court,
which is to be inferior to the Supreme Court of the United
States: —That from an undue bias which they are supposed
to have for the citizens of their own States, they shall not be
competent to determine title to your real estate, disputes
which may arise upon a protested Bill of Exchange, a
simple note of hand, or book debt, wherein your citizens
shall be unfortunately involved with disputes of such or
any other kind, with citizens either of other States or foreign States: In all such cases they shall have a right to
carry their causes to the Supreme Court of the United
States, whether for delay only or vexation; however distant
from the place of your abode, or inconsistent with your
circumstances: —That such appeals shall be extended to
matters of fact as well as law, and a trial of the cause by
jury you shall not have a right to insist upon. —In short,
my fellow citizens, previous to a capacity of giving a compleat answer to these proceedings, you must determine
that the Constitution of your Commonwealth, which is
instructive, beautiful and consistent in practice, which has
been justly admired in Europe, as a model of perfection,
and which the present Convention have affected to imi-

tate, a Constitution which is especially calculated for your territory, and is made conformable to your genius, your habits, the mode of holding your estates, and your particular interests, shall be reduced in its powers to those of a City Corporation: —The skeleton of it may remain, but its vital principle shall be transferred to the new Government: Nay, you must go still further, and agree to invest the new Congress with powers, which you have yet thought proper to withhold from your own present Government. —All these, and more, which are contained in the proceedings of the Federal Convention, may be highly proper and necessary. —In this overturn of all individual Government, in this new-fashioned set of ideas, and in this total dereliction of those sentiments which animated us in 1775, the Political Salvation of the United States may be very deeply interested, but BE CAUTIOUS.

III

[November 5, 1787]

TO THE FREE CITIZENS OF THE COMMONWEALTH OF MASSACHUSETTS

Civil Liberty, in all countries, hath been promoted by a free discussion of publick measures, and the conduct of publick men, The FREEDOM OF THE PRESS hath, in consequence thereof, been esteemed one of its safe guards. That freedom gives the right, at all times, to every citizen to lay his sentiments, in a decent manner, before the people. If he will take that trouble upon himself, whether they are in point or not, his countrymen are obliged to him for so doing; for, at least, they lead to an examination of the subject upon which he writes. —If any possible situation makes it a duty, it is our present important one, for in the course of sixty or ninety days you are to approve of or reject the present proceedings of your Convention, which, if established, will certainly effect, in a greater or less degree, during the remainder of your lives, those privileges which you esteem dear to you, and not improbably those of your children for succeeding ages. Now therefore is unquestionably the proper time to examine it, and see if it really is what, upon paper, it appears to be. If with your eyes open, you deliberately accept it, however different it may prove in practice from what it appears in theory, you will have nobody to blame but yourselves; and what is infinitely worse, as I have before endeavoured to observe to you, you will be wholly without a remedy. It has many zealous advocates, and they have attempted, at least as far as their modesty would permit, to monopolize our gazettes, with their encomiums upon it. With the people they have to manage, I would hint to them, their zeal is not their best weapon, and exertions of such a kind, artful attempts to seize the moment, do seldom tend either to elucidate and explain principles, or ensure success. Such conduct ought to be an additional stimulous for those persons who are not its professed admirers, to speak their sentiments with freedom however unpopular. Such conduct ought to inspire caution, for as a man is invariably known by his company, so is the tendency of principles known by their advocates. Nay, it ought to lead you to enquire who are its advocates? Whether ambitious men throughout America, waiting with impatience to make it a stepping stone to posts of honour and emolument, are not of this class? Whether men who openly profess to be tired of republican governments, and sick to the heart of republican measures; who daily ridicule a government of choice, and pray ardently for one of force, are not of the same class? And, whether there are not men among us, who disapprove of it only because it is not an absolute monarchy, but who, upon the whole, are among its advocates? In such examinations as these, you cannot mispend a proportion of the sixty days.

All contracts are to be construed according to the meaning of the parties at the time of making them. By which is meant, that mutual communications shall take place, and each shall explain to the other their ideas of the contract before them. —If any unfair practices are made use of, if its real tendency is concealed by either party, or any advantage taken in the execution of it, it is in itself fraudulent and may be avoided. There is no difference in the constitution of government. —Consent it is allowed is the spring. —The form is the mode in which the people choose to direct their affairs, and the magistrates are but trustees to put the mode in force. —It will not be denied, that this people, of any under Heaven, have a right of living under a government of their own choosing. —That government, originally consented to, which is in practice, what it purports to be in theory, is a government of choice; on the contrary, that which is essentially different in practice, from its appearance in theory, however it may be in letter a government of choice, it never can be so in spirit. Of this latter kind appear to me to be the proceedings of the Federal Convention. —They are presented as a Frame of Government purely Republican, and perfectly consistent with the individual governments in the Union. It is declared to be constructed for national purposes only, and not calculated to interfere with domestic concerns. You are told, that the rights of the people are very amply secured, and when the wheels of it are put in motion, it will wear a milder aspect than its present one. Whereas the very contrary of all this doctrine appears to be the case. Upon an attentive examination you can pronounce it nothing less, than a government which in a few years, will degenerate to a compleat Aristocracy, armed with powers unnecessary in any case to bestow, and which in its vortex swallows up every other Government upon the Continent. In short, my fellow citizens, it can be said to be nothing less than a hasty stride to Universal Empire in this Western World, flattering, very flattering to young ambitious minds, but fatal to the liberties of the people. The cord is strained to the very utmost. — There is every spice of the Sic. Jubeo possible in the composition. Your consent is requested, because it is essential to the introduction of it; after having received confirmation, your complaints may encrease the whistling of the wind, and they will be equally regarded.

It cannot be doubted at this day by any men of common sense, that there is a charm in politicks. That persons who enter reluctantly into office become habituated, grow fond of it, and are loath to resign it. —They feel themselves flattered and elevated, and are apt to forget their constituents, until the time returns that they again feel the want of them. —They uniformly exercise all the powers granted to them, and ninety-nine in a hundred are for grasping for more. It is this passionate thirst for power, which has produced different branches to exercise different departments and mutual checks upon those branches. The aristocratical hath ever been found to have the most influence, and the people in most countries have been particularly attentive in providing checks against it. Let us see if it is the case here. —A President, a Senate, and a House of Representatives are proposed. The Judicial Department is at present out of the question, being separated excepting in impeachments. The Legislature is divided between the People who are the Democratical, and the Senate who are the Aristocratical part, and the Executive between the same Senate and the President who represents the Monarchical Branch—In the construction of this System, their interests are put in opposite scales. If they are exactly balanced, the Government will remain perfect; if there is a prepondency, it will finally prevail. After the first four years, each Senator will hold his seat for the term of six years. This length of time will be amply sufficient of itself to remove any checks that he may have upon his independency, from the fear of a future election. He will consider that it is a serious portion of his life after the age of thirty; that places of honour and trust are not generally obtained unsolicited. The same means that placed him there may again be made use of; his influence and his abilities arising from his opportunities, will, during the whole term encrease those means; he will have a compleat negative upon all laws that shall be general, or that shall favor individuals, and a voice in the appointment of all officers in the United States. —Thus habituated to power, and living in the daily practice of granting favors and receiving solicitations, he may hold himself compleatly independent of the people, and at the same time ensure his election. If there remains even a risque, the blessed assistance of a little well-distributed money, will remove it.

With respect to the Executive, the Senate excepting in nomination, have a negative upon the President, and if we but a moment attend to their situation and to his, and to the power of persuasion over the human mind, especially when employed in behalf of friends and favotits [*sic*], we cannot hesitate to say, that he will be infinitely less apt to disoblige them, than they to refuse him. It is far easier for twenty to gain over one, than one twenty; besides, in the one case, we can ascertain where the denial comes from, and the other we cannot. It is also highly improbable but some of the members, perhaps a major part, will hold their seats during their lives. We see it daily in our own Government, and we see it in every Government we are acquainted with, however many the cautions and however frequent the elections.

These considerations, added to their share above mentioned in the Executive department must give them a decided superiority over the House of Representatives. —But that superiority is greatly enhanced, when we consider the difference of time for which they are chosen. They will have become adepts in the mystery of administration, while the House of Representatives may be composed perhaps two thirds of members, just entering into office, little used to the course of business, and totally unacquainted with the means made use of to accomplish it. —Very possible also in a country where they are total strangers. —But, my fellow citizens, the important question here arises, who are this House of Representatives? "A representative Assembly, says the celebrated Mr. Adams, is the sense of the people, and the perfection of the portrait, consists in the likeness." —Can this Assembly be said to contain the sense of the people? —Do they resemble the people in any one single feature? —Do they represent your wants, your grievances, your wishes, in person? If that is impracticable, have you a right to send one of your townsmen for that purpose? —Have you a right to send one from your county? Have you a right to send more than one for every thirty thousand of you? Can he be presumed knowing to your different, peculiar situations —your abilities to pay publick taxes, when they ought to be abated, and when encreased? Or is there any possibility of giving him information? All these questions must be answered in the negative. But how are these men to be chosen? Is there any other way than by dividing the States into districts? May not you as well at once invest your annual Assemblies with the power of choosing them —where is the essential difference? The nature of the thing will admit of none. Nay, you give them the power to prescribe the mode. They may invest it in themselves. —If you choose them yourselves, you must take them upon credit, and elect those persons you know only by common fame. Even this privilege is denied you annually, through fear that you might withhold the shadow of controul over them. In this view of the System, let me sincerely ask you, where is the people in this House of Representatives? —Where is the boasted popular part of this much admired System? Are they not couzin germans in every sense to the Senate? May they not with propriety be termed an Assistant Aristocratical Branch, who will be infinitely more inclined to co-operate and compromise with each other, than to be the careful guardians of the rights of their constituents? Who is there among you would not start at being told, that instead of your present House of Representatives, consisting of members chosen from every town, your future Houses were to consist of but ten in number, and these to be chosen by districts? —What man among you would betray his country and approve of it? And yet how infinitely preferable to the plan proposed? —In the one case the elections would be annual, the persons elected would reside in the center of you, their interests would be yours, they would be subject to your immediate controul, and nobody to consult in their deliberations. —But in the other, they are chosen for double the time, during which, however well disposed, they become strangers to the very people choosing them, they reside at a distance from you, you have no controul over them, you cannot observe their conduct, and they have to consult and finally be guided by twelve other States, whose interests are, in all material points, directly opposed to yours. Let me again ask you, What citizen is there in the Commonwealth of Massachusetts, that would deliberately consent laying aside the mode proposed, that the several Senates of the several States, should be the popular Branch, and together, form one National House of Representatives? —And yet one moment's attention will evince to you, that this blessed proposed Representation of the people, this apparent faithful Mirror, this striking Likeness, is to be still further refined, and more Aristocratical four times fold. —Where now is the exact balance which has been so diligently attended to? Where lies the security of the people? What assurance have they that either their taxes will not be exacted but in the greatest emergencies, and then sparingly, or that standing armies will be raised and supported for the very plausible purpose only of cantoning them upon their frontiers? There is but one answer to these questions. —They have none. Nor was it intended by the makers they should have, for meaning to make a different use of the latter, they never will be at a loss for ways and means to expend the former. They do not design to beg a second time. Knowing the danger of frequent applications to the people, they ask for the whole at once, and are now by their conduct, teazing and absolutely haunting of you into a compliance. —If you choose all these things should take place, by all means gratify them. Go, and establish this Government, which is unanimously confessed imperfect, yet incapable of alteration. Intrust it to men, subject it to the same unbounded passions and infirmities, as yourselves, possessed with an insatiable thirst for power, and many of them,carrying in them vices, tho' tinsel'd and concealed, yet, in themselves, not less dangerous than those more naked and exposed. But in the mean time, add an additional weight to the stone that now covers the remains of the Great WARREN and MONTGOMERY; prepare an apology for the blood and treasure, profusely spent to obtain those rights which you now so tamely part with. Conceal yourselves from the ridicule of your enemies, and bring your New-England spirits to a level with the contempt of mankind. Henceforth you may sit yourselves down with propriety, and say, Blessed are they that never expect, for they shall not be disappointed.

6. *The Letters of "A Republican Federalist"*

The identity of "A Republican Federalist" is not known, but the author was clearly a person of considerable ability. It is equally clear that his use of logic produced striking and sometimes seemingly bizarre results. The first four letters expound the dual propositions that the proposed constitution, if adopted, would be unconstitutional, and that it would alter the Massachusetts constitution of 1780 in a manner contrary to the amending procedures of that constitution. The reasoning used to support these positions provides an excellent example of the American talent for combining law and logic to create an impressive structure of constitutional interpretation. For example, "A Republican Federalist" reaches the conclusion that the three-fifths clause respecting representation and slavery lays the basis (after the states have been abolished) for apportioning representation in accordance with property rather than population. Thus one man worth £50,000 would have as many votes as a thousand men worth £50 each.

The reader may not agree with all of "A Republican Federalist's" conclusions, but it is difficult not to admire the ingenuity of his very fertile mind.

II

[January 2, 1788]

To the Members of the Convention of Massachusetts

Honourable Friends, and Fellow Citizens,
It clearly appeared by the resolutions quoted in my last
address, that the utmost extent of the views of Congress,
and of the Legislature of this State in calling a Federal
Convention, was, that it should revise the articles of Confederation, and report such *alterations* and *provisions
therein,* as shall render the Federal Constitution adequate
to the exigencies of government and preservation of the
union—that neither Congress or the Legislature had the
most distant idea of conducting the matter in a mode different from that prescribed by the Confederation—but that
on the other hand, they expressly provided, and would
have acted unconstitutionally to have done otherwise, that
the proceedings of the Convention, before they become a
part of the Federal Constitution, should be agreed to by
Congress and confirmed by the Legislatures of the several
states.

No one I presume will deny that the powers of the delegates of this state, were as *full* and *extensive* as either
Congress or any of the Legislatures had *authority* to
give—that the powers of the other delegate were in general, more *limited*—and that had any of them been more
ample than those of Massachusetts, they must have been
founded in *usurpation* and therefore have been *null* and
void. And have the Federal Convention, in pursuance of
their powers, reported the *alterations* and *provisions* men-

Reprinted from *The Massachusetts Centinel* [Boston], December 29,
1787 – February 6, 1788.

tioned in the recited resolve of Congress? If they have, let us call on Congress, to inform us, whether they have agreed to the report, and to transmit it when approved to the Legislature for their consideration: This would be conducting upon constitutional principles, but the *call* would be vain, there is no such report, *and the original design of forming the Convention has not been carried into effect.*

The Convention nevertheless have reported a new system, and the object of it is, *a consolidation of the union.* Mr. Wilson[1] denies this fact, and says "if this was *a just objection,* it would be *strongly against the system."* But unfortunately for that gentleman, his *memory* appears to be very *defective,* for he forgot that he has said, in the letter to Congress, signed "George Washington, president, *by unanimous order of the Convention"*—"In all our deliberations on this subject, we kept steadily in our view, that which appears to us the greatest interest of every true American, *the consolidation of the union."* There the Convention have candidly avowed their intentions, and how Mr. Wilson can reconcile his *jarring* and *contradictory* assertions, I am at a loss to determine. The Convention having then kept *"steadily in view"* "a consolidation of the union," it is incumbent on every one who is zealous for the *infallibility* of the Convention, and liberal in abusing those who *dare* to think for themselves, to admit that the proposed plan *compleatly embraces* the object of *consolidation,* for otherwise he will call in question the *ability* of the Convention to execute their design—indeed it must be evident to every one who will attentively read the new system, that it secures to all intents and purposes the *consolidation intended.* And here permit me to remark on an argument, in favour of the new plan, often urged and drawn from the respectable characters of George Washington and Doctor Franklin: Let those gentlemen have *every*

[1]James Wilson, delegate to the Convention from Pennsylvania, whose defences of the Constitution in that state were widely published [Ed.].

honour that can be paid them, they are justly entitled to *it*—but of what consequence is it to the publick, whether the members who assented or dissented to the new plan, were influenced by *virtuous* and *disinterested*, or by *vicious* and *selfish* motives? If the plan is *properly* before the States, is *good*, and will secure to them "peace, liberty and safety" should it not be adopted, were they even sure that every member who subscribed it was in principle a *Caligula* or a *Nero*? And if the plan is bad and will entail *slavery on the land*, ought it not to be rejected should every subscriber excel in wisdom and integrity *Lycrugus* or *Solon.* Surely the *good* or *bad* effects of the system, depend not on the *characters* of the original *framers*, but on the *system* itself, and on those who may administer it; and no man of candour and discernment will urge *characters*, as an argument for or against this system, however repectable the characters of any particular members, or of the members in general of the federal convention, may be: They had no other authority to act in this matter, than what was derived from their *commissions*—when they ceased to act *in conformity thereto*, they ceased to be a federal convention, and had no more *right* to propose to the United States the new form of government, than an equal number of other gentlemen, who might voluntarily have assembled for this purpose—The members of the convention therefore, admitting they have the merit of a work of supererogation, have thereby inferred no kind of obligation on the States to *consider*, much less to adopt *this plan of consolidation.* The consolidation of the union! What a question is this, to be *taken up* and *decided* by *thirty nine gentlemen*, who had no publick authority whatever for *discussing it*! —To be submitted to the people at large, before it has been *considered* or even *agitated* by Congress, or any of the Legislatures, and to be transmitted with such precipitation to the States *merely* "for their assent and ratification?"

True it is, that neither Congress or the Legislatures could decide this great question; the first are restrained by the confederation, and the last by the federal and state constitutions—but Congress and the Legislatures, if they thought it necessary, might at any time have considered the subject, expressed their sentiments on it, and recommended to the people an election of State conventions to have taken up the matter. Had this been done the important question would have been previously canvassed; and understood by Congress and the Legislatures; and explained to the people; and the publick opinion would have been thus *united* in some salutary measure—but as the matter has been conducted, a *system of consolidation* has been formed with the most *profound secrecy*, and without the *least authority*: And has been *suddenly* and *without any previous notice* transmitted by the federal convention for ratification—*Congress not disposed to give any opinion on the plan, have transmitted it to the legislatures*—The *legislatures have followed the example, and sent it to the people. The people* of this State, *unassisted* by Congress or their *legislature*, have not had time to investigate the subject, have referred to the news-papers for information, have been divided by contending writers, and *under such circumstances* have elected members for the *State Convention*—and these members are to consider whether they will accept the plan of the federal convention, *with* ALL *its imperfection*, and *bind* the people by a *system of government*, of the nature and principle of which they have not at present a clearer idea, than they have *of the Copernican system.*

What are we to expect, from such a mode of proceeding? Are not the people already thrown into great confusion? Are not heats, animosities, and a party spirit very prevalent and daily increasing? Are the citizens of this State in a proper temper to receive information, either of the ratification, or rejection, of the new constitution? Is there a probability of *its being supported,* if so *precipitately adopted?* Surely it must appear that the plan, although *improperly before the State,* cannot with safety be rejected —that it cannot as it stands, be safely *accepted*—that the people will not be satisfied with a *ratification,* and the *delusive prospect of future alterations*—and that the only hope that remains of preserving the peace and happiness of this Commonwealth, is *from amending the plan in order to its adoption.*

III

[January 9, 1788]

TO THE MEMBERS OF THE CONVENTION OF MASSACHU-
SETTS.

Honourable Friends, and Fellow Citizens,
In the preceding numbers it has been shewn, that the
original design of calling the federal convention has not
been carried into effect—That they nevertheless reported a
system of government with a professed intention of consolidating the union—That they had not the least publick
authority to discuss, much less to decide this great question—That neither Congress or the Legislatures have been
disposed to express any opinion on the new system—That
although they were constitutionally restrained from deciding, yet they had a right at any time, to have agitated and
considered the question, to have explained it to the people,
and to have recommended their electing State Conventions
to have taken up the matter—That had this been done, the
people would have had every necessary information, and
probably have united in some salutary measure—That they
are now without that information, and by the mode of
conducting this matter, are thrown into great confusion—
That a party spirit prevails, and is daily increasing—That
in the present temper of the people, it will not restore
peace or tranquility to reject the system, or to ratify it with
or without the *delusive prospect* of future alterations—
That if accepted in its present form, there is not a probability of supporting it—and that amendments are indispen-
sibly necessary, in order to its adoption. —There are facts
which if any one doubts, will I think, clearly appear when
we consider the system itself.

The revolution which separated the United States from Great-Britain, was not more important to the liberties of America, than that which will result from the adoption of the new system. The *former* freed us from a *foreign subjugation*, and there is too much reason to apprehend, that the *latter* will reduce us to a *federal domination*. Had the Convention thought proper, *merely* to have formed the plan, and to have sent it to Congress, and the legislatures, the consequences would not have been so serious, as from their accompanying it with the following resolutions. — "*Resolved*, That the preceeding Constitution be laid before the United States in Congresss assembled, and that is the opinion of this Convention, that it should afterwards be submitted to a Convention of Delegates chosen in each state by the PEOPLE thereof, under the recommendation of its legislature, *for their assent and ratification*, and that each Convention, assenting to and ratifying the same, should give notice thereof to the United States in Congress assembled." "*Resolved*, That it is the opinion of the Convention, that as soon as the Conventions of *nine* States shall have ratified the Constitution, the United States in Congress assembled shall fix a day on which electors should be appointed by the States which shall have ratified the same, and a day on which the electors should assemble to vote for the President, and the time and place for commencing proceedings under this Constitution: That after such publication, the electors should be appointed, and the Senators and Representatives elected: That the electors should meet on the day fixed for the election of the President; and should transmit *their votes*, certified, signed, sealed and directed, as the Constitution requires, to the secretary of the United States in Congress assembled, that the Senators and Representatives should convene at the time and place assigned—that the Senators should appoint a President of the Senate, for the sole purpose of receiving, opening and counting the votes for President, and that after he shall be chosen, the Congress together with the President, should without delay, *proceed to execute this Constitution."* In consequence of these resolutions of the federal convention, Congress *"Resolved,* That the Constitution so reported be transmitted to the several legislatures, in order to be submitted to a Convention of the Delegates, chosen in each State by the people thereof, *in conformity to the resolves of the said Convention in that case made and provided"*—and in pursuance thereof, the legislature of this State resolved, "That it be, and it is hereby recommended to the people of this Commonwealth, that a Convention of Delegates be chosen *agreeably to and for the purposes mentioned in the resolution of Congress aforesaid.*—It is evident, therefore, that the proposed Constitution is, agreeably to the recommendation of the federal Convention, submitted to the State Convention, *that is,* to a *majority* of its members, for their assent and ratification. Should the plan be adopted by this and eight other States, *every part of the Constitution of this Commonwealth which is contrary to the new Constitution, to the laws that may be made in pursuance thereof, or to treaties of the United States,* will be null and void for the plan expressly provides, that "this Constitution, and the laws of the United States, which shall be made in pursuance thereof, and all treaties made, or which shall be made under the authority of the United States, shall be the supreme law of the land, and the judges in every State shall be bound thereby, *any thing in the Constitution or laws of any State to the contrary notwithstanding"*—And will not such a subjection of the Constitution of this Commonwealth, not only *to the Constitution,* but *to the laws of the union,* and to *treaties,* that are or may be made under the *authority of Congress,* be in effect, A DISSOLUTION OF THE GOVERNMENT OF MASSACHU-

SETTS? Surely it will. Mr. *Locke*, in his treatise of civil government, chap. 19, in *Sect.* 212, says, "Governments are dissolved from within, when the legislative is altered," and in *Sect.* 215, *"for it is not a certain number of men, no, nor their meeting,* unless they have also freedom of debating, and leisure of perfecting, what is for the good of the society, wherein the legislative consists: when these are taken away, or altered, so as to deprive the society of the due exercise of this power, the *legislative* is *truly altered;* for it is *not names that constitute governments, but the use and exercise of those powers that were intended to accompany them."* What were the *powers* originally intended by the people of this State, *to be used and exercised by their legislature;* they are contained in a Constitution of the Commonwealth, *part 2, chap. I, Section 1,* under the head of "the legislative power," qualified nevertheless by certain reservations in the Bill of Rights. *Some* of the most *important* of those *powers* will, by the new plan, be transferred to the *federal government,* and *others* be exercised by *their* permission. This, I presume, is too evident to be denied, and will hereafter more fully appear. Our government will then have the *name* that it now *has,* but not "the use and exercise of those powers that were intended to accompany it." Indeed, it is inconceivable, that a plan of consolidation can be established, without destroying the sovereignty of the respective States, and thus *dissolving their present governments.*

But supposing the adoption of the new plan would only *alter* the Constitution of this State, *by what mode should that alteration be made?* Should it be effected pursuant to the recommendation of a federal Convention, and in direct violation of the Constitution of this State? or should the alteration be made consistently with the Constitution itself? This expressly provides, "That, in order the more effectually to adhere to the principles of the Constitution, and to correct those violations which by any means may be made therein, as well as to form such alterations as from experience shall be found necessary, the General Court, which shall be in the year of our Lord 1795, shall issue precepts to the selectmen of the several towns, and to the assessors of the unincorporated plantations, directing them to convene the qualified voters of their respective towns and plantations for the purpose of collecting their sentiments on the *necessity* or *expediency* of *revising the Constitution, in order to amendments*: And if it shall appear by the returns made, that two thirds of the qualified voters throughout the State, who shall assemble and vote in consequence of the said precepts, are in favour of such revision or amendment, the General Court shall issue precepts, or direct them to be issued, from the secretary's office to the several towns to elect delegates to meet in Convention, for the purpose aforesaid: The said delegates to be chosen in the same manner and proportion as their representatives," etc. —Here we see, that by the Constitution of this State in the year 1795; the sentiments of the qualified voters on the *necessity* or *expediency* of *revising* the Constitution, are to be collected, and if it shall then appear that *two thirds* of them are in favour of a *revision* and *amendment*, in that case only, is a Convention to be called *for these purposes*. Should it be a question, whether an alteration in the Constitution can be made before the year 1795, there is nothing in the clause recited, that I can conceive to prevent it: because although in the year 1795, precepts must issue for the purposes mentioned, there is no provision to prevent their issuing, if necessary, before that period. But surely, if any alteration should be made in the Constitution, it must be *in a mode provided by the Constitution itself*, for otherwise *the clause recited must become a nullity*, which is inadmissible, or, which is the same thing, *the Constitution itself must be violated.*

Of all compacts, a Constitution or frame of Government, is the most solemn and important, and should be strictly adhered to. The object of it is the preservation of that property, which every individual of the community has, in his *life, liberty* and *estate*: Every measure therefore, that only approaches to an infraction of such a covenant, ought to be avoided, because it will injure that sacred regard to the Constitution which should be deeply impressed on the minds of the whole community—How much more careful then should we be to avoid an open violation of such a compact? Such a violation must take place, if a majority, or every member of the Convention, should vote for an acceptance of the new Constitution, because a Convention cannot be called for *altering,* much less *dissolving* the government of Massachusetts, before the sentiments of the qualified voters are collected on the *necessity* or *expediency* of *revising* the Constitution in order to *amendment,* and *two thirds* of them shall be in favour of the measure. A ratification, therefore, of the new Constitution by the State Convention, cannot be binding on the citizens of this State, being directly repugnant to an existing covenant. But suppose such a ratification should be supported by a majority of the Convention and of the citizens of this State: What must be the consequence of thus destroying all publick faith and confidence? Are not these the principles that bind and cement the community, and that establish them as a body politick? Are they not the foundation of a free Government? If every individual by such a measure, should have his faith and confidence in the honour and integrity of the community effectually destroyed, (and this must inevitably be the consequence) will he not decline entering into such a nugatory compact in future, or entering into it, will he not disregard it as a mere matter of form, and rather than be at any pains or expense to support it, suffer it to share the fate of the other? Certainly he will, and instead of a government founded in compact, we must hereafter be content with one founded in fraud or force.

V

[January 19, 1788]

To the Members of the Convention of Massachu-setts.

Honourable Friends, and Fellow Citizens,
The proceedings of the federal Convention, having, as has been shewn, originated in usurpation, and being founded in tyranny, cannot be ratified by the State Convention, *without breaking down the barriers of liberty; trampling on the authority of federal and State Constitutions, and annihilating in America, governments founded in compact.* In this predicament, there appears but two measures which can with safety be adopted by the Convention of this State. One has been hinted at, *an adjournment,* until the sense of Virginia can be known. The great danger in this business is, from *precipitation, not* from *delay:* The *latter* cannot injure whilst the *former* may *irretrievably* ruin us; an adjournment would not only ripen the judg-ment of our own citizens, but give them an opportunity of benefiting by the opinions of those States, which are atten-tive to, but not *extravagantly* zealous in this matter. The other measure is, to return the proceedings of the federal Convention to the legislature of this State, to be by them transmitted to Congress, and *amended* agreeably to the articles of Confederation: For the system being *improperly* before the State Convention, and they being *incompetent* to a ratification of it, cannot thereby bind the citizens of Massachusetts. Had the system been in itself unobjection-able, it is evident from what has been said, that the sen-

timents of the qualified voters *on the necessity* of a revision,*must* have been taken, and two thirds of them *must*
have been in favour of it, before a State Convention could
be called for amending the Constitution, much more for
dissolving the government.

Let us once more particularly attend to the system itself.
It begins, "We the People of the United States, in order to
form a more perfect union," &c. "do ordain and establish
this Constitution for the United States of America"—In
other words, *We the people, do hereby publickly declare
the violation of the faith which we have solemnly pledged
to each other—do give the most unequivocal evidence,
that we cannot ourselves, neither can any others, place the
least confidence in our most solemn covenants, do
effectually put an end in America, to governments founded
in compact—do relinquish that security for life, liberty
and property, which we had in the Constitutions of these
States, and of the Union—do give up governments which
we well understood, for a new system which we have no
idea of—and we do, by this act of ratification and political
suicide, destroy the new system itself, and prepare the way
for a despotism, if agreeable to our rulers.* All this we do,
for the *honour of having a system of consolidation formed
by us the people.* This is not *magnifying,* for such are the
facts, and such will be the consequences. Indeed we find
despotism not only in contemplation of the Pennsylvanians,
but openly avowed in their State Convention, in the words
following—"Despotism, if wisely administered, is the best
system invented by the ingenuity of man." This was declared by chief justice M'Kean; and in such an high office,
we must suppose him a man of too much precaution to
have made the declaration, had he not known, that a majority of the Convention, and of the citizens, who so highly
applauded his speeches, were of his opinion. M. Montesquieu, in his "Spirit of Laws," 1st vol. book 3, chap. 9,
says, "As *virtue* is necessary in a *republick,* and *honour* in

a monarchy, so *fear* is necessary in a *despotick* government: With regard to *virtue*, there is no occasion for it, and *honour* would be extremely dangerous." Thus has a declaration been made in Pennsylvania, in favour of a government which substitues *fear* for *virtue*, and reduces men *from rational beings* to the *level of brutes*; and if the citizens of Massachusetts are disposed to follow the example, and *submit their necks to the yoke*, they must expect to be governed by the *whip* and *goad*. But it is remarkable, that the resolution of the federal Convention, for transmitting the system to the people, provided, "that the Constitution should *be laid before the United States in Congress assembled*, and afterwards submitted to a Convention of Delegates, chosen in each State by the people thereof, *under the recommendation of its legislature*; thus making Congress and the legislatures, *vehicles of conveyance*, but precluding them from passing their judgments on the system. Had it been submitted to their consideration, their members were men of such discernment, that the *defects* as well as *excellencies* of the plan, would have been clearly explained to the people; but immediately on the publication of it, we find measures were taken to prejudice the people against all persons in the legislative, executive and judicial departments of the States and Confederacy (if opposed to the plan) as being actuated by motives of private interest. Mr. Wilson, a member of the federal and Pennsylvania Convention, in his town meeting speech, adopted this practice, which, to say the least of it, was very illiberal. Indeed, it is but justice to observe, that many artful advocates of this plan, to cover their designs of creating a government which will afford *abundance* of *legislative offices for placemen and pensioners, proclaimed suspicions* of others, and diverted the attention of the people from themselves, on whom the odium should fall.

Let us now proceed to the provision in the system for a representation of the people, which is the *corner stone* of a free government. The Constitution provides, art. 1st, sect. 2, "that representatives and direct taxes shall be apportioned among the several States, which may be included within this union, according to their respective numbers, which shall be determined by adding to the whole number of free persons, including those bound to service for a term of years, and excluding Indians not taxed, three fifths of all other persons." Representatives "then are to be" apportioned among the several States, according to their respective numbers," and *five* slaves, in computing those numbers, are to be classed with *three* freemen — By which rule, fifty thousand slaves, having neither *liberty* or *property*, will have a representative in that branch of the legislature—to which more especially will be committed, the *protection of the liberties*, and *disposal of all the property* of the freemen of the Union—for thus stands the new Constitution. Should it be said, that not *the slaves* but their *masters* are to send a representative, the answer is plain—If the *slaves* have a *right* to be represented, they are *on a footing* with *freemen*, *three* of *whom* can then have no more than an equal right of representation with *three slaves*, and these when qualified by property, may elect or be elected representatives, *which is not the case*: But if they have not a right to be represented, their masters can have no right derived from their *slaves*, for *these* cannot transfer to others what they have not themselves. Mr. Locke, in treating of political or civil societies, chap. 7, sect. 85, says, that men "being in the state of slavery, not capable of any property, cannot, in that state, be considered as any part of civil society, the chief end whereof, is the preservation of property." If slaves, then, are no part of civil society, there can be no more reason in admitting them, than there would be in admitting the *beasts* of the field, or *trees* of the forest, to be classed with *free electors*. What covenant are the freemen of Massachusetts about to ratify? A covenant that will degrade them to the *level of slaves,* and give to the States who have as many blacks as whites, *eight* representatives, *for the same number of freemen* as will enable this State to elect *five*—Is this an *equal,* a *safe,* or a *righteous* plan government? Indeed it is not. But if to encrease these objections, it should be urged, "that representation being regulated by the same rule as taxation, and taxation being regulated by a rule intended to ascertain the relative property of the States, representation will then be regulated by the principle of property." This *answer* would be the only one that could be made, for representation, according to the new Constitution is to be regulated, either by *numbers* or *property.*

Let us now inquire of those who take this ground, what right they have to put a construction on the constitution, which is repugnant to the express terms of the Constitution itself? This provides, "that representatives shall be apportioned among the several States, *according to their respective numbers.*" Not a word of *property* is mentioned, but the word "numbers" is repeatedly expressed—Admitting however that property was intended by the Constitution as the rule of representation, does this *mend the matter?* It will be but a short time, after the adoption of the new Constitution, before the State *legislatures,* and *establishments in general* will be so *burthensome* and *useless* as to make the people desirous of being rid of them, for they will not be able to support them. The *State appointment* of Representatives will then cease, *but the principle of representation according to property,* will undoubtedly be retained, and before *it is established* it is necessary to consider whether it is a just *one,* for if *once* it is *adopted* it will *not be easily altered*—According to this principle, a man worth £50,000 is to have as many votes for repsentatives in the new Congress, as *one thousand men,* worth £50 each: And *sixty such nabobs* may send *two repre-*

sentatives, while *sixty thousand* freemen having £50 *each* can only send the same number. Does not this establish in the representative branch of the new Congress, a principle of aristocracy, with a vengeance? The Constitution of the several States, admit of no such principle, neither can any freeman with safety thus surrender, not only the intire disposition of their property, but also, the controul of their liberties and lives to a few opulent ciitizens. Should it be said that the rule of federal taxation, being advantageous to the State, it should be content with the same rule for representation. The answer is plain, the rule gives no advantage, but is supposed to be advantageous to Massachusetts, and to be an accommodation very beneficial to the southern States; But admitting this State will be benefited by the rule, is it disposed to sell its birthright, the right of an equal representation in the federal councils *for so small a consideration*? Would this State give up that right to any State that would pay our whole proportion of *direct* and *indirect taxes*? Shall we relinquish some of the most essential rights of government, which are our only security for every thing dear to us, to avoid our proportion of the publick expense? Shall we give up all we have, for a small part of it? This if agreed to, would be no great evidence of our wisdom or foresight. But it is not probable, in the opinion of some of the ablest advocates for the new system, that *direct taxes* will ever be levied on the States, and if not, the provision for levying such taxes will be *nugatory*; We shall receive no kind of benefit from it, and shall have committed ourselves to the mercy of the states having slaves, *without any consideration whatever*. Indeed, should direct taxes be necessary, shall we not by increasing the representation of those States, put it in their power to prevent the levying such taxes, and thus defeat our own purpose? Certainly we shall, and having given up a substantial and *essential* right, shall in lieu of it, have a mere *visionary advantage.* Upon the whole then, it must be evident, that we might as well have committed ourselves to the parliament of Great Britain, under the idea of a *virtual representation* as in this manner resign ourselves to the federal government.

James Winthrop [?] *The Letters of "Agrippa"*

The authorship of these letters is not definitely known. They were attributed by his contemporaries to James Winthrop (1752–1821), of Cambridge, Massachusetts, who neither denied nor confirmed this attribution. "Agrippa," whoever he was, stated in his tenth letter that speculations as to his identity up to that time were erroneous. Paul Leicester Ford leaves standing the attribution to Winthrop.

Selections from the series are included here because they represent an interesting attempt to demonstrate that adoption of the Constitution would be adverse to the commercial and manufacturing interests of the nation, and especially of Massachusetts. "Agrippa" argued that the economy was basically sound and prosperous, and that centralized government would hinder rather than help its future growth. He advocated amendment of the Articles of Confederation to give Congress limited powers over foreign relations and commerce; if the Constitution were adopted at all, he thought it should be drastically amended, as specified in the eighteenth letter. "Agrippa" also articulated with force and clarity the common Antifederalist belief that republican government could not operate over large and heterogeneous nations. His is an outspoken brief for decentralization, for the legitimacy of individual, local, and state interests, and for maintaining the status quo with only minor changes.

Lesser points of interest in his theory are his preference for limited immigration, his critical allusion to the absence of a religious qualification for the President, and his refusal to accept the usual version of social contract theory.

From "The Letters of Agrippa," a series of eighteen essays which appeared in *The Massachusetts Gazette* (Boston), IV, IX, XIII, XVII–XVIII are reprinted here from the text in Ford, *Essays*, pp. 63–65, 79–81, 93–101, 110–122.

IV.

[December 3, 1787]

To the People.

Having considered some of the principal advantages of the happy form of government under which it is our peculiar good fortune to live, we find by experience, that it is the best calculated of any form hitherto invented, to secure to us the rights of our persons and of our property, and that the general circumstances of the people shew an advanced state of improvement never before known. We have found the shock given by the war, in a great measure obliterated, and the public debt contracted at that time to be considerably reduced in the nominal sum. The Congress lands are full adequate to the redemption of the principal of their debt, and are selling and populating very fast. The lands of this state, at the west, are, at the moderate price of eighteen pence an acre, worth near half a million pounds in our money. They ought, therefore, to be sold as quick as possible. An application was made lately for a large tract at that price, and continual applications are made for other lands in the eastern part of the state. Our resources are daily augmenting.

We find, then, that after the experience of near two centuries our separate governments are in full vigor. They discover, for all the purposes of internal regulation, every symptom of strength, and none of decay. The new system is, therefore, for such purposes, useless and burdensome.

Let us now consider how far it is practicable consistent with the happiness of the people and their freedom. It is the opinion of the ablest writers on the subject, that no extensive empire can be governed upon republican principles, and that such a government will degenerate to a despotism, unless it be made up of a confederacy of smaller states, each having the full powers of internal regulation. This is precisely the principle which has hitherto preserved our freedom. No instance can be found of any free government of considerable extent which has been supported upon any other plan. Large and consolidated empires may indeed dazzle the eyes of a distant spectator with their splendour, but if examined more nearly are always found to be full of misery. The reason is obvious. In large states the same principles of legislation will not apply to all the parts. The inhabitants of warmer climates are more dissolute in their manners, and less industrious, than in colder countries. A degree of severity is, therefore, necessary with one which would cramp the spirit of the other. We accordingly find that the very great empires have always been despotick. They have indeed tried to remedy the inconveniences to which the people were exposed by local regulations; but these contrivances have never answered the end. The laws not being made by the people, who felt the inconveniences, did not suit their circumstances. It is under such tyranny that the Spanish provinces languish, and such would be our misfortune and degradation, if we should submit to have the concerns of the whole empire managed by one legislature. To promote the happiness of the people it is necessary that there should be local laws; and it is necessary that those laws should be made by the representatives of those who are immediately subject to the want of them. By endeavouring to suit both extremes, both are injured.

It is impossible for one code of laws to suit Georgia and Massachusetts. They must, therefore, legislate for themselves. Yet there is, I believe, not one point of legislation that is not surrendered in the proposed plan. Questions of every kind respecting property are determinable in a continental court, and so are all kinds of criminal causes. The continental legislature has, therefore, a right to make rules in all cases by which their judicial courts shall proceed and decide causes. No rights are reserved to the citizens. The laws of Congress are in all cases to be the supreme law of the land, and paramount to the constitutions of the individual states. The Congress may institute what modes of trial they please, and no plea drawn from the constitution of any state can avail. This new system is, therefore, a consolidation of all the states into one large mass, however diverse the parts may be of which it is to be composed. The idea of an uncompounded republick, on an average one thousand miles in length, and eight hundred in breadth, and containing six millions of white inhabitants all reduced to the same standard of morals, of habits, and of laws, is in itself an absurdity, and contrary to the whole experience of mankind. The attempt made by Great Britain to introduce such a system, struck us with horrour, and when it was proposed by some theorist that we should be represented in parliament, we uniformly declared that one legislature could not represent so many different interests for the purposes of legislation and taxation. This was the leading principle of the revolution, and makes an essential article in our creed. All that part, therefore, of the new system, which relates to the internal government of the states, ought at once to be rejected.

IX.

[December 28, 1787.]

To the People.

We come now to the second and last article of complaint against the present confederation, which is, that Congress has not the sole power to regulate the intercourse between us and foreigners. Such a power extends not only to war and peace, but to trade and naturalization. This last article ought never to be given them; for though most of the states may be willing for certain reasons to receive foreigners as citizens, yet reasons of equal weight may induce other states, differently circumstanced, to keep their blood pure. Pennsylvania has chosen to receive all that would come there. Let any indifferent person judge whether that state in point of morals, education, energy is equal to any of the eastern states; the small state of Rhode Island only excepted. Pennsylvania in the course of a century has acquired her present extent and population at the expense of religion and good morals. The eastern states have, by keeping separate from the foreign mixtures, acquired their present greatness in the course of a century and an half, and have preserved their religion and morals. They have also preserved that manly virtue which is equally fitted for rendering them respectable in war, and industrious in peace.

The remaining power for peace and trade might perhaps be safely enough lodged with Congress under some limitations. Three restrictions appear to me to be essentially necessary to preserve that equality of rights to the states, which it is the object of the state governments to secure to each citizen. 1st. It ought not to be in the power of Congress, either by treaty or otherwise, to alienate part of any state without the consent of the legislature. 2d. They ought not to be able, by treaty or other law, to give any legal preference to one part above another. 3d. They ought to be restrained from creating any monopolies. Perhaps others may propose different regulations and restrictions. One of these is to be found in the old confederation, and another in the newly proposed plan. The third scenes [*sic*] to be equally necessary.

After all that has been said and written on this subject, and on the difficulty of amending our old constitution so as to render it adequate to national purposes, it does not appear that any thing more was necessary to be done, than framing two new articles. By one a limited revenue would be given to Congress with a right to collect it, and by the other a limited right to regulate our intercourse with foreign nations. By such an addition we should have preserved to each state its power to defend the rights of the citizens, and the whole empire would be capable of expanding and receiving additions without altering its former constitution. Congress, at the same time, by the extent of their jurisdiction, and the number of their officers, would have acquired more respectability at home, and a sufficient influence abroad. If any state was in such a case to invade the rights of the Union, the other states would join in defence of those rights, and it would be in the power of Congress to direct the national force to that object. But it is certain that the powers of Congress over the citizens should be small in proportion as the empire is extended; that, in order to preserve the balance, each state may supply by energy what is wanting in numbers. Congress would be able by such a system as we have proposed to regulate trade with foreigners by such duties as should effectually give the preference to the produce and manufactures of our own country. We should then have a friendly intercourse established between the states, upon the principles of mutual interest. A moderate duty upon foreign vessels would give an advantage to our own people, while it would avoid all the disadvantages arising from a prohibition, and the consequent deficiency of vessels to transport the produce of the southern states.

Our country is at present upon an average a thousand miles long from north to south, and eight hundred broad from the Mississippi to the Ocean. We have at least six millions of white inhabitants, and the annual increase is about two hundred and fifty thousand souls, exclusive of emigrants from Europe. The greater part of our increase is employed in settling the new lands, while the older settlements are entering largely into manufactures of various kinds. It is probable that the extraordinary exertions of this state in the way of industry for the present year only, exceed in value five hundred thousand pounds. The new settlements, if all made in the same tract of country, would form a large state annually; and the time seems to be literally accomplished when a nation shall be born in a day. Such an immense country is not only capable of yielding all the produce of Europe, but actually does produce by far the greater part of the raw materials. The restrictions on our trade in Europe, necessarily oblige us to make use of those materials, and the high price of labour operates as an encouragement to mechanical improvements. In this way we daily make rapid advancements towards independence in resources as well as in empire. If we adopt the new system of government we shall, by one rash vote, lose the fruit of the toil and expense of thirteen years, at the time when the benefits of that toil and expense are rapidly increasing. Though the imposts of Congress on foreign trade may tend to encourage manufactures, the excise and dry tax will destroy all the beneficial effects of the impost, at the same time that they diminish our capital. Be careful then to give only a limited revenue, and the limited power of managing foreign concerns. Once surrender the rights of internal legislation and taxation, and instead of being respected abroad, foreigners will laugh at us, and posterity will lament our folly.

XIII.

[January 14, 1788].

TO THE MASSACHUSETTS CONVENTION.

Gentlemen,
The question then arises, what is the kind of government best adapted to the object of securing our persons and possessions from violence? I answer, a *Federal Republick.* By this kind of government each state reserves to itself the right of making and altering its laws for internal regulation, and the right of executing those laws without any external restraint, while the general concerns of the empire are committed to an assembly of delegates, each accountable to his own constituents. This is the happy form under which we live, and which seems to mark us out as a people chosen of God. No instance can be produced of any other kind of government so stable and energetick as the republican. The objection drawn from the Greek and Roman states does not apply to the question. Republicanism appears there in its most disadvantageous form. Arts and domestic employments were generally committed to slaves, while war was almost the only business worthy of a citizen. Hence arose their internal dissensions. Still they exhibited proofs of legislative wisdom and judicial integrity hardly to be found among their monarchick neighbors. On the other hand we find Carthage cultivating commerce, and extending her dominions for the long space of seven centuries, during which term the internal tranquillity was never disturbed by her citizens. Her national power was so respectable, that for a long time it was doubtful whether Carthage or Rome should rule. In the

form of their government they bore a strong resemblance to each other. Rome might be reckoned a free state for about four hundred and fifty years. We have then the true line of distinction between those two nations, and a strong proof of the hardy materials which compose a republican government. If there was no other proof, we might with impartial judges risk the issue upon this alone. But our proof rests not here. The present state of Europe, and the vigour and tranquillity of our own governments, after experiencing this form for a century and an half, are decided proofs in favour of those governments which encourage commerce. A comparison of our own country, first with Europe and then with the other parts of the world, will prove, beyond a doubt, that the greatest share of freedom is enjoyed by the citizens, so much more does commerce flourish. The reason is, that every citizen has an influence in making the laws, and thus they are conformed to the general interests of the state; but in every other kind of government they are frequently made in favour of a part of the community at the expense of the rest.

The argument against republicks, as it is derived from the Greek and Roman states, is unfair. It goes on the idea that no other government is subject to be disturbed. As well might we conclude, that a limited monarchy is unstable, because that under the feudal system the nobles frequently made war upon their king, and disturbed the publick peace. We find, however, in practice, that limited monarchy is more friendly to commerce, because more friendly to the rights of the subject, than an absolute government; and that it is more liable to be disturbed than a republick, because less friendly to trade and the rights of individuals. There cannot, from the history of mankind, be produced an instance of rapid growth in extent, in numbers, in arts, and in trade, that will bear any comparison with our country. This is owing to what the friends of the new system, and the enemies of the revolution, for I take them to be nearly the same, would term *our extreme liberty*. Already, have our ships visited every part of the world, and brought us their commodities in greater perfection, and at a more moderate price, than we ever before experienced. The ships of other nations crowd to our ports, seeking an intercourse with us. All the estimates of every party make the balance of trade for the present year to be largely in our favour. Already have some very useful, and some elegant manufactures got established among us, so that our country every day is becoming independent in her resources. Two-thirds of the continental debt has been paid since the war, and we are in alliance with some of the most respectable powers of Europe. The western lands, won from Britain by the sword, are an ample fund for the principal of all our public debts; and every new sale excites that manly pride which is essential to national virtue. All this happiness arises from the freedom of our institutions and the limited nature of our government; a government that is respected from principles of affection, and obeyed with alacrity. The sovereigns of the old world are frequently, though surrounded with armies, treated with insult; and the despotick monarchies of the east, are the most fluctuating, oppressive and uncertain governments of any form hitherto invented. These considerations are sufficient to establish the excellence of our own form, and the goodness of our prospects.

Let us now consider the probable effects of a consolidation of the separate states into one mass; for the new system extends so far. Many ingenious explanations have been given of it; but there is this defect, that they are drawn from maxims of the common law, while the system itself cannot be bound by any such maxims. A legislative assembly has an inherent right to alter the common law, and to abolish any of its principles, which are not particularly guarded in the constitution. Any system therefore which appoints a legislature, without any reservation of the rights of individuals, surrenders all power in every branch of legislation to the government. The universal practice of every government proves the justness of this remark; for in every doubtful case it is an established rule to decide in favour of authority. The new system is, therefore, in one respect at least, essentially inferior to our state constitutions. There is no bill of rights, and consequently a continental law may controul any of those principles, which we consider at present as sacred; while not one of those points, in which it is said that the separate governments misapply their power, is guarded. Tender acts and the coinage of money stand on the same footing of a consolidation of power. It is a mere fallacy, invented by the deceptive powers of Mr. Wilson, that what rights are not given are reserved. The contrary has already been shewn. But to put this matter of legislation out of all doubt, let us compare together some parts of the book; for being an independent system, this is the only way to ascertain its meaning.

In article III, section 2, it is declared, that "the judicial power shall extend to all cases in law and equity arising under this constitution, the laws of the United States, and treaties made or which shall be made under their authority." Among the cases arising under this new constitution are reckoned, "all controversies between citizens of different states," which include all kinds of civil causes between those parties. The giving Congress a power to appoint courts for such a purpose is as much, there being no stipulation to the contrary, giving them power to legislate for such causes, as giving them a right to raise an army, is giving them a right to direct the operations of the army when raised. But it is not left to implication. The last clause of article I, section 8, expressly gives them power "to make all laws which shall be needful and proper for carrying into execution the foregoing powers, and all other powers vested by this constitution in the government of the United States, or in any department or officer thereof." It is, therefore, as plain as words can make it, that they have a right by this proposed form to legislate for all kinds of causes respecting property between citizens of different states. That this power extends to all cases between citizens of the same state, is evident from the sixth article, which declares all continental laws and treaties to be the *supreme law* of the land, and that all state judges are bound thereby, *"anything in the constitution or laws of any state to the contrary notwithstanding."* If this is not binding the judges of the separate states in their own office, by continental rules, it is perfect nonsense. There is then a complete consolidation of the legislative powers in all cases respecting property. This power extends to all cases between a state and citizens of another state. Hence a citizen, possessed of the notes of another state, may bring his action, and there is no limitation that the execution shall be levied on the publick property of the state; but the property of individuals is liable. This is a foundation for endless confusion and discord. This right to try causes between a state and citizens of another state, involves in it all criminal causes; and a man who has accidentally transgressed the laws of another state, must be transported, with all his witnesses, to a third state, to be tried. He must be ruined to prove his innocence. These are necessary parts of the new system, and it will never be complete till they are reduced to practice. They effectually prove a consolidation of the states, and we have before shewn the ruinous tendency of such a measure.

By sect. 8 of article 1, Congress are to have the unlimited right to regulate commerce, external and *internal*, and may therefore create monopolies which have been universally injurious to all the subjects of the countries that have adopted them, excepting the monopolists themselves. They have also the unlimited right to imposts and all kinds of taxes, as well to levy as to collect them. They have indeed very nearly the same powers claimed formerly by the British parliament. Can we have so soon forgot our glorious struggle with that power, as to think a moment of surrendering it now? It makes no difference in principle whether the national assembly was elected for seven years or for six. In both cases we should vote to great disadvantage, and therefore ought never to agree to such an article. Let us make provision for the payment of the interest of our part of the debt, and we shall be fairly acquitted. Let the fund be an impost on our foreign trade, and we shall encourage our manufactures. But if we surrender the unlimited right to regulate trade, and levy taxes, imposts will oppress our foreign trade for the benefit of other states, while excises and taxes will discourage our internal industry. The right to regulate trade, without any limitations, will, as certainly as it is granted, transfer the trade of this state to Pennsylvania. That will be the seat of business and of wealth, while the extremes of the empire will, like Ireland and Scotland, be drained to fatten an overgrown capital. Under our present equal advantages, the citizens of this state come in for their full share of commercial profits. Surrender the rights of taxation and commercial regulation, and the landed states at the southward will all be interested in draining our resources; for whatever can be got by impost on our trade and excises on our manufactures, will be considered as so much saved to a state inhabited by planters. All savings of this sort ought surely to be made in favour of our own state; and we ought never to surrender the unlimited powers of revenue and trade to uncommercial people. If we do, the glory of the state from that moment departs, never to return.

The safety of our constitutional rights consists in having the business of governments lodged in different departments, and in having each part well defined. By this means each branch is kept within the constitutional limits. Never was a fairer line of distinction than what may be easily drawn between the continental and state governments. The latter provide for all cases, whether civil or criminal, that can happen ashore, because all such causes must arise within the limits of some state. Transactions between citizens may all be fairly included in this idea, even although they should arise in passing by water from one state to another. But the intercourse between us and foreign nations properly forms the department of Congress. They should have the power of regulating trade under such limitations as should render their laws equal. They should have the right of war and peace, saving the equality of rights, and the territory of each state. But the power of naturalization and internal regulation should not be given them. To give my scheme a more systematick appearance, I have thrown it into the form of a resolve, which is submitted to your wisdom for amendment, but not as being perfect.

"Resolved, that the form of government proposed by the federal convention, lately held in Philadelphia, be rejected on the part of this commonwealth; and that our delegates in Congress are hereby authorised to propose on the part of this commonwealth, and, if the other states for themselves agree thereto, to sign an article of confederation, as an addition to the present articles, in the form following, provided such agreement be made on or before the first day of January, which will be in the year of our Lord 1790; the said article shall have the same force and effect as if it had been inserted in the original confederation, and is to be construed consistently with the clause in the former articles, which restrains the United States from exercising such powers as are not expressly given.

"XIV. The United States shall have power to regulate, whether by treaty, ordinance or law, the intercourse between these states and foreign dominions and countries, under the following restrictions. No treaty, ordinance, or law shall give a preference to the ports of one state over those of another; nor 2d. impair the territory or internal authority of any state; nor 3d. create any monopolies or exclusive companies; nor 4th. naturalize any foreigners. All their imposts and prohibitions shall be confined to foreign produce and manufactures imported, and to foreign ships trading in our harbours. All imposts and confiscations shall be to the use of the state where they shall accrue, excepting only such branches of impost as shall be assigned by the separate states to Congress for a fund to defray the interest of their debt, and their current charges. In order the more effectually to execute this and the former articles, Congress shall have authority to appoint courts, supreme and subordinate, with power to try all crimes, not relating to state securities, between any foreign state, or subject of such state, actually residing in a foreign country, and not being an absentee or person who has alienated himself from these states on the one part, and any of the United States or citizens thereof on the other part; also all causes in which foreign ambassadours or other foreign ministers resident here shall be immediately concerned, respecting the jurisdiction or immunities only. And the Congress shall have authority to execute the judgment of such courts by their own affairs. Piracies and felonies committed on the high seas shall also belong to the department of Congress for them to define, try, and punish, in the same manner as the other causes shall be defined, tried, and determined. All the before-mentioned causes shall be tried by jury and in some sea-port town. And it is recommended to the general court at their next meeting to provide and put Congress in possession of funds arising from foreign imports and ships sufficient to defray our share of the present annual expenses of the continent."

Such a resolve, explicitly limiting the powers granted, is the farthest we can proceed with safety. The scheme of accepting the report of the Convention, and amending it afterwards, is merely delusive. There is no intention among those who make the proposition to amend it at all. Besides, if they have influence enough to get it accepted in its present form, there is no probability that they will consent to an alteration when possessed of an unlimited revenue. It is an excellence in our present confederation, that it is extremely difficult to alter it. An unanimous vote of the states is required. But this newly proposed form is founded in injustice, as it proposes that a fictitious consent of only nine states shall be sufficient to establish it. Nobody can suppose that the consent of a state is any thing more than a fiction, in the view of the federalists, after the mobbish influence used over the Pennsylvania convention. The two great leaders of the plan, with a modesty of Scotsmen, placed a rabble in the gallery to applaud their speeches, and thus supplied their want of capacity in the argument. Repeatedly were Wilson and M'Kean worsted in the argument by the plain good sense of Findley and Smilie. But reasoning or knowledge had little to do with the federal party. Votes were all they wanted, by whatever means obtained. Means not less criminal have been mentioned among us. But votes that are bought can never justify a treasonable conspiracy. Better, far better, would it be to reject the whole, and remain in possession of present advantages. The authority of Congress to decide disputes between states is sufficient to prevent their recurring to hostility: and their different situation, wants and produce is a sufficient foundation for the most friendly intercourse. All the arts of delusion and legal chicanery will be used to elude your vigilance, and obtain a majority. But keeping the constitution of the state and the publick interest in view, will be your safety.

[We are obliged, contrary to our intention, to postpone the remainder of Agrippa till our next.]

XVII.

[January 20, 1788]

To the Massachusetts Convention.

Gentlemen,
As it is essentially necessary to the happiness of a free people, that the constitution of government should be established in principles of truth, I have endeavoured, in a series of papers, to discuss the proposed form with that degree of freedom which becomes a faithful citizen of the commonwealth. It must be obvious to the most careless observer that the friends of the new plan appear to have nothing more in view than to establish it by a popular current, without any regard to the truth of its principles. Propositions, novel, erroneous and dangerous, are boldly advanced to support a system, which does not appear to be founded in, but in every instance to contradict, the experience of mankind. We are told that a constitution is in itself a bill of rights; that all power not expressly given, is reserved; that no powers are given to the new government which are not already vested in the state governments, and that it is for the security of liberty that the persons elected should have the absolute controul over the time, manner and place of election. These, and an hundred other things of a like kind, though they have gained the hasty assent of men, respectable for learning and ability, are false in themselves and invented merely to serve a present purpose.

This will, I trust, clearly appear from the following considerations:

It is common to consider man at first as in a state of nature, separate from all society. The only historical evidence, that the human species ever actually existed in this state, is derived from the book of Gen. There it is said, that Adam remained a while alone. While the whole species was comprehended in his person was the only instance in which this supposed state of nature really existed. Ever since the completion of the first pair, mankind appear as natural to associate with their own species, as animals of any other kind herd together. Wherever we meet with their settlements, they are found in clans. We are therefore justified in saying, that a state of society is the natural state of man. Wherever we find a settlement of men, we find also some appearance of government. The state of government is therefore as natural to mankind as a state of society. Government and society appear to be co-eval. The most rude and artless form of government is probably the most ancient. This we find to be practised among the Indian tribes in America. With them the whole authority of government is vested in the whole tribe. Individuals depend upon their reputation of valour and wisdom to give them influence. Their government is genuinely democratical. This was probably the first kind of government among mankind, as we meet with ño mention of any other kind, till royalty was introduced in the person of Nimrod. Immediately after that time, the Asiatick nations seem to have departed from the simple democracy, which is still retained by their American brethern, and universally adopted the kingly form. We do indeed meet with some vague rumors of an aristocracy in India so late as the time of Alexander the Great. But such stories are altogether uncertain and improbable. For in the time of Abraham, who lived about sixteen hundred years before Alexander, all

the little nations mentioned in the Mosaick history appear
to be governed by kings. It does not appear from any accounts of the Asiatick kingdoms that they have practised at
all upon the idea of a limited monarchy. The whole power
of society has been delegated to the kings; and though
they may be said to have constitutions of government,
because the succession to the crown is limited by certain
rules, yet the people are not benefitted by their constitutions, and enjoy no share of civil liberty. The first attempt
to reduce republicanism to a system, appears to be made
by Moses when he led the Israelites out of Egypt. This
government stood a considerable time, about five centuries, till in a frenzy the people demanded a king, that they
might resemble the nations about them. They were dissat-
isfied with their judges, and instead of changing the administration, they madly changed their constitution. However they might flatter themselves with the idea, that an
high-spirited people could get the power back again when
they pleased; they never did get it back, and they fared
like the nations about them. Their kings tyrannized over
them for some centuries, till they fell under a foreign yoke.
This is the history of that nation. With a change of names,
it describes the progress of political changes in other
countries. The people are dazzled with the splendour of
distant monarchies, and a desire to share their glory induces them to sacrifice their domestick happiness.

From this general view of the state of mankind it appears that all the powers of government originally reside
in the body of the people; and that when they appoint
certain persons to administer the government, they delegate all the powers of government not expressly reserved.
Hence it appears that a constitution does not in itself imply any more than a declaration of the relation which the
different parts of the government bear to each other, but
does not in any degree imply security to the rights of indi-

viduals. This has been the uniform practice. In all doubtful cases the decision is in favour of the government. It is therefore impertinent to ask by what right government exercises powers not expressly delegated. Mr. Wilson, the great oracle of federalism, acknowledges, in his speech to the Philadelphians, the truth of these remarks, as they respect the state governments, but attempts to set up a distinction between them and the continental government. To anybody who will be at the trouble to read the new system, it is evidently in the same situation as the state constitutions now possess. It is a compact among the *people* for the purposes of government, and not a compact between states. It begins in the name of the people, and not of the states.

It has been shown in the course of this paper, that when people institute government, they of course delegate all rights not expressly reserved. In our state constitution the bill of rights consists of thirty articles. It is evident therefore that the new constitution proposes to delegate greater powers than are granted to our own government, sanguine as the person was who denied it. The complaints against the separate governments, even by the friends of the new plan, are not that they have not power enough, but that they are disposed to make a bad use of what power they have. Surely then they reason badly, when they purpose to set up a government possess'd of much more extensive powers than the present, and subject to much smaller checks.

Bills of rights, reserved by authority of the people, are, I believe, peculiar to America. A careful observance of the abuse practised in other countries has had its just effect by inducing our people to guard against them. We find the happiest consequences to flow from it. The separate governments know their powers, their objects, and operations. We are therefore not perpetually tormented with new experiments. For a single instance of abuse among us there are thousands in other countries. On the other hand, the people know their rights, and feel happy in the possession of their freedom, both civil and political. Active industry is the consequence of their security, and within one year the circumstances of the state and of individuals have improved to a degree never before known in this commonwealth. Though our bill of rights does not, perhaps, contain all the cases in which power might be safely reserved, yet it affords a protection to the persons and possessions of individuals not known in any foreign country. In some respects the power of government is a little too confined. In many other countries we find the people resisting their governours for exercising their power in an unaccustomed mode. But for want of a bill of rights the resistance is always, by the principles of their government, a rebellion which nothing but success can justify. In our constitution we have aimed at delegating the necessary powers of government and confining their operation to beneficial purposes. At present we appear to have come very near the truth. Let us therefore have wisdom and virtue enough to preserve it inviolate. It is a stale contrivance, to get the people into a passion, in order to make them sacrifice their liberty. Repentance always comes, but it comes too late. Let us not flatter ourselves that we shall always have good men to govern us. If we endeavour to be like other nations we shall have more bad men than good ones to exercise extensive powers. That circumstance alone will corrupt them. While they fancy themselves the viceregents of God, they will resemble him only in power, but will always depart from his wisdom and goodness.

XVIII.

[February 5, 1788]

To the Massachusetts Convention.

Gentlemen,
In my last address I ascertained, from historical records,
the following principles: that, in the original state of government, the whole power resides in the whole body of
the nation, that when a people appoint certain persons to
govern them, they delegate their whole power; that a
constitution is not in itself a bill of rights; and that, whatever is the form of government, a bill of rights is essential
to the security of the persons and property of the people. It
is an idea favourable to the interest of mankind at large,
that government is founded in compact. Several instances
may be produced of it, but none is more remarkable than
our own. In general, I have chosen to apply to such facts as
are in the reach of my readers. For this purpose I have
chiefly confined myself to examples drawn from the history of our own country, and to the Old Testament. It is in
the power of every reader to verify examples thus substan-
tiated. Even in the remarkable arguments on the fourth
section, relative to the power over election I was far from
stating the worst of it, as it respects the adverse party. A
gentleman, respectable in many points, but more especially for his systematick and perspicuous reasoning in his
profession, has repeatedly stated to the Convention,
among his reasons in favour of that section, that *the Rhode
Island assembly have for a considerable time past had a
bill lying on their table for altering the manner of elections for representatives in that state.* He has stated it with

all the zeal of a person who believed his argument to be a good one. But surely a *bill lying on a table* can never be considered as any more than an *intention* to pass it, and nobody pretends that it ever actually did pass. It is in strictness only the intention of a part of the assembly, for nobody can aver that it ever will pass. I write not with an intention to deceive, but that the whole argument may be stated fairly. Much eloquence and ingenuity have been employed in shewing that side of the argument in favor of the proposed constitution, but it ought to be considered that if we accept it upon mere verbal explanations, we shall find ourselves deceived. I appeal to the knowledge of every one, if it does not frequently happen, that a law is interpreted in practice very differently from the intention of the legislature. Hence arises the necessity of acts to amend and explain former acts. This is not an inconvenience in the common and ordinary business of legislation, but is a great one in a constitution. A constitution is a legislative act of the whole people. It is an excellence that it should be permanent, otherwise we are exposed to perpetual insecurity from the fluctuation of government. We should be in the same situation as under absolute government, sometimes exposed to the pressure of greater, and sometimes unprotected by the weaker power in the sovereign.

It is now generally understood that it is for the security of the people that the powers of the government should be lodged in different branches. By this means publick business will go on when they all agree, and stop when they disagree. The advantage of checks in government is thus manifested where the concurrence of different branches is necessary to the same act, but the advantage of a division of business is advantageous in other respects. As in every extensive empire, local laws are necessary to suit the different interests, no single legislature is adequate to the business. All human capacities are limited to a narrow space, and as no individual is capable of practising a great variety of trades, no single legislature is capable of managing all the variety of national and state concerns. Even if a legislature was capable of it, the business of the judicial department must, from the same cause, be slovenly done. Hence arises the necessity of a division of the business into national and local. Each department ought to have all the powers necessary for executing its own business, under such limitations as tend to secure us from any inequality in the operations of government. I know it is often asked against whom in a government by representation is a bill of rights to secure us? I answer, that such a government is indeed a government by ourselves; but as a just government protects all alike, it is necessary that the sober and industrious part of the community should be defended from the rapacity and violence of the vicious and idle. A bill of rights, therefore, ought to set forth the purposes for which the compact is made, and serves to secure the minority against the usurpation and tyranny of the majority. It is a just observation of his excellency, doctor Adams, in his learned defence of the American constitutions that unbridled passions produce the same effect, whether in a king, nobility, or a mob. The experience of all mankind has proved the prevalence of a disposition to use power wantonly. It is therefore as necessary to defend an individual against the majority in a republick as against the king in a monarchy. Our state constitution has wisely guarded this point. The present confederation has also done it.

I confess that I have yet seen no sufficient reason for not amending the confederation, though I have weighed the argument with candour; I think it would be much easier to amend it than the new constitution. But this is a point on which men of very respectable character differ. There is another point in which nearly all agree, and that is, that the new constitution would be better in many respects if it had been differently framed. Here the question is not so much what the amendments ought to be, as in what manner they shall be made; whether they shall be made as conditions of our accepting the constitution, or whether we shall first accept it, and then try to amend it. I can hardly conceive that it should seriously be made a question. If the first question, whether we will receive it as it stands, be negatived, as it undoubtedly ought to be, while the conviction remains that amendments are necessary; the next question will be, what amendments shall be made? Here permit an individual, who glories in being a citizen of Massachusetts, and who is anxious that her character may remain undiminished, to propose such articles as appear to him necessary for preserving the rights of the state. He means not to retract anything with regard to the expediency of amending the old confederation, and rejecting the new one totally; but only to make a proposition which he thinks comprehends the general idea of all parties. If the new constitution means no more than the friends of it acknowledge, they certainly can have no objection to affixing a declaration in favor of the rights of states and of citizens, especially as a majority of the states have not yet voted upon it.

"Resolved, that the constitution lately proposed for the United States be received only upon the following conditions:

"1. Congress shall have no power to alter the time, place or manner of elections, nor any authority over elections, otherwise than by fining such state as shall neglect to send its representatives or senators, a sum not exceeding the expense of supporting its representatives or senators one year.

"2. Congress shall not have the power of regulating the intercourse between the states, nor to levy any direct tax on polls or estates, or any excise.

"3. Congress shall not have power to try causes between a state and citizens of another state, nor between citizens of different states; nor to make any laws relative to the transfer of property between those parties, nor any other matter which shall originate in the body of any state.

"4. It shall be left to every state to make and execute its own laws, except laws impairing contracts, which shall not be made at all.

"5. Congress shall not incorporate any trading companies, nor alienate the territory of any state. And no treaty, ordinance or law of the United States shall be valid for these purposes.

"6. Each state shall have the command of its own militia.

"7. No continental army shall come within the limits of any state, other than garrison to guard the publick stores, without the consent of such states in time of peace.

"8. The president shall be chosen annually and shall serve but one year, and shall be chosen successively from the different states, changing every year.

"9. The judicial department shall be confined to cases in which ambassadours are concerned, to cases depending upon treaties, to offences committed upon the high seas, to the capture of prizes, and to cases in which a foreigner residing in some foreign country shall be a party, and an American state or citizen shall be the other party, provided no suit shall be brought upon a state note.

"10. Every state may emit bills of credit without making them a tender, and may coin money, of silver, gold or copper, according to the continental standard.

"11. No powers shall be exercised by Congress or the president but such as are expressly given by this constitution and not excepted against by this declaration. And any officer of the United States offending against an individual state shall be held accountable to such state, as any other citizen would be.

"12. No officer of Congress shall be free from arrest for debt [but] by authority of the state in which the debt shall be due.

"13. Nothing in this constitution shall deprive a citizen of any state of the benefit of the bill of rights established by the constitution of the state in which he shall reside, and such bill of rights shall be considered as valid in any court of the United States where they shall be pleaded.

"14. In all those causes which are triable before the continental courts, the trial by jury shall be held sacred."

These at present appear to me the most important points to be guarded. I have mentioned a reservation of excise to the separate states, because it is necessary, that they should have some way to discharge their own debts, and because it is placing them in an humiliating & disgraceful situation to depute them to transact the business of international government without the means to carry it on. It is necessary also, as a check on the national government, for it has hardly been known that any government having the powers of war, peace, and revenue, has failed to engage in needless and wanton expense. A reservation of this kind is therefore necessary to preserve the importance of the state governments: without this the extremes of the empire will in a very short time sink into the same degradation and contempt with respect to the middle state as Ireland, Scotland, & Wales, are in with regard to England. All the men of genius and wealth will resort to the seat of government, that will be center of revenue, and of business, which the extremes will be drained to supply.

This is not mere vision, it is justified by the whole course of things. We shall, therefore, if we neglect the present opportunity to secure ourselves, only increase the number of proofs already too many, that mankind are incapable of enjoying their liberty. I have been the more particular in stating the amendments to be made, because many gentlemen think it would be preferable to receive the new system with corrections. I have by this means brought the corrections into one view, and shown several of the principal points in which it is unguarded. As it is agreed, at least professedly, on all sides, that those rights should be guarded, it is among the inferior questions in what manner it is done, provided it is absolutely and effectually done. For my own part, I am fully of opinion that it would be best to reject this plan, and pass an explicit resolve, defining the powers of Congress to regulate the intercourse between us and foreign nations, under such restrictions as shall render their regulations equal in all parts of the empire. The impost, if well collected, would be fully equal to the interest of the foreign debt, and the current charges of the national government. It is evidently for our interest that the charges should be as small as possible. It is also for our interest that the western lands should, as fast as possible, be applied to the purpose of paying the home debt. Internal taxation and that fund have already paid two-thirds of the whole debt, notwithstanding the embarrassments usual at the end of a war.

We are now rising fast above our difficulties; everything at home has the appearance of improvement, government is well established, manufactures increasing rapidly, and trade expanding. Till since the peace we never sent a ship to India, and the present year, it is said, sends above a dozen vessels from this state only, to the countries round the Indian ocean. Vast quantities of our produce are exported to those countries. It has been so much the practice of European nations to farm out this branch of trade, that we ought to be exceedingly jealous of our right. The manufactures of the state probably exceed in value one million pounds for the last year. Most of the useful and some ornamental fabricks are established. There is great danger of these improvements being injured unless we practice extreme caution at setting out. It will always be for the interest of the southern states to raise a revenue from the more commercial ones. It is said that the consumer pays it. But does not a commercial state consume more foreign goods than a landed one? The people are more crowded, and of consequence the land is less able to support them. We know it is to be a favourite system to raise the money where it is. But the money is to be expended at another place, and is therefore so much withdrawn annually from our stock. This is a single instance of the difference of interest; it would be very easy to produce others. Innumerable as the differences of manners, and these produce differences in the laws. Uniformity in legislation is of no more importance than in religion. Yet the framers of this new constitution did not even think it necessary that the president should believe that there is a God, although they require an oath of him. It would be easy to shew the propriety of a general declaration upon that subject. But this paper is already extended to so far [*sic*].

Another reason which I had in stating the amendments to be made, was to shew how nearly those who are for admitting the system with the necessary alterations, agree with those who are for rejecting this system and amending the confederation. In point of convenience, the confederation amended would be infinitely preferable to the proposed constitution. In amending the former, we know the powers granted, and are subject to no perplexity; but in reforming the latter, the business is excessively intricate, and great part of the checks on Congress are lost. It is to be remembered too, that if you are so far charmed with eloquence, and misled by fair representations and charitable constructions, as to adopt an undefined system, there will be no saying afterwards that you were mistaken, and wish to correct it. *It will then be the constitution of our country, and entitled to defence.* If Congress should chuse to avail themselves of a popular commotion to continue in being, as the fourth section justifies, and as the British parliament has repeatedly done, the only answer will be, that it is the constitution of our country, and the people chose it. It is therefore necessary to be exceedingly critical. Whatsoever way shall be chosen to secure our rights, the same resolve ought to contain the whole system of amendment. If it is rejected, the resolve should contain the amendments of the old system; and if accepted, it should contain the corrections of the new one.

AGRIPPA.

A writer in the Gazette of 29th January, under the signature of Captain M'Daniel, having with civility and apparent candour, called for an explanation of what was said in one of my former papers, I have chosen to mention him with respect, as the only one of my reviewers who deserves an answer.

8. *A Letter of Luther Martin*

The document printed herewith is the fourth in a series of letters written by Luther Martin in reply to Oliver Ellsworth's "The Letters of a Landholder."[1] Ellsworth, a member of the Federal Convention, had attacked two fellow-members who had refused to sign the Constitution, George Mason of Virginia and Elbridge Gerry of Massachusetts. Martin's first letters were in defense of Gerry. Ellsworth in turn wrote a stinging letter attacking Martin, who had also been a delegate to the Convention, including such personal remarks as references to "your endless garrulity" and, ". . . you exhausted the politeness of the Convention, which at length prepared to slumber when you rose to speak. . . ." Martin's fourth letter was written in reply to Ellsworth's attack.[2] It is reproduced here partly because it represents the opinion of one of the leading Antifederalists, but primarily because it gives an insight into the working procedures and spirit of the Philadelphia Convention, as reported by a member of the opposition. Ellsworth's attempt to attribute the "supreme law clause" to Martin was made in an effort to undermine the sharp Antifederalist attack on that clause. Martin's reply indicates the evolution of that clause—and by example other clauses—in the course of the Convention debates. It may be said that both Ellsworth and Martin violated the spirit if not the letter of the rule of secrecy agreed upon by the Convention, and that the exchange between them illustrated the virtue of that rule. The rule, when obeyed,

---

From "The Letters of Luther Martin," printed in *The Maryland Journal,* January–March 1788. The text here is that of Ford, *Essays,* pp. 360–371.
[1] Published in *The Connecticut Courant* and *The American Mercury,* November 1787–March 1788. Reprinted in Ford, *Essays,* pp. 134–202.
[2] Reprinted in Ford, *op. cit.,* pp. 182 ff.

helped to avoid arguments *ad hominem,* and to force debate on
the actual structure of the Constitution. Martin (*ca.* 1748–1826)
had a distinguished career as politician and lawyer. He was for
many years attorney-general of Maryland, and had represented
that state in the Continental Congress. He opposed the Constitution largely because of its centralization of power, but later became a staunch Federalist. He defended Samuel Chase in his
impeachment trial of 1804, and Aaron Burr in the treason trial of
1807. In the famous case of McCulloch *v.* Maryland, 4 Wheaton,
316 (1819), he represented the state of Maryland. Shortly
thereafter he was incapacitated by a paralytic stroke, and died in
1826.

NUMBER II.

[March 21, 1788]

To the Citizens of Maryland.

In the recognition which the Landholder professes to
make "of what occurred to my advantage," he equally
deals in the arts of misrepresentation, as while he was
"only the record of the bad," and I am equally obliged
from a regard to truth to disclaim his pretended approbation as his avowed censure. He declares that I originated
the clause which enacts that "this Constitution and the
laws of the United States, which shall be made in pursuance thereof, and all treaties made, or which shall be
made, under the authority of the United States, shall be
the supreme law of the land, and the judges in every state
shall be bound thereby, any thing in the Constitution or
the laws of any state to the contrary notwithstanding." To
place this matter in a proper point of view, it will be necessary to state, that as the propositions were reported by
the committee of the whole house, a power was given to

the general government to negative the laws passed by the state legislatures, a power which I considered as totally inadmissible; in substitution of this I proposed the following clause, which you will find very materially different from the clause adopted by the Constitution, "that the legislative acts of the United States, made by virtue and in pursuance of the articles of the union, and all treaties made and ratified under the authority of the United States, shall be the supreme law of the respective states, so far as those acts or treaties shall relate to the said states or their citizens, and that the judiciaries of the several states shall be bound thereby in their decisions, any thing in the respective laws of the individual states to the contrary notwithstanding." When this clause was introduced, it was not established that inferior continental courts should be appointed for trial of all questions arising on treaties and on the laws of the general government, and it was my wish and hope that every question of that kind would have been determined in the first instance in the courts of the respective states; had this been the case, the propriety and the necessity that treaties duly made and ratified, and the laws of the general government, should be binding on the state judiciaries which were to decide upon them, must be evident to every capacity, while at the same time, if such treaties or laws were inconsistent with our constitution and bill of rights, the judiciaries of this state would be bound to reject the first and abide by the last, since in the form I introduced the clause, notwithstanding treaties and the laws of the general government were intended to be superior to the laws of our state government, where they should be opposed to each other, yet that they were not proposed nor meant to be superior to our constitution and bill of rights. It was afterwards altered and amended (if it can be called an amendment) to the form in which it stands in the system now published, and as inferior continental, and not state courts, are originally to decide on those questions, it is now worse than useless, for being so altered as to render the treaties and laws made under the general government superior to our constitution, if the system is adopted it will amount to a total and unconditional surrender to that government, by the citizens of this state, of every right and privilege secured to them by our constitution, and an express compact and stipulation with the general government that it may, at its discretion, make laws in direct violation of those rights. But on this subject I shall enlarge in a future number.

That I "voted an appeal should lay to the supreme judiciary of the United States, for the correction of all errors both in law and fact," in rendering judgment is most true, and it is equally true that if it had been so ordained by the Constitution, the supreme judiciary would only have had an appellate jurisdiction, of the same nature with that possessed by our high court of appeals, and could not in any respect intermeddle with any fact decided by a jury; but as the clause now stands, an appeal being given in general terms from the inferior courts, both as to law and fact, it not only doth, but is avowedly intended, to give a power very different from what our court of appeals, or any court of appeals in the United States or in England enjoys, a power of the most dangerous and alarming nature, that of setting at nought the verdict of a jury, and having the same facts which they had determined, without any regard or respect to their determination, examined and ultimately decided by the judges themselves, and that by judges immediately appointed by the government. But the Landholder also says that "I agreed to the clause that declares nine states to be sufficient to put the government in motion." I cannot take to myself the merit even of this without too great a sacrifice of truth. It was proposed that if seven states agreed that should be sufficient; by a rule of

Convention in filling up blanks, if different numbers were mentioned, the question was always to be taken on the highest. It was my opinion, that to agree upon a ratification of the constitution by any less number than the whole thirteen states, is so directly repugnant to our present articles of confederation, and the mode therein prescribed for their alteration, and such a violation of the compact which the states, in the most solemn manner, have entered into with each other, that those who could advocate a contrary proposition, ought never to be confided in, and entrusted in public life. I availed myself of this rule, and had the question taken on thirteen, which was rejected. Twelve, eleven, ten and nine were proposed in succession; the last was adopted by a majority of the members. I voted successively for each of these members, to prevent a less number being agreed on. Had nine not been adopted, I should on the same principle have voted for eight. But so far was I from giving my approbation that the assent of a less number of states than thirteen should be sufficient to put the government in motion, that I most explicitly expressed my sentiments to the contrary, and always intended, had I been present when the ultimate vote was taken on the constitution, to have given it my decided negative, accompanied with a solemn protest against it, assigning this reason among others for my dissent. Thus, my fellow citizens, that candour with which I have conducted myself through the whole of this business obliges me, however reluctantly, and however "mortifying it may be to my vanity," to disavow all "those greater positive virtues" which the Landholder has so obligingly attributed to me in Convention, and which he was so desirous of conferring upon me as to consider the guilt of misrepresentation and falsehood but a trifling sacrifice for that purpose, and to increase my mortification, you will find I am equally compelled to yield up every pretence even to those of a negative nature, which a regard to justice has, as he says, obliged him not to omit. These consist, as he tells us, in giving my entire approbation to the system as to those parts which are said to endanger a trial by jury, and as to its want of a bill of rights, and in having too much candour there to signify that I thought it deficient in either of these respects. But how, I pray, can the Landholder be certain that I deserve this encomium? Is it not possible, as I so frequently exhausted the politeness of the Convention, that some of those marks of fatigue and disgust, with which he intimates I was mortified as oft as I attempted to speak, might at that time have taken place, and have been of such a nature as to attract his attention; or, perhaps, as the Convention was prepared to slumber whenever I rose, the Landholder, among others, might have sunk into sleep, and at that very moment might have been feasting his imagination with the completion of his ambitious views, and dreams of future greatness. But supposing I never did declare in Convention that I thought the system defective in those essential points, will it amount to a positive proof that I approved the system in those respects, or that I culpably neglected an indispensable duty? Is it not possible, whatever might have been my insolence and assurance when I first took my seat, and however fond I might be at that time of obtruding my sentiments, that the many rebuffs with which I met, the repeated mortifications I experienced, the marks of fatigue and disgust with which my eyes were sure to be assailed wherever I turned them—one gaping here, another yawning there, a third slumbering in this place, and a fourth snoring in that —might so effectually have put to flight all my original arrogance, that, as we are apt to run into extremes, having at length become convinced of my comparative nothingness, in so august an assembly and one in which the science of government was so perfectly understood, I might sink into such a state of modesty and diffidence as not to be able to muster up resolution enough to break the seal of silence and open my lips even after the rays of light had begun to penetrate my understanding, and in some measure to chase away those clouds of error and ignorance in which it was enveloped on my first arrival? Perhaps had I been treated with a more forbearing indulgence while committing those memorable blunders, for a want of a sufficient knowledge in the science of government, I might, after the rays of light had illuminated my mind, have rendered my country much more important services, and not only assisted in raising some of the pillars, but have furnished the edifice with a new roof of my own construction, rather better calculated for the convenience and security of those who might wish to take shelter beneath it, than that which it at present enjoys. Or even admitting I was not mortified, as I certainly ought to have been, from the Landholder's account of the matter, into a total loss of speech, was it in me, who considered the system, for a variety of reasons, absolutely inconsistent with your political welfare and happiness, a culpable neglect of duty in not endeavouring, and that against every chance of success, to remove one or two defects, when I had before ineffectually endeavoured to clear it of the others, which therefore, I knew must remain? But to be serious, as to what relates to the appellate jurisdiction in the extent given by the system proposed, I am positive there were objections made to it, and as far as my memory will serve me, I think I was in the number of those who actually objected; but I am sure that the objections met with my approbation. With respect to a bill of rights, had the government been formed upon principles truly federal, as I wished it, legislating over and acting upon the states only in their collective or political capacity, and not on individuals, there would have been no need of a bill of rights, as far as related to the rights of individuals, but only as to the rights of states. But the proposed constitution being intended and empowered to act not only on states, but also immediately on individuals, it renders a recognition and a stipulation in favour of the rights both of states and of men, not only proper, but in my opinion absolutely necessary. I endeavoured to obtain a restraint on the powers of the general government, as to standing armies, but it was rejected. It was my wish that the general government should not have the power of suspending the privilege of the writ of habeas corpus, as it appears to me altogether unnecessary, and that the power given to it may and will be used as a dangerous engine of oppression, but I could not succeed. An honorable member from South Carolina most anxiously sought to have a clause inserted securing the liberty of the Press, and repeatedly brought this subject before the Convention, but could not obtain it. I am almost positive he made the same attempt to have a stipulation in favour of liberty of conscience, but in vain. The more the system advanced the more was I impressed with the necessity of not merely attempting to secure a few rights, but of digesting and forming a complete bill of rights, including those of states and of individuals, which should be assented to, and prefixed to the Constitution, to serve as a barrier between the general government and the respective states and their citizens; because the more the system advanced the more clearly it appeared to me that the framers of it did not consider that either states or men had any rights at all, or that they meant to secure the enjoyment of any to either the one or the other; accordingly, I devoted a part of my time to the actually preparing and draughting such a bill of rights, and had it in readiness before I left the Convention, to have laid it before a committee. I conversed with several members on the subject; they agreed with me on the propriety of the measure, but at the same time expressed their sentiments that it would be impossible to procure its adoption if attempted. A very few days before I left the Convention, I shewed to an honorable member sitting by me a proposition, which I then had in my hand, couched in the following words: "Resolved that a committee be appointed to prepare and report a bill of rights, to be prefixed to the proposed Constitution," and I then would instantly have moved for the appointment of a committee for that purpose, if he would have agreed to second the motion, to do which he hesitated, not as I understand from any objection to the measure, but from a conviction in his own mind that the motion would be in vain.

Thus my fellow citizens, you see that so far from having no objections to the system on this account, while I was at Convention, I not only then thought a bill of rights necessary, but I took some pains to have the subject brought forward, which would have been done, had it not been for the difficulties I have stated. At the same time I declare that when I drew up the motion, and was about to have proposed it to the Convention, I had not the most distant hope it would meet with success. The rejection of the clauses attempted in favour of particular rights, and to check and restrain the dangerous and exorbitant powers of the general government from being abused, had sufficiently taught me what to expect. And from the best judgment I could form while in Convention, I then was, and yet remained, decidedly of the opinion that ambition and interest had so far blinded the understanding of some of the principal framers of the Constitution, that while they were labouring to erect a fabrick by which they themselves might be exalted and benefited, they were rendered insensible to the sacrifice of the freedom and happiness of the states and their citizens, which must, inevitably be the consequence. I most sacredly believe their object is the total abolition and destruction of all state governments, and the erection on their ruins of one great and extensive empire, calculated to aggrandize and elevate its rulers and chief officers far above the common herd of mankind, to enrich them with wealth, and to encircle them with honours and glory, and which according to my judgment on the maturest reflection, must inevitably be attended with the most humiliating and abject slavery óf their fellow citizens, by the sweat of whose brows, and by the toil of whose bodies, it can only be effected. And so anxious were its zealous promoters to hasten to a birth this misshapened heterogenous monster of ambition and interest, that, for some time before the Convention rose, upon the least attempt to alter its form, or modify its powers, the most fretful impatience was shown, such as would not have done much honour to a State Assembly, had they been sitting as long a time, and their treasury empty; while it was repeatedly urged on the contrary, but urged in vain, that in so momentous an undertaking, in forming a system for such an extensive continent, on which the political happiness of so many millions, even to the latest ages, may depend, no time could be too long—no thoughts and reflections too great—and that if by continuing six months, or even as many years, we could free the system from all its errors and defects, it would be the best use to which we could possibly devote our time. Thus my fellow citizens am I under necessity of resigning again into the hands of the Landholder, all those virtues both of a positive and negative kind, which from an excess of goodness he bestowed upon me, and give him my full permission to dispose of them hereafter in favour of some other person, who may be more deserving, and to whom they will be more acceptable: at the same time, I must frankly acknowledge, however it may operate as a proof of my dullness and stupidity, that the "ignorance in the science of government" under which I laboured at first was not removed by more than two months close application under those august and enlightened masters of the science with which the Convention abounded, nor was I able to discover during that time, either by my own researches, or by any light borrowed from those luminaries, anything in the history of mankind or in the sentiments of those who have favoured the world with their ideas on government, to warrant or countenance the motley mixture of a system proposed: a system which is an innovation in government of the most extraordinary kind; a system neither wholly federal, nor wholly national—but a strange hotch-potch of both—just so much federal in appearance as to give its advocates in some measure, an opportunity of passing it as such upon the unsuspecting multitude, before they had time and opportunity to examine it, and yet so predominantly national as to put it in the power of its movers, whenever the machine shall be set agoing, to strike out every part that has the appearance of being federal, and to render it wholly and entirely a national government: And if the framing and approving the Constitution now offered to our acceptance, is a proof of knowledge in the science of government, I not only admit, but I glory in my ignorance; and if my rising to speak had such a somnific influence on the Convention as the Landholder represents, I have no doubt the time will come, should this system be adopted, when my countrymen will ardently wish I had never left the Convention, but remained there to the last, daily administering to my associates the salutary opiate. Happy, thrice happy, would it have been for my country, if the whole of that time had been devoted to sleep, or been a blank in our lives, rather than employed in forging its chains. As I fully intended to have returned to the Convention before the completion of its business, my colleagues very probably might, and were certainly well warranted to, give that information the Landholder mentions; but whether the Convention was led to conclude that I "would have honoured the Constitution with my signature had not indispensable business called me away," may be easily determined after stating a few facts. The

Landholder admits I was at first against the system—when the compromise took place on the subject of representation, I in the most explicit manner declared in Convention, that though I had concurred in the report, so far as to consent to proceed upon it that we might see what kind of a system might be formed, yet I disclaimed every idea of being bound to give it my assent, but reserved to myself the full liberty of finally giving it my negative, if it appeared to me inconsistent with the happiness of my country. In a desultory conversation which long after took place in Convention, one morning before our honourable president took the chair, he was observing how unhappy it would be should there be such a diversity of sentiment as to cause any of the members to oppose the system when they returned to their states; on that occasion I replied that I was confident no state in the union would more readily accede to a proper system of government than Maryland, but that the system under consideration was of such a nature, that I never could recommend it for acceptance; that I thought the state never ought to adopt it, and expressed my firm belief that it never would.

An honourable member from Pennsylvania objected against that part of the sixth article which requires an oath to be taken by the persons there mentioned, in support of the constitution, observing (as he justly might from the conduct the convention was then pursuing) how little such oaths were regarded. I immediately joined in the objection, but declared my reason to be, that I thought it such a constitution as no friend of his country ought to bind himself to support. And not more than two days before I left Philadelphia, another honourable member from the same state urged most strenuously that the Convention ought to hasten their deliberations to a conclusion, assigning as a reason that the Assembly of Pennsylvania was just then about to meet, and that it would be of the greatest impor-

tance to bring the system before that session of the legislature, in order that a Convention of the State might be immediately called to ratify it, before the enemies of the
system should have an opportunity of making the people
acquainted with their objections, at the same time declaring that if the matter should be delayed and the people
have time to hear the variety of objections which would be
made to it by its opposers, he thought it doubtful whether
that state or any other state in the union would adopt it.*
As soon as the honourable member took his seat, I rose
and observed, that I was precisely of the same opinion,
that the people of America never would, nor did I think
they ought to, adopt the system, if they had time to consider
and understand it; whereas a proneness for novelty and
change—a conviction that some alteration was necessary,
and a confidence in the members who composed the
Convention—might possibly procure its adoption, if
brought hastily before them, but that these sentiments
induced me to wish that a very different line of conduct
should be pursued from that recommended by the honourable member. I wished the people to have every opportunity of information, as I thought it much preferable that a bad
system should be rejected at first, than hastily adopted and
afterwards be unavailingly repented of. If these were instances of my "high approbation," I gave them in abundance as all the Convention can testify, and continued so to
do till I left them. That I expressed great regret at being
obliged to leave Philadelphia, and a fixed determination to
return if possible before the Convention rose, is certain.
That I might declare that I had rather lose an hundred guineas than not to be there at the close of the business is very

---

*How exactly agreeable to the sentiments of that honourable member
has been the conduct of the friends of the Constitution in Pennsylvania
and some other states, I need not mention.

probable—and it is possible that some who heard me say this, not knowing my reasons, which could not be expressed without a breach of that secrecy to which we were enjoined, might erroneously have concluded that my motive was the gratification of vanity, in having my name enrolled with those of a Franklin and a Washington. As to the first, I cordially join in the tribute of praise so justly paid to the enlightened philosopher and statesman, while the polite, friendly and affectionate treatment myself and my family received from that venerable sage and the worthy family in which he is embosomed, will ever endear him to my heart. The name of Washington is far above my praise. I would to Heaven that on this occasion one more wreath had been added to the number of those which are twined around his amiable brow—that those with which it is already surrounded may flourish with immortal verdure, nor wither or fade till time shall be no more, is my fervent prayer, and may that glory which encircles his head ever shine with undiminished rays. To find myself under the necessity of opposing such illustrious characters, whom I venerated and loved, filled me with regret; but viewing the system in the light I then did, and yet do view it, to have hesitated would have been criminal; complaisance would have been guilt. If it was the idea of my state that whatever a Washington or Franklin approved, was to be blindly adopted, she ought to have spared herself the expence of sending any members to the Convention, or to have instructed them implicitly to follow where they led the way. It was not to have my "name enrolled with the other labourers," that I wished to return to Philadelphia—that sacrifice which I must have made of my principles by putting my name to the Constitution, could not have been effaced by any derivative lustre it could possibly receive from the bright constellation with which it would have been surrounded. My object was in truth the very reverse; as I had uniformly opposed the system in its progress, I wished to have been present at the conclusion, to have then given it my solemn negative, which I certainly should have done, even had I stood single and alone, being perfectly willing to leave it to the cool and impartial investigation both of the present and of future ages to decide who best understood the science of government —who best knew the rights of men and of states, who best consulted the true interest of America, and who most faithfully discharged the trust reposed in them, those who agreed to or those who opposed the new Constitution —and so fully have I made up my own mind on this subject, that as long as the history of mankind shall record the appointment of the late Convention, and the system which has been proposed by them, it is my highest ambition that my name may also be recorded as one who considered the system injurious to my country, and as such opposed it. Having shown that I did not "alter my opinion after I left Philadelphia," and that I acted no "contradictory parts on the great political stage," and therefore that there are none such to reconcile, the reason assigned by the Landholder for that purpose doth not deserve my notice, except only to observe that he shrewdly intimates there is already a Junto established, who are to share in and deal out the offices of this new government at their will and pleasure, and that they have already fixed upon the character who is to be "Deputy Attorney General of the United States for the State of Maryland." If this is true, it is worth while to inquire of whom this Junto consists, as it might lead to a discovery of the persons for the gratification of whose ambition and interest this system is prepared, and is, if possible, to be enforced, and from the disposition of offices already allotted in the various and numerous departments, we possibly might discover whence proceeds the conviction and zeal of some of its advocates.

9. *Debates in the South Carolina Legislature and Convention*

The leader of the South Carolina Antifederalists was Rawlins Lowndes (1721–1800), long prominent in state and colonial politics. He had served in legislative and judicial offices before the Revolution, and while defending South Carolina's right to representative government, had at first been opposed to independence. He was a member of the commission that drafted the first state constitution, and later was chosen as chief executive. The speeches printed here were delivered in the legislature during the debate over whether to call a ratifying convention. Lowndes did not expect to be elected to the latter, because, as he reported, his constituents were in favor of the Constitution. He was, in fact, elected, but chose not to attend.

In his speeches against the Constitution, Lowndes defended the Articles of Confederation, the slave trade, and paper money. He expressed fear that the South would suffer in a new union dominated by a majority from the Eastern states, deplored the loss of state sovereignty that would result from ratification, and predicted that the new government would probably end in monarchy. He said, nevertheless, that if the people approved of it, it would have his "hearty concurrence and support." The convention ratified the Constitution by a vote of 149–73.

Speeches by James Lincoln and Patrick Dollard are included in order to represent the attitudes of more obscure opponents of the Constitution.

These selections are reprinted from Elliot *Debates*, IV, 287–291, 312–315, 336–338. The speeches of Lowndes and Lincoln were delivered in the legislature, that of Dollard in the convention.

[RAWLINS LOWNDES]

Hon. RAWLINS LOWNDES declared himself almost willing
to give up his post, finding he was opposed by such a
phalanx of able antagonists, any one of them possessing
sufficient abilities to contend with him; but as a number of
respectable members, men of good sense, though not in
the habit of speaking in public, had requested that he
would state his sentiments, for the purpose of gaining
information on such points as seemed to require it,—rather
in compliance, therefore, with their wishes, than any inclination on his part, he should make a few further observations on the subject. Much had been said, from different
parts of the house, against the old Confederation—that it
was such a futile, inefficient, impolitic government as to
render us the objects of ridicule and contempt in the eyes
of other nations. He could not agree to this, because there
did not appear any evidence of the fact, and because the
names of those gentlemen who had signed the old Confederation were eminent for patriotism, virtue, and wisdom,—as much so as any set of men that could be found in
America,—and their prudence and wisdom particularly
appeared in the care which they had taken sacredly to
guaranty the sovereignty of each state. The treaty of peace
expressly agreed to acknowledge us as free, sovereign, and
independent states, which privileges we lived at present
in the exercise of. But this new Constitution at once swept
those privileges away, being sovereign over all; so that this
state would dwindle into a mere skeleton of what it was;
its legislative powers would be pared down to little more
than those now vested in the corporation; and he should

value the honor of a seat in the legislature in no higher estimation than a seat in the city council. Adverting to the powers given to the President, he considered them as enormous, particularly in being allowed to interfere in the election of members in the House of Representatives; astonishing that we had not this reserved to us, when the senators were to be chosen from that body:—thinks it might be so managed that the different legislatures should be limited to the passing a few laws for regulating ferries and roads.

The honorable gentleman went into an investigation of the weight of our representation in the proposed government, which he thought would be merely virtual, similar to what we were allowed in England, whilst under the British government. We were then told that we were represented in Parliament; and this would, in the event, prove just such another. The mode of choosing senators was exceedingly exceptionable. It had been the practice formerly to choose the Senate or council for this state from that house, which practice proved so inconvenient and oppressive, that, when we framed our present Constitution, great care was taken to vest the power of electing the Senate originally with the people, as the best plan for securing their rights and privileges. He wished to know in what manner it was proposed to elect the five representatives. Was it to be done in this city? or would some districts return one member, and others none at all?

Still greater difficulties would be found in the choice of a President, because he must have a majority of ninety-one votes in his favor. For the first President there was one man to whom all America looked up, (General Washing-

ton,) and for whom he most heartily would vote; but after
that gentleman's administration ceased, where could they
point out another so highly respected as to concentre a
majority of ninety-one persons in his favor? and if no gentleman should be fully returned, then the government
must stand still. He went over much of the ground which
he had trod the preceding day, relative to the Eastern
States having been so guarded in what they had conceded
to gain the regulation of our commerce, which threw into
their hands the carrying trade, and put it in their power to
lay us under payment of whatever freightage they thought
proper to impose. It was their interest to do so, and no
person could doubt but they would promote it by every
means in their power. He wished our delegates had sufficiently attended to this point in the Convention—had been
more attentive to this object, and taken care to have it
expressed, in this Constitution, that all our ports were
open to all nations; instead of putting us in the power of a
set of men who may fritter away the value of our produce
to a little or nothing, by compelling payment of exorbitant
freightage. Neither did he believe it was in the power of
the Eastern States to furnish a sufficient number of ships to
carry our produce. It was, indeed, a general way of talking,
that the Eastern States had a great number of seamen, a
vast number of ships; but where were they? Why did they
not come here now, when ships are greatly wanted? He
should always wish to give them a preference, and so, no
doubt, would many other gentlemen; and yet very few
ships come here from the Eastern States. Another exceptionable point was, that we were to give up the power of
taxing ourselves. During our connection with Great
Britain, she left us the power of raising money in any way
most convenient: a certain sum was only required to de-

fray the public wants, but no mode of collecting it ever prescribed. In this new Constitution, every thing is transferred, not so much power being left us as Lord North offered to guaranty to us in his consiliatory plan. Look at the articles of union ratified between England and Scotland. How cautiously had the latter taken care of her interest in reserving all the forms of law—her representation in Parliament—the right of taxation—the management of her revenue—and all her local and municipal interests! Why take from us the right of paying our delegates, and pay them from the federal treasury? He remembered formerly what a flame was raised in Massachusetts, on account of Great Britain assuming the payment of salaries to judges and other state officers; and that this conduct was considered as originating in a design to destroy the independence of their government. Our local expenses had been nearly defrayed by our impost duty; but now that this was given away, and thrown into a general fund, for the use of all the states indiscriminately, we should be obliged to augment our taxes to carry on our local government, notwithstanding we were to pay a poll tax for our negroes. Paper money, too, was another article of restraint, and a popular point with many; but what evils had we ever experienced by issuing a little paper money to relieve ourselves from any exigency that pressed us? We had now a circulating medium which every body took. We used formerly to issue paper bills every year, and recall them every five, with great convenience and advantage. Had not paper money carried us triumphantly through the war, extricated us from difficulties generally supposed to be insurmountable, and fully established us in our independence? and now every thing is so changed that an entire stop must be put to any more paper emissions, however great our distress may be. It was true, no article of the Constitution declared there should not be jury trials in civil cases; yet this must be implied, because it stated that all crimes, except in cases of impeachment, shall be tried by a jury. But even if trials by jury were allowed, could any person rest satisfied with a mode of trial which prevents the parties from being obliged to bring a cause for discussion before a jury of men chosen from the vicinage, in a manner conformable to the present administration of justice, which had stood the test of time and experience, and ever been highly approved of? Mr. Lowndes expatiated some time on the nature of compacts, the sacred light in which they were held by all nations, and solemnly called on the house to consider whether it would not be better to add strength to the old Confederation, instead of hastily adopting another; asking whether a man could be looked on as wise, who, possessing a magnificent building, upon discovering a flaw, instead of repairing the injury, should pull it down, and build another. Indeed, he could not understand with what propriety the Convention proceeded to change the Confederation; for every person with whom he had conversed on this subject concurred in opinion that the sole object of appointing a convention was to inquire what alterations were necessary in the Confederation, in order that it might answer those salutary purposes for which it was originally intended.

He recommended that another convention should be called; and as the general sense of America appeared now to be known, every objection could be met on fair grounds, and adequate remedies applied where necessary. This mode of proceeding would conciliate all parties, because it was candid, and had a more obvious tendency to do away all inconveniences than the adoption of a government which perhaps might require the bayonet to enforce it; for it could not be expected that the people, who had disregarded the requisitions of Congress, though expressed in language the most elegant and forcible that he ever remembered to have read, would be more obedient to the government until an irresistible force compelled them to be so. Mr. Lowndes concluded a long speech with a glowing eulogy on the old Confederation, and challenged his opponents, whilst one state objected, to get over that section which said, "The Articles of this Confederation shall be inviolably observed in every state, and the Union shall be perpetual; nor shall any alteration at any time hereafter be made in them, unless such alteration be agreed to in a Congress of the United States, and be afterwards confirmed by the legislature of every state." . . .

[James Lincoln]

Hon. JAMES LINCOLN, of *Ninety-six*, declared, that if ever any person rose in a public assembly with diffidence, he then did; if ever any person felt himself deeply interested in what he thought a good cause, and at the same time lamented the want of abilities to support it, it was he. On a question on which gentlemen, whose abilities would do honor to the senate of ancient Rome, had enlarged with so much eloquence and learning, who could venture without anxiety and diffidence? He had not the vanity to oppose his opinion to such men; he had not the vanity to suppose he could place this business in any new light; but the justice he owed to his constituents—the justice he owed to his own feelings, which would perhaps upbraid him hereafter, if he indulged himself so far as to give merely a silent vote on this great question—impelled him, reluctantly impelled him, to intrude himself on the house. He had, for some years past, turned his thoughts towards the politics of this country; he long since perceived that not only the federal but the state Constitution required much the hand of correction and revision. They were both formed in times of confusion and distress, and it was a matter of wonder they were so free from defects as we found them. That they were imperfect, no one would deny; and that something must be done to remedy those imperfections, was also evident; but great care should be taken that, by endeavoring to do some good, we should not do an infinite deal of mischief. He had listened with eager attention to all the arguments in favor of the Constitution; but he solemnly declared that the more he heard, the more he was persuaded of its evil tendency. What does this proposed Constitution do? It changes, totally changes, the form of your present government. From a well-digested, well-formed democratic, you are at once rushing into an aristocratic government. What have you been contending for these ten years past? Liberty! What is liberty? The power of governing yourselves. If you adopt this Constitution, have you this power? No: you give it into the hands of a set of men who live one thousand miles distant from you. Let the people but once trust their liberties out of their own hands, and what will be the consequence? First, a haughty, imperious aristocracy; and ultimately, a tyrannical monarchy. No people on earth are, at this day, so free as the people of America. All other nations are, more or less, in a state of slavery. They owe their constitutions partly to chance, and partly to the sword; but that of America is the offspring of their choice—the darling of their bosom: and was there ever an instance in the world that a people in this situation, possessing all that Heaven could give on earth, all that human wisdom and valor could procure—was there ever a people so situated, as calmly and deliberately to convene themselves together for the express purpose of considering whether they should give away or retain those inestimable blessings? In the name of God, were we a parcel of children, who would cry and quarrel for a hobby-horse, which, when we were once in possession of, we quarrel with and throw it away? It is said this Constitution is an experiment; but all regular-bred physicians are cautious of experiments. If the constitution be crazed a little, or somewhat feeble, is it therefore necessary to kill it in order to cure it? Surely not. There are many parts of this Constitution he objected to: some few of them had not been mentioned; he would therefore request some information thereon. The President holds his employment for four years; but he may hold it for fourteen times four years: in short, he may hold it so long that it will be impossible, without another revolution, to displace him. You do not put the same check on him that you do on your own state governor—a man born and bred among you; a man over whom you have a continual and watchful eye; a man who, from the very nature of his situation, it is almost impossible can do you any injury: this man, you say, shall not be elected for more than four years; and yet this mighty, this omnipotent governor-general may be elected for years and years.

He would be glad to know why, in this Constitution, there is a total silence with regard to the liberty of the press. Was it forgotten? Impossible! Then it must have been purposely omitted; and with what design, good or bad, he left the world to judge. The liberty of the press was the tyrant's scourge—it was the true friend and firmest supporter of civil liberty; therefore why pass it by in silence? He perceived that not till almost the very end of the Constitution was there any provision made for the nature or form of government we were to live under: he contended it should have been the very first article; it should have been, as it were, the groundwork or founda-

tion on which it should have been built. But how is it? At
the very end of the Constitution, there is a clause which
says,— "The Congress of the United States shall guaranty
to each state a republican form of government." But pray,
who are the United States?—A President and four or five
senators? Pray, sir, what security have we for a republican
form of government, when it depends on the mere will and
pleasure of a few men, who, with an army, navy, and rich
treasury at their back, may change and alter it as they
please? It may be said they will be sworn. Sir, the king of
Great Britain, at his coronation, swore to govern his subjects with justice and mercy. We were then his subjects,
and continued so for a long time after. He would be glad to
know how he observed his oath. If, then, the king of Great
Britain forswore himself, what security have we that a
future President and four or five senators—men like himself—will think more solemnly of so sacred an obligation
than he did?

Why was not this Constitution ushered in with the bill of
rights? Are the people to have no rights? Perhaps this
same President and Senate would, by and by, declare
them. He much feared they would. He concluded by re-
turning his hearty thanks to the gentleman who had so
nobly opposed this Constitution: it was supporting the
cause of the people; and if ever any one deserved the
title of man of the people, he, on this occasion, most certainly did.

[Patrick Dollard]

Mr. PATRICK DOLLARD, *of Prince Frederick's.* Mr. President, I rise, with the greatest diffidence, to speak on this
occasion, not only knowing myself unequal to the task, but
believing this to be the most important question that ever
the good people of this state were called together to deliberate upon. This Constitution has been ably supported,

and ingeniously glossed over by many able and respectable gentlemen in this house, whose reasoning, aided by the most accurate eloquence, might strike conviction even in the predetermined breast, had they a good cause to support. Conscious that they have not, and also conscious of my inability to point out the consequences of its defects, which have in some measure been defined by able gentlemen in this house, I shall therefore confine myself within narrow bounds: that is, concisely to make known the sense and language of my constituents. The people of Prince Frederick's Parish, whom I have the honor to represent, are a brave, honest, and industrious people. In the late bloody contest, they bore a conspicuous part, when they fought, bled, and conquered, in defence of their civil rights and privileges, which they expected to transmit untainted to their posterity. They are nearly all, to a man, opposed to this new Constitution, because, they say, they have omitted to insert a bill of rights therein, ascertaining and fundamentally establishing, the unalienable rights of men, without a full, free, and secure enjoyment of which there can be no liberty, and over which it is not necessary that a good government should have the control. They say that they are by no means against vesting Congress with ample and sufficient powers; but to make over to them, or any set of men, their birthright, comprised in Magna Charta, which this new Constitution absolutely does, they can never agree to. Notwithstanding this, they have the highest opinion of the virtues and abilities of the honorable gentlemen from this state, who represented us in the General Convention; and also a few other distinguished characters, whose names will be transmitted with honor to future ages; but I believe, at the same time, they are but mortal, and, therefore, liable to err; and as the virtue and abilities of those gentlemen will consequently recommend their being first employed in jointly conducting the reins

of this government, they are led to believe it will commence in a moderate aristocracy: but, that it will, in its
future operations, produce a monarchy, or a corrupt and
oppressive aristocracy, they have no manner of doubt. Lust
of dominion is natural in every soil, and the love of power
and superiority is as prevailing in the United States, at
present, as in any part of the earth; yet in this country,
depraved as it is, there still remains a strong regard for
liberty: an American bosom is apt to glow at the sound of
it, and the splendid merit of preserving that best gift of
God, which is mostly expelled from every country in Europe, might stimulate Indolence, and animate even Luxury
to consecrate herself at the altar of freedom.

My constituents are highly alarmed at the large and
rapid strides which this new government has taken towards despotism. They say it is big with political mischiefs, and pregnant with a greater variety of impending
woes to the good people of the Southern States, especially
South Carolina, than all the plagues supposed to issue
from the poisonous box of Pandora. They say it is particularly calculated for the meridian of despotic aristocracy;
that it evidently tends to promote the ambitious views of a
few able and designing men, and enslave the rest; that it
carries with it the appearance of an old phrase, formerly
made use of in despotic reigns, and especially by "Arch-
bishop Laud, in the reign of Charles I., that is, non-resistance." They say they will resist against it; that they will
not accept of it unless compelled by force of arms, which
this new Constitution plainly threatens; and then, they
say, your standing army, like Turkish janizaries enforcing
despotic laws, must ram it down their throats with the
points of bayonets. They warn the gentlemen of this Convention, as the guardians of their liberty, to beware how
they will be accessory to the disposal of, or rather sacrificing, their dear-bought rights and privileges. This is the

sense and language, Mr. President, of the people; and it is an old saying, and I believe a very true one, that the general voice of the people is the voice of God. The general voice of the people, to whom I am responsible, is against it. I shall never betray the trust resposed in me by them; therefore, shall give my hearty dissent.

10. *George Mason, Objections to the Proposed Federal Constitution*

Of all the Antifederalists who wrote and spoke against ratification of the Constitution, George Mason is the most interesting. Already experienced in the making of constitutions—he was the principal author of the Virginia Declaration of Rights of 1776—he was one of the first of the delegates to arrive for the Philadelphia convention in May of 1787 and was an active participant throughout its sessions. Until very near the end, he gave little indication that he was strongly opposed to the decisions made there, but was nevertheless one of the three members who refused to sign the Constitution when it was completed. The very brief essay printed herewith must have been written hastily, and very shortly after the close of the Convention, since it was sent to George Washington with a letter dated October 7, 1787. From one who knew so much about the work of the Convention and the ideas of its members, and one who had at one time been strongly in favor of some form of new national government, it would have been eminently satisfying to have a longer and more elaborate critique. Mason did make several speeches months later in the Virginia ratifying convention, but at that time and in those circumstances he appeared to be more polemical than in the first, early summary of his objections. An analysis and comparison of Mason's remarks in the Philadelphia convention, in these "Objections," and in the state convention makes an inter-

---

The Objections of the Hon. George Mason, to the Proposed Federal Constitution. Addressed to the Citizens of Virginia. Printed by Thomas Nicholas. From the text reprinted in Ford, *Pamphlets*, pp. 327–332.

esting study of a statesman operating on the same subject in three different contexts.

There is no declaration of rights: and the laws of the general government being paramount to the laws and constitutions of the several states, the declarations of rights, in the separate states, are no securiity. Nor are the people secured even in the enjoyment of the benefit of the common law, which stands here upon no other foundation than its having been adopted by the respective acts forming the constitutions of the several states.

In the House of Representatives there is not the substance, but the shadow only of representation; which can never produce proper information in the legislature, or inspire confidence in the people.—The laws will, therefore, be generally made by men little concerned in, and unacquainted with their effects and consequences.[*]

The Senate have the power of altering all money-bills, and of originating appropriations of money, and the salaries of the officers of their appointment, in conjunction with the President of the United States—Although they are not the representatives of the people, or amenable to them. These, with their other great powers, (viz. their powers in the appointment of ambassadors, and all public officers, in making treaties, and in trying all impeachments) their influence upon, and connection with, the supreme executive from these causes, their duration of office, and their being a constant existing body, almost continually sitting, joined with their being one complete branch of the legislature, will destroy any balance in the government, and enable them to accomplish what usurpations they please, upon the rights and liberties of the people.

---

[*]This objection has been in some degree lessened, by an amendment, often before refused, and at last made by an erasure, after the engrossment upon parchment, of the word forty, and inserting thirty, in the third clause of the second section of the first article.

The judiciary of the United States is so constructed and extended, as to absorb and destroy the judiciaries of the several states; thereby rendering laws as tedious, intricate, and expensive, and justice as unattainable by a great part of the community, as in England; and enabling the rich to oppress and ruin the poor.

The President of the United States has no constitutional council (a thing unknown in any safe and regular government.) he will therefore be unsupported by proper information and advice; and will generally be directed by minions and favorites—or he will become a tool to the Senate—or a council of state will grow out of the principal officers of the great departments—the worst and most dangerous of all ingredients for such a council, in a free country; for they may be induced to join in any dangerous or oppressive measures, to shelter themselves, and prevent an inquiry into their own misconduct in office. Whereas, had a constitutional council been formed (as was proposed) of six members, viz., two from the eastern, two from the middle, and two from the southern states, to be appointed by vote of the states in the House of Representatives, with the same duration and rotation of office as the Senate, the executive would always have had safe and proper information and advice; the president of such a council might have acted as Vice-President of the United States, *pro tempore*, upon any vacancy or disability of the chief magistrate; and long continued sessions of the Senate, would in a great measure have been prevented. From this fatal defect of a constitutional council, has arisen the improper power of the Senate, in the appointment of the public officers, and the alarming dependence and connexion between that branch of the legislature and the supreme executive. Hence, also, sprung that unnecessary officer, the Vice-President, who, for want of other employment, is made President of the Senate; thereby dangerously blending the executive and legislative powers; besides always giving to some one of the states an unnecessary and unjust pre-eminence over the others.

The President of the United States has the unrestrained power of granting pardon for treason; which may be sometimes exercised to screen from punishment those whom he had secretly instigated to commit the crime, and thereby prevent a discovery of his own guilt. By declaring all treaties supreme laws of the land, the executive and the Senate have, in many cases, an exclusive power of legislation, which might have been avoided, by proper distinctions with respect to treaties, and requiring the assent of the House of Representatives, where it could be done with safety.

By requiring only a majority to make all commercial and navigation laws, the five southern states (whose produce and circumstances are totally different from those of the eight northern and eastern states) will be ruined: for such rigid and premature regulations may be made, as will enable the merchants of the northern and eastern states not only to demand an exorbitant freight, but to monopolize the purchase of the commodities, at their own price, for many years, to the great injury of the landed interest, and the impoverishment of the people: and the danger is the greater, as the gain on one side will be in proportion to the loss on the other. Whereas, requiring two-thirds of the members present in both houses, would have produced mutual moderation, promoted the general interest, and removed an insuperable objection to the adoption of the government.

Under their own construction of the general clause at the end of the enumerated powers, the Congress may grant monopolies in trade and commerce, constitute new crimes, inflict unusual and severe punishments, and extend their power as far as they shall think proper; so that the state legislatures have no security for the powers now presumed to remain to them; or the people for their rights. There is no declaration of any kind for preserving the liberty of the press, the trial by jury in civil cases, nor against the danger of standing armies in time of peace.

The state legislatures are restrained from laying export duties on their own produce—the general legislature is restrained from prohibiting the further importation of slaves for twenty odd years, though such importations render the United States weaker, more vulnerable, and less capable of defence. Both the general legislature, and the state legislatures are expressly prohibited making *ex post facto* laws, though there never was, nor can be, a legislature, but must and will make such laws, when necessity and the public safety require them, which will hereafter be a breach of all the constitutions in the union, and afford precedents for other innovations.

This government will commence in a moderate aristocracy; it is at present impossible to foresee whether it will, in its operation, produce a monarchy, or a corrupt oppressive aristocracy; it will most probably vibrate some years between the two, and then terminate in the one or the other.

11. Richard Henry Lee, Letters from the Federal Farmer

These five letters by one of the leading Antifederalists in Virginia were written within a month after the end of the Philadelphia Convention, and being widely circulated, were influential in helping to articulate reasons for opposition to the Constitution. Though somewhat rambling and discursive, less incisive and more moderate than some of the later Antifederalist literature, Lee's commentaries reflect a thoughtful, analytical approach to the subject under debate. They also reveal a very perceptive observer of political polemics, and a superb master of the same. Lee notes the purpose and practice of reformers who describe the times and conditions they would reform in the language of exaggeration—clearly a reference to the Federalist tactics being used in 1787–1788. Lee's own polemical style was more subtle. He identifies the proposed new plan with "the young visionary man, and the consolidating aristocracy," and contrasts the "uneasy and fickle" (those ready to accept the new plan) with the "enlightened and substantial" (those ready to lean to the "Federal Farmer"). For an example of extremely skillful and subtle political propaganda, Lee's *Letters* are difficult to beat. Lee, a prominent Virginia statesman, had been selected as a delegate to the Federal Convention, but had declined to serve. The first three letters are reprinted here.

LETTER I.

[October 8th, 1787]

DEAR SIR,

My letters to you last winter, on the subject of a well balanced national government for the United States, were the result of a free enquiry; when I passed from that subject to

enquiries relative to our commerce, revenues, past administration, &c. I anticipated the anxieties I feel, on carefully
examining the plan of government proposed by the convention. It appears to be a plan retaining some federal
features; but to be the first important step, and to aim
strongly at one consolidated government of the United
States. It leaves the powers of government, and the representation of the people, so unnaturally divided between
the general and state governments, that the operations of
our system must be very uncertain. My uniform federal
attachments, and the interest I have in the protection of
property, and a steady execution of the laws, will convince
you, that, if I am under any bias at all, it is in favor of any
general system which shall promise those advantages. The
instability of our laws increases my wishes for firm and
steady government; but then, I can consent to no government, which, in my opinion, is not calculated equally to
preserve the rights of all orders of men in the community.
My object has been to join with those who have endeavoured to supply the defects in the forms of our governments by a steady and proper administration of them.
Though I have long apprehended that fraudalent debtors,
and embarrassed men, on the one hand, and men, on the
other, unfriendly to republican equality, would produce an
uneasiness among the people, and prepare the way, not for
cool and deliberate reforms in the governments, but for
changes calculated to promote the interests of particular
orders of men. Acquit me, sir, of any agency in the formation of the new system; I shall be satisfied with seeing, if it
shall be adopted with a prudent administration. Indeed I

"Observations leading to a fair examination of the system of government,
proposed by the late Convention; and to several essential and necessary
alterations in it." *In a number of Letters from the Federal Farmer to the
Republican*. Printed in New York by Thomas Greenleaf, 1787. From the
text as reprinted in Ford, *Pamphlets*, pp. 277–309.

am so much convinced of the truth of Pope's maxim, that "That which is best administered is best," that I am much inclined to subscribe to it from experience. I am not disposed to unreasonably contend about forms. I know our situation is critical, and it behoves us to make the best of it. A federal government of some sort is necessary. We have suffered the present to languish; and whether the confederation was capable or not originally of answering any valuable purposes, it is now but of little importance. I will pass by the men, and states, who have been particularly instrumental in preparing the way for a change, and perhaps, for governments not very favourable to the people at large. A constitution is now presented which we may reject, or which we may accept with or without amendments, and to which point we ought to direct our exertions is the question. To determine this question with propriety; we must attentively examine the system itself, and the probable consequences of either step. This I shall endeavour to do, so far as I am able, with candor and fairness; and leave you to decide upon the propriety of my opinions, the weight of my reasons, and how far my conclusions are well drawn. Whatever may be the conduct of others, on the present occasion, I do not mean hastily and positively to decide on the merits of the constitution proposed. I shall be open to conviction and always disposed to adopt that which, all things considered, shall appear to me to be most for the happiness of the community. It must be granted, that if men hastily and blindly adopt a system of government, they will as hastily and as blindly be led to alter or abolish it; and changes must ensue, one after another, till the peaceable and better part of the community will grow weary with changes, tumults and disorders, and be disposed to accept any government however despotic, that shall promise stability and firmness.

The first principal question that occurs, is, Whether,

considering our situation, we ought to precipitate the adoption of the proposed constitution? If we remain cool and temperate, we are in no immediate danger of any commotions; we are in a state of perfect peace, and in no danger of invasions; the state governments are in the full exercise of their powers; and our governments answer all present exigencies, except the regulation of trade, securing credit, in some cases, and providing for the interest, in some instances, of the public debts; and whether we adopt a change three or nine months hence, can make but little odds with the private circumstances of individuals; their happiness and prosperity, after all, depend principally upon their own exertions. We are hardly recovered from a long and distressing war: The farmers, fishmen, &c. have not fully repaired the waste made by it. Industry and frugality are again assuming their proper station. Private debts are lessened, and public debts incurred by the war have been, by various ways, diminished; and the public lands have now become a productive source for diminishing them much more. I know uneasy men, who with very much to precipitate, do not admit all these facts; but they are facts well known to all men who are thoroughly informed in the affairs of this country. It must, however, be admitted, that our federal system is defective, and that some of the state governments are not well administered; but, then, we impute to the defects in our governments many evils and embarrassments which are most clearly the result of the late war. We must allow men to conduct on the present occasion, as on all similar ones. They will urge a thousand pretences to answer their purposes on both sides. When we want a man to change his condition, we describe it as wretched, miserable, and despised; and draw a pleasing picture of that which we would have him assume. And when we wish the contrary, we reverse our descriptions. Whenever a clamor is raised, and idle men get to work, it is highly necessary to examine facts carefully, and without unreasonably suspecting men of falshood, to examine, and enquire attentively, under what impressions they act. It is too often the case in political concerns that men state facts not as they are, but as they wish them to be; and almost every man, by calling to mind past scenes, will find this to be true.

Nothing but the passions of ambitious, impatient, or disorderly men, I conceive, will plunge us into commotions, if time should be taken fully to examine and consider the system proposed. Men who feel easy in their circumstances, and such as are not sanguine in their expectations relative to the consequences of the proposed change, will remain quiet under the existing governments. Many commercial and monied men, who are uneasy, not without just cause, ought to be respected; and by no means, unreasonably disappointed in their expectations and hopes; but as to those who expect employments under the new constitution; as to those weak and ardent men who always expect to be gainers by revolutions, and whose lot it generally is to get out of one difficulty into another, they are very little to be regarded; and as to those who designedly avail themselves of this weakness and ardor, they are to be despised. It is natural for men, who wish to hasten the adoption of a measure, to tell us, now is the crisis—now is the critical moment which must be seized or all will be lost; and to shut the door against free enquiry, whenever conscious the thing presented has defects in it, which time and investigation will probably discover. This has been the custom of tyrants, and their dependants in all ages. If it is true, what has been so often said, that the people of this country cannot change their condition for the worse, I presume it still behoves them to endeavour deliberately to change it for the better. The fickle and ardent, in any community are the proper tools for establishing despotic government. But it is deliberate and thinking men, who must establish and secure governments on free principles. Before they decide on the plan proposed, they will enquire whether it will probably be a blessing or a curse to this people.

The present moment discovers a new face in our affairs. Our object has been all along, to reform our federal system, and to strengthen our governments—to establish peace, order and justice in the community—but a new object now presents. The plan of government now proposed is evidently calculated totally to change, in time, our condition as a people. Instead of being thirteen republics, under a federal head, it is clearly designed to make us one consolidated government. Of this, I think I shall fully convince you, in my following letters on this subject. This consolidation of the states has been the object of several men in this country for some time past. Whether such a change can ever be effected, in any manner; whether it can be effected without convulsions and civil wars; whether such a change will not totally destroy the liberties of this country—time only can determine.

To have a just idea of the government before us, and to shew that a consolidated one is the object in view, it is necessary not only to examine the plan, but also its history, and the politics of its particular friends.

The confederation was formed when great confidence was placed in the voluntary exertions of individuals, and of the respective states; and the framers of it, to guard against usurpation, so limited, and checked the powers, that, in many respectts, they are inadequate to the exigencies of the union. We find, therefore, members of congress urging alterations in the federal system almost as soon as it was adopted. It was early proposed to vest congress with powers to levy an impost, to regulate trade, &c. but such was known to be the caution of the states in parting with power, that the vestment even of these, was proposed to be under several checks and limitations. During the war, the general confusion, and the introduction of paper money, infused in the minds of people vague ideas respecting government and credit. We expected too much from the return of peace, and of course we have been disappointed. Our governments have been new and unsettled; and several legislatures, by making tender, suspension, and paper money laws, have given just cause of uneasiness to creditors. By these and other causes, several orders of men in the community have been prepared, by degrees, for a change of government; and this very abuse of power in the legislatures, which in some cases has been charged upon the democratic part of the community, has furnished aristocratical men with those very weapons, and those very means, with which, in great measure, they are rapidly effecting their favourite object. And should an oppressive government be the consequence of the proposed change, prosperity may reproach not only a few overbearing, unprincipled men, but those parties in the states which have misused their powers.

The conduct of several legislatures, touching paper money, and tender laws, has prepared many honest men for changes in government, which otherwise they would not have thought of—when by the evils, on the one hand, and by the secret instigations of artful men, on the other, the minds of men were become sufficiently uneasy, a bold step was taken, which is usually followed by a revolution, or a civil war. A general convention for mere commercial purposes was moved for—the authors of this measure saw that the people's attention was turned solely to the amendment of the federal system; and that, had the idea of a total change been started, probably no state would have appointed members to the convention. The idea of destroying ultimately, the state government, and forming one consolidated system, could not have been admitted—a convention, therefore, merely for vesting in congress power to regulate trade was proposed. This was pleasing to the commercial towns; and the landed people had little or no concern about it. September, 1786, a few men from the middle states met at Annapolis, and hastily proposed a convention to be held in May, 1787, for the purpose, generally, of amending the confederation—this was done before the delegates of Massachusetts, and of the other states arrived—still not a word was said about destroying the old constitution, and making a new one—The states still unsuspecting, and not aware that they were passing the Rubicon, appointed members to the new convention, for the sole and express purpose of revising and amending the confederation—and, probably, not one man in ten thousand in the United States, till within these ten or twelve days, had an idea that the old ship was to be destroyed, and he put to the alternative of embarking in the new ship presented, or being left in danger of sinking—The States, I believe, universally supposed the convention would report alterations in the confederation, which would pass an examination in congress, and after being agreed to there, would be confirmed by all the legislatures, or be rejected. Virginia made a very respectable appointment, and placed at the head of it the first man in America. In this appointment there was a mixture of political characters; but Pennsylvania appointed principally those men who are esteemed aristocratical. Here the favourite moment for changing the government was evidently discerned by a few men, who seized it with address. Ten other states appointed, and tho' they chose men principally connected with commerce and the judicial department yet they appointed many good republican characters—had they all attended we should now see, I am persuaded, a better system presented. The non-attendance of eight or nine men, who were appointed members of the convention, I shall ever consider as a very fortunate event to the United States.——Had they attended, I am pretty clear that the result of the convention would not have had that strong tendency to aristocracy now discernable in every part of the plan. There would not have been so great an accumulation of powers, especially as to the internal police of this country in a few hands as the constitution reported proposes to vest in them—the young visionary men, and the consolidating aristocracy, would have been more restrained than they have been. Eleven states met in the convention, and after four months close attention presented the new constitution, to be adopted or rejected by the people. The uneasy and fickle part of the community may be prepared to receive any form of government; but I presume the enlightened and substantial part will give any constitution presented for their adoption a candid and thorough examination; and silence those designing or empty men, who weakly and rashly attempt to precipitate the adoption of a system of so much importance —We shall view the convention with proper respect— and, at the same time, that we reflect there were men of abilities and integrity in it, we must recollect how disproportionately the democratic and aristocratic parts of the community were represented——Perhaps the judicious friends and opposers of the new consituation will agree, that it is best to let it reply solely on its own merits, or be condemned for its own defects.

In the first place, I shall premise, that the plan proposed is a plan of accommodation—and that is in this way only, and by giving up a part of our opinions, that we can ever expect to obtain a government founded in freedom and compact. This circumstance candid men will always keep in view, in the discussion of this subject.

The plan proposed appears to be partly federal, but

Consolidated government [handwritten margin note]

principally however, calculated ultimately to make the states one consolidated government.

The first interesting question, therefore suggested, is how far the states can be consolidated into one entire government on free principles. In considering this question extensive objects are to be taken into view, and important changes in the forms of government to be carefully attended to in all their consequences. The happiness of the people at large must be the great object with every honest statesman, and he will direct every movement to this point. If we are so situated as a people, as not to be able to enjoy equal happiness and advantages under one government, the consolidation of the states cannot be admitted.

There are three different forms of free government under which the United States may exist as one nation; and now is, perhaps, the time to determine to which we will direct our views. 1. Distinct republics connected under a federal head. In this case the respective state governments must be the principal guardians of the peoples rights, and exclusively regulate their internal police; in them must rest the balance of government. The congress of the states, or federal head, must consist of delegates amenable to, and removable by the respective states: This congress must have general directing powers; powers to require men and monies of the states; to make treaties; peace and war; to direct the operations of armies, &c. Under this federal modification of government, the powers of congress would be rather advisory or recommendatory than coercive. 2. We may do away the federal state governments, and form or consolidate all the states into one entire government, with one executive, one judiciary, and one legislature, consisting of senators and representatives collected from all parts of the union: In this case there would be a compleat consolidation of the states. 3. We may consolidate the states as to certain national objects, and leave them severally distinct independent republics, as to internal police generally. Let the general government consist of an executive, a judiciary, and balanced legislature, and its powers extend exclusively to all foreign concerns, causes arising on the seas to commerce, imports, armies, navies, Indian affairs, peace and war, and to a few internal concerns of the community; to the coin, post-offices, weights and measures, a general plan for the militia, to naturalization, *and, perhaps to bankruptcies,* leaving the internal police of the community, in other respects, exclusively to the state governments; as the administration of justice in all causes arising internally, the laying and collecting of internal taxes, and the forming of the militia according to a general plan prescribed. In this case there would be a compleat consolidation, *quoad* certain objects only.

Touching the first, or federal plan, I do not think much can be said in its favor: The sovereignity of the nation, without coercive and efficient powers to collect the strength of it, cannot always be depended on to answer the purposes of government; and in a congress of representatives of foreign states, there must necessarily be an unreasonable mixture of powers in the same hands.

As to the second, or compleat consolidating plan, it deserves to be carefully considered at this time by every American: If it be impracticable, it is a fatal error to model our governments, directing our views ultimately to it.

The third plan, or partial consolidation, is, in my opinion, the only one that can secure the freedom and happiness of this people. I once had some general ideas that the second plan was practicable, but from long attention, and the proceedings of the convention, I am fully satisfied, that this third plan is the only one we can with safety and propriety proceed upon. Making this the standard to point out, with candor and fairness, the parts of the new constitution which appear to be improper, is my object. The convention appears to have proposed the partial consolidation evidently with a view to collect all powers ultimately, in the United States into one entire government; and from its views in this respect, and from the tenacity of the small states to have an equal vote in the senate, probably originated the greatest defects in the proposed plan.

Independent of the opinions of many great authors, that a free elective government cannot be extended over large territories, a few reflections must evince, that one government and general legislation alone never can extend equal benefits to all parts of the United States: Different laws, customs, and opinions exist in the different states which by a uniform system of laws would be unreasonably invaded. The United States contain about a million of square miles, and in half a century will, probably, contain ten millions of people; and from the center to the extremes is about 800 miles.

Before we do away the state governments or adopt measures that will tend to abolish them, and to consolidate the states into one entire government several principles should be considered and facts ascertained:——These, and my examination into the essential parts of the proposed plan, I shall pursue in my next.

Your's, &c.

LETTER II.

[October 9, 1787]

DEAR SIR,

The essential parts of a free and good government are a

full and equal representation of the people in the legislature, and the jury trial of the vicinage in the administration
of justice—a full and equal representation, is that which
possesses the same interests, feelings, opinions, and views
the people themselves would were they all assembled—a
fair representation, therefore, should be so regulated, that
every order of men in the community, according to the
common course of elections, can have a share in it—in
order to allow professional men, merchants, traders, farmers, mechanics, &c. to bring a just proportion of their best
informed men respectively into the legislature, the representation must be considerably numerous—We have about
200 state senators in the United States. and a less number
than that of federal representatives cannot, clearly, be a
full representation of this people, in the affairs of internal
taxation and police, were there but one legislature for the
whole union. The representation cannot be equal, or the
situation of the people proper for one government only—if
the extreme parts of the society cannot be represented as
fully as the central—It is apparently impracticable that this
should be the case in this extensive country——it would be
impossible to collect a representation of the parts of the
country five, six, and seven hundred miles from the seat of
government.

Under one general government alone, there could be
but one judiciary, one supreme and a proper number of
inferior courts. I think it would be totally impracticable in
this case to preserve a due administration of justice, and
the real benefits of the jury trial of the vicinage——there
are now supreme courts in each state in the union, and a
great number of county and other courts subordinate to
each supreme court——most of these supreme and inferior
courts are itinerant, and hold their sessions in different
parts every year of their respective states, counties and
districts—with all these moving courts, our citizens, from

the vast extent of the country, must travel very considerable distances from home to find the place where justice is administered. I am not for bringing justice so near to individuals as to afford them any temptation to engage in law suits; though I think it one of the greatest benefits in a good government, that each citizen should find a court of justice within a reasonable distance, perhaps, within a day's travel of his home; so that, without great inconveniences and enormous expense, he may have the advantages of his witnesses and jury—it would be impracticable to derive these advantages from one judiciary—the one supreme court at most could only set in the centre of the union, and move once a year into the centre of the eastern and southern extremes of it—and, in this case, each citizen, on an average, would travel 150 or 200 miles to find this court——that, however, inferior courts might be properly placed in the different counties, and districts of the union, the appellate jurisdiction would be intolerable and expensive.

If it were possible to consolidate the states, and preserve the features of a free government, still it is evident that the middle states, the parts of the union, about the seat of government, would enjoy great advantages, while the remote states would experience the many inconveniences of remote provinces. Wealth, offices, and the benefits of government would collect in the centre: and the extreme states; and their principal towns, become much less important.

There are other considerations which tend to prove that the idea of one consolidated whole, on free principles, is ill-founded——the laws of a free government rest on the confidence of the people, and operate gently—and never can extend the influence very far—if they are executed on free principles, about the centre, where the benefits of the government induce the people to support it voluntarily; yet they must be executed on the principles of fear and force in the extremes——This has been the case with every extensive republic of which we have any accurate account.

There are certain unalienable and fundamental rights, which in forming the social compact, ought to be explicitly ascertained and fixed—a free and enlightened people, in forming this compact, will not resign all their rights to those who govern, and they will fix limits to their legislators and rulers, which will soon be plainly seen by those who are governed, as well as by those who govern: and the latter will know they cannot be passed unperceived by the former, and without giving a general alarm——These rights should be made the basis of every constitution; and if a people be so situated, or have such different opinions that they cannot agree in ascertaining and fixing them, it is a very strong argument against their attempting to form one entire society, to live under one system of laws only.——I confess, I never thought the people of these states differed essentially in these respects; they having derived all these rights from one common source, the British systems; and having in the formation of their state constitutions, discovered that their ideas relative to these rights are very similar. However, it is now said that the states differ so essentially in these respects, and even in the important article of the trial by jury, that when assembled in convention, they can agree to no words by which to establish that trial, or by which to ascertain and establish many other of these rights, as fundamental articles in the social compact. If so, we proceed to consolidate the states on no solid basis whatever.

But I do not pay much regard to the reasons given for not bottoming the new constitution on a better bill of rights. I still believe a complete federal bill of rights to be very practicable. Nevertheless I acknowledge the proceedings of the convention furnish my mind with many new and strong reasons, against a complete consolidation of the states. They tend to convince me, that it cannot be carried with propriety very far—that the convention have gone much farther in one respect than they found it practicable to go in another; that is, they propose to lodge in the general government very extensive powers—*powers* nearly, if not altogether, complete and unlimited, over the purse and the sword. But, in its organization, they furnish the strongest proof that the proper limbs, or parts of a government, to support and execute those powers on proper principles (or in which they can be safely lodged) cannot be formed. These powers must be lodged somewhere in every society; but then they should be lodged where the strength and guardians of the people are collected. They can be wielded, or safely used, in a free country only by an able executive and judiciary, a respectable senate, and a secure, full, and equal representation of the people. I think the principles I have premised or brought into view, are well founded—I think they will not be denied by any fair reasoner. It is in connection with these, and other solid principles, we are to examine the constitution. It is not a few democratic phrases, or a few well formed features, that will prove its merits; or a few small omissions that will produce its rejection among men of sense; they will enquire what are the essential powers in a community, and what are nominal ones; where and how the essential powers shall be lodged to secure government, and to secure true liberty.

In examining the proposed constitution carefully, we must clearly perceive an unnatural separation of these powers from the substantial representation of the people. The state government will exist, with all their governors, senators, representatives, officers and expences; in these will be nineteen twentieths of the representatives of the people; they will have a near connection, and their members an immediate intercourse with the people; and the probability is, that the state governments will possess the confidence of the people, and be considered generally as their immediate guardians.

The general government will consist of a new species of executive, a small senate, and a very small house of representatives. As many citizens will be more than three hundred miles from the seat of this government as will be nearer to it, its judges and officers cannot be very numerous, without making our governments very expensive. Thus will stand the state and the general governments, should the constitution be adopted without any alterations in their organization; but as to powers, the general government will possess all essential ones, at least on paper, and those of the states a mere shadow of power. And therefore, unless the people shall make some great exertions to restore to the state governments their powers in matters of internal police; as the powers to lay and collect, exclusively, internal taxes, to govern the militia, and to hold the decisions of their own judicial courts upon their own laws final, the balance cannot possibly continue long; but the state governments must be annihilated, or continue to exist for no purpose.

It is however to be observed, that many of the essential powers given the national government are not exclusively given; and the general government may have prudence enough to forbear the exercise of those which may still be exercised by the respective states. But this cannot justify the impropriety of giving powers, the exercise of which prudent men will not attempt, and imprudent men will, or probably can, exercise only in a manner destructive of free government. The general government, organized as it is, may be adequate to many valuable objects, and be able to carry its laws into execution on proper principles in several cases; but I think its warmest friends will not contend, that it can carry all the powers proposed to be lodged in it into effect, without calling to its aid a military force, which must very soon destroy all elective governments in the country, produce anarchy, or establish despotism. Though we cannot have now a complete idea of what will be the operations of the proposed system, we may, allowing things to have their common course, have a very tolerable one. The powers lodged in the general government, if exercised by it, must intimately effect the internal police of the states, as well as external concerns; and there is no reason to expect the numerous state governments, and their connections, will be very friendly to the execution of federal laws in those internal affairs, which hitherto have been under their own immediate management. There is more reason to believe, that the general government, far removed from the people, and none of its members elected oftener than once in two years, will be forgot or neglected, and its laws in many cases disregarded, unless a multitude of officers and military force be continually kept in view, and employed to enforce the execution of the laws, and to make the government feared and respected. No position can be truer than this. That in this country either neglected laws, or a military execution of them, must lead to a revolution, and to the destruction of freedom. Neglected laws must first lead to anarchy and confusion; and a military execution of laws is only a shorter way to the same point—despotic government.

Your's, &c.

LETTER III.

[October 10th, 1787.]

DEAR SIR,

The great object of a free people must be so to form their government and laws, and so to administer them, as to create a confidence in, and respect for the laws; and thereby induce the sensible and virtuous part of the community to declare in favor of the laws, and to support them without an expensive military force. I wish, though I confess I have not much hope, that this may be the case with the laws of congress under the new constitution. I am fully convinced that we must organize the national government on different principals, and make the parts of it more efficient, and secure in it more effectually the different interests in the community; or else leave in the state governments some powers proposed to be lodged in it—at least till such an organization shall be found to be practicable. Not sanguine in my expectations of a good federal administration, and satisfied, as I am, of the impracticability of consolidating the states, and at the same time of preserving the rights of the people at large, I believe we ought still to leave some of those powers in the state governments, in which the people, in fact, will still be represented—to define some other powers proposed to be vested in the general government, more carefully, and to establish a few principles to secure a proper exercise of the powers given it. It is not my object to multiply objections, or to contend about inconsiderable powers or amendments. I wish the system adopted with a few alterations; but those, in my mind, are essential ones; if adopted without, every good citizen will acquiesce, though I shall consider the duration of our governments, and the liberties of this people, very much dependant on the administration of the general government. A wise and honest administration, may make the people happy under any government; but necessity only can justify even our leaving open avenues to the abuse of power, by wicked, unthinking, or ambitious men, I will examine, first, the organization of the proposed government, in order to judge; 2d, with propriety, what powers are improperly, at least prematurely lodged in it. I shall examine, 3d, the undefined powers; and 4th, those powers, the exercise of which is not secured on safe and proper ground.

First. As to the organization——the house of representatives, the democrative branch, as it is called, is to consist of 65 members: that is, about one representative for fifty thousand inhabitants, to be chosen biennially——the federal legislature may increase this number to one for each thirty thousand inhabitants, abating fractional numbers in each state.——Thirty-three representatives will make a quorum for doing business, and a majority of those present determine the sense of the house.——I have no idea that the interests, feelings, and opinions of three or four millions of people, especially touching internal taxation, can be collected in such a house.——In the nature of things, nine times in ten, men of the elevated classes in the community only can be chosen——Connecticut, for instance, will have five representatives——not one man in a hundred of those who form the democrative branch in the state legislature, will, on a fair computation, be one of the five.—The people of this country, in one sense, may all be democratic; but if we make the proper distinction between the few men of wealth and abilities, and consider them, as we ought, as the natural aristocracy of the country, and the great body of the people, the middle and lower classes, as the democracy, this federal representative branch will have but very little democracy in it, even this small representation is not secured on proper principles.——The branches of the legislature are essential parts of the fundamental compact, and ought to be so fixed by the people, that the legislature cannot alter itself by modifying the elections of its own members. This, by a part of Art. 1, Sect. 4, the general legislature may do, it may evidently so regulate elections as to secure the choice of any particular description of men.——It may make the whole state one district—make the capital, or any places in the state, the place or places of election—it may declare that the five men (or whatever the number may be the state may chuse) who shall have the most votes shall be considered as chosen.——In this case it is easy to perceive how the people who live scattered in the inland towns will bestow their votes on different men—and how a few men in a city, in any order or profession, may unite and place any five men they please highest among those that may be voted for—— and all this may be done constitutionally, and by those silent operations, which are not immediately perceived by the people in general.——I know it is urged, that the general legislature will be disposed to regulate elections on fair and just principles:——This may be true—good men will generally govern well with almost any constitution: but why in laying the foundation of the social system, need we unnecessarily leave a door open to improper regulations?—This is a very general and unguarded clause, and many evils may flow from that part which authorises the congress to regulate elections.——Were it omitted, the regulations of elections would be solely in the respective states, where the people are substantially represented; and where the elections ought to be regulated, otherwise to secure a representation from all parts of the community, in making the constitutions, we ought to provide for dividing each state into a proper number of districts, and for confining the electors in each district to the choice of some men, who shall have a permanent interest and residence in it; and also for this essential object, that the representative elected shall have a majority of the votes of those electors who shall attend and give their votes.

In considering the practicability of having a full and equal representation of the people from all parts of the union, not only distances and different opinions, customs and views, common in extensive tracts of country, are to be taken into view, but many differences peculiar to Eastern, Middle, and Southern States. These differences are not so perceivable among the members of congress, and men of general information in the states, as among the men who would properly form the democratic branch. The Eastern states are very democratic, and composed chiefly of moderate freeholders; they have but few rich men and no slaves; the Southern states are composed chiefly of rich planters and slaves; they have but few moderate freeholders, and the prevailing influence, in them is generally a dissipated aristocracy: The Middle states partake partly of the Eastern and partly of the Southern character.

Perhaps, nothing could be more disjointed, unwieldy and incompetent to doing business with harmony and dispatch, than a federal house of representatives properly numerous for the great objects of taxation, &c. collected from the federal states; whether such men would ever act in concert; whether they would not worry along a few years, and then be the means of separating the parts of the union, is very problematical?——View this system in whatever form we can, propriety brings us still to this point, a federal government possessed of general and complete powers, as to those national objects which cannot well come under the cognizance of the internal laws of the respective states, and this federal government, accordingly, consisting of branches not very numerous.

The house of representatives is on the plan of consolidation, but the senate is entirely on the federal plan; and Delaware will have as much constitutional influence in the senate, as the largest state in the union: and in this senate are lodged legislative, executive and judicial powers: Ten states in this union urge that they are small states, nine of which were present in the convention.—They were interested in collecting large powers into the hands of the senate, in which each state still will have its equal share of power. I suppose it was impracticable for the three large states, as they were called, to get the senate formed on any other principles: But this only proves, that we cannot form one general government on equal and just principles—and proves, that we ought not to lodge in it such extensive powers before we are convinced of the practicability of organizing it on just and equal principles. The senate will consist of two members from each state, chosen by the state legislatures, every sixth year. The clause referred to, respecting the elections of representatives, empowers the general legislature to regulate the elections of senators also, "except as to the places of chusing senators."—There is, therefore, but little more security in the elections than in those of representatives: Fourteen senators make a quorum for business, and a majority of the senators present give the vote of the senate, except in giving judgment upon an impeachment, or in making treaties, or in expelling a member, when two-thirds of the senators present must agree—The members of the legislature are not excluded from being elected to any military offices, or any civil offices, except those created, or the emoluments of which shall be increased by themselves: two-thirds of the members present, of either house, may expel a member at pleasure. The senate is an independant branch of the legislature, a court for trying impeachments, and also a part of the executive, having a negative in the making of all treaties, and in appointing almost all officers.

The vice president is not a very important, if not an unnecessary part of the system—he may be a part of the senate at one period, and act as the supreme executive magistrate at another——The election of this officer, as well as of the president of the United States seems to be properly secured; but when we examine the powers of the president, and the forms of the executive, we shall perceive that the general government, in this part, will have a strong tendency to aristocracy, or the government of the few. The executive is, in fact, the president and senate in all transactions of any importance; the president is connected with, or tied to the senate; he may always act with the senate, but never can effectually counteract its views: The president can appoint no officer, civil or military, who shall not be agreeable to the senate; and the presumption is, that the will of so important a body will not be very easily controuled, and that it will exercise its powers with great address.

In the judicial department, powers ever kept distinct in well balanced governments, are no less improperly blended in the hands of the same men—in the judges of the supreme court is lodged the law, the equity and the fact. It is not necessary to pursue the minute organical parts of the general government proposed.—There were various interests in the convention, to be reconciled, especially of large and small states; of carrying and non-carrying states; and of states more and states less democratic—vast labour and attention were by the convention bestowed on the organization of the parts of the constitution offered; still it is acknowledged there are many things radically wrong in the essential parts of this constitution—but it is said that these are the result of our situation: On a full examination of the subject, I believe it; but what do the laborious inquiries and determination of the convention prove? If they prove any thing, they prove that we cannot consolidate the states on proper principles: The organization of the government presented proves, that we cannot form a general government in which all power can be safely lodged; and a little attention to the parts of the one proposed will make it appear very evident, that all the powers proposed to be lodged in it, will not be then well deposited, either for the purposes of government, or the preservation of liberty. I will suppose no abuse of power in those cases, in which the abuse of it is not well guarded against—I will suppose the words authorizing the general government to regulate the elections of its own members struck out of the plan, or free district elections, in each state, amply secured.—That the small representation provided for shall be as fair and equal as it is capable of being made—I will suppose the judicial department regulated on pure principles, by future laws, as far as it can be by the constitution, and consist with the situation of the country—still there will be an unreasonable accumulation of powers in the general government if all be granted, enumerated in the plan proposed. The plan does not present a well balanced government: The senatorial branch of the legislative and the executive are substantially united, and the president, or the state executive magistrate, may aid the senatorial interest when weakest, but never can effectually support the democratic, however it may be opposed;—the excellency, in my mind, of a well-balanced government is that it consists of distinct branches, each sufficiently strong and independant to keep its own station, and to aid either of the other branches which may occasionally want aid.

The convention found that any but a small house of representatives would be expensive, and that it would be impracticable to assemble a large number of representatives. Not only the determination of the convention in this case, but the situation of the states, proves the impracticability of collecting, in any one point, a proper representation.

The formation of the senate, and the smallness of the house, being, therefore, the result of our situation, and the actual state of things, the evils which may attend the exercise of many powers in this national government may be considered as without a remedy.

All officers are impeachable before the senate only—before the men by whom they are appointed, or who are consenting to the appointment of these officers. No judgment of conviction, on an impeachment, can be given unless two thirds of the senators agree. Under these circumstances the right of impeachment, in the house, can be of but little importance; the house cannot expect often to convict the offender; and, therefore, probably, will but seldom or never exercise the right. In addition to the insecurity and inconveniences attending this organization beforementioned, it may be observed, that it is extremely difficult to secure the people against the fatal effects of corruption and influence. The power of making any law will be in the president, eight senators, and seventeen representatives, relative to the important objects enumerated in the constitution. Where there is a small representation a sufficient number to carry any measure, may, with ease, be influenced by bribes, offices and civilities; they easily form private juntoes, and out-door meetings, agree on measures, and carry them by silent votes.

Impressed, as I am, with a sense of the difficulties there are in the way of forming the parts of a federal government on proper principles, and seeing a government so unsubstantially organized, after so arduous an attempt has been made, I am led to believe, that powers ought to be given to it with great care and caution.

In the second place it is necessary, therefore, to examine

the extent, and the probable operations of some of those extensive powers proposed to be vested in this government. These powers, legislative, executive, and judicial, respect internal as well as external objects. Those respecting external objects, as all foreign concerns, commerce, imposts, all causes arising on the seas, peace and war, and Indian affairs, can be lodged no where else, with any propriety, but in this government. Many powers that respect internal objects ought clearly to be lodged in it; as those to regulate trade between the states, weights and measures, the coin or current monies, post-offices, naturalization, &c. These powers may be exercised without essentially effecting the internal police of the respective states: But powers to lay and collect internal taxes, to form the militia, to make bankrupt laws, and to decide on appeals, questions arising on the internal laws of the respective states, are of a very serious nature, and carry with them almost all other powers. These taken in connection with the others, and powers to raise armies and build navies, proposed to be lodged in this government, appear to me to comprehend all the essential powers in this community, and those which will be left to the states will be of no great importance.

A power to lay and collect taxes at discretion, is, in itself, of very great importance. By means of taxes, the government may command the whole or any part of the subject's property. Taxes may be of various kinds; but there is a strong distinction between external and internal taxes. External taxes are import duties, which are laid on imported goods; they may usually be collected in a few seaport towns, and of a few individuals, though ultimately paid by the consumer; a few officers can collect them, and they can be carried no higher than trade will bear, or smuggling permit—that in the very nature of commerce, bounds are set to them. But internal taxes, as poll and land taxes, excises, duties on all written instruments, &c. may fix themselves on every person and species of property in the community; they may be carried to any lengths, and in proportion as they are extended, numerous officers must be employed to assess them, and to enforce the collection of them. In the United Netherlands the general government has compleat powers, as to external taxation; but as to internal taxes, it makes requisitions on the provinces. Internal taxation in this country is more important, as the country is so very extensive. As many assessors and collectors of federal taxes will be above three hundred miles from the seat of the federal government as will be less. Besides, to lay and collect taxes, in this extensive country, must require a great number of congressional ordinances, immediately operating upon the body of the people; these must continually interfere with the state laws, and thereby produce disorder and general dissatisfaction, till the one system of laws or the other, operating on the same subjects, shall be abolished. These ordinances alone, to say nothing of those respecting the milita, coin, commerce, federal judiciary, &c. &c. will probably soon defeat the operations of the state laws and governments.

Should the general government think it politic, as some administration (if not all) probably will, to look for a support in a system of influence, the government will take every occasion to multiply laws, and officers to execute them, considering these as so many necessary props for its own support. Should this system of policy be adopted, taxes more productive than the impost duties will, probably, be wanted to support the government, and to discharge foreign demands, without leaving any thing for the domestic creditors. The internal sources of taxation then must be called into operation, and internal tax laws and federal assessors and collectors spread over this immense country. All these circumstances considered, is it wise, prudent, or safe, to vest the powers of laying and collecting internal taxes in the general government, while imperfectly organized and inadequate; and to trust to amending it hereafter, and making it adequate to this purpose? It is not only unsafe but absurd to lodge power in a government before it is fitted to receive it? It is confessed that this power and representation ought to go together. Why give the power first? Why give the power to the few, who, when possessed of it, may have address enough to prevent the increase of representation? Why not keep the power, and, when necessary, amend the constitution, and add to its other parts this power, and a proper increase of representation at the same time? Then men who may want the power will be under strong inducements to let in the people, by their representatives, into the government, to hold their due proportion of this power. If a proper representation be impracticable, then we shall see this power resting in the states, where it at present ought to be, and not inconsiderately given up.

When I recollect how lately congress, conventions, legislatures, and people contended in the cause of liberty, and carefully weighed the importance of taxation, I can scarcely believe we are serious in proposing to vest the powers of laying and collecting internal taxes in a government so imperfectly organized for such purposes. Should the United States be taxed by a house of representatives of two hundred members, which would be about fifteen members for Connecticut, twenty-five for Massachusetts, &c. still the middle and lower classes of people could have no great share, in fact, in taxation. I am aware it is said, that the representation proposed by the new constitution is sufficiently numerous; it may be for many purposes; but to suppose that this branch is sufficiently numerous to guard the rights of the people in the administration of the government, in which the purse and sword is placed, seems to argue that we have forgot what the true meaning of representation is. I am sensible also, that it is said that congress will not attempt to lay and collect internal taxes; that it is necessary for them to have the power, though it cannot probably be exercised.——I admit that it is not probable that any prudent congress will attempt to lay and collect internal taxes, especially direct taxes: but this only proves, that the power would be improperly lodged in congress, and that it might be abused by imprudent and designing men.

I have heard several gentlemen, to get rid of objections to this part of the constitution, attempt to construe the powers relative to direct taxes, as those who object to it would have them; as to these, it is said, that congress will only have power to make requisitons, leaving it to the states to lay and collect them. I see but very little colour for this construction, and the attempt only proves that this part of the plan cannot be defended. By this plan there can be no doubt, but that the powers of congress will be complete as to all kinds of taxes whatever—Further, as to internal taxes, the state governments will have concurrent powers with the general government, and both may tax the same objects in the same year; and the objection that the general government may suspend a state tax, as a necessary measure for the promoting the collection of a federal tax, is not without foundation.——As the states owe large debts, and have large demands upon them individually, there clearly will be a propriety in leaving in their possession exclusively, some of the internal sources of taxation, at least until the federal representation shall be properly encreased: The power in the general government to lay and collect internal taxes, will render its powers respecting armies, navies and the militia, the more exceptionable. By the constitution it is proposed that congress shall have power "to raise and support armies, but no appropriation of money to that use shall be for a longer term than two years; to provide and maintain a navy; to provide for calling forth the militia to execute the laws of the union; suppress insurrections, and repel invasions: to provide for organizing, arming, and disciplining the militia;" reserving to the states the right to appoint the officers, and to train the militia according to the discipline prescribed by congress; congress will have unlimited power to raise armies, and to engage officers and men for any number of years; but a legislative act applying money for their support can have operation for no longer term than two years, and if a subsequent congress do not within the two years renew the appropriation, or further appropriate monies for the use of the army, the army will be left to take care of itself. When an army shall once be raised for a number of years, it is not probable that it will find much difficulty in getting congress to pass laws for applying monies to its support. I see so many men in America fond of a standing army, and especially among those who probably will have a large share in administering the federal system; it is very evident to me, that we shall have a large standing army as soon as the monies to support them can be possibly found. An army is not a very agreeable place of employment for the young gentlemen of many families. A power to raise armies must be lodged some where; still this will not justify the lodging this power in a bare majority of so few men without any checks; or in the government in which the great body of the people, in the nature of things, will be only nominally represented. In the state governments the great body

of the people, the yeomanry, &c. of the country, are represented: It is true they will chuse the members of congress,
and may now and then chuse a man of their own way of
thinking; but it is not impossible for forty, or thirty thousand people in this country, one time in ten to find a man
who can possess similar feelings, views, and interests with
themselves: Powers to lay and collect taxes and to raise
armies are of the greatest moment; for carrying them into
effect, laws need not be frequently made, and the yeomanry, &c. of the country ought substantially to have a
check upon the passing of these laws; this check ought to
be placed in the legislatures, or at least, in the few men
the common people of the country, will, probably, have in
congress, in the true sense of the word, "from among themselves." It is true, the yeomanry of the country possess the
lands, the weight of property, possess arms, and are too
strong a body of men to be openly offended—and, therefore, it is urged, they will take care of themselves, that
men who shall govern will not dare pay any disrespect to
their opinions. It is easily perceived, that if they have not
their proper negative upon passing laws in congress, or on
the passage of laws relative to taxes and armies, they may
in twenty or thirty years be by means inperceptible to
them, totally deprived of that boasted weight and strength:
This may be done in a great measure by congress, if disposed to do it, by modelling the militia. Should one fifth or
one eighth part of the men capable of bearing arms, be
made a select militia, as has been proposed, and those the
young and ardent part of the community, possessed of but
little or no property, and all the others put upon a plan that
will render them of no importance, the former will answer
all the purposes of an army, while the latter will be defenceless. The state must train the militia in such form and
according to such systems and rules as congress shall prescribe: and the only actual influence the respective states

will have respecting the militia will be in appointing the officers. I see no provision made for calling out the *posse comitatus* for executing the laws of the union, but provision is made for congress to call forth the militia for the execution of them—and the militia in general, or any select part of it, may be called out under military officers, instead of the sheriff to enforce an execution of federal laws, in the first instance, and thereby introduce an entire military execution of the laws. I know that powers to raise taxes, to regulate the military strength of the community on some uniform plan, to provide for its defence and internal order, and for duly executing the laws, must be lodged somewhere; but still we ought not so to lodge them, as evidently to give one-order of men in the community, undue advantages over others; or commit the many to the mercy, prudence, and moderation of the few. And so far as it may be necessary to lodge any of the peculiar powers in the general government, a more safe exercise of them ought to be secured, by requiring the consent of two-thirds or three-fourths of congress thereto—until the federal representation can be increased, so that the democratic members in congress may stand some tolerable chance of a reasonable negative, in behalf of the numerous, important, and democratic part of the community.

I am not sufficiently acquainted with the laws and internal police of all the states to discern fully, how general bankrupt laws, made by the union, would effect them, or promote the public good. I believe the property of debtors, in the several states, is held responsible for their debts in modes and forms very different. If uniform bankrupt laws can be made without producing real and substantial inconveniences, I wish them to be made by congress.

There are some powers proposed to be lodged in the general government in the judicial department, I think very unnecessarily, I mean powers respecting questions arising upon the internal laws of the respective states. It is proper the federal judiciary should have powers co-extensive with the federal legislature—that is, the power of deciding finally on the laws of the union. By Art. 3, Sec. 2. the powers of the federal judiciary are extended (among other things) to all cases between a state and citizens of another state—between citizens of different states—between a state or the citizens thereof, and foreign states, citizens or subjects. Actions in all these cases, except against a state government, are now brought and finally determined in the law courts of the states respectively and as there are no words to exclude these courts of their jurisdiction in these cases, they will have concurrent jurisdiction with the inferior federal courts in them; and, therefore, if the new constitution be adopted without any amendment in this respect, all those numerous actions, now brought in the state courts between our citizens and foreigners, between citizens of different states, by state governments against foreigners, and by state governments against citizens of other states, may also be brought in the federal courts; and an appeal will lay in them from the state courts or federal inferior courts to the supreme judicial court of the union. In almost all these cases, either party may have the trial by jury in the state courts; except paper money and tender laws, which are wisely guarded against in the proposed constitution; justice may be obtained in these courts on reasonable terms; they must be more competent to proper decisions on the laws of their respective states, than the federal states can possibly be. I do not, in any point of view, see the need of opening a new jurisdiction in these causes—of opening a new scene of expensive law suits, of suffering foreigners, and citizens of different states, to drag each other many hundred miles into the federal courts. It is true, those courts may be so organized by a wise and prudent legislature, as to make the obtaining of justice in them tolerably easy; they may in general be organized on the common law principles of the country: But this benefit is by no means secured by the constitution. The trial by jury is secured only in those few criminal cases, to which the federal laws will extend—as crimes committed on the seas, against the laws of nations, treason and counterfeiting the federal securities and coin: But even in these cases, the jury trial of the vicinage is not secured—particularly in the large states, a citizen may be tried for a crime committed in the state, and yet tried in some states 500 miles from the place where it was committed; but the jury trial is not secured at all in civil causes. Though the convention have not established this trial, it is to be hoped that congress, in putting the new system into execution, will do it by a legislative act, in all cases in which it can be done with propriety. Whether the jury trial is not excluded the supreme judicial court is an important question. By Art. 3, Sec. 2, all cases affecting ambassadors, other public ministers, and consuls, and in those cases in which a state shall be party, the supreme court shall have jurisdiction. In all the other cases before-mentioned, the supreme court shall have appellate jurisdiction, both as to *law and fact*, with such exception, and under such regulations as the congress shall make. By court is understood a court consisting of judges; and the idea of a jury is excluded. This court, or the judges, are to have jurisdiction on appeals, in all the cases enumerated, as to law and fact; the judges are to decide the law and try the fact, and the trial of the fact being assigned to the judges by the constitution, a jury for trying the fact is excluded; however, under the exceptions and powers to make regulations, congress may, perhaps, introduce the jury, to try the fact in most necessary cases.

There can be but one supreme court in which the final jurisdiction will centre in all federal causes—except in cases where appeals by law shall not be allowed: The judicial powers of the federal courts extend in law and equity to certain cases: and, therefore, the powers to determine on the law, in equity, and as to the fact, all will concentrate in the supreme court:—These powers, which by this constitution are blended in the same hands, the same judges, are in Great-Britain deposited in different hands—to wit, the decision of the law in the law judges, the decision in equity in the chancellor, and the trial of the fact in the jury. It is a very dangerous thing to vest in the same judge power to decide on the law, and also general powers in equity; for if the law restrain him, he is only to step into his shoes of equity, and give what judgment his reason or opinion may dictate; we have no precedents in this country, as yet, to regulate the divisions in equity as in Great Britain; equity, therefore, in the supreme court for many years will be mere discretion. I confess in the constitution of this supreme court, as left by the constitution, I do not see a spark of freedom or a shadow of our own or the British common law.

This court is to have appellate jurisdiction in all the other cases before mentioned: Many sensible men suppose that cases before mentioned respect, as well the criminal cases as the civil ones mentioned antecedently in the constitution, if so an appeal is allowed in criminal cases—contrary to the usual sense of law. How far it may be proper to admit a foreigner or the citizen of another state to bring actions against state governments, which have failed in performing so many, promises made during the war is doubtful: How far it may be proper so to humble a state, as to oblige it to answer to an individual in a court of law, is worthy of consideration; the states are now subject to no such actions; and this new jurisdiction will subject the states, and many defendants to actions, and processes, which were not in the contemplation of the parties, when the contract was made; all engagements existing between citizens of different states, citizens and foreigners, states and foreigners; and states and citizens of other states were made the parties contemplating the remedies then existing on the laws of the states——and the new remedy proposed to be given in the federal courts, can be founded on no principle whatever.

Your's, &c,

12. *Debates in the Virginia Convention*

Virginia was the tenth state to ratify the Constitution, on June 25, 1788, after a long debate and by the close vote of 89–79. Federalists and Antifederalists had chosen men of distinction for their leaders, and the list of major speakers on both sides included names that were or would become famous in Virginia and in the nation. There were also at least nine and possibly ten of the forty-nine members of the original chapter of Phi Beta Kappa organized in December of 1776. About one-fourth of the total membership were military veterans of the Revolution. Some had attended the Stamp Act Congress, and a goodly number had served in the succeeding Continental Congresses or in Congress under the Articles of Confederation. Many had held legislative, executive, or judicial office in the Virginia government both before and after the achievement of independence. It was indeed a convention that could rival the one which had met to draft the Constitution for political experience, sophistication, and fame. The selections reprinted here are chosen from the speeches of Patrick Henry, George Mason, William Grayson.

Patrick Henry (1736–1799). No member of the Virginia convention was more widely known than Patrick Henry. He first became prominent when, as a young lawyer, he argued for the colony against the Anglican clergy and the British government in the famous "Parsons' Cause" of 1763–1764. In 1765 he took his seat in the House of Burgesses and almost immediately introduced resolutions severely critical of the Stamp Act and radical in their implications with respect to colonial relations with Great Britain. Ten years later came his "Give me liberty or give me death" oration, and Henry's reputation as the orator of the Revolution was established forever. He served five terms as governor of Virginia, and had been chosen as a delegate to represent the state in the Philadelphia Convention, but had declined the appointment; he expressed skepticism about, if not hostility to, the proposals to strengthen the central government. It was believed that he would be a formidable opponent in the state ratifying convention, and apparently he was. To the modern reader, his speeches seem overly long, discursive, and patently demagogic, but in an age with a very different style of oratory from our own, they may have been impressive. Although Henry was defeated in the convention, he remained powerful enough in state politics to see that Virginia's delegation to the first Congress was heavily Antifederalist. By the mid-1790's, however, he was veering toward the Federalists, and just before his death in 1799 was elected as a Federalist to the Virginia legislature. His shift in political orientation was apparently related to a long-standing feud with Thomas Jefferson, whose administration as governor of Virginia Henry had severely criticized, and whose Statute for Religious Liberty Henry had bitterly opposed.

The speech printed below was Henry's first in the convention. Although the rules adopted by the delegates—on the motion of George Mason—provided for a clause-by-clause consideration of the Constitution, Henry chose to ignore the procedure which this entailed with respect to germaness, and to deliver a rambling commentary on the defects of the Constitution and the dangers of adopting it.

George Mason (1725–1792). George Mason's outstanding contribution to the American political tradition was the Virginia Declaration of Rights of 1776, which influenced the Declaration of Independence, many of the state constitutions of the Revolutionary period, and the federal Bill of Rights. A wealthy planter in the Northern Neck of Virginia, Mason participated in the usual county and parish governmental functions common to his class, but showed a disinclination to serve in the Virginia House of Burgesses after one term there. He was an active participant in the events that led up to the Revolution, however, and had a hand in preparing some of the Virginia papers of protest against British policy. During the period after 1776, he took part in drafting the revisions of Virginia laws to adapt them to the new status of republicanism, and he supported Jefferson's bill for the disestablishment of religion in Virginia. Long a member of the Ohio Company and a speculator in Western lands, he was vitally interested in the territories and their political future, and was influential both in securing Virginia's cession of them to the Union, and in the shaping of the Northwest Ordinance, which was to serve as their fundamental law.

Mason's complex position on the Constitution has already been noted (see this volume, Document 10). The speech reprinted here expresses his opposition to consolidation of power in the national government. It is directed specifically to the jurisdiction of the federal judiciary.

William Grayson (1736?–1790). Although William Grayson does not rank with Henry, Mason, and Monroe (to whom he was related) in the annals of our national history, he was well-known among contemporary Virginians, and according to tradition, was a superb orator. A lawyer, he entered the Continental Army on the outbreak of the Revolution and served both as a combat officer and as an aide to George Washington. In 1784 he was elected to the Virginia legislature, and represented that state in the Congress of the Confederation from 1785 to 1787. In that body he was particularly interested in the Western lands, was influential in securing the enactment of the Northwest Ordinance, and was opposed to a much discussed treaty that would have waived American rights of navigation on the Mississippi in exchange for commercial privileges advantageous to the Eastern states. This issue was extremely important in the Virginia convention, and appeared to be one of the principal reasons for opposition to the

Constitution among delegates from the western part of what was then Virginia but later became Kentucky. After serving in the Virginia convention, he was selected as one of Virginia's first senators to the national Congress in 1789, but died shortly thereafter in 1790.

Grigsby states that he made much use of humor, wit, sarcasm, and ridicule in his speeches, and that each was "a specimen in dialectics."[1] In refuting the Federalist portrayal of the various internal and external dangers which would ensue if the Constitution were not ratified, which he termed "imaginary and ridiculous," Grayson pictured an invasion of Virginia by South Carolinians, "(mounted on alligators, I presume,) . . . come to destroy our cornfields, and eat up our little children." This is said to have brought roars of laughter from both sides of the house. Though much of the speech reprinted here contains familiar and oft-repeated Antifederalist arguments, there are also insights and observations that mark Grayson as an astute political thinker and while leading one to regret his early death, strengthen the conviction that Revolutionary America was blessed with an extraordinarily high degree of political sophistication. One such observation, made in answer to Federalist fears about our foreign creditors, is worth repeating: "Nations lend money, and grant assistance, to one another, from views of national interest."

[PATRICK HENRY]

MR. HENRY. Mr. Chairman, I am much obliged to the very worthy gentleman for his encomium. I wish I was possessed with talents, or possessed of any thing that might

---

[1]Hugh Blair Grigsby, *The History of the Virginia Federal Convention of 1788*, R. A. Brock, ed. (Richmond, Virginia: Virginia Historical Society, 1891, 2 vols.), I, 200–201.

Elliot, *Debates* III, 43–64, 521–530 273–293.

enable me to elucidate this great subject. I am not free
from suspicion: I am apt to entertain doubts. I rose yesterday to ask a question which arose in my own mind. When I
asked that question, I thought the meaning of interro-
gation was obvious. The fate of this question and of America may depend on this. Have they said, We, the states?
Have they made a proposal of a compact between states? If
they had, this would be a confederation. It is otherwise
most clearly a consolidated government. The question
turns, sir, on that poor little thing—the expression, We, the
people, instead of the *states*, of America. I need not take
much pains to show that the principles of this system are
extremely pernicious, impolitic, and dangerous. Is this a
monarchy, like England—a compact between prince and
people, with checks on the former to secure the liberty of
the latter? Is this a confederacy, like Holland—an association of a number of independent states, each of which
retains its individual sovereignty? It is not a democracy,
wherein the people retain all their rights securely. Had
these principles been adhered to, we should not have
been brought to this alarming transition, from a confederacy to a consolidated government. We have no detail of
these great considerations, which, in my opinion, ought to
have abounded before we should recur to a government of
this kind. Here is a resolution as radical as that which
separated us from Great Britain. It is radical in this transition; our rights and privileges are endangered, and the
sovereignty of the states will be relinquished: and cannot
we plainly see that this is actually the case? The rights of
conscience, trial by jury, liberty of the press, all your immunities and franchises, all pretensions to human rights
and privileges, are rendered insecure, if not lost, by this
change, so loudly talked of by some, and inconsiderately
by others. Is this tame relinquishment of rights worthy of
freemen? Is it worthy of that manly fortitude that ought to

characterize republicans? It is said eight states have adopted this plan. I declare that if twelve states and a half had adopted it, I would, with manly firmness, and in spite of an erring world, reject it. You are not to inquire how your trade may be increased, nor how you are to become a great and powerful people, but how your liberties can be secured; for liberty ought to be the direct end of your government.

Having premised these things, I shall, with the aid of my judgment and information, which, I confess, are not extensive, go into the discussion of this system more minutely. Is it necessary for your liberty that you should abandon those great rights by the adoption of this system? Is the relinquishment of the trial by jury and the liberty of the press necessary for your liberty? Will the abandonment of your most sacred rights tend to the security of your liberty? Liberty. the greatest of all earthly blessings—give us that precious jewel, and you may take everything else! But I am fearful I have lived long enough to become an old-fashioned fellow. Perhaps an invincible attachment to the dearest rights of man may, in these refined, enlightened days, be deemed old-fashioned; if so, I am contented to be so. I say, the time has been when every pulse of my heart beat for American liberty, and which, I believe, had a counterpart in the breast of every true American; but suspicions have gone forth—suspicions of my integrity—publicly reported that my professions are not real. Twenty-three years ago was I supposed a traitor to my country? I was then said to be the bane of sedition, because I supported the rights of my country. I may be thought suspicious when I say our privileges and rights are in danger. But, sir, a number of the people of this country are weak enough to think these things are too true. I am happy to find that the gentleman on the other side declares they are groundless. But, sir, suspicion is a virtue as long as its object is the preservation of the public good, and as long as it stays within proper bounds: should it fall on me, I am contented: conscious rectitude is a powerful consolation. I trust there are many who think my professions for the public good to be real. Let your suspicion look to both sides. There are many on the other side, who possibly may have been persuaded to the necessity of these measures, which I conceive to be dangerous to your liberty. Guard with jealous attention the public liberty. Suspect every one who approaches that jewel. Unfortunately, nothing will preserve it but downright force. Whenever you give up that force, you are inevitably ruined. I am answered by gentlemen, that, though I might speak of terrors, yet the fact was, that we were surrounded by none of the dangers I apprehended. I conceive this new government to be one of those dangers: it has produced those horrors which distress many of our best citizens. We are come hither to preserve the poor commonwealth of Virginia, if it can be possibly done: something must be done to preserve your liberty and mine. The Confederation, this same despised government, merits, in my opinion, the highest encomium: it carried us through a long and dangerous war; it rendered us victorious in that bloody conflict with a powerful nation; it has secured us a territory greater than any European monarch possesses: and shall a government which has been thus strong and vigorous, be accused of imbecility, and abandoned for want of energy? Consider what you are about to do before you part with the government. Take longer time in reckoning things; revolutions like this have happened in almost every country in Europe; similar examples are to be found in ancient Greece and ancient Rome—instances of the people losing their liberty by their own carelessness and the ambition of a few. We are cautioned by the honorable gentleman, who presides, against faction and turbulence. I acknowledge that licentiousness is dangerous, and that it ought to be provided against: I acknowledge, also, the new form of government may effectually prevent it: yet there is another thing it will as effectually do—it will oppress and ruin the people.

There are sufficient guards placed against sedition and licentiousness; for, when power is give to this government to suppress these, or for any other purpose, the language it assumes is clear, express, and unequivocal; but when this Constitution speaks of privileges, there is an ambiguity, sir, a fatal ambiguity—an ambiguity which is very astonishing. In the clause under consideration, there is the strangest language that I can conceive. I mean, when it says that there shall not be more representatives than one for every thirty thousand. Now, sir, how easy is it to evade this privilege! "The number shall not exceed one for every thirty thousand." This may be satisfied by one representative from each state. Let our numbers be ever so great, this immense continent may, by this artful expression, be reduced to have but thirteen representatives. I confess this construction is not natural; but the ambiguity of the expression lays a good ground for a quarrel. Why was it not clearly and unequivocally expressed, that they should be entitled to have one for every thirty thousand? This would have obviated all disputes; and was this difficult to be done? What is the inference? When population increases, and a state shall send representatives in this proportion, Congress *may* remand them, because the right of having one for every thirty thousand is not clearly expressed. This possibility of reducing the number to one for each state approximates to probability by that other expression—"but each state shall at least have one representative." Now, is it not clear that, from the first expression, the number might be reduced so much that some states should have no representatives at all, were it not for the insertion of this last expression? And as this is the only restriction upon them, we may fairly conclude that they *may* restrain the number to one from each state. Perhaps the same horrors may hang over my mind again. I shall be told I am continually afraid: but, sir, I have strong cause of apprehension. In some parts of the plan before you, the great rights of freemen are endangered; in other parts, absolutely taken away. How does your trial by jury stand? In civil cases gone—not sufficiently secured in criminal—this best privilege is gone. But we are told that we need not fear; because those in power, being our representatives, will not abuse the powers we put in their hands. I am not well versed in history, but I will submit to your recollection, whether liberty has been destroyed most often by the licentiousness of the people, or by the tyranny of rulers. I imagine, sir, you will find the balance on the side of tyranny. Happy will you be if you miss the fate of those nations, who, omitting to resist their oppressors, or negligently suffering their liberty to be wrested from them, have groaned under intolerable despotism! Most of the human race are now in this deplorable condition; and those nations who have gone in search of grandeur, power, and splendor, have also fallen a sacrifice, and been the victims of their own folly. While they acquired those visonary blessings, they lost their freedom. My great objection to this government is, that it does not leave us the means of defending our rights, or of waging war against tyrants. It is urged by some gentlemen, that this new plan will bring us an acquisition of strength—an army and the militia of the states. This is an idea extremely ridiculous; gentlemen cannot be earnest. This acquisition will trample on our fallen liberty. Let my beloved Americans guard against that fatal lethargy that has pervaded the universe. Have we the means of resisting disciplined armies, when our only defence, the militia, is put into the hands of Congress? The honorable gentleman said that great danger would ensue if the Convention rose without adopting this system. I ask, Where is that danger? I see none. Other gentlemen have told us, within these walls, that the union is gone, or that the union will be gone. Is not this trifling with the judgment of their fellow-citizens? Till they tell us the grounds of their fears, I will consider them as imaginary. I rose to make inquiry where those dangers were; they could make no answer: I believe I never shall have that answer. Is there a disposition in the people of this country to revolt against the dominion of laws? Has there been a single tumult in Virginia? Have not the people of Virginia, when laboring under the severest pressure of accumulated distresses, manifested the most cordial acquiescence in the execution of the laws? What could be more awful than their unanimous acquiescence under general distresses? Is there any revolution in Virginia? Whither is the spirit of America gone? Whither is the genius of America fled? It was but yesterday, when our enemies marched in triumph through our country. Yet the people of this country could not be appalled by their pompous armaments: they stopped their career, and victoriously captured them. Where is the peril, now, compared to that? Some minds are agitated by foreign alarms. Happily for us, there is no real danger from Europe; that country is engaged in more arduous business: from that quarter there is no cause of fear: you may sleep in safety forever for them.

Where is the danger? If, sir, there was any, I would recur to the American spirit to defend us; that spirit which has enabled us to surmount the greatest difficulties: to that illustrious spirit I address my most fervent prayer to prevent our adopting a system destructive to liberty. Let not gentlemen be told that it is not safe to reject this government. Wherefore is it not safe? We are told there are dangers, but those dangers are ideal; they cannot be demonstrated. To encourage us to adopt it, they tell us that there is a plain, easy way of getting amendments. When I come to contemplate this part, I suppose that I am mad, or that my countrymen are so. The way to amendment is, in my conception, shut. Let us consider this plain, easy way. "The Congress, whenever two thirds of both houses shall deem it necessary, shall propose amendments to this Constitution, or on the application of the legislatures of two thirds of the several states, shall call a Convention for proposing amendments, which, in either case, shall be valid to all intents and purposes, as part of this Constitution, when ratified by the legislatures of three fourths of the several states, or by the Conventions in three fourths thereof, as the one or the other mode of ratification may be proposed by the Congress. Provided, that no amendment which may be made prior to the year 1808, shall in any manner affect the 1st and 4th clauses in the 9th section of the 1st article; and that no state, without its consent, shall be deprived of its equal suffrage in the Senate."

Hence it appears that three fourths of the states must ultimately agree to any amendments that may be necessary. Let us consider the consequence of this. However uncharitable it may appear, yet I must tell my opinion— that the most unworthy characters may get into power, and prevent the introduction of amendments. Let us suppose—for the case is supposable, possible, and probable—that you happen to deal those powers to unworthy hands; will they relinquish powers already in their possession, or agree to amendments? Two thirds of the Congress, or of the state legislatures, are necessary even to propose amendments. If one third of these be unworthy men, they may prevent the application for amendments; but what is destructive and mischievous, is, that three fourths of the state legislatures, or of the state conventions, must concur in the amendments when proposed! In such numerous bodies, there must necessarily be some designing, bad men. To suppose that so large a number as three fourths of the states will concur, is to suppose that they will possess genius, intelligence, and integrity, approach-

ing to miraculous. It would indeed be miraculous that
they should concur in the same amendments, or even in
such as would bear some likeness to one another; for
four of the smallest states, that do not collectively contain
one tenth part of the population of the United States, may
obstruct the most salutary and necessary amendments.
Nay, in these four states, six tenths of the people may
reject these amendments; and suppose that amendments
shall be opposed to amendments, which is highly probable,—is it possible that three fourths can ever agree to the
same amendments? A bare majority in these four small
states may hinder the adoption of amendments; so that we
may fairly and justly conclude that one twentieth part of
the American people may prevent the removal of the most
grievous inconveniences and oppression, by refusing to
accede to amendments. A trifling minority may reject the
most salutary amendments. Is this an easy mode of securing the public liberty? It is, sir, a most fearful situation,
when the most contemptible minority can prevent the
alteration of the most oppressive government; for it may,
in many respects, prove to be such. Is this the spirit of
republicanism?

What, sir, is the genius of democracy? Let me read that
clause of the bill of rights of Virginia which relates to this:
3d clause:—that government is, or ought to be, instituted
for the common benefit, protection, and security of the
people, nation, or community. Of all the various modes
and forms of government, that is best, which is capable of
producing the greatest degree of happiness and safety, and
is most effectually secured against the danger of mal-
administration; and that whenever any government shall
be found inadequate, or contrary to those purposes, a
majority of the community hath an indubitable, unalienable,
and indefeasible right to reform, alter, or abolish it, in such

manner as shall be judged most conducive to the public weal.

This, sir, is the language of democracy—that a majority of the community have a right to alter government when found to be oppressive. But how different is the genius of your new Constitution from this! How different from the sentiments of freemen, that a contemptible minority can prevent the good of the majority! If, then, gentlemen, standing on this ground, are come to that point, that they are willing to bind themselves and their posterity to be oppressed, I am amazed and inexpressibly astonished. If this be the opinion of the majority, I must submit; but to me, sir, it appears perilous and destructive. I cannot help thinking so. Perhaps it may be the result of my age. These may be feelings natural to a man of my years, when the American spirit has left him, and his mental powers, like the members of the body, are decayed. If, sir, amendments are left to the twentieth, or tenth part of the people of America, your liberty is gone forever. We have heard that there is a great deal of bribery practised in the House of Commons, in England, and that many of the members raise themselves to preferments by selling the rights of the whole of the people. But, sir, the tenth part of that body cannot continue oppressions on the rest of the people. English liberty is, in this case, on a firmer foundation than American liberty. It will be easily contrived to procure the opposition of one tenth of the people to any alteration, however judicious. The honorable gentleman who presides told us that, to prevent abuses in our government, we will assemble in Convention, recall our delegated powers, and punish our servants for abusing the trust reposed in them. O sir, we should have fine times, indeed, if, to punish tyrants, it were only sufficient to assemble the people! Your arms, wherewith you could defend yourselves, are gone; and you have no longer an aristocratical, no longer a democratical spirit. Did you ever read of any revolution in a nation, brought about by the punishment of those in power, inflicted by those who had no power at all? You read of a riot act in a country which is called one of the freest in the world, where a few neighbors cannot assemble without the risk of being shot by a hired soldiery, the engines of despotism. We may see such an act in America.

A standing army we shall have, also, to execute the execrable commands of tyranny; and how are you to punish them? Will you order them to be punished? Who shall obey these orders? Will your mace-bearer be a match for a disciplined regiment? In what situation are we to be? The clause before you gives a power of direct taxation, unbounded and unlimited, exclusive power of legislation, in all cases whatsoever, for ten miles square, and over all places purchased for the erection of forts, magazines, arsenals, dockyards, &c. What resistance could be made? The attempt would be madness. You will find all the strength of this country in the hands of your enemies; their garrisons will naturally be the strongest places in the country. Your militia is given up to Congress, also, in another part of this plan: they will therefore act as they think proper: all power will be in their own possession. You cannot force them to receive their punishment: of what service would militia be to you, when, most probably, you will not have a single musket in the state? for, as arms are to be provided by Congress, they may or may not furnish them.

Let me here call your attention to that part which gives the Congress power "to provide for organizing, arming, and disciplining the militia, and for governing such part of them as may be employed in the service of the United States—reserving to the states, respectively, the appointment of the officers, and the authority of training the militia according to the discipline prescribed by Congress."

By this, sir, you see that their control over our last and best defence is unlimited. If they neglect or refuse to discipline or arm our militia, they will be useless: the states can do neither—this power being exclusively given to Congress. The power of appointing officers over men not disciplined or armed is ridiculous; so that this pretended little remains of power left to the states may, at the pleasure of Congress, be rendered nugatory. Our situation will be deplorable indeed: nor can we ever expect to get this government amended, since I have already shown that a very small minority may prevent it, and that small minority interested in the continuance of the oppression. Will the oppressor let go the oppressed? Was there ever an instance? Can the annals of mankind exhibit one single example where rulers overcharged with power willingly let go the oppressed, though solicited and requested most earnestly? The application for amendments will therefore be fruitless. Sometimes, the oppressed have got loose by one of those bloody struggles that desolate a country; but a willing relinquishment of power is one of those things which human nature never was, nor ever will be, capable of.

The honorable gentleman's observations, respecting the people's right of being the agents in the formation of this government, are not accurate, in my humble conception. The distinction between a national government and a confederacy is not sufficiently discerned. Had the delegates, who were sent to Philadelphia, a power to propose a consolidated government instead of a confederacy? Were they not deputed by states, and not by the people? The assent of the people, in their collective capacity, is not necessary to the formation of a federal government. The people have no right to enter into leagues, alliances, or confederations, they are not the proper agents for this purpose. States and foreign powers are the only proper agents for this kind of government. Show me an instance where the people have exercised this business. Has it not always gone through the legislatures? I refer you to the treaties with France, Holland, and other nations. How were they made? Were they not made by the states? Are the people, therefore, in their aggregate capacity, the proper persons to form a confederacy? This, therefore, ought to depend on the consent of the legislatures, the people having never sent delegates to make any proposition for changing the government. Yet I must say, at the same time, that it was made on grounds the most pure; and perhaps I might have been brought to consent to it so far as to the change of government. But there is one thing in it which I never would acquiesce in. I mean, the changing it into a consolidated government, which is so abhorrent to my mind. [The honorable gentleman then went on to the figure we make with foreign nations; the contemptible one we make in France and Holland; which, according to the substance of the notes, he attributes to the present feeble government.] An opinion has gone forth, we find, that we are contemptible people: the time has been when we were thought otherwise. Under the same despised government, we commanded the respect of all Europe: wherefore are we now reckoned otherwise? The American spirit has fled from hence: it has gone to regions where it has never been expected; it has gone to the people of France, in search of a splendid government—a strong, energetic government. Shall we imitate the example of those nations who have gone from a simple to a splendid government? Are those nations more worthy of our imitation? What can make an adequate satisfaction to them for the loss they have suffered in attaining such a government—for the loss of their liberty? If we admit this consolidated government, it will be because we like a great, splendid one. Some way or other we must be a great and mighty empire; we must have an army, and a navy, and a number of things. When the American spirit was in its youth, the language of America was different: liberty, sir, was then the primary object. We are descended from a people whose government was founded on liberty: our glorious forefathers of Great Britain made liberty the foundation of every thing. That country is become a great, mighty, and splendid nation; not because their government is strong and energetic, but, sir, because liberty is its direct end and foundation. We drew the spirit of liberty from our British ancestors: by that spirit we have triumphed over every difficulty. But now, sir, the American spirit, assisted by the ropes and chains of consolidation, is about to convert this country into a powerful and mighty empire. If you make the citizens of this country agree to become the subjects of one great consolidated empire of America, your government will not have sufficient energy to keep them together. Such a government is incompatible with the genius of republicanism. There will be no checks, no real balances, in this government. What can avail your specious, imaginary balances, your rope-dancing, chain-rattling, ridiculous ideal checks and contrivances? But, sir, we are not feared by foreigners; we do not make nations tremble. Would this constitute happiness, or secure liberty? I trust, sir, our political hemisphere will ever direct their operations to the security of those objectes.

Consider our situation, sir: go to the poor man, and ask him what he does. He will inform you that he enjoys the fruits of his labor, under his own fig-tree, with his wife and children around him, in peace and security. Go to every other member of society,—you will find the same tranquil ease and content; you will find no alarms or disturbances. Why, then, tell us of danger, to terrify us into an adoption of this new form of government? And yet who knows the dangers that this new system may produce? They are out of the sight of the common people: they cannot foresee latent consequences. I dread the operation of it on the middling and lower classes of people: it is for them I fear the adoption of this system. I fear I tire the patience of the committee; but I beg to be indulged with a few more observations. When I thus profess myself an advocate for the liberty of the people, I shall be told I am a designing man, that I am to be a great man, that I am to be a demagogue; and many similar illiberal insinuations will be thrown out: but, sir, conscious rectitude outweighs those things with me. I see great jeopardy in this new government. I see none from our present one. I hope some gentleman or other will bring forth, in full array, those dangers, if there be any, that we may see and touch them. I have said that I thought this a consolidated government: I will now prove it. Will the great rights of the people be secured by this government? Suppose it should prove oppressive, how can it be altered? Our bill of rights declares, "that a majority of the community hath an indubitable, unalienable, and indefeasible right to reform, alter, or abolish it, in such manner as shall be judged most conducive to the public weal."

I have just proved that one tenth, or less, of the people of America—a most despicable minority—may prevent this reform or alteration. Suppose the people of Virginia should wish to alter their government; can a majority of them do it? No; because they are connected with other men, or, in other words, consolidated with other states. When the people of Virginia, at a future day, shall wish to alter their government, though they should be unanimous in this desire, yet they may be prevented therefrom by a despicable minority at the extremity of the United States. The founders of your own Constitution made your government changeable: but the power of changing it is gone from you. Whither is it gone? It is placed in the same hands that hold the rights of twelve other states; and those who hold those rights have right and power to keep them. It is not the particular government of Virginia: one of the leading features of that government is, that a majority can alter it, when necesssary for the public good. This government is not a Virginian, but an American government. Is it not, therefore, a consolidated government? The sixth clause of your bill of rights tells you, "that elections of members to serve as representatives of the people in Assembly ought to be free, and that all men having sufficient evidence of permanent common interest with, and attachment to, the community, have the right of suffrage, and cannot be *taxed*, or deprived of their property for public uses, without their own consent, or that of their representatives so elected, nor bound by any law to which they have not in like manner assented for the public good." But what does this Constitution say? The clause under consideration gives an unlimited and unbounded power of taxation. Suppose every delegate from Virginia opposes a law laying a tax; what will it avail? They are opposed by a majority; eleven members can destroy their efforts; those feeble ten cannot prevent the passing the most oppressive tax law; so that, in direct opposition to the spirit and express language of your declaration of rights, you are taxed, not by your own consent, but by people who have no connection with you.

The next clause of the bill of rights tells you, "that all power of suspending law, or the execution of laws, by any authority, without the consent of the representatives of the people, is injurious to their rights, and ought not to be exercised." This tells us that there can be no suspension of government or laws without our own consent; yet this Constitution can counteract and suspend any of our laws that contravene its oppressive operation; for they have the power of direct taxation, which suspends our bill of rights; and it is expressly provided that they can make all laws necessary for carrying their powers into execution; and it is declared paramount to the laws and constitutions of the states. Consider how the only remaining defence we have left is destroyed in this manner. Besides the expenses of maintaining the Senate and other house in as much splendor as they please, there is to be a great and mighty President, with very extensive powers—the powers of a king. He is to be supported in extravagant magnificence; so that the whole of our property may be taken by this American government, by laying what taxes they please, giving themselves what salaries they please, and suspending our laws at their pleasure. I might be thought too inquisitive, but I believe I should take up very little of your time in enumerating the little power that is left to the government of Virginia; for this power is reduced to little or nothing: their garrisons, magazines, arsenals, and forts, which will be situated in the strongest places within the states; their ten miles square, with all the fine ornaments of human life, added to their powers, and taken from the states, will reduce the power of the latter to nothing.

The voice of tradition, I trust, will inform posterity of our struggles for freedom. If our descendants be worthy the name of Americans, they will preserve, and hand down to their latest posterity, the transactions of the present times; and though I confess my exclamations are not worthy the hearing, they will see that I have done my utmost to preserve their liberty; for I never will give up the power of direct taxation but for a scourge. I am willing to give it conditionally; that is, after non-compliance with requisitions. I will do more, sir, and what I hope will convince the most skeptical man that I am a lover of the American Union—that, in case Virginia shall not make punctual payment, the control of our custom-houses, and the whole regulation of trade, shall be given to Congress, and that Virginia shall depend on Congress even for passports, till

Virginia shall have paid the last farthing, and furnished the last soldier. Nay, sir there is another alternative to which I would consent;—even that they should strike us out of the Union, and take away from us all federal privileges, till we comply with federal requisitions: but let it depend upon our own pleasure to pay our money in the most easy manner for our people. Were all the states, more terrible than the mother country, to join against us, I hope Virginia could defend herself; but, sir, the dissolution of the Union is most abhorrent to my mind. The first thing I have at heart is American liberty: the second thing is American union; and I hope the people of Virginia will endeavor to preserve that union. The increasing population of the Southern States is far greater than that of New England; consequently, in a short time, they will be far more numerous than the people of that country. Consider this, and you will find this state more particularly interested to support American liberty, and not bind our posterity by an improvident relinquishment of our rights. I would give the best security for a punctual compliance with requisitions; but I beseech gentlemen, at all hazards, not to give up this unlimited power of taxation. The honorable gentleman has told us that these powers, given to Congress, are accompanied by a judiciary which will correct all. On examination, you will find this very judiciary oppressively constructed; your jury trial destroyed, and the judges dependent on Congress.

In this scheme of energetic government, the people will find two sets of tax-gatherers—the state and the federal sheriffs. This, it seems to me, will produce such dreadful oppression as the people cannot possibly bear. The federal sheriff may commit what oppression, make what distresses, he pleases, and ruin you with impunity; for how are you to tie his hands? Have you any sufficiently decided means of preventing him from sucking your blood by speculations, commissions, and fees? Thus thousands of your people will be most shamefully robbed: our state sheriffs, those unfeeling blood-suckers, have, under the watchful eye of our legislature, committed the most horrid and barbarous ravages on our people. It has required the most constant vigilance of the legislature to keep them totally from ruining the people; a repeated succession of laws has been made to suppress their iniquitous speculations and cruel extortions; and as often has their nefarious ingenuity devised methods of evading the force of those laws: in the struggle they have generally triumphed over the legislature.

It is a fact that lands have been sold for five shillings, which were worth one hundred pounds: if sheriffs, thus immediately under the eye of our state legislature and judiciary, have dared to commit these outrages, what would they not have done if their masters had been at Philadelphia or New York? If they perpetrate the most unwarrantable outrage on your person or property, you cannot get redress on this side of Philadelphia or New York; and how can you get it there? If your domestic avocations could permit you to go thither, there you must appeal to judges sworn to support this Constitution, in opposition to that of any state, and who may also be inclined to favor their own officers. When these harpies are aided by excisemen, who may search, at any time, your houses, and most secret recesses, will the people bear it? If you think so, you differ from me. Where I thought there was a possibility of such mischiefs, I would grant power with a niggardly hand; and here there is a strong probability that these oppressions shall actually happen. I may be told that it is safe to err on that side, because such regulations may be made by Congress as shall restrain these officers, and because laws are made by our representatives, and judged by righteous judges: but, sir, as these regulations may be made, so they may not; and many reasons there are to induce a belief that they will not. I shall therefore be an infidel on that point till the day of my death.

This Constitution is said to have beautiful features; but when I come to examine these features, sir, they appear to me horribly frightful. Among other deformities, it has an awful squinting; it squints towards monarchy; and does not this raise indignation in the breast of every true American?

Your President may easily become king. Your Senate is so imperfectly constructed that your dearest rights may be sacrificed by what may be a small minority; and a very small minority may continue forever unchangeably this government, although horridly defective. Where are your checks in this government? Your strongholds will be in the hands of your enemies. It is on a supposition that your American governors shall be honest, that all the good qualities of this government are founded; but its defective and imperfect construction puts it in their power to perpetrate the worst of mischiefs, should they be bad men; and, sir, would not all the world, from the eastern to the western hemisphere, blame our distracted folly in resting our rights upon the contingency of our rulers being good or bad? Show me that age and country where the rights and liberties of the people were placed on the sole chance of their rulers being good men, without a consequent loss of liberty! I say that the loss of that dearest privilege has ever followed, with absolute certainty, every such mad attempt.

If your American chief be a man of ambition and abilities, how easy is it for him to render himself absolute! The army is in his hands, and if he be a man of address, it will be attached to him, and it will be the subject of long meditation with him to seize the first auspicious moment to accomplish his design; and, sir, will the American spirit solely relieve you when this happens? I would rather infinitely—and I am sure most of this Convention are of the same opinion—have a king, lords, and commons, than a government so replete with such insupportable evils. If we make a king, we may prescribe the rules by which he shall rule his people, and interpose such checks as shall prevent him from infringing them; but the President, in the field, at the head of his army, can prescribe the terms on which he shall reign master, so far that it will puzzle any American ever to get his neck from under the galling yoke. I cannot with patience think of this idea. If ever he violates the laws, one of two things will happen: he will come at the head of his army, to carry every thing before him; or he will give bail, or do what Mr. Chief Justice will order him. If he be guilty, will not the recollection of his crimes teach him to make one bold push for the American throne? Will not the immense difference between being master of every thing, and being ignominiously tried and punished, powerfully excite him to make this bold push? But, sir, where is the existing force to punish him? Can he not, at the head of his army, beat down every opposition? Away with your President! we shall have a king: the army will salute him monarch: your militia will leave you, and assist in making him king, and fight against you: and what have you to oppose this force? What will then become of you and your rights? Will not absolute despotism ensue?

[*Here* MR. HENRY *strongly and pathetically expatiated on the probability of the President's enslaving America, and the horrid consequences that must result.*]

What can be more defective than the clause concerning the elections? The control given to Congress over the time, place, and manner of holding elections, will totally destroy the end of suffrage. The elections may be held at one place, and the most inconvenient in the state; or they may be at remote distances from those who have a right of suffrage: hence nine out of ten must either not vote at all, or vote for strangers; for the most influential characters will be applied to, to know who are the most proper to be chosen. I repeat, that the control of Congress over the *manner*, &c., of electing, well warrants this idea. The natural consequence will be, that this democratic branch will possess none of the public confidence; the people will be prejudiced against representatives chosen in such an injudicious manner. The proceedings in the northern conclave will be hidden from the yeomanry of this country. We are told that the yeas and nays shall be taken, and entered on the journals. This, sir, will avail nothing: it may be locked up in their chests, and concealed forever from the people; for they are not to publish what parts they think require secrecy: they *may* think, and *will think*, the whole requires it. Another beautiful feature of this Constitution is, the publication from time to time of the receipts and expenditures of the public money.

This expression, *from time to time*, is very indefinite and indeterminate: it may extend to a century. Grant that any of them are wicked; they may squander the public money so as to ruin you, and yet this expression will give you no redress. I say they may ruin you; for where, sir, is the responsibility? The yeas and nays will show you nothing, unless they be fools as well as knaves; for, after having wickedly trampled on the rights of the people, they would act like fools indeed, were they to publish and divulge their iniquity, when they have it equally in their power to suppress and conceal it. Where is the responsibility—that leading principle in the British government? In that government, a punishment certain and inevitable is provided; but in this, there is no real, actual punishment for the grossest mal-administration. They may go without punishment, though they commit the most outrageous violation on our immunities. That paper may tell me they will be punished. I ask, By what law? They must make the law, for there is no existing law to do it. What! will they make a law to punish themselves?

This, sir, is my great objection to the Constitution, that there is no true responsibility—and that the preservation of our liberty depends on the single chance of men being virtuous enough to make laws to punish themselves.

In the country from which we are descended, they have real and not imaginary responsibility; for their mal-administration has cost their heads to some of the most saucy geniuses that ever were. The Senate, by making treaties, may destroy your liberty and laws for want of responsibility. Two thirds of those that shall happen to be present, can, with the President, make treaties that shall be the supreme law of the land; they may make the most ruinous treaties; and yet there is no punishment for them. Whoever shows me a punishment provided for them will oblige me. So, sir, notwithstanding there are eight pillars, they want another. Where will they make another? I trust, sir, the exclusion of the evils wherewith this system is replete in its present form, will be made a condition precedent to its adoption by this or any other state. The transition, from a general unqualified admission to offices, to a consolidation of government, seems easy; for, though the American states are dissimilar in their structure, this will assimilate them. This, sir, is itself a strong consolidating feature, and is not one of the least dangerous in that system. Nine states are sufficient to establish this government over those nine. Imagine that nine have come into it. Virginia has certain scruples. Suppose she will, consequently, refuse to join with those states; may not she still continue in friendship and union with them? If she sends her annual requisitions in dollars, do you think their stomachs will be so squeamish as to refuse her dollars? Will they not accept her regiments? They would intimidate you into an inconsiderate adoption, and frighten you with ideal evils, and that the Union shall be dissolved. 'Tis a bugbear, sir: the fact is, sir, that the eight adopting states can hardly stand on their own legs. Public fame tells us that the adopting states have already heart-burnings and animosity, and repent their precipitate hurry: this, sir, may occasion exceeding great mischief. When I reflect on these and many other circumstances, I must think those states will be found to be in confederacy with us. If we pay our quota of money annually, and furnish our ratable number of men, when necessary, I can see no danger from a rejection.

The history of Switzerland clearly proves that we might be in amicable alliance with those states without adopting this Constitution. Switzerland is a confederacy, consisting of dissimilar governments. This is an example which proves that governments of dissimilar structures may be confederated. That confederate republic has stood upwards of four hundred years; and, although several of the individual republics are democratic, and the rest aristocratic, no evil has resulted from this dissimilarity; for they have braved all the power of France and Germany during that long period. The Swiss spirit, sir, has kept them together; they have encountered and overcome immense difficulties with patience and fortitude. In the vicinity of powerful and ambitious monarchs, they have retained their independence, republican simplicity, and valor. [Here he makes a comparison of the people of that country and those of France, and makes a quotation from Addison illustrating the subject.] Look at the peasants of that country and of France; and mark the difference. You will find the condition of the former far more desirable and comfortable. No matter whether the people be great, splendid, and powerful, if they enjoy freedom. The Turkish Grand Signior, alongside of our President, would put us to disgrace; but we should be as abundantly consoled for this disgrace, when our citizens have been put in contrast with the Turkish slave. The most valuable end of government is the liberty of the inhabitants. No possible advantages can compensate for the loss of this privilege. Show me the reason why the American Union is to be dissolved. Who are those eight adopting states? Are they averse to give us a little time to consider, before we conclude? Would such a disposition render a junction with them eligible; or is it the genius of that kind of government to precipitate people hastily into measures of the utmost importance, and grant no indulgence? If it be, sir, is it for us to accede to such a government? We have a right to have time to consider; we shall therefore insist upon it. Unless the government be amended, we can never accept it. The adopting states will doubtless accept our money and our regiments; and what is to be the consequence, if we are disunited? I believe it is yet doubtful, whether it is not proper to stand by a while, and see the effect of its adoption in other states. In forming a government, the utmost care should be taken to prevent its becoming oppressive; and this government is of such an intricate and complicated nature, that no man on this earth can know its real operation. The other states have no reason to think, from the antecedent conduct of Virginia, that she has any intention of seceding from the Union, or of being less active to support the general welfare. Would they not, therefore, acquiesce in our taking time to deliberate—deliberate whether the measure be not perilous, not only for us, but the adopting states?

Permit me, sir, to say, that a great majority of the people, even in the adopting states, are averse to this government. I believe I would be right to say, that they have been egregiously misled. Pennsylvania has, *perhaps*, been tricked into it. If the other states who have adopted it have not been tricked, still they were too much hurried into its adoption. There were very respectable minorities in several of them; and if reports be true, a clear majority of the people are averse to it. If we also accede, and it should prove grievous, the peace and prosperity of our country, which we all love, will be destroyed. This government has not the affection of the people at present. Should it be oppressive, their affections will be totally estranged from it; and, sir, you know that a government, without their affections, can neither be durable nor happy. I speak as one poor individual; but when I speak, I speak the language of thousands. But, sir, I mean not to breathe the spirit, nor utter the language, of secession.

I have trespassed so long on your patience, I am really concerned that I have something yet to say. The honorable member has said, we shall be properly represented. Remember, sir, that the number of our representatives is but ten, whereof six is a majority. Will those men be possessed of sufficient information? A particular knowledge of particular districts will not suffice. They must be well acquainted with agriculture, commerce, and a great variety of other matters throughout the continent; they must know not only the actual state of nations in Europe and America, the situations of their farmers, cottagers, and mechanics, but also the relative situations and intercourse of those nations. Virginia is as large as England. Our proportion of representatives is but ten men. In England they have five hundred and fifty-eight. The House of Commons, in England, numerous as they are, we are told, are bribed, and have bartered away the rights of their constituents: what, then, shall become of us? Will these few protect our rights? Will they be incorruptible? You say they will be better men than the English commoners. I say they will be infinitely worse men, because they are to be chosen blindfolded: their election (the term, as applied to their appointment, is inaccurate) will be an involuntary nomination, and not a choice.

I have, I fear, fatigued the committee; yet I have not said the one hundred thousandth part of what I have on my mind, and wish to impart. On this occasion, I conceived myself bound to attend strictly to the interest of the state, and I thought her dearest rights at stake. Having lived so long—been so much honored—my efforts, though small, are due to my country. I have found my mind hurried on, from subject to subject, on this very great occasion. We have been all out of order, from the gentleman who opened to-day to myself. I did not come prepared to speak, on so multifarious a subject, in so general a manner. I trust you will indulge me another time. Before you abandon the present system, I hope you will consider not only its defects, most maturely, but likewise those of that which you are to substitute for it. May you be fully apprized of the dangers of the latter, not by fatal experience, but by some abler advocate than I!

[GEORGE MASON]

MR. GEORGE MASON. Mr. Chairman, I had some hopes that the candor and reason of the warmest friends of this Constitution would have led them to point out objections so important. They must occur, more or less, to the mind of every one. It is with great reluctance I speak of this department, as it lies out of my line. I should not tell my sentiments upon it, did I not conceive it to be so constructed as to destroy the dearest rights of the community. After having read the first section, Mr. Mason asked, What is there left to the state courts? Will any gentleman be pleased, candidly, fairly, and without sophistry, to show us what remains? There is no limitation. It goes to every thing. The inferior courts are to be as numerous as Congress may think proper. They are to be of whatever nature they please. Read the 2d section, and contemplate attentively the extent of the jurisdiction of these courts, and consider if there be any limits to it.

I am greatly mistaken if there be any limitation whatsoever, with respect to the nature or jurisdiction of these courts. If there be any limits, they must be contained in one of the clauses of this section; and I believe, on a dispassionate discussion, it will be found that there is none of any check. All the laws of the United States are paramount to the laws and constitution of any single state. "The judicial power shall extend to all cases in law and equity arising under this Constitution." What objects will not this expression extend to? Such laws may be formed as will go to every object of private property. When we consider the nature of these courts, we must conclude that their effect and operation will be utterly to destroy the state governments; for they will be the judges how far their laws will operate. They are to modify their own courts, and you can make no state law to counteract them. The discrimination between their judicial power, and that of the states, exists, therefore, but in name. To what disgraceful and dangerous length does the principle of this go! For if your state judiciaries are not to be trusted with the administration of common justice, and decision of disputes respecting property between man and man, much less ought the state governments to be trusted with power of legislation. The principle itself goes to the destruction of the legislation of the states, whether or not it was intended. As to my own opinion, I most religiously and conscientiously believe that it was intended, though I am not absolutely certain. But I think it will destroy the state governments, whatever may have been the intention. There are many gentlemen in the United States who think it right that we should have one great, national, consolidated government, and that it was better to bring it about slowly and imperceptibly rather than all at once. This is no reflection on any man, for

I mean none. To those who think that one national, consolidated government is best for America, this extensive judicial authority will be agreeable; but I hope there are many in this Convention of a different opinion, and who see their political happiness resting on their state governments. I know, from my own knowledge, many worthy gentlemen of the former opinion.

[*Here Mr. Madison interrupted Mr. Mason, and demanded an unequivocal explanation. As these insinuations might create a belief that every member of the late federal Convention was of that opinion, he wished him to tell who the gentlemen were to whom he alluded.*]

Mr. MASON then replied, I shall never refuse to explain myself. It is notorious that this is a prevailing principle. It was at least the opinion of many gentlemen in Convention, and many in the United States. I do not know what explanation the honorable gentleman asks. I can say, with great truth, that the honorable gentleman, in private conversation with me, expressed himself against it; neither did I ever hear any of the delegates from this state advocate it.

Mr. MADISON declared himself satisfied with this, unless the committee thought themselves entitled to ask a further explanation.

After some desultory remarks, Mr. MASON continued: I have heard that opinion advocated by gentlemen for whose abilities, judgment, and knowledge, I have the highest reverence and respect. I say that the general description of the judiciary involves the most extensive jurisdiction. Its cognizance, in all cases arising under the system and the laws of Congress, may be said to be unlimited. In the next place, it extends to treaties made, or which shall be made, under their authority. This is one of the powers which ought to be given them. I also admit that they ought to have judicial cognizance in all cases affecting ambassadors, foreign ministers and consuls, as well as in cases of maritime jurisdiction. There is an additional reason now to give them this last power; because Congress, besides the general powers, are about to get that of regulating commerce with foreign nations. This is a power which existed before, and is a proper subject of federal jurisdiction. The next power of the judiciary is also necessary under some restrictions. Though the decision of controversies to which the United States shall be a party may at first view seem proper, it may, without restraint, be extended to a dangerously oppressive length. The next, with respect to disputes between two or more states, is right. I cannot see the propriety of the next power, in disputes between a state and the citizens of another state. As to controversies between citizens of different states, their power is improper and inadmissible. In disputes between citizens of the same state, claiming lands under the grants of different states, the power is proper. It is the only case in which the federal judiciary ought to have appellate cognizance of disputes between private citizens. Unless this was the case, the suit must be brought and decided in one or the other state, under whose grant the lands are claimed, which would be injurious, as the decision must be consistent with the grant.

The last clause is still more improper. To give them cognizance in disputes between a state and the citizens there of is utterly inconsistent with reason or good policy.

Here Mr. NICHOLAS arose, and informed Mr. Mason that his interpretation of this part was not warranted by the words.

Mr. MASON replied, that, if he recollected rightly, the propriety of the power, as explained by him, had been contended for; but that, as his memory had never been good, and was now impaired much from his age, he would not insist on that interpretation. He then proceeded: Give me leave to advert to the operation of this judicial power. Its jurisdiction in the first case will extend to all cases affecting revenue, excise, and custom-house officers. If I am mistaken, I will retract. "All cases in law and equity arising under this Constitution, and the laws of the United States," take in all the officers of the government. They comprehend all those who act as collectors of taxes, excisemen, &c. It will take in, of course, what others do to them, and what is done by them to others. In what predicament will our citizens then be? We know the difficulty we are put in by our own courts, and how hard it is to bring officers to justice even in them. If any of the federal officers should be guilty of the greatest oppressions, or behave with the most insolent and wanton brutality to a man's wife or daughter, where is this man to get relief? If you suppose in the inferior courts, they are not appointed by the states. They are not men in whom the community can place confidence. It will be decided by federal judges. Even suppose the poor man should be able to obtain judgment in the inferior court, for the greatest injury, what justice can he get on appeal? Can he go four or five hundred miles? Can he stand the expense attending it? On this occasion they are to judge of fact as well as law. He must bring his witnesses where he is not known, where a new evidence may be brought against him, of which he never heard before, and which he cannot contradict.

The honorable gentleman who presides here has told us that the Supreme Court of appeals must embrace every object of maritime, chancery, and common-law controversy. In the two first, the indiscriminate appellate jurisdiction as to fact must be generally granted; because, otherwise, it could exclude appeals in those cases. But why not discriminate as to matters of fact with respect to common-law controversies? The honorable gentleman has allowed that it was dangerous, but hopes regulations will be made to suit the convenience of the people. But mere hope is not a sufficient security. I have said that it appears to me (though I am no lawyer) to be very dangerous. Give me leave to lay before the committee an amendment, which I think convenient, easy, and proper.

[Here Mr. Mason proposed an alteration nearly the same as the first part of the fourteenth amendment recommended by the Convention which see at the conclusion.]

Thus, sir, said Mr. Mason, after limiting the cases in which the federal judiciary could interpose, I would confine the appellate jurisdiction to matters of law only, in common-law controversies.

It appears to me that this will remove oppressions, and answer every purpose of an appellate power.

A discrimination arises between common-law trials and trials in courts of equity and admiralty. In these two last, depositions are committed to record, and therefore, on an appeal, the whole fact goes up; the equity of the whole case, comprehending fact and law, is considered, and no new evidence requisite. Is it so in courts of common law? There evidence is only given *viva voce*. I know not a single case where there is an appeal of fact as to common law. But I may be mistaken. Where there is an appeal from an inferior to a superior court, with respect to matters of fact, a new witness may be introduced, who is perhaps suborned by the other party, a thousand miles from the place where the first trial was had. These are some of the inconveniences and insurmountable objections against this general power being given to the federal courts. Gentlemen will perhaps say there will be no occasion to carry up the evidence by *viva voce* testimony, because Congress may order it to be committed to writing, and transmitted in that manner with the rest of the record. It is true they may, but it is as true that they may not. But suppose they do;

little conversant as I am in this subject, I know there is a great difference between *viva voce* evidence given at the bar, and testimony given in writing. I leave it to gentlemen more conversant in these matters to discuss it. They are also to have cognizance in controversies to which the United States shall be a party. This power is superadded, that there might be no doubt. and that all cases arising under the government might be brought before the federal court. Gentlemen will not, I presume, deny that all revenue and excise controversies, and all proceedings relative to the duties of the officers of government, from the highest to the lowest, may and must be brought by these means to the federal courts; in the first instance, to the inferior federal court, and afterwards to the superior court. Every fact proved with respect to these, in the court below, may be revived in the superior court. But this appellate jurisdiction is to be under the regulations of Congress. What these regulations may be, God only knows.

Their *jurisdiction* further extends to controversies between citizens of different states. Can we not trust our state courts with the decision of these? If I have a controversy with a man in Maryland, —if a man in Maryland has my bond for a hundred pounds. —are not the state courts competent to try it? It is suspected that they would enforce the payment if unjust, or refuse to enforce it if just? The very idea is ridiculous. What! carry me a thousand miles from home—from my family and business—to where, perhaps, it will be impossible for me to prove that I paid it? Perhaps I have a respectable witness who saw me pay the money; but I must carry him one thousand miles to prove it, or be compelled to pay it again. Is there any necessity for this power? It ought to have no unnecessary or dangerous power. Why should the federal courts have this cognizance? Is it because one lives on one side of the Potomac, and the other on the other? Suppose I have your

Objected to settlement of British debts in federal court. Fed ct obliged under peace treaty to consider British claims

bond for a thousand pounds: if I have any wish to harass you, or if I be of a litigious disposition, I have only to assign it to a gentleman in Maryland. This assignment will involve you in trouble and expense. What effect will this power have between British creditors and the citizens of this state? This is a ground on which I shall speak with confidence. Every one, who heard me speak on the subject, knows that I always spoke for the payment of the British debts. I wish every honest debt to be paid. Though I would wish to pay the British creditor, yet I would not put it in his power to gratify private malice to our injury. Let me be put right if I be mistaken; but there is not, in my opinion, a single British creditor but can bring his debtors to the federal court.

An unusual position for Mason!

There are a thousand instances where debts have been paid, and yet must, by this appellate cognizance, be paid again. Are these imaginary cases? Are they only possible cases, or are they certain and inevitable? "To controversies between a state and the citizens of another state." How will their jurisdiction in this case do? Let gentlemen look at the westward. Claims respecting those lands, every liquidated account, or other claim against this state, will be tried before the federal court. Is not this disgraceful? Is this state to be brought to the bar of justice like a delinquent individual? Is the sovereignty of the state to be arraigned like a culprit, or private offender? Will the states undergo this mortification? I think this power perfectly unnecessary. But let us pursue this subject farther. What is to be done if a judgment be obtained against a state? Will you issue a *fieri facias*? It would be ludicrous to say that you could put the state's body in jail. How is the judgment, then, to be enforced? A power which cannot be executed ought not to be granted.

Let us consider the operation of the last subject of its *cognizance*. "Controversies between a state, or the citizens thereof, and foreign states, citizens, or subject." There is a confusion in this case. This much, however, may be raised out of it—that a suit will be brought against Virginia. She may be sued by a foreign state. What reciprocity is there in it? In a suit between Virginia and a foreign state, is the foreign state to be bound by the decision? Is there a similar privilege given to us in foreign states? Where will you find a parallel regulation? How will the decision be enforced? Only by the *ultima ratio regum.* A dispute between a foreign citizen or subject and a Virginian cannot be tried in our own courts, but must be decided in the federal court. Is this the case in any other country? Are not men obliged to stand by the laws of the country where the disputes are? This is an innovation which is utterly unprecedented and unheard-of. Cannot we trust the state courts with disputes between a Frenchman, or an Englishman, and a citizen; or with disputes between two Frenchmen? This is disgraceful; it will annihilate your state judiciary: it will prostrate your legislature.

Thus, sir, it appears to me that the greater part of these powers are unnecessary, and dangerous, as tending to impair, and ultimately destroy, the state judiciaries, and, by the same principle, the legislation of the state governments. To render it safe, there must be an amendment, such as I have pointed out. After mentioning the original jurisdiction of the Supreme Court, which extends to but three cases, it gives it appellate jurisdiction, in all other cases mentioned, both as to law and fact, indiscriminately and without limitation. Why not remove the cause of fear and danger? But it is said that the regulations of Congress will remove these. I say that, in my opinion, they will have a contrary effect, and will utterly annihilate your state courts. Who are the court? The judges. It is a familiar distinction. We frequently speak of a court in contradistinction from a jury. I think the court are to be the judges of this. The judges on the bench are to be judges of fact and law, with such exceptions, &c., as Congress shall make. Now, give me leave to ask, Is not a jury excluded absolutely? By way of illustration, were Congress to say that a jury, instead of a court, should judge the fact, will not the court be still judges of the fact consistently with this Constitution? Congress may make such a regulation, or may not. But suppose they do; what sort of a jury would they have in the ten miles square? I would rather, a thousand times, be tried by a court than by such a jury. This great palladium of national safety, which is secured to us by our own government, will be taken from us in those courts; or, if it be reserved, it will be but in name, and not in substance. In the government of Virginia, we have secured an impartial jury of the vicinage. We can except to jurors, and peremptorily challenge them in criminal trials. If I be tried in the federal court for a crime which may affect my life, have I a right of challenging or excepting to the jury? Have not the best men suffered by weak and partial juries? This sacred right ought, therefore, to be secured. I dread the ruin that will be brought on thirty thousand of our people, with respect to disputed lands. I am personally endangered as an inhabitant of the Northern Neck. The people of that part will be obliged, by the operation of this power, to pay the quitrent of their lands. Whatever other gentlemen may think, I consider this as a most serious alarm. It will little avail a man to make a profession of his candor. It is to his character and reputation they will appeal. Let gentlemen consider my public and private character. To these I wish gentlemen to appeal for an interpretation of my motives and views. Lord Fairfax's title was clear and undisputed. After the revolution, we taxed his lands as private property. After his death, an act of Assembly was made, in 1782, to sequester the quitrents due, at his death, in the hands of his debtors. Next year, an act was made restoring them to the executor of the proprietor. Subsequent to this, the treaty of peace was made, by which it was agreed that there should be no further confiscations. But, after this, an act of Assembly passed, confiscating his whole property. As Lord Fairfax's title was indisputably good, and as treaties are to be the supreme law of the land, will not his representatives be able to recover all in the fedesal court? How will gentlemen like to pay an additional tax on lands in the Northern Neck? This the operation of this system will compel them to do. They now are subject to the same tax that other citizens are; and if the quitrents be recovered in the federal court, they are doubly taxed. This may be called an assertion; but were I going to my grave, I would appeal to Heaven that I think it true. How will a poor man, who is injured or dispossessed unjustly, get a remedy? Is he to go to the federal court, seven or eight hundred miles? He might as well give his claim up. He may grumble, but, finding no relief, he will be contented.

Again, all that tract of country between the Blue Ridge and the Alleghany Mountains will be claimed, and probably recovered in the federal court, from the present possessors, by those companies who have a title to them. These *lands* have been sold to a great number of people. Many settled on them, on terms which were advertised. How will this be with respect to *ex post facto* laws? We have not only confirmed the title of those who made the contract, but those who did not, by a law, in 1779, on their paying the original price. Much was paid in a depreciated value, and much was not paid at all. Again, the great Indiana purchase, which was made to the westward, will, by this judicial power, be rendered a cause of dispute. The possessors may be ejected from those lands. That company paid a consideration of ten thousand pounds to the crown, before the lands were taken up. I have heard gentlemen of the law say (and I believe it is right) that, after the consideration was paid to the crown, the purchase was legally made, and ought to be valid. That company may come in, and show that they have paid the money, and have a full right to the land. Of the Indiana company I need not say much. It is well known that their claims will be brought before these courts. Three or four counties are settled on the land to which that company claims a title, and have long enjoyed it peaceably. All these claims before those courts, if they succeed, will introduce a scene of distress and confusion never heard of before. Our peasants will be, like those mentioned by Virgil, reduced to ruin and misery, driven from their farms, and obliged to leave their country:—

"Nos patriam fugimus, et dulcia linquimus arva."

Having mentioned these things, give me leave to submit an amendment, which I think would be proper and safe, and would render our citizens secure in their possessions justly held. I mean, sir, "that the judicial power shall extend to no case where the cause of action shall have originated before the ratification of this Constitution, except in suits for debts due to the United States, disputes between states about their territory, and disputes between persons claiming lands under grants of different states." In these cases, there is an obvious necessity for giving it a retrospective power. I have laid before you my idea on the subject, and expressed my fears, which I most conscientiously believe to be well founded.

[WILLIAM GRAYSON]

Mr. GRAYSON. Mr. Chairman, I must make a few observations on this subject; and, if my arguments are desultory I hope I shall stand justified by the bad example which has been set me, and the necessity I am under of following my opponents through all their various recesses. I do not in the smallest degree blame the conduct of the gentlemen who represented this state in the general Convention. I believe that they endeavored to do all the good to this commonwealth which was in their power, and that all the members who formed that Convention did every thing within the compass of their abilities to procure the best terms for their particular states. That they did not do more for the general good of America, is perhaps a misfortune. They are entitled, however, to our thanks and those of the people. Although I do not approve of the result of their deliberations, I do not criminate or suspect the principles on which they acted. I desire that what I may say may not be improperly applied. I make no allusions to any gentleman whatever.

I do not pretend to say that the present Confederation is not defective. Its defects have been actually experienced. But I am afraid that they cannot be removed. It has defects arising from reasons which are inseparable from the nature of such governments, and which cannot be removed but by death. All such governments, that ever existed, have uniformly produced this consequence—that particular interests have been consulted, and the general good, to which all wishes ought to be directed, has been neglected. But the particular disorders of Virginia ought not to be attributed to the Confederation. I was concerned to hear the local affairs of Virginia mentioned. If these make impressions on the minds of the gentlemen, why did not the Convention provide for the removing the evils of the government of Virginia? If I am right, the states, with respect to their internal affairs, are left precisely as before, except in a few instances. Of course, the judiciary, should this government be adopted, would not be improved; the state government would be in this respect nearly the same;

and the Assembly may, without judge or jury, hang as many men as they may think proper to sacrifice to the good of the public. Our judiciary has been certainly improved in some respects since the revolution. The proceedings of our courts are not, at least, as rapid as they were under the royal government.

[*Here Mr. Grayson mentioned a particular cause which had been thirty-one years on the docket.*]

The adoption of this government will not meliorate our own particular system. I beg leave to consider the circumstances of the Union antecedent to the meeting of the Convention at Philadelphia. We have been told of phantoms and ideal dangers to lead us into measures which will, in my opinion, be the ruin of our country. If the existence of those dangers cannot be proved, if there be no apprehension of wars, if there be no rumors of wars, it will place the subject in a different light, and plainly evince to the world that there cannot be any reason for adopting measures which we apprehend to be ruinous and destructive. When this state proposed that the general government should be improved, Massachusetts was just recovered from a rebellion which had brought the republic to the brink of destruction—from a rebellion which was crushed by that federal government which is now so much contemned and abhorred: a vote of that august body for fifteen hundred men, aided by the exertions of the state, silenced all opposition, and shortly restored the public tranquillity. Massachusetts was satisfied that these internal commotions were so happily settled, and was unwilling to risk any similar distresses by theoretic experiments. Were the Eastern States willing to enter into this measure? Were they willing to accede to the proposal of Virginia? In what manner was it received? Connecticut revolted at the idea. The Eastern States, sir, were unwilling to recommend a meeting of a convention. They were well aware of the dangers of revolutions and changes. Why was every effort used, and such uncommon pains taken, to bring it about? This would have been unnecessary, had it been approved of by the people. Was Pennsylvania disposed for the reception of this project of reformation? No, sir. She was even unwilling to amend her revenue laws, so as to make the five per centum operative. She was satisfied with things as they were. There was no complaint, that ever I heard of, from any other part of the Union, except Virginia. This being the case among ourselves, what dangers were there to be apprehended from foreign nations? It will be easily shown that dangers from that quarter were absolutely imaginary. Was not France friendly? Unequivocally so. She was devising new regulations of commerce for our advantage. Did she harass us with applications for her money? Is it likely that France will quarrel with us? Is it not reasonable to suppose that she will be more desirous than ever to cling, after losing the Dutch republic, to her best ally? How are the Dutch? We owe them money, it is true; and are they not willing that we should owe them more? Mr Adams applied to them for a new loan to the poor, despised Confederation. They readily granted it. The Dutch have a fellow-feeling for us. They were in the same situation with ourselves.

I believe that the money which the Dutch borrowed of Henry IV. is not yet paid. How did they pass Queen Elizabeth's loan? At a very considerable discount. They took advantage of the weakness and necessities of James I., and made their own terms with that contemptible monarch. Loans from nations are not like loans from private men. Nations lend money, and grant assistance, to one another, from views of national interest. France was willing to pluck the fairest feather out of the British crown. This was her object in aiding us. She will not quarrel with us on pecuniary considerations. Congress considered it in this point of view; for when a proposition was made to make it a debt of private persons, it was rejected without hesitation. That respectable body wisely considered, that, while we remained their debtors in so considerable a degree, they would not be inattentive to our interest.

With respect to Spain, she is friendly in a high degree. I wish to know by whose interposition was the treaty with Morocco made. Was it not by that of the king of Spain? Several predatory nations disturbed us, on going into the Mediterranean: the influence of Charles III. at the Barbary court, and four thousand pounds, procured as good a treaty with Morocco as could be expected. But I acknowledge it is not of any consequence, since the Algerines and people of Tunis have not entered into similar measures. We have nothing to fear from Spain; and, were she hostile, she could never be formidable to this country. Her strength is so scattered, that she never can be dangerous to us either in peace or war.

As to Portugal, we have a treaty with her, which may be very advantageous, though it be not yet ratified.

The domestic debt is diminished by considerable sales of western lands to Cutler, Sergeant, and Company; to Simms; and to Royal, Flint, and Company. The board of treasury is authorized to sell in Europe, or any where else, the residue of those lands.

An act of Congress has passed, to adjust the public debts between the individual states and the United States.

Was our trade in a despicable situation? I shall say nothing of what did not come under my own observation. When I was in Congress, sixteen vessels had had sea letters in the East India trade, and two hundred vessels entered and cleared out, in the French West India Islands, in one year.

I must confess that public credit has suffered, and that

our public creditors have been ill used. This was owing to a fault at the head-quarters, —to Congress themselves, —in not apportioning the debts on the different states, and in not selling the western lands at an earlier period. If requisitions have not been complied with, it must be owing to Congress, who might have put the unpopular debts on the back lands. Commutation is abhorrent to New England ideas. Speculation is abhorrent to the Eastern States. Those inconveniences have resulted from the bad policy of Congress.

There are certain modes of governing the people which will succeed. There are others which will not. The idea of consolidation is abhorrent to the people of this country. How were the sentiments of the people before the meeting of the Convention at Philadelphia? They had only one object in view. Their ideas reached no farther than to give the general government the five per centum impost, and the regulation of trade. When it was agitated in Congress, in a committee of the whole, this was all that was asked, or was deemed necessary. Since that period, their views have extended much farther. Horrors have been greatly magnified since the rising of the Convention.

We are now told by the honorable gentleman (Governor Randolph) that we shall have wars and rumors of wars, that every calamity is to attend us, and that we shall be ruined and disunited forever, unless we adopt this Constitution. Pennsylvania and Maryland are to fall upon us from the north, like the Goths and Vandals of old; the Algerines, whose flat-sided vessels never came farther than Madeira, are to fill the Chesapeake with mighty fleets, and to attack us on our front; the Indians are to invade us with numerous armies on our rear, in order to convert our cleared lands into hunting-grounds; and the Carolinians, from the South, (mounted on alligators, I presume,) are to come and destroy our cornfields, and eat up our little children!

These, sir, are the mighty dangers which await us if we reject—dangers which are merely imaginary, and ludicrous in the extreme! Are we to be destroyed by Maryland and Pennsylvania? What will democratic states make war for, and how long since have they imbibed a hostile spirit?

But the generality are to attack us. Will they attack us after violating their faith in the first Union? Will they not violate their faith if they do not take us into their confederacy? Have they not agreed, by the old Confederation, that the Union shall be perpetual, and that no alteration should take place without the consent of Congress, and the confirmation of the legislatures of every state? I cannot think that there is such depravity in mankind as that, after violating public faith so flagrantly, they should make war upon us, also, for not following their example.

The large states have divided the back lands among themselves, and have given as much as they thought proper to the generality. For the fear of disunion, we are told that we ought to take measures which we otherwise should not. Disunion is impossible. The Eastern States hold the fisheries, which are their cornfields, by a hair. They have a dispute with the British government about their limits at this moment. Is not a general and strong government necessary for their interest? If ever nations had inducements to peace, the Eastern States now have. New York and Pennsylvania anxiously look forward for the fur trade. How can they obtain it but by union? Can the western posts be got or retained without union? How are the little states inclined? They are not likely to disunite. Their weakness will prevent them from quarrelling. Little men are seldom fond of quarrelling among giants. Is there not a strong inducement to union, while the British are on one side and the Spaniards on the other? Thank Heaven, we have a Carthage of our own!

But we are told that, if we do not embrace the present

moment, we are lost forever. Is there no difference between productive states and carrying states? If we hold out, will not the tobacco trade enable us to make terms with the carrying states? Is there nothing in a similarity of laws, religion, language, and manners? Do not these, and the intercourse and intermarriage between the people of the different states, invite them in the strongest manner to union?

But what would I do on the present occasion to remedy the existing defects of the present Confederation? There are two opinions prevailing in the world—the one, that mankind can only be governed by force; the other, that they are capable of freedom and a good government. Under a supposition that mankind can govern themselves, I would recommend that the present Confederation should be amended. Give Congress the regulation of commerce. Infuse new strength and spirit into the state governments; for, when the component parts are strong, it will give energy to the government, although it be otherwise weak. This may be proved by the union of Utrecht.

Apportion the public debts in such a manner as to throw the unpopular ones on the back lands. Call only for requisitions for the foreign interest, and aid them by loans. Keep on so till the American character be marked with some certain features. We are yet too young to know what we are fit for. The continual migration of people from Europe, and the settlement of new countries on our western frontiers, are strong arguments against making new experiments now in government. When these things are removed, we can, with greater prospect of success, devise changes. We ought to consider, as Montesquieu says, whether the construction of the government be suitable to the genius and disposition of the people, as well as a variety of other circumstances.

But if this position be not true, and men can only be

governed by force, then be as gentle as possible. What, then, would I do? I would not take the British monarchy for my model. We have not materials for such a government in this country, although I will be bold to say, that it is one of the governments in the world by which liberty and property are best secured. But I would adopt the following government. I would have a President for life, choosing his successor at the same time; a Senate for life, with the powers of the House of Lords; and a triennial House of Representatives, with the powers of the House of Commons in England.

By having such a President, we should have more independence and energy in the executive, and not be encumbered with the expense, &c., of a court and an hereditary prince and family. By such a Senate, we should have more stability in the laws, without having an odious hereditary aristocracy. By the other branch, we should be fully and fairly represented. If, sir, we are to be consolidated at all, we ought to be fully represented, and governed with sufficient energy, according to numbers, in both houses.

I admit that coercion is necessary in every government in some degree; that it is manifestly wanting in our present government, and that the want of it has ruined many nations. But I should be glad to know what great degree of coercion is in this Constitution, more than in the old government, if the states will refuse to comply with requisitions, and they can only be compelled by means of an army. Suppose the people will not pay the taxes; is not the sword to be then employed? The difference is this—that, by this Constitution, the sword is employed against individuals, by the other, it is employed against the states, which is more honorable. Suppose a general resistance to pay taxes in such a state as Massachusetts; will it not be precisely the same thing as a non-compliance with requisitions?

Will this Constitution remedy the fatal inconveniences of the clashing state interests? Will not every member that goes from Virginia be actuated by state influence? So they will also from every other state. Will the liberty and property of this country be secure under such a government? What, sir, is the present Constitution? A republican government founded on the principles of monarchy, with the three estates. Is it like the model of Tacitus or Montesquieu? Are there checks in it, as in the British monarchy? There is an executive fetter in some parts, and as unlimited in others as a Roman dictator. A democratic branch marked with the strong features of aristocracy, and an aristocratic branch with all the impurities and imperfections of the British House of Commons, arising from the inequality of representation and want of responsibility. There will be plenty of Old Sarums, if the new Constitution should be adopted. Do we love the British so well as to imitate their imperfections? We could not effect it more than in that particular instance. Are not all defects and corruption founded on an inequality of representation and want of responsibility? How is the executive? Contrary to the opinion of all the best writers, blended with the legislative. We have asked for bread, and they have given us a stone. I am willing to give the government the regulation of trade. It will be serviceable in regulating the trade among the states. But I believe that it will not be attended with the advantages generally expected.

As to direct taxation—give up this, and you give up every thing, as it is the highest act of sovereignty: surrender up this inestimable jewel, and you throw away a pearl richer than all your tribe. But it has been said by an honorable gentleman, (Mr. Pendleton,) as well as I recollect, that there could be no such thing as an interference between the two legislatures, either in point of direct taxation, or in any other case whatsoever. An honorable gentleman (Mr. Mason) has replied that they might interfere in the case of a poll tax. I will go farther, and say, that the case may happen in the judiciary. Suppose a state execution and a federal execution issued against the same man, and the state officer and federal officer seize him at the same moment; would they divide the man in two, as Solomon directed the child to be divided who was claimed by two women? I suppose the general government, as being paramount, would prevail. How are two legislatures to coincide, with powers transcendent, supreme, and omnipotent? for such is the definition of a legislature. There must be an external interference, not only in the collection of taxes, but in the judiciary. Was there ever such a thing in any country before? Great Britain never went so far in the stamp act. Poyning's law—the abhorrence of the Irish—never went so far. I never heard of two supreme coördinate powers in one and the same country before. I cannot conceive how it can happen. It surpasses every thing that I have read of concerning other governments, or that I can conceive by the utmost exertion of my faculties.

But, sir, as a cure for every thing, the democratic branch is elected by the people. What security is there in that? as has already been demanded. Their number is too small. Is not a small number more easy to be corrupted than a large one? Were not the tribunes at Rome the choice of the people? Were not the *decemviri* chosen by them? Was not Caesar himself the choice of the people? Did this secure them from oppression and slavery? Did this render these agents so chosen by the people upright? If five hundred and sixty members are corrupted in the British House of Commons, will it not be easier to corrupt ninety-one members of the new Constitution? But the British House of Commons are corrupted from the same cause that our representatives will be: I mean, *from the Old Sarums* among them—from the inequality of the representation.

How many are legislating in this country yearly? It is thought necessary to have fifteen hundred representatives, for the great purposes of legislation, throughout the Union, exclusive of one hundred and sixty senators, which form a proportion of about one for every fifteen hundred persons. By the present Constitution, these extensive powers are to be exercised by the small number of ninety-one persons—a proportion almost twenty times less than the other. It must be degrading indeed to think that so small a number should be equal to so many! Such a preferential distinction must presuppose the happiest selection. They must have something divine in their composition, to merit such a preëminence But my greatest objection is, that it will, in its operation, be found unequal, grievous, and oppressive. If it have any efficacy at all, it must be by a faction—a faction of one part of the Union against the other. I think that it has a great natural imbecility within itself, too weak for a consolidated and too strong for a confederate government. But if it be called into action by a combination of seven states, it will be terrible indeed. We need be at no loss to determine how this combination will be formed. There is a great difference of circumstances between the states. The interest of the carrying states is strikingly different from that of the productive states. I mean not to give offence to any part of America, but mankind are governed by interest. The carrying states will assuredly unite, and our situation will be then wretched indeed. Our commodities will be transported on their own terms, and every measure will have for its object their particular interest. Let ill-fated Ireland be ever present to our view. We ought to be wise enough to guard against the abuse of such a government. Republics, in fact, oppress more than monarchies. If we advert to the page of history, we shall find this disposition too often manifested in republican governments. The Romans, in ancient, and the

Dutch, in modern times, oppressed their provinces in a remarkable degree.

I hope that my fears are groundless; but I believe it as I do my creed, that this government will operate as a faction of seven states to oppress the rest of the union. But it may be said that we are represented, and cannot therefore be injured. A poor representation it will be! The British would have been glad to take America into the union, like the Scotch, by giving us a small representation. The Irish might be indulged with the same favor by asking for it. Will that lessen our misfortunes? A small representation gives a pretence to injure and destroy. But, sir, the Scotch union is introduced by an honorable gentleman as an argument in favor of adoption. Would he wish his country to be on the same foundation as Scotland? They have but forty-five members in the House of Commons, and sixteen in the House of Lords.

These go up regularly in order to be bribed. The smallness of their number puts it out of their power to carry any measure. And this unhappy nation exhibits the only instance, perhaps, in the world, where corruption becomes a virtue. I devoutly pray that this description of Scotland may not be picturesque of the Southern States, in three years from this time! The committee being tired, as well as myself, I will take another time to give my opinion more fully on this great and important subject.

Mr. Monroe, seconded by Mr. Henry, moved that the committee should rise, that Mr. Grayson might have an opportunity of continuing his argument next day. Mr. Madison insisted on going through the business regularly, according to the resolution of the house.

THURSDAY, *June* 12, 1788.

[The 1st and 2d sections still under consideration.]

Mr. GRAYSON. Mr. Chairman, I asserted yesterday that

there were two opinions in the world—the one that mankind were capable of governing themselves, the other that
it required actual force to govern them. On the principle
that the first position was true, and which is consonant to
the rights of humanity, the house will recollect that it was
my opinion to amend the present Confederation, and infuse a new portion of health and strength into the state
governments; to apportion the public debts in such a manner as to throw the unpopular ones on the back lands; to
divide the rest of the domestic debt among the different
states; and to call for requisitions only for the interest of
the foreign debt. If, contrary to this maxim, force is necessary to govern men, I then did propose, as an alternative,
not a monarchy like that of Great Britain, but a milder
government, one which, under the idea of a general corruption of manners, and the consequent necessity of force,
should be as gentle as possible. I showed, in as strong a
manner as I could, some of the principal defects in the
Constitution. The greatest defect is the opposition of the
component parts to the interests of the whole; for, let gentlemen ascribe its defects to as many causes as their imagination may suggest, this is the principal and radical
one. I urged that, to remedy the evils which must result
from this government, a more equal representation in the
legislature, and proper checks against abuse, were indis-
pensably necessary. I do not pretend to propose for your
adoption the plan of government which I mentioned as an
alternative to a monarchy, in case mankind were incapable
of governing themselves. I only meant, if it were once
established that force was necessary to govern men, that
such a plan would be more eligible for a free people than
the introduction of crowned heads and nobles. Having
premised this much, to obviate misconstruction, I shall
proceed to the clause before us with this observation—that
I prefer a complete consolidation to a partial one, but a

federal government to either. In my opinion, the states which give up the power of taxation have nothing more to give. The people of that state which suffers any power but her own immediate government to interfere with the sovereign right of taxation are gone forever. Giving the right of taxation is giving a right to increase the miseries of the people. Is it not a political absurdity to suppose that there can be two concurrent legislatures, each possessing the supreme power of direct taxation? If two powers come in contact, must not the one prevail over the other? Must it not strike every man's mind, that two unlimited, coëqual, coördinate authorities, over the same objects, cannot exist together? But we are told that there is one instance of coëxisting powers, in cases of petty corporations, as well here as in other parts of the world. The case of petty corporations does not prove the propriety or possibility of two coëqual, transcendent powers over the same object. Although these have the power of taxation, it only extends to certain degrees and for certain purposes. The powers of corporations are defined, and operate on limited objects. Their power originates by the authority of the legislature, and can be destroyed by the same authority. Persons carrying on the powers of a petty corporation may be punished for interfering with the power of the legislature. Their acts are entirely nugatory, if they contravene those of the legislature.

Scotland is also introduced to show that two different bodies may, with convenience, exercise power of taxation in the same country. How is the land tax there? There is a fixed apportionment. When England pays four shillings in the pound, Scotland only pays forty-five thousand pounds. This proportion cannot be departed from, whatever augmentation may take place. There are stannary courts, and a variety of other inferior private courts, in England. But when they pass the bounds of their jurisdiction, the su-

preme courts in Westminster Hall may, on appeal, correct
the abuse of their power. Is there any connection between
the federal courts and state courts? What power is there to
keep them in order? Where is there any authority to terminate disputes between these two contending powers?
An observation came from an honorable gentleman, (Mr.
Mason,) when speaking of the propriety of the general
government's exercising this power, that, according to the
rules and doctrine of representation, the thing was entirely
impracticable. I agreed with him in sentiment. I waited to
hear the answer from the admirers of the new Constitution. What was the answer? Gentlemen were obliged to
give up the point with respect to general, uniform taxes.
They have the candor to acknowledge that taxes on slaves
would not affect the Eastern States, and that taxes on fish
or potash would not affect the Southern States. They are
then reduced to this dilemma. In order to support this part
of the system, they are obliged to controvert the first maxims of representation. The best writers on this subject lay
it down as a fundamental principle, that he who lays a tax
should bear his proportion of paying it. A tax that might
with propriety be laid, and with ease collected, in Delaware, might be highly improper in Virginia. The taxes
cannot be uniform throughout the states without being
oppressive to some. If they be not uniform, some of the
members will lay taxes, in the payment of which they will
bear no proportion. The members of Delaware will assist
in laying a tax on our slaves, of which they will pay no part
whatever. The members of Delaware do not return to
Virginia, to give an account of their conduct. This total
want of responsibility and fellow-feeling will destroy the
benefits of representation. In order to obviate this objection, the gentleman has said that the same evil exists, in
some degree, in the present Confederation:—to which I
answer, that the present Confederation has nothing to do

but to say how much money is necessary, and to fix the proportion to be paid by each state. They cannot say in what manner the money shall be raised. This is left to the state legislatures.

But, says the honorable gentleman, (Mr. Madison,) if we were in danger, we should be convinced of the necessity of the clause. Are we to be terrified into a belief of its necessity? It is proposed by the opposition to amend it in the following manner—that requisitions shall be first made, and if not paid, that direct taxes shall be laid by way of punishment. If this ultimate right be in Congress, will it not be in their power to raise money on any emergency? Will not their credit be competent to procure any sum they may want? Gentlemen agree that it would be proper to imitate the conduct of other countries, and Great Britain particularly, in borrowing money, and establishing funds for the payment of the interest on the loans, that, when the government is properly organized, and its competency to raise money made known, public and private confidence will be the result, and men will readily lend it any sums it may stand in need of. If this should be a fact, and the reasoning well founded, it will clearly follow that it will be practicable to borrow money in cases of great difficulty and danger, on the principles contended for by the opposition; and this observation must supersede the necessity of granting them the powers of direct taxation in the first instance, provided the right is secured in the second.

As to the idea of making extensive loans for extinguishing the present domestic debt, it is what I have not by any means in contemplation. I think it would be unnecessary, unjust, and impolitic. This country is differently situated and circumstanced from all other countries in the world. It is now thinly inhabited, but daily increasing in numbers. It would not be politic to lay grievous taxes and burdens at present. If our numbers double in twenty-five years, as is generally believed, we ought to spare the present race, because there will be double the number of persons to pay in that period of time; so that, were our matters so arranged that the interest could be paid regularly, and that any one might get his money when he thought proper, as is the case now in England, it would be all that public faith would require. Place the subject, however, in every point of view—whether as it relates to raising money for the immediate exigencies of the state, or for the extinction of the foreign or the domestic debt—still it must be obvious, if a proper confidence is placed in the acknowledgment of the right of taxation in the second instance, that every purpose can be answered.

However, sir, if the states are not blameless, why has not the Congress used that coercion which is vested in their government? It is an unquestionable fact that the Belgic republic, on a similar occasion, by an actual exertion of force, brought a delinquent province to a proper sense of justice. The gentleman said that, in case of a partial compliance with requisitions, the alternative proposed will operate unequally, by taxing those who may have already paid, as well as those who have not, and involving the innocent in the crimes of the guilty. Suppose the new government fully vested with authority to raise taxes; it will also operate unequally. To make up antecedent deficiencies, they will lay more taxes the next succeeding year. By this means, those persons from whom a full proportion shall have been extracted will be saddled with a share of the deficiencies, as well as those who shall not have discharged their full portion. This mode, then, will have precisely the same unequal and unjust operation as the other.

I said, yesterday, that there were one thousand five hundred representatives, and one hundred and sixty senators, who transacted the affairs of the different states. But we are told that this great number is unnecessary, and that in the multitude of counsellors there is folly instead of wisdom; that they are a dead weight on the public business, which is said in all public assemblies to devolve on a few. This may in some degree be true, but it will not apply in the great latitude as mentioned by the gentleman. If ten men in our Assembly do the public business, may not the same observation extend to Congress? May not five men do the public business of the Union? But there is a great difference between the objects of legislation in Congress and those of the state legislatures. If the former be more complicated, there is a greater necessity of a full and adequate representation. It must be confessed that it is highly improper to trust our liberty and property in the hands of so few persons, if they were any thing less than divine. But it seems that, in this contest of power, the state governments have the advantage. I am of opinion that it will be directly the reverse. What influence can the state governments be supposed to have, after the loss of their most important rights? Will not the diminution of their power and influence be an augmentation of those of the general government? Will not the officers of the general government receive higher compensation for their services than those of the state governments? Will not the most influential men be employed by Congress? I think the state governments will be contemned and despised as soon as they give up the power of direct taxation; and a state, says Montesquieu, should lose her existence sooner than her importance.

But, sir, we are told that, if we do not give up this power to Congress, the impost will be stretched to the utmost extent. I do suppose this might follow, if the thing did not correct itself. But we know that it is the nature of this kind of taxation, that a small duty will bring more real money than a large one. The experience of the English nation proves the truth of this assertion. There has been much said of the necessity of the five per cent. impost. I have been ever of opinion, that two and a half per cent. would produce more real money into the treasury. But we need not be alarmed on this account, because, when smugglers will be induced, by heavy imposts, to elude the laws, the general government will find it their interest again to reduce them within reasonable and moderate limits. But it is suggested that, if direct taxation be inflicted by way of punishment, it will create great disturbances in the country. This is an assertion without argument. If man is a reasonable being, he will submit to punishment, and acquiesce in the justice of its infliction, when he knows he deserves it. The states will comply with the requisitions of Congress more readily when they know that this power may be ultimately used; and if they do not comply, they will have no reasons to complain of its exercise.

We are then told of the armed neutrality of the empress of Russia, the opposition to it by Great Britain, and the acquiescence of other powers. We are told that, in order to become the carriers of contending nations, it will be necessary to be formidable at sea—that we must have a fleet in case of a war between Great Britain and France. I think that the powers who formed that treaty will be able to support it. But if we were certain that this would not be the case, still I think that the profits that might arise from such a transient commerce could not compensate for the expenses of rendering ourselves formidable at sea, or the dangers that would probably result from the attempt. To have a fleet, in the present limited population of America, is, in my opinion, impracticable and inexpedient. Is America in a situation to have a fleet? I take it to be a rule founded on common sense, that manufacturers, as well as sailors, proceed from a redundancy of inhabitants. Our numbers, compared to our territory, are very small indeed.

I think, therefore, that all attempts to have a fleet, till our western lands are fully settled, are nugatory and vain. How will you induce your people to go to sea? Is it not more agreeable to follow agriculture than to encounter the dangers and hardships of the ocean? The same reasoning will apply in a greater degree to manufacturers. Both are the result of necessity. It would, besides, be dangerous to have a fleet in our present weak, dispersed, and defenceless situation. The powers of Europe, who have West India possessions, would be alarmed at any extraordinary maritime exertions, and, knowing the danger of our arrival at manhood, would crush us in our infancy. In my opinion, the great objects most necessary to be promoted and attended to, in America, are agriculture and population. First take care that you are sufficiently strong, by land, to guard against European partition; secure your own house before you attack that of other people. I think that the sailors who would be prevailed on to go to sea would be a real loss to the community: neglect of agriculture and loss of labor would be the certain consequence of such an irregular policy.

I hope that, when these objections are thoroughly considered, all ideas of having a fleet, in our infant situation, will be given over. When the American character is better known, and the government established on permanent principles,—when we shall be sufficiently populous, and our situation secure,—then come forward with a fleet; not with a small one, but with one sufficient to meet any of the maritime powers.

The honorable gentleman (Mr. Madison) said that the imposts will be less productive hereafter, on account of the increase of population. I shall not controvert this principle. When all the lands are settled, and we have manufactures sufficient, this may be the case. But I believe that for a very long time this cannot possibly happen. In islands and thick-settled countries, where they have manufactures, the principle will hold good, but will not apply in any degree to our country. I apprehend that, among us, as the people in the lower country find themselves straitened, they will remove to the frontiers, which, for a considerable period, will prevent the lower country from being very populous, or having recourse to manufactures. I cannot, therefore, but conclude that the amount of the imposts will continue to increase, at least for a great number of years.

Holland, we are informed, is not happy, because she has not a constitution like this. This is but an unsupported assertion. Do we not know the cause of her misfortunes? The evil is coeval with her existence—there are always opposite parties in that republic. There are now two parties—the aristocratic party, supporting the Prince of Orange, and the Lovestein party, supporting the rights of the people. France foments the one, and Great Britain the other. Is it known, if Holland had begun with such a government as this, that the violence of faction would not produce the same evils which they experience at this present moment? It is said that all our evils result from requisitions on the states. I did not expect to hear of complaints for noncompliance during the war. Do not gentlemen recollect our situation during the war? Our ports were blocked up, and all means of getting money destroyed, and almost every article taken from the farmer for the public service—so as, in many instances, not to leave him enough to support his own family with tolerable decency and comfort. It cannot be forgot that another resort of government was applied to, and that press-warrants were made to answer for non-compliance of requisitions. Every person must recollect our miserable situation during the arduous contest; therefore, I shall make no further apology for the states, during the existence of the war. Since the peace, there have been various causes for not furnishing the necessary quotas to the general government. In some of the flourishing states, the requisitions have been attended to; in others, their non-compliance is to be attributed more to the inability of the people than to their unwillingness to advance the general interests. Massachusetts attempted to correct the nature of things by extracting more from the people than they were able to part with What did it produce? A revolution which shook that state to its centre.

Paper money has been introduced. What did we do a few years ago? Struck off many millions, and by the charms of magic made the value of the emissions diminish by a forty-fold ratio. However unjust or unreasonable this might be, I suppose it was warranted by the inevitable laws of necessity. But, sir, there is no disposition now of having paper money; this engine of iniquity is universally reprobated. But conventions give power, and conventions can take it away. This observation does not appear to me well founded. It is not so easy to dissolve a government like this. Its dissolution may be prevented by a trifling minority of the people of America. The consent of so many states is necessary to introduce amendments, that I fear they will with great difficulty be obtained. It is said that a strong government will increase our population by the addition of immigrants. From what quarter is immigration to proceed? From the arbitrary monarchies of Europe? I fear this kind of population would not add much to our happiness or improvement. It is supposed that, from the prevalence of the Orange faction, numbers will come hither from Holland, although it is not imagined the strength of the government will form the inducement. The exclusive power of legislation over the ten miles square is introduced by many gentlemen. I would not deny the utility of vesting the general government with a power of this kind, were it properly guarded. Perhaps I am mistaken, but it occurs to me that Congress may give exclusive privileges to merchants residing within the ten miles square, and that the same exclusive power of legislation will enable them to grant similar privileges to merchants in the strongholds within the states. I wish to know if there be any thing in the Constitution to prevent it. If there be, I have not been able to discover it. I may, perhaps, not thoroughly comprehend this part of the Constitution; but it strikes my mind that there is a possibility that, in process of time, and from the simple operation of effects from causes, the whole commerce of the United States may be exclusively carried on by merchants residing within the seat of government, and those places of arms which may be purchased of the state legislatures. How detrimental and injurious to the community, and how repugnant to the equal rights of mankind, such exclusive emoluments would be, I submit to the consideration of the committee. Things of a similar nature have happened in other countries; or else from whence have issued the Hanse Towns, Cinque Ports, and other places in Europe, which have peculiar privileges in commerce as well as in other matters? I do not offer this sentiment as an opinion, but a conjecture, and, in this doubtful agitation of mind on a point of such infinite magnitude, only ask for information from the framers of the Constitution, whose superior opportunities must have furnished them with more ample lights on the subject than I am possessed of. Something is said on the other side with respect to the Mississippi. An honorable gentleman has mentioned, that he was satisfied that no member of Congress had any idea of giving up that river. Sir, I am not at liberty, from my situation, to enter into any investigation on the subject. I am free, however, to acknowledge that I have frequently heard the honorable member declare, that he conceived the object then in contemplation was the only method by which the right of that river could be ultimately secured. I have heard similar declarations from other members.

I must beg leave to observe, at the same time, that I most decidedly differed with them in sentiment. With respect to the citizens of the Eastern and some of the Middle States, perhaps the best and surest means of discovering their general dispositions may be by having recourse to their interests. This seems to be the pole-star to which the policy of nations is directed. If this supposition should be well founded, I think they must have reasons of considerable magnitude for wishing the exclusion of that river. If the Mississippi was yielded to Spain, the migration to the western country would be stopped, and the Northern States would not only retain their inhabitants, but preserve their superiority and influence over those of the South. If matters go on in their present direction, there will be a number of new states to the westward—population may become greater in the Southern States—the ten miles square may approach us! This they must naturally wish to prevent. I think gentlemen may know the disposition of the different states, from the geography of the country, and from the reason and nature of things. Is it not highly imprudent to vest a power in the generality, which will enable those states to relinquish that river? There are but feeble restrictions at present to prevent it. By the old Confederation, nine states are necessary to form any treaty. By this Constitution, the President, with two thirds of the members present in the Senate, can make any treaty. Ten members are two thirds of a quorum. Ten members are the representatives of five states. The Northern States may then easily make a treaty relinquishing this river. In my opinion, the power of making treaties, by which the territorial rights of any of the states may be essentially affected, ought to be guarded against every possibility of abuse; and the precarious situation to which those rights will be exposed is one reason, with me, among a number of others, for voting against its adoption.

13. *George Clinton: The Letters of "Cato".*

These letters, attributed to George Clinton, Governor of New York and leader of one of the two powerful factions in state politics that had emerged since the Revolution, summarize in comparatively brief compass some of the major arguments of the Antifederalists in that state and elsewhere. "Cato's" method of argument offers an interesting comparison with that of "Agrippa," the intellectual from Cambridge and Harvard. Whereas the latter offers his criticisms of the Constitution and then sets down a long list of proposed amendments, which would have almost completely emasculated that document if adopted, the practical politician of New York was content with negative criticisms alone. Thus he touches on the indirect election of the Senate and the President, but does not actually propose direct election of either. He criticizes the two-year term of the House of Representatives, but does not explore the problems of a one-year term. He criticizes two of the compromises made at Philadelphia, the equal representation of all states in the Senate regardless of population, and the guarantee of a continuation of the slave trade until 1808, without considering whether such compromises were necessary to secure agreement among the various groups whose interests and ideas were in conflict. "Cato's" *Letters* thus raise the difficult problem of interpreting much Antifederalist argumentation: What were the Antifederalists *really* opposed to? Any central government at all? This particular form? This particular feature of this particular form? Any proposal that came from or was supported by the opposing faction in state politics? No final answer can be given in most instances, but it is essential that the question should be asked.

IV.

[November 8, 1787]

To the Citizens of the State of New York.

Admitting, however, that the vast extent of America, together with the various other reasons which I offered you in my last number, against the practicability of the just exercise of the new government are insufficient to convince; still it is an undesirable truth, that its several parts are either possessed of principles, which you have heretofore considered as ruinous and that others are omitted which you have established as fundamental to your political security, and must in their operation, I will venture to assert, fetter your tongues and minds, enchain your bodies, and ultimately extinguish all that is great and noble in man.

In pursuance of my plan I shall begin with observations on the executive branch of this new system; and though it is not the first in order, as arranged therein, yet being the *chief*, is perhaps entitled by the rules of rank to the first consideration. The executive power as described in the 2d article, consists of a president and vice-president, who are to hold their offices during the term of four years; the same article has marked the manner and time of their election, and established the qualifications of the president; it also provides against the removal, death, or inability of the president and vice-president—regulates the salary of the

---

"The Letters of Cato," seven in number, were first published in *The New York Journal*, September 27, 1787, to January 3, 1788. The fourth through the seventh letters are reprinted here from the text in Ford, *Essays*, pp. 260–278.

president, delineates his duties and powers; and, lastly, declares the causes for which the president and vice-president shall be removed from office.

Notwithstanding the great learning and abilities of the gentlemen who composed the convention, it may be here remarked with deference, that the construction of the first paragraph of the first section of the second article is vague and inexplicit, and leaves the mind in doubt as to the election of a president and vice-president, after the expiration of the election for the first term of four years; in every other case, the election of these great officers is expressly provided for; but there is no explicit provision for their election in case of expiration of their offices, subsequent to the election which is to set this political machine in motion; no certain and express terms as in your state constitution, that *statedly* once in every four years, and as often as these offices shall become vacant, by expiration or otherwise, as is therein expressed, an election shall be held as follows, &c., this inexplicitness perhaps may lead to an establishment for life.

It is remarked by Monesquieu, in treating of republics, that *in all magistracies, the greatness of the power must be compensated by the brevity of the duration, and that a longer time than a year would be dangerous.* It is, therefore, obvious to the least intelligent mind to account why great power in the hands of a magistrate, and that power connected with considerable duration, may be dangerous to the liberties of a republic, the deposit of vast trusts in the hands of a single magistrate, enables him in their exercise to create a numerous train of dependents; this tempts his *ambition*, which in a republican magistrate is also remarked, *to be pernicious*, and the duration of his office for any considerable time favors his views, gives him the means and time to perfect and execute his designs, *he therefore fancies that he may be great and glorious by*

oppressing his fellow-citizens, and raising himself to per-
manent grandeur on the ruins of his country. And here it
may be necessary to compare the vast and important powers of the president, together with his continuance in office, with the foregoing doctrine—his eminent magisterial
situation will attach many adherents to him, and he will be
surrounded by expectants and courtiers, his power of nomination and influence on all appointments, the strong posts
in each state comprised within his superintendence, and
garrisoned by troops under his direction, his control over
the army, militia, and navy, the unrestrained power of
granting pardons for treason, which may be used to screen
from punishment those whom he had secretly instigated to
commit the crime, and thereby prevent a discovery of his
own guilt, his duration in office for four years: these, and
various other principles evidently prove the truth of the
position, that if the president is possessed of ambition, he
has power and time sufficient to ruin his country.

Though the president, during the sitting of the legislature, is assisted by the senate, yet he is without a constitutional council in their recess; he will therefore be unsupported by proper information and advice, and will
generally be directed by minions and favorites, or a
council of state will grow out of the principal officers of the
great departments, the most dangerous council in a free
country.

The ten miles square, which is to become the seat of
government, will of course be the place of residence for
the president and the great officers of state; the same observations of a great man will apply to the court of a president possessing the powers of a monarch, that is observed
of that of a monarch—*ambition with idleness—baseness*
with pride—the thirst of riches without labor—aversion to
truth—flattery—treason—perfidy—violation of engage-
ments—contempt of civil duties—hope from the mag-

istrate's weakness; but above all, the perpetual ridicule of virtue—these, he remarks, are the characteristics by which the courts in all ages have been distinguished.

The language and the manners of this court will be what distinguishes them from the rest of the community, not what assimilates them to it; and in being remarked for a behavior that shows they are not *meanly born*, and in adulation to people of fortune and power.

The establishment of a vice-president is as unnecessary as it is dangerous. This officer, for want of other employment, is made president of the senate, thereby blending the executive and legislative powers, besides always giving to some one state, from which he is to come, an unjust pre-eminence.

It is a maxim in republics that the representative of the people should be of their immediate choice; but by the manner in which the president is chosen, he arrives to this office at the fourth or fifth hand, nor does the highest vote, in the way he is elected, determine the choice, for it is only necessary that he should be taken from the highest of five, who may have a plurality of votes.

Compare your past opinions and sentiments with the present proposed establishment, and you will find, that if you adopt it, that it will lead you into a system which you heretofore reprobated as odious. Every American Whig, not long since, bore his emphatic testimony against a monarchical government, though limited, because of the dangerous inequality that it created among citizens as relative to their rights and property; and wherein does this president, invested with his powers and prerogatives, essentially differ from the king of Great Britain (save as to name, the creation of nobility, and some immaterial incidents, the offspring of absurdity and locality). The direct prerogatives of the president, as springing from his political character, are among the following: It is necessary, in order to distinguish him from the rest of the community, and enable him to keep, and maintain his court, that the compensation for his services, or in other words, his revenue, should be such as to enable him to appear with the splendor of a prince; he has the power of receiving ambassadors from, and a great influence on their appointments to foreign courts; as also to make treaties, leagues, and alliances with foreign states, assisted by the Senate, which when made become the supreme law of land: he is a constituent part of the legislative power, for every bill which shall pass the House of Representatives and Senate is to be presented to him for approbation; if he approves of it he is to sign it, if he disapproves he is to return it with objections, which in many cases will amount to a complete negative; and in this view he will have a great share in the power of making peace, coining money, etc., and all the various objects of legislation, expressed or implied in this Constitution: for though it may be asserted that the king of Great Britain has the express power of making peace or war, yet he never thinks it prudent to do so without the advice of his Parliament, from whom he is to derive his support, and therefore these powers, in both president and king, are substantially the same: he is the generalissimo of the nation, and of course has the command and control of the army, navy and militia; he is the general conservator of the peace of the union—he may pardon all offences, except in cases of impeachment, and the principal fountain of all offices and employments. Will not the exercise of these powers therefore tend either to the establishment of a vile and arbitrary aristocracy or monarchy? The safety of the people in a republic depends on the share or proportion they have in the government; but experience ought to teach you, that when a man is at the head of an elective government invested with great powers, and interested in his re-election, in what circle appointments will be made;

by which means an *imperfect aristocracy* bordering on monarchy may be established.

You must, however, my countrymen, beware that the advocates of this new system do not deceive you by a fallacious resemblance between it and your own state government which you so much prize; and, if you examine, you will perceive that the chief magistrate of this state is your immediate choice, controlled and checked by a just and full representation of the people, divested of the prerogative of influencing war and peace, making treaties, receiving and sending embassies, and commanding standing armies and navies, which belong to the power of the confederation, and will be convinced that this government is no more like a true picture of your own than an Angel of Darkness resembles an Angel of Light.

V.

[November 22, 1787]

TO THE CITIZENS OF THE STATE OF NEW YORK.

In my last number I endeavored to prove that the language of the article relative to the establishment of the executive of this new government was vague and inexplicit; that the great powers of the president, connected with his duration in office, would lead to oppression and ruin; that he would be governed by favorites and flatterers, or that a dangerous council would be collected from the great officers of state; that the ten miles square, if the remarks of one of the wisest men, drawn from the experience of mankind, may be credited, would be the asylum of the base, idle, avaricious and ambitious, and that the court would possess a language and manners different from yours; that a vice-president is as unnecessary as he is dangerous in his influence;

that the president cannot represent you because he is not of your own immediate choice; that if you adopt this government you will incline to an arbitrary and odious aristocracy or monarchy; that the president, possessed of the power given him by this frame of government, differs but very immaterially from the establishment of monarchy in Great Britain; and I warned you to beware of the fallacious resemblance that is held out to you by the advocates of this new system between it and your own state governments.

And here I cannot help remarking that inexplicitness seems to pervade this whole political fabric; certainly in political compacts, which Mr. Coke calls *the mother and nurse of repose and quietness* the want of which induced men to engage in political society, has ever been held by a wise and free people as essential to their security; as on the one hand it fixes barriers which the ambitious and tyrannically disposed magistrate dare not overleap, and on the other, becomes a wall of safety to the community—otherwise stipulations between the governors and governed are nugatory; and you might as well deposit the important powers of legislation and execution in one or a few and permit them to govern according to their disposition and will; but the world is too full of examples, which prove that *to live by one man's will became the cause of all men's misery*. Before the existence of express political compacts it was reasonably implied that the magistrate should govern with wisdom and justice; but mere implication was too feeble to restrain the unbridled ambition of a bad man, or afford security against negligence, cruelty or any other defect of mind. It is alleged that the opinions and manners of the people of America are capable to resist and prevent an extension of prerogative or oppression, but you must recollect that opinion and manners are mutable, and may not always be a permanent obstruction against the encroachments of government; that the progress of a commercial society begets luxury, the parent of inequality, the foe to virtue, and the enemy to restraint; and that ambition and voluptuousness, aided by flattery, will teach magistrates where limits are not explicitly fixed to have separate and distinct interests from the people; besides, it will not be denied that government assimilates the manners and opinions of the community to it. Therefore, a general presumption that rulers will govern well is not a sufficient security. You are then under a sacred obligation to provide for the safety of your posterity, and would you now basely desert their interests, when by a small share of prudence you may transmit to them a beautiful political patrimony, which will prevent the necessity of their travelling through seas of blood to obtain that which your wisdom might have secured? It is a duty you owe likewise to your own reputation, for you have a great name to lose; you are characterized as cautious, prudent and jealous in politics; whence is it therefore that you are about to precipitate yourselves into a sea of uncertainty, and adopt a system so vague, and which has discarded so many of your valuable rights? Is it because you do not believe that an American can be a tyrant? If this be the case, you rest on a weak basis: Americans are like other men in similar situations, when the manners and opinions of the community are changed by the causes I mentioned before; and your political compact inexplicit, your posterity will find that great power connected with ambition, luxury and flattery, will as readily produce a Caesar, Caligula, Nero and Domitain in America, as the same causes did in the Roman Empire.

But the next thing to be considered, in conformity to my plan, is the first article of this new government, which comprises the erection of the house of representatives and the senate, and prescribes their various powers and objects of legislation. The most general objections to the first article, that biennial elections for representatives are a departure from the safe democratic principles of annual ones—that the number of representatives are too few; that the apportionment and principles of increase are unjust; that no attention has been paid to either the numbers or property in each state in forming the senate; that the mode in which they are appointed and their duration will lead to the establishment of an aristocracy; that the senate and president are improperly connected, both as to appointments and the making of treaties, which are to become the supreme law of the land; that the judicial, in some measure, to wit, as to the trial of impeachments, is placed in the senate, a branch of the legislative, and sometimes a branch of the executive; that Congress have the improper power of making or altering the regulations prescribed by the different legislatures, respecting the time, place and manner of holding elections for representatives, and the time and manner of chosing senators; that standing armies may be established, and appropriation of money made for their support for two years; that the militia of the most remote state may be marched into those states situated at the opposite extreme of this continent; that the slave trade is, to all intents and purposes, permanently established, and a slavish capitation or poll-tax may at any time be levied; these are some of the many evils that will attend the adoption of this government.

But, with respect to the first objection, it may be remarked that a well-digested democracy has this advantage over all others, to wit: that it affords to many the opportunity to be advanced to the supreme command, and the honors they thereby enjoy fill them with a desire of rendering themselves worthy of them; hence this desire becomes part of their education, is matured in manhood, and produces an ardent affection for their country, and it is the opinion of Sidney and Montesquieu that this is, in a great measure, produced by annual election of magistrates.

If annual elections were to exist in this government, and learning and information to become more prevalent, you never would want men to execute whatever you could design. Sidney observes *that a well-governed state is as fruitful to all good purposes as the seven-headed serpent is said to have been in evil; when one head is cut off, many rise up in the place of it.* He remarks further that *it was also thought that free cities, by frequent election of magistrates, became nurseries of great and able men, every man endeavoring to excel others, that he might be advanced to the honor he had no other title to, than what might arise from his merit or reputation;* but the framers of this *perfect government*, as it is called, have departed from this democratical principle, and established biennial elections for the house of representatives, who are to be chosen by the people, and sextennial for the senate, who are to be chosen by the legislatures of the different states, and have given to the executive the unprecedented power of making temporary senators, in case of vacancies by resignation or otherwise, and so far forth establishing a precedent for virtual representation (though, in fact, their original appointment is virtual), thereby influencing the choice of the legislatures, or if they should not be so complaisant as to conform to his appointment, offence will be given to the executive, and the temporary members will appear ridiculous by rejection; this temporary member, during his time of appointment, will of course act by a power derived from the executive, and for, and under his immediate influence.

It is a very important objection to this government, that the representation consists of so few; too few to resist the influence of corruption, and the temptation to treachery, against which all governments ought to take precautions—how guarded you have been on this head, in your own state constitution, and yet the number of senators and representatives proposed for this vast continent does not equal those of your own state; how great the disparity, if you compare them with the aggregate numbers in the United States. The history of representation in England, from which we have taken our model of legislation, is briefly this: before the institution of legislating by deputies, the whole free part of the community usually met for that purpose; when this became impossible, by the increase of numbers, the community was divided into districts, from each of which was sent such a number of deputies as was a complete representation of the various numbers and orders of citizens within them; but can it be asserted with truth, that six men can be a complete and full representation of the numbers and various orders of the people in this state? Another thing that may be suggested against the small number of representatives is, that but few of you will have a chance of sharing even in this branch of the legislature; and that the choice will be confined to a very few. The more complete it is, the better will your interests be preserved, and the greater the opportunity you will have to participate in government, one of the principal securities of a free people; but this subject has been so ably and fully treated by a writer under the signature of Brutus, that I shall content myself with referring you to him thereon, reserving further observations on the other objections I have mentioned, for my future numbers.

VI.

[December 16, 1787.]

To the People of the State of New York.

The next objection that arises against this proffered constitution is, that the apportionment of representatives and direct taxes are unjust. The words, as expressed in this article, are "representatives and direct taxes shall be apportioned among the several states which may be included in this union, according to their respective numbers, which shall be determined by adding to the whole number of free persons, including those bound to service for a term of years, and excluding Indians not taxed, three-fifths of all other persons." In order to elucidate this, it will be necessary to repeat the remark in my last number, that the mode of legislation in the infancy of free communities was by the collective body, and this consisted of free persons, or those whose age admitted them to the right of mankind and citizenship, whose sex made them capable of protecting the state, and whose birth may be denominated Free Born; and no traces can be found that ever women, children, and slaves, or those who were not sui juris, in the early days of legislation, meeting with the free members of the community to deliberate on public measures; hence is derived this maxim in free governments, that representation ought to bear a proportion to the number of free inhabitants in a community; this principle your own state constitution, and others, have observed in the establishment of a future census, in order to apportion the representatives, and to increase or diminish the representation to the ratio of the increase or diminution of electors. But, what aid can the community derive from the assistance of women, infants and slaves, in their deliberation, or in their defence? and what motives, therefore, could the convention have in departing from the just and rational principle of representation, which is the governing principle of this state and of all America?

The doctrine of taxation is a very important one, and nothing requires more wisdom and prudence than the regulation of that portion, which is taken from, and of that which is left to the subject—and if you anticipate what will be the enormous expense of this new government added also to your own, little will that portion be which will be left to you. I know there are politicians who believe that you should be loaded with taxes, in order to make you industrious, and, perhaps, there are some of this opinion in the convention, but it is an erroneous principle. For, what can inspire you with industry, if the greatest measure of your labors are to be swallowed up in taxes? The advocates for this new system hold out an idea, that you will have but little to pay, for that the revenues will be so managed as to be almost wholly drawn from the source of trade or duties on imports, but this is delusive—for this government to discharge all its incidental expenses, besides paying the interest on the home and foreign debts, will require more money than its commerce can afford; and if you reflect one moment, you will find, that if heavy duties are laid on merchandise, as must be the case if government intends to make this the prime medium to lighten the people of taxes, that the price of the commodities, useful as well as luxurious, must be increased; the consumers will be fewer; the merchants must import less; trade will languish, and this source of revenue in a great measure be dried up; but if you examine this a little further you will find that this revenue, managed in this way, will come out of you, and be a very heavy and ruinous one, at least. The merchant no more than advances the money for you to the public and will not, nor cannot pay any part of it himself; and if he pays more duties, he will sell his commodities at a price portionably raised. Thus the laborer, mechanic, and farmer must feel it in the purchase of their utensils and clothing—wages, etc., must rise with the price of things or they must be ruined; and that must be the case with the farmer, whose produce will not increase, in the ratio, with labor, utensils and clothing; for that he must sell at the usual price or lower perhaps, caused by the decrease of trade; the consequence will be that he must mortgage his farm, and then comes inevitable bankruptcy.

In what manner then will you be eased, if the expenses of government are to be raised solely out of the commerce of this country; do you not readily apprehend the fallacy of this argument? But government will find that to press so heavily on commerce will not do, and therefore must have recourse to other objects; these will be a capitation or poll-tax, window lights, etc., etc., and a long train of impositions which their ingenuity will suggest; but will you submit to be numbered like the slaves of an arbitrary despot; and what will be your reflections when the tax-master thunders at your door for the duty on that light which is the bounty of heaven. It will be the policy of the great landholders who will chiefly compose this senate, and perhaps a majority of this house of representatives, to keep their lands free from taxes; and this is confirmed by the failure of every attempt to lay a land-tax in this state; hence recourse must and will be had to the sources I mentioned before. The burdens on you will be insupportable—your complaints will be inefficacious—this will beget public disturbances; and I will venture to predict, without the spirit of prophecy, that you and the government, if it is adopted, will one day be at issue on this point. The force of government will be exerted, this will call for an increase of revenue, and will add fuel to the fire. The result will be that either you will revolve to some other form, or that government will give peace to the country by destroying the opposition. If government therefore can, notwithstanding every opposition, raise a revenue on such things as are odious and burdensome to you, they can do anything.

But why should the number of individuals be the principle to apportion the taxes in each state, and to include in that number women, children and slaves? The most natural and equitable principle of apportioning taxes would be in a ratio to their property, and a reasonable impost in a ratio to their trade; but you are told to look for the reason of these things in accommodation; but this much-admired principle, when stripped of its mystery, will in this case appear to be no less than a basis for an odious poll-tax—the offspring of despotic governments, a thing so detestable that the state of Maryland, in their bill of rights, declares "that the levying taxes by the poll is grievous and oppressive, and ought to be abolished." A poll-tax is at all times oppressive to the poor, and their greatest misfortune will consist in having more prolific wives than the rich.

In every civilized community, even in those of the most democratic kind, there are principles which lead to an aristocracy—these are superior talents, fortunes and public employments. But in free governments the influence of the two former is resisted by the equality of the laws, and the latter by the frequency of elections, and the chance that every one has in sharing in public business; but when this natural and artificial eminence is assisted by principles interwoven in this government; when the senate, so important a branch of the legislature, is so far removed from the people as to have little or no connection with them; when their duration in office is such as to have the resemblance to perpetuity; when they are connected with the executive, by the appointment of all officers, and also to become a judiciary for the trial of officers of their own appointments; added to all this, when none but men of opulence will hold a seat, what is there left to resist and repel this host of influence and power? Will the feeble efforts of the house of representatives, in whom your security ought to subsist, consisting of about seventy-three, be able to hold the balance against them, when, from the fewness of members in this house, the senate will have in their power to poison even a majority of that body by douceurs of office for themselves or friends? From causes like this both Montesquieu and Hume have predicted the decline of the British government into that of an absolute one; but the liberties of this country, it is probable, if this system is adopted, will be strangled in their birth; for whenever the executive and senate can destroy the independence of the majority in the house of representatives, then where is your security? They are so intimately connected, that their interests will be one and the same; and will the slow increase of numbers be able to afford a repelling principle? But you are told to adopt this government first, and you will always be able to alter it afterwards; this would first be submitting to be slaves and then taking care of your liberty; and when your chains are on, then to act like freemen.

Complete acts of legislation, which are to become the supreme law of the land, ought to be the united act of all the branches of government; but there is one of the most important duties may be managed by the Senate and executive alone, and to have all the force of the law paramount without the aid or interference of the House of Representatives; that is the power of making treaties. This power is a very important one, and may be exercised in various ways, so as to affect your person and property, and even the domain of the nation. By treaties you may defalcate part of the empire; engagements may be made to raise an army, and you may be transported to Europe, to fight the wars of ambitious princes; money may be contracted for, and you must pay it; and a thousand other obligations may be entered into; all which will become the supreme law of the land, and you are bound by it. If treaties are erroneously or wickedly made who is there to punish,—the executive can always cover himself with the plea that he was advised by the senate, and the senate being a collective body are not easily made accountable for mal-administration. On this account we are in a worse situation than Great Britain, where they have secured by a ridiculous fiction, the king from accountability, by declaring that he can do no wrong, by which means the nation can have redress against his minister; but with us infallibility pervades every part of the system, and neither the executive nor his council, who are a collective body, and his advisers, can be brought to punishment for mal-administration.

VII.

[January 3, 1788.]

To the Citizens of the State of New York.

That the president and senate are further improperly connected will appear, if it is considered that their dependence on each other will prevent either from being a check upon the other; they must act in concert, and whether the power and influence of the one or the other is to prevail, will depend on the character and abilities of the men who hold those offices at the time. The senate is vested with such a proportion of the executive that it would be found necessary that they should be constantly sitting. This circumstance did not escape the convention, and they have provided for the event, in the 2d article, which declares that the executive may, on extraordinary occasions, *convene both houses or either of them.* No occasion can exist for calling the assembly without the senate; the words *or either of them* must have been intended to apply only to the senate. Their wages are already provided for, and it will be therefore readily observed that the partition between a perpetuation of their sessions, and a perpetuation of offices in the progress of the government, will be found to be but thin and feeble. Besides, the senate, who have the sole power to try all impeachments, in case of the impeachment of the president are to determine, as judges, the propriety of the advice they gave him as senators. Can the senate in this, therefore, be an impartial judicature? And will they not rather serve as a screen to great public defaulters?

Among the many evils that are incorporated in this new system of government is that of congress having the power of making or altering the regulations prescribed by the different legislatures respecting the time, place and manner of holding elections for representatives, and the time and manner of choosing senators. If it is enquired in what manner this regulation may be exercised to your injury, the answer is easy. By the first article the house of representatives shall consist of members, chosen every second year by the people of the several states who are qualified to vote for members of their several state assemblies; it can therefore readily be believed, that the different state legislatures, provided such can exist after the adoption of this government, will continue those easy and convenient modes for the election of representatives for the national legislature that are in use for the election of members of assembly for their own states; but the congress have, by the constitution, a power to make other regulations or alter those in practice, prescribed by your own state legislatures; hence, instead of having the places of elections in the precincts and brought home almost to your own doors, congress may establish a place, or places, at either the extremes, center or outer parts of the states; at a time and season, too, when it may be very inconvenient to attend; and by these means destroy the rights of election. But in opposition to this reasoning, it is asserted, that it is a necessary power, because the states might omit making rules for the purpose, and thereby defeat the existence of that branch of the government; this is what logicians call *argu-*

mentum absurdum; for the different states, if they will have any security at all in this government, will find it in the house of representatives, and they, therefore, would be very ready to eradicate a principle in which it dwells, or involve their country in an instantaneous revolution. Besides, if this was the apprehension of the framers, and the ground of that provision, why did not they extend this controlling power to the other duties of the several state legislatures? To exemplify this, the states are to appoint senators and electors for choosing of a president; but the time is to be under the direction of congress. Now, suppose they were to omit the appointment of senators and electors, though congress was to appoint the time, which might well be apprehended, as the omission of regulations for the election of members of the house of representatives, provided they had that power; or suppose they were not to meet at all; of course, the government cannot proceed in its exercise. And from this motive or apprehension, congress ought to have taken these duties entirely in their own hands, and, by a decisive declaration, annihilated them, which they in fact have done by leaving them without the means of support, or at least resting on their bounty. To this the advocates for this system oppose the common, empty declamation, that there is no danger that congress will abuse this power; but such language, as relative to so important a subject, is mere vapor, and formed without sense. Is it not in their power, however, to make such regulations as may be inconvenient to you? It must be admitted, because the words are unlimited in their sense. It is a good rule, in the construction of a contract, to suppose that what may be done will be; therefore, in considering this subject, you are to suppose that in the exercise of this government, a regulation of congress will be made for holding an election for the whole state at Poughkeepsie, at New York, or, perhaps, at Fort Stanwix;

who will then be the actual electors for the house of representatives? You ought certainly to have as much or more distrust with respect to the exercise of these powers by congress, than congress ought to have with respect to the exercise of those duties which ought to be entrusted to the several states, because over them congress can have a legislative controlling power.

Hitherto we have tied up our rulers in the exercise of their duties by positive restrictions; if the cord has been drawn too tight, loosen it to the necessary extent, but do not entirely unbind them. I am no enemy to placing a reasonable confidence in them, but such an unbounded one as the advocates and framers of this new system advise you to, would be dangerous to your liberties; it has been the ruin of other governments, and will be yours, if you adopt with all its latitudinal power. Unlimited power in governors as well as individuals is frequently the parent of deception. What facilitated the corrupt designs of Philip of Macedon and caused the ruin of Athens, but the unbounded confidence in their statesmen and rulers? Such improper confidence Demosthenes was so well convinced had ruined his country, that in his second Philippic oration he remarks "that there is one common bulwark with which men of prudence are naturally provided, the guard and security of all people, particularly of free states, against the assaults of tyrants. What is this? Distrust. Of this be mindful; to this adhere; preserve this carefully, and no calamity can affect you." Montesquieu observes that "the course of government is attended with an insensible descent to evil, and there is no reascending to good without very great efforts." The plain influence from this doctrine is, that rulers in all governments will erect an interest separate from the ruled, which will have a tendency to enslave them. There is, therefore, no other way of interrupting this insensible descent and warding off the evil as long as possible, than by establishing principles of distrust on your constituents, and cultivating the sentiment among yourselves. But let me inquire of you, my countrymen, whether the freedom and independence of elections is a point of magnitude? If it is, what kind of a spirit of amity, deference and concession is that which has put in the power of congress, at one stroke, to prevent your interference in government, and do away your liberties forever? Does either the situation or circumstances of things warrant it?

14. Robert Yates, The Letters of Brutus

The Antifederalists had no publicist more able than Robert Yates. The long series of letters signed "Brutus" appeared in *The New York Journal* in the winter and spring of 1787–1788, and must have contributed greatly to the landslide victory won by the Antifederalists in the election of delegates to the state convention. The letters are outstanding for their logical development of possible implications and ramifications of specific clauses in the Constitution, and of the relationships between various clauses. The sixth letter in the series is included here as an example of this logic, for in it Yates argued that the combination of the concurrent tax powers of the national and state governments, and the supreme law clause of the Constitution, would effect the destruction of the states. It is an argument that experience, not logic, has refuted. The other essays reprinted here contain an extended analysis of the principle of judicial review and predictions regarding its probable operation. Again, the logic is powerful, and the insights acute. Yates preferred the legislature, being accountable to the people, to be the final governmental interpreter of the Constitution.

Yates was a leading figure in New York politics. He was a member of several important committees during the Revolution, including that which drafted the state constitution of 1777, and was shortly thereafter appointed to the New York Supreme Court. In the 1780's he sided with George Clinton in opposing measures designed to strengthen the central government. He was appointed a delegate to the Philadelphia convention, but withdrew in early July on the grounds that the convention was exceeding its instructions.

Reprinted from *The New York Journal and Weekly Register* [New York City], December 27, 1787; January 31, 1788; February 7, 14; March 20, 1788.

NO. VI.

[December 27, 1787]

It is an important question, whether the general government of the United States should be so framed, as to absorb and swallow up the state governments? or whether, on the contrary, the former ought not to be confined to certain defined national objects, while the latter should retain all the powers which concern the internal police of the states?

I have, in my former papers, offered a variety of arguments to prove, that a simple free government could not be exercised over this whole continent, and that therefore we must either give up our liberties and submit to an arbitrary one, or frame a constitution on the plan of confederation. Further reasons might be urged to prove this point—but it seems unnecessary, because the principal advocates of the new constitution admit of the position. The question therefore between us, this being admitted, is, whether or not this system is so formed as either directly to annihilate the state governments, or that in its operation it will certainly effect it. If this is answered in the affirmative, then the system ought not to be adopted, without such amendments as will avoid this consequence. If on the contrary it can be shewn, that the state governments are secured in their rights to manage the internal police of the respective states, we must confine ourselves in our enquiries to the organization of the government and the guards and provisions it contains to prevent a misuse or abuse of power. To determine this question, it is requisite, that we fully investigate the nature, and the extent of the powers intended to be granted by this constitution to the rulers.

In my last number I called your attention to this subject, and proved, as I think, uncontrovertibly, that the powers given the legislature under the 8th section of the 1st article, had no other limitation than the discretion of the Congress. It was shewn, that even if the most favorable construction was given to this paragraph, that the advocates for the new constitution could wish, it will convey a power to lay and collect taxes, imposts, duties, and excises, according to the discretion of the legislature, and to make all laws which they shall judge proper and necessary to carry this power into execution. This I shewed would totally destroy all the power of the state governments. To confirm this, it is worth while to trace the operation of the government in some particular instances.

The general government is to be vested with authority to levy and collect taxes, duties, and excises; the separate states have also power to impose taxes, duties, and excises, except that they cannot lay duties on exports and imports without the consent of Congress. Here then the two governments have concurrent jurisdiction; both may lay impositions of this kind. But then the general government have superadded to this power, authority to make all laws which shall be necessary and proper for carrying the foregoing power into execution. Suppose then that both governments should lay taxes, duties, and excises, and it should fall so heavy on the people that they would be unable, or be so burdensome that they would refuse to pay them both—would it not be necessary that the general legislature should suspend the collection of the state tax? It certainly would. For, if the people could not, or would not pay both, they must be discharged from the tax to the state, or the tax to the general government could not be collected. The conclusion therefore is inevitable, that the respective state governments will not have the power to raise one shilling in any way, but by the permission of the

Congress. I presime no one will pretend, that the states can exercise legislative authority, or administer justice among their citizens for any length of time, without being able to raise a sufficiency to pay those who administer their governments.

If this be true, and if the states can raise money only by permission of the general government, it follows that the state governments will be dependent on the will of the general government for their existence.

What will render this power in Congress effectual and sure in its operation is, that the government will have complete judicial and executive authority to carry all their laws into effect, which will be paramount to the judicial and executive authority of the individual states: in vain therefore will be all interference of the legislatures, courts, or magistrates of any of the states on the subject; for they will be subordinate to the general government, and engaged by oath to support it, and will be constitutionally bound to submit to their decisions.

The general legislature will be empowered to lay any tax they chuse, to annex any penalties they please to the breach of their revenue laws; and to appoint as many officers as they may think proper to collect the taxes. They will have authority to farm the revenues and to vest the farmer general, with his subalterns, with plenary powers to collect them, in any way which to them may appear eligible. And the courts of law, which they will be authorized to institute, will have cognizance of every case arising under the revenue laws, the conduct of all the officers employed in collecting them; and the officers of these courts will execute their judgments. There is no way, therefore, of avoiding the destruction of the state governments, whenever the Congress please to do it, unless the people rise up, and, with a strong hand, resist and prevent the execution of constitutional laws. The fear of this, will, it is presumed, restrain the general government, for some time, within proper bounds; but it will not be many years before they will have a revenue, and force, at their command, which will place them above any apprehensions on that score.

How far the power to lay and collect duties and excises, may operate to dissolve the state governments, and oppress the people, it is impossible to say. It would assist us much in forming a just opinion on this head, to consider the various objects to which this kind of taxes extend, in European nations, and the infinity of laws they have passed respecting them. Perhaps, if leisure will permit, this may be essayed in some future paper.

It was observed in my last number, that the power to lay and collect duties and excises, would invest the Congress with authority to impose a duty and excise on every necessary and convenience of life. As the principal object of the government, in laying a duty or excise, will be, to raise money, it is obvious, that they will fix on such articles as are of the most general use and consumption; because, unless great quantities of the article, on which the duty is laid, is used, the revenue cannot be considerable. We may therefore presume, that the articles which will be the object of this species of taxes will be either the real necessaries of life; or if not these, such as from custom and habit are esteemed so. I will single out a few of the productions of our own country, which may, and probably will, be of the number.

Cider is an article that most probably will be one of those on which an excise will be laid, because it is one, which this country produces in great abundance, which is in very general use, is consumed in great quantities, and which may be said too not to be a real necessary of life. An excise on this would raise a large sum of money in the United States. How would the power, to lay and collect an excise on cider, and to pass all laws proper and necessary to carry it into execution, operate in its exercise? It might be necessary, in order to collect the excise on cider, to grant to one man, in each county, an exclusive right of building and keeping cider mills, and oblige him to give bonds and security for payment of the excise; or, if this was not done, it might be necessary to license the mills, which are to make this liquor, and to take from them security, to account for the excise; or, if otherwise, a great number of officers must be employed, to take account of the cider made, and to collect the duties on it.

Porter, ale, and all kinds of malt-liquors, are articles that would probably be subject also to an excise. It would be necessary, in order to collect such an excise, to regulate the manifactory of these, that the quantity made might be ascertained, or otherwise security could not be had for the payment of the excise. Every brewery must then be licensed, and officers appointed, to take account of its product, and to secure the payment of the duty, or excise, before it is sold. Many other articles might be named, which would be objects of this species of taxation, but I refrain from enumerating them. It will probably be said, by those who advocate this system, that the observations already made on this head, are calculated only to inflame the minds of the people, with the apprehension of dangers merely imaginary. That there is not the least reason to apprehend, the general legislature will exercise their power in this manner. To this I would only say, that these kinds of taxes exist in Great Britain, and are severely felt. The excise on cider and perry, was imposed in that nation a few years ago, and it is in the memory of every one, who read the history of the transaction, what great tumults it occasioned.

This power, exercised without limitation, will introduce

itself into every corner of the city, and country—It will wait upon the ladies at their toilett, and will not leave them in any of their domestic concerns; it will accompany them to the ball, the play, and the assembly; it will go with them when they visit, and will, on all occasions, sit beside them in their carriages, nor will it desert them even at church; it will enter the house of every gentleman, watch over his cellar, wait upon his cook in the kitchen, follow the servants into the parlour, preside over the table, and note down all he eats or drinks; it will attend him to his bedchamber, and watch him while he sleeps; it will take cognizance of the professional man in his office, or his study; it will watch the merchant in the counting-house, or in his store; it will follow the mechanic to his shop, and in his work, and will haunt him in his family, and in his bed; it will be a constant companion of the industrious farmer in all his labour, it will be with him in the house, and in the field, observe the toil of his hands, and the sweat of his brow; it will penetrate into the most obscure cottage; and finally, it will light upon the head of every person in the United States. To all these different classes of people, and in all these circumstances, in which it will attend them, the language in which it will address them will be GIVE! GIVE!

A power that has such latitude, which reaches every person in the community in every conceivable circumstance, and lays hold of every species of property they possess, and which has no bounds set to it, but the discretion of those who exercise it. I say, such a power must necessarily, from its very nature, swallow up all the power of the state governments.

I shall add but one other observation on this head, which is this—It appears to me a solecism, for two men, or bodies of men, to have unlimited power respecting the same object. It contradicts the scripture maxim which saith, "no man can serve two masters," the one power or the other must prevail, or else they will destroy each other, and neither of them effect their purpose. It may be compared to two mechanic powers, acting upon the same body in opposite directions, the consequence would be, if the powers were equal, the body would remain in a state of rest, or if the force of the one was superior to that of the other, the stronger would prevail, and overcome the resistance of the weaker.

But it is said, by some of the advocates of this system, "That the idea that Congress can levy taxes at pleasure, is false, and the suggestion wholly unsupported: that the preamble to the constitution is declaratory of the purposes of the union, and the assumption of any power not necessary to establish justice, &c. to provide for the common defence, &c., will be unconstitutional. Besides, in the very clause which gives the power of levying duties and taxes, the purposes to which the money shall be appropriated, are specified, viz. to pay the debts, and provide for the common defence and general welfare."*

I would ask those, who reason thus, to define what ideas are included under the terms, to provide for the common defence and general welfare? Are these terms definite, and will they be understood in the same manner, and to apply to the same cases by every one? No one will pretend they will. It will then be a matter of opinion, what tends to the general welfare; and the Congress will be the only judges in the matter. To provide for the general welfare, is an abstract proposition, which mankind differ in the explanation of, as much as they do on any political or moral proposition that can be proposed; the most opposite measures

---

*Vide an examination into the leading principles of the federal constitution, printed in Philadelphia, p. 34.

may be pursued by different parties, and both may profess, that they have in view the general welfare; and both sides may be honest in their professions, or both may have sinister views. Those who advocate this new constitution declare, they are influenced by a regard to the general welfare; those who oppose it, declare they are moved by the same principle; and I have no doubt but a number on both sides are honest in their professions; and yet nothing is more certain than this, that to adopt this constitution, and not to adopt it, cannot both of them be promotive of the general welfare.

It is absurd to say, that the power of Congress is limited by these general expressions, "to provide for the common safety, and general welfare," as it would be to say, that it would be limited, had the constitution said they should have power to lay taxes, &c. at will and pleasure. Were this authority given, it might be said, that under it the legislature could not do injustice, or pursue any measures, but such as were calculated to promote the public good, and happiness. For every man, rulers as well as others, are bound by the immutable laws of God and reason, always to will what is right. It is certainly right and fit, that the governors of every people should provide for the common defence and general welfare; every government, therefore, in the world, even the greatest despot, is limited in the exercise of his power. But however just this reasoning may be, it would be found, in practice, a most pitiful restriction. The government would always say, their measures were designed and calculated to promote the public good; and there being no judge between them and the people, the rulers themselves must, and would always, judge for themselves.

There are others of the favourers of this system, who admit, that the power of the Congress under it, with respect to revenue, will exist without limitation, and contend, that so it ought to be.

It is said, "The power to raise armies, to build and equip fleets, and to provide for their support, ought to exist without limitation, because it is impossible to foresee, or to define, the extent and variety of national exigencies, or the correspondent extent and variety of the means which may be necessary to satisfy them."

This, it is said, "is one of those truths which, to correct and unprejudiced minds, carries its own evidence along with it. It relies upon axioms as simple as they are universal: the means ought to be proportioned to the end; the person, from whose agency the attainment of any end is expected, ought to possess the means by which it is to be attained."*

This same writer insinuates, that the opponents to the plan promulgated by the convention, manifests a want of candor, in objecting to the extent of the powers proposed to be vested in this government; because he asserts, with an air of confidence, that the powers ought to be unlimited as to the object to which they extend; and that this position, if not self-evident, is at least clearly demonstrated by the foregoing mode of reasoning. But with submission to the author's better judgment, I humbly conceive his reasoning will appear, upon examination, more specious than solid. The means, says the gentleman, ought to be proportioned to the end: admit the proposition to be true it is then necessary to enquire, what is the end of the government of the United States, in order to draw any just conclusions from it. Is this end simply to preserve the general government, and to provide for the common defence and general welfare of the union only? certainly not: for beside this, the state governments are to be supported, and provision made for the managing such of their internal concerns as are allotted to them. It is admitted, "that the cir-

---

*Vide the *Federalist*, No. 23.

cumstances of our country are such, as to demand a compound, instead of a simple, a confederate, instead of a sole government," that the objects of each ought to be pointed out, and that each ought to possess ample authority to execute the powers committed to them. The government then, being complex in its nature, the end it has in view is so also; and it is as necessary, that the state governments should possess the means to attain the ends expected from them, as for the general government, Neither the general government, nor the state governments, ought to be vested with all the powers proper to be exercised for promoting the ends of government. The powers are divided between them—certain ends are to be attained by the one, and other certain ends by the other; and these, taken together, include all the ends of good government. This being the case, the conclusion follows, that each should be furnished with the means, to attain the ends, to which they are designed.

To apply this reasoning to the case of revenue; the general government is charged with the care of providing for payment of the debts of the United States; supporting the general government, and providing for the defence of the union. To obtain these ends, they should be furnished with means. But does it thence follow, that they should command all the revenues of the United States! Most certainly it does not. For if so, it will follow, that no means will be left to attain other ends, as necessary to the happiness of the country, as those committed to their care. The individual states have debts to discharge; their legislatures and executives are to be supported, and provision is to be made for the administration of justice in the respective states. For these objects the general government has no authority to provide; nor is it proper it should. It is clear then, that the states should have the command of such revenues, as to answer the ends they have to obtain. To say, "that the circumstances that endanger the safety of nations are infinite," and from hence to infer, that all the sources of revenue in the states should be yielded to the general government, is not conclusive reasoning: for the Congress are authorized only to controul in general concerns, and not regulate local and internal ones; and these are as essentially requisite to be provided for as those. The peace and happiness of a community is as initimately connected with the prudent direction of their domestic affairs, and the due administration of justice among themselves, as with a competent provision for their defence against foreign invaders, and indeed more so.

Upon the whole, I conceive, that there cannot be a clearer position than this, that the state governments ought to have an uncontroulable power to raise a revenue, adequate to the exigencies of their governments; and, I presume, no such power is left them by this constitution.

NO. XI.

[January 31, 1788]

The nature and extent of the judicial power of the United States, proposed to be granted by this constitution, claims our particular attention.

Much has been said and written upon the subject of this new system on both sides, but I have not met with any writer, who has discussed the judicial powers with any degree of accuracy. And yet it is obvious, that we can form but very imperfect ideas of the manner in which this government will work, or the effect it will have in changing the internal police and mode of distributing justice at present subsisting in the respective states, without a thorough investigation of the powers of the judiciary and of the manner in which they will operate. This government is a complete system, not only for making, but for executing laws. And the courts of law, which will be constituted by it, are not only to decide upon the constitution and the laws made in pursuance of it, but by officers subordinate to them to execute all their decisions. The real effect of this system of government, will therefore be brought home to the feelings of the people, through the medium of the judicial power. It is, moreover, of great importance, to examine with care the nature and extent of the judicial power, because those who are to be vested with it, are to be placed in a situation altogether unprecedented in a free country. They are to be rendered totally independent, both of the people and the legislature, both with respect to their offices and salaries. No errors they may commit can be corrected by any power above them, if any such power there be, nor can they be removed from office for making ever so many erroneous adjudications.

The only causes for which they can be displaced, is, conviction of treason, bribery, and high crimes and misdemeanors.

This part of the plan is so modelled, as to authorize the courts, not only to carry into execution the powers expressly given, but where these are wanting or ambiguously expressed, to supply what is wanting by their own decisions.

That we may be enabled to form a just opinion on this subject, I shall, in considering it,

1st. Examine the nature and extent of the judicial powers—and

2d. Enquire, whether the courts who are to exercise them, are so constituted as to afford reasonable ground of confidence, that they will exercise them for the general good.

With a regard to the nature and extent of the judicial powers, I have to regret my want of capacity to give that full and minute explanation of them that the subject merits. To be able to do this, a man should be possessed of a degree of law knowledge far beyond what I pretend to. A number of hard words and technical phrases are used in this part of the system, about the meaning of which gentlemen learned in the law differ.

Its advocates know how to avail themselves of these phrases. In a number of instances, where objections are made to the powers given to the judicial, they give such an explanation to the technical terms as to avoid them.

Though I am not competent to give a perfect explanation of the powers granted to this department of the government, I shall yet attempt to trace some of the leading features of it, from which I presume it will appear, that they will operate to a total subversion of the state judiciaries, if not, to the legislative authority of the states.

In article 3d, sect 2d, it is said, "The judicial power shall extend to all cases in law and equity arising under this constitution, the laws of the United States, and treaties made, or which shall be made, under their authority, &c."

The first article to which this power extends, is, all cases in law and equity arising under this constitution.

What latitude of construction this clause should receive, it is not easy to say. At first view, one would suppose, that it meant no more than this, that the courts under the general government should exercise, not only the powers of courts of law, but also that of courts of equity, in the manner in which those powers are usually exercised in the different states. But this cannot be the meaning, because the next clause authorises the courts to take cognizance of all cases in law and equity arising under the laws of the United States; this last article, I conceive, conveys as much power to the general judicial as any of the State courts possess.

The cases arising under the constitution must be different from those arising under the laws, or else the two clauses mean exactly the same thing.

The cases arising under the constitution must include such, as bring into question its meaning, and will require an explanation of the nature and extent of the powers of the different departments under it.

This article, therefore, vests the judicial with a power to resolve all questions that may arise on any case on the construction of the constitution, either in law or in equity.

1st. They are authorised to determine all questions that may arise upon the meaning of the constitution in law. This article vests the courts with authority to give the constitution a legal construction, or to explain it according to the rules laid down for construing a law.—These rules give a certain degree of latitude of explanation. According to this mode of construction, the courts are to give such meaning to the constitution as comports best with the common, and generally received acceptation of the words in which it is expressed, regarding their ordinary and popular use, rather than their grammatical propriety. Where words are dubious, they will be explained by the context. The end of the clause will be attended to, and the words will be understood, as having a view to it; and the words will not be so understood as to bear no meaning or a very absurd one.

2d. The judicial are not only to decide questions arising upon the meaning of the constitution in law, but also in equity.

By this they are empowered, to explain the constitution according to the reasoning spirit of it, without being confined to the words or letter.

"From this method of interpreting laws (says Blackstone) by the reason of them, arises what we call equity;" which is thus defined by Grotius, "the correction of that, wherein the law, by reason of its universality, is deficient; for since in laws of all cases cannot be foreseen, or expressed, it is necessary, that when the decrees of the law cannot be applied to particular cases, there should some where be a power vested of defining those circumstances, which had they been foreseen the legislator would have expressed; and these are the cases, which according to Grotius, lex non exacte definit, fed arbitrio boni viri permittet."

The same learned author observes, "That equity, thus depending essentially upon each individual case, there can be no established rules and fixed principles of equity laid down, without destroying its very essence, and reducing it to a positive law."

From these remarks, the authority and business of the courts of law, under this clause, may be understood.

They will give the sense of every article of the constitution, that may from time to time come before them. And in their decisions they will not confine themselves to any fixed or established rules, but will determine, according to what appears to them, the reason and spirit of the constitution. The opinions of the supreme court, whatever they may be, will have the force of law; because there is no power provided in the constitution, that can correct their errors, or controul their adjudications. From this court there is no appeal. And I conceive the legislature themselves, cannot set aside a judgment of this court, because they are authorised by the constitution to decide in the last resort. The legislature must be controuled by the constitution, and not the constitution by them. They have therefore no more right to set aside any judgment pronounced upon the construction of the constitution, than they have to take from the president, the chief command of the army and navy, and commit it to some other person. The reason is plain; the judicial and executive derive their authority from the same source, that the legislature do theirs; and therefore in all cases, where the constitution does not make the one responsible to, or controulable by the other, they are altogether independent of each other.

The judicial power will operate to effect, in the most certain, but yet silent and imperceptible manner, what is evidently the tendency of the constitution: —I mean, an entire subversion of the legislative, executive and judicial powers of the individual states. Every adjudication of the supreme court, on any question that may arise upon the nature and extent of the general government, will affect the limits of the state jurisdiction. In proportion as the former enlarge the exercise of their powers, will that of the latter be restricted.

That the judicial power of the United States, will lean strongly in favour of the general government, and will give such an explanation to the constitution, as will favour an extension of its jurisdiction, is very evident from a variety of considerations.

1st. The constitution itself strongly countenances such a mode of construction. Most of the articles in this system, which convey powers of any considerable importance, are conceived in general and indefinite terms, which are either equivocal, ambiguous, or which require long definitions to unfold the extent of their meaning. The two must important powers committed to any government, those of raising money, and of raising and keeping up troops, have already been considered, and shewn to be unlimited by any thing but the discretion of the legislature. The clause which vests the power to pass all laws which are proper and necessary, to carry the powers given into execution, it has been shewn, leaves the legislature at liberty, to do every thing, which in their judgment is best. It is said, I know, that this clause confers no power on the legislature, which they would not have had without it—though I believe this is not the fact, yet, admitting it to be, it implies that the constitution is not to receive an explanation strictly, according to its letter; but more power is implied than is expressed. And this clause, if it is to be considered, as explanatory of the extent of the powers given, rather than giving a new power, is to be understood as declaring, that in construing any of the articles conveying power, the spirit, intent and design of the clause, should be attended to, as well as the words in their common acceptation.

This constitution gives sufficient colour for adopting an equitable construction, if we consider the great end and design it professedly has in view—this appears from its preamble to be, "to form a more perfect union, establish justice, insure domestic tranquillity, provide for the common defence, promote the general welfare, and secure the blessings of liberty to ourselves and posterity." The design of this system is here expressed, and it is proper to give such a meaning to the various parts, as will best promote the accomplishment of the end; this idea suggests itself naturally upon reading the preamble, and will countenance the court in giving the several articles such a sense, as will the most effectually promote the ends the constitution had in view—how this manner of explaining the constitution will operate in practice, shall be the subject of future enquiry.

2d. Not only will the constitution justify the courts in inclining to this mode of explaining it, but they will be interested in using this latitude of interpretation. Every body of men invested with office are tenacious of power; they feel interested, and hence it has become a kind of maxim, to hand down their offices, with all its rights and privileges, unimpared to their successors; the same principle will influence them to extend their power, and increase their rights; this of itself will operate strongly upon the courts to give such a meaning to the constitution in all cases where it can possibly be done, as will enlarge the sphere of their own authority. Every extension of the power of the general legislature, as well as of the judicial powers, will increase the powers of the courts; and the dignity and importance of the judges, will be in proportion to the extent and magnitude of the powers they exercise. I add, it is highly probable the emolument of the judges will be increased, with the increase of the business they will have to transact and its importance. From these considerations the judges will be interested to extend the powers of the courts, and to construe the constitution as much as possible, in such a way as to favour it; and that they will do it, appears probable.

3d. Because they will have precedent to plead, to justify them in it. It is well known, that the courts in England, have by their own authority, extended their jurisdiction far beyond the limits set them in their original institution, and by the laws of the land.

The court of exchequer is a remarkable instance of this. It was originally intended principally to recover the king's debts, and to order the revenues of the crown. It had a common law jurisdiction, which was established merely for the benefit of the king's accomptants. We learn from Blackstone, that the proceedings in this court are grounded on a writ called quo minus, in which the plaintiff suggests, that he is the king's farmer or debtor, and that the defendant hath done him the damage complained of, by which he is less able to pay the king. These suits, by the statute of Rutland, are expressly directed to be confined to such matters as specially concern the king, or his ministers in the exchequer. And by the articuli super cartas, it is enacted, that no common pleas be thenceforth held in the exchequer contrary to the form of the great charter: but now any person may sue in the exchequer. The surmise of being debtor to the king being matter of form, and mere words of course; and the court is open to all the nation.

When the courts will have a precedent[1] before them of a

---

[1]The original text reads "president," but this would appear to be in error [Ed.].

court which extended its jurisdiction in opposition to an act of the legislature, is it not to be expected that they will extend theirs, especially when there is nothing in the constitution expressly against it? and they are authorised to construe its meaning, and are not under any controul?.

This power in the judicial, will enable them to mould the government, into almost any shape they please.—The manner in which this may be effected we will hereafter examine.

NO. XII (PART I)

[February 7, 1788]

In my last, I shewed, that the judicial power of the United States under the first clause of the second section of article eight, would be authorized to explain the constitution, not only according to its letter, but according to its spirit and intention; and having this power, they would strongly incline to give it such a construction as to extend the powers of the general government, as much as possible, to the diminution, and finally to the destruction, of that of the respective states.

I shall now proceed to shew how this power will operate in its exercise to effect these purposes. In order to perceive the extent of its influence, I shall consider,

First. How it will tend to extend the legislative authority.

Second. In what manner, it will increase the jurisdiction of the courts, and

Third. The way in which it will diminish, and destroy, both the legislative and judicial authority of the United States.

First. Let us enquire how the judicial power will effect an extension of the legislative authority.

Perhaps the judical power will not be able, by direct and positive decrees, ever to direct the legislature, because it is not easy to conceive how a question can be brought before them in a course of legal discussion, in which they can give a decision, declaring, that the legislature have certain powers which they have not exercised, and which, in consequence of the determination of the judges, they will be bound to exercise. But it is easy to see, that in their adjudications they may establish certain principles, which being received by the legislture, will enlarge the sphere of their power beyond all bounds.

It is to be observed, that the supreme court has the power, in the last resort, to determine all questions that may arise in the course of legal discussion, on the meaning and construction of the constitution. This power they will hold under the constitution, and independent of the legislature. The latter can no more deprive the former of this right, than either of them, or both of them together, can take from the president, with the advice of the senate, the power of making treaties, or appointing ambassadors.

In determining these questions, the court must and will assume certain principles, from which they will reason, in forming their decisions. These principles, whatever they may be, when they become fixed, by a course of decisions, will be adopted by the legislature, and will be the rule by which they will explain their own powers. This appears evident from this consideration, that if the legislature pass laws, which, in the judgment of the court, they are not authorised to do by the constitution, the court will not take notice of them; for it will not be denied, that the constitution is the highest or supreme law. And the courts are vested with the supreme and uncontroulable power, to determine, in all cases that come before them, what the constitution means; they cannot, therefore, execute a law, which, in their judgment, opposes the constitution, unless we can suppose they can make a superior law give way to an inferior. The legislature, therefore, will not go over the limits by which the courts may adjudge they are confined. And there is little room to doubt but that they will come up to those bounds, as often as occasion and opportunity may offer, and they may judge it proper to do it. For as on the one hand, they will not readily pass laws which they know the courts will not execute, so on the other, we may be sure they will not scruple to pass such as they know they will give effect, as often as they may judge it proper.

From these observations it appears, that the judgment of the judicial, on the constitution, will become the rule to guide the legislature in their construction of their powers.

What the principles are, which the courts will adopt, it is impossible for us to say; but taking up the powers as I have explained them in my last number, which they will possess under this clause, it is not difficult to see, that they may, and probably will, be very liberal ones.

We have seen, that they will be authorized to give the constitution a construction according to its spirit and reason, and not to confine themselves to its letter.

To discover the spirit of the constitution, it is of the first importance to attend to the principal ends and designs it has in view. These are expressed in the preamble, in the following words, viz. "We, the people of the United States, in order to form a more perfect union, establish justice, insure domestic tranquility, provide for the common defence, promote the general welfare, and secure the blessings of liberty to ourselves and our posterity, do ordain and establish this constitution," &c. If the end of the government is to be learned from these words, which are clearly designed to declare it, it is obvious it has in view every object which is embraced by any government. The preservation of internal peace—the due administration of justice—and to provide for the defence of the community, seems to include all the objects of government; but if they do not, they are certainly comprehended in the words, "to provide for the general welfare". If it be further considered, that this constitution, if it is ratified, will not be a compact entered into by states, in their corporate capacities, but an agreement of the people of the United States, as one great body politic, no doubt can remain, but that the great end of the constitution, if it is to be collected from the preamble, in which its end is declared, is to constitute a government which is to extend to every case for which any government is instituted, whether external or internal. The courts, therefore, will establish this as a principle in expounding the constitution, and will give every part of it such an explanation, as will give latitude to every department under it, to take cognizance of every matter, not only that affects the general and national concerns of the union, but also of such as relate to the administration of private justice, and to regulating the internal and local affairs of the different parts.

Such a rule of exposition is not only consistent with the general spirit of the preamble, but it will stand confirmed by considering more minutely the different clauses of it.

The first object declared to be in view is, "To form a perfect union." It is to be observed, it is not an union of states of bodies corporate; had this been the case the existence of the state governments, might have been secured. But it is a union of the people of the United States considered as one body, who are to ratify this constitution, if it is adopted. Now to make a union of this kind perfect, it is necessary to abolish all inferior governments, and to give the general one compleat legislative, executive and judicial powers to every purpose. The courts therefore will establish it as a rule in explaining the constitution. To give it such a construction as will best tend to perfect the union or take from the state governments every power of either making or executing laws. The second object is "to establish justice." This must include not only the idea of instituting the rule or of justice, or of making laws which shall be the measure or rule of right, but also of providing for the application of this rule of administering justice under it. And under this the courts will in their decisions extend the power of the government to all cases they possibly can, or otherwise they will be restricted in doing what appears to be the intent of the constitution they should do, to wit, pass laws and provide for the execution of them, for the general distribution of justice between man and man. Another end declared is "to insure domestic tranquility." This comprehends a provision against all private breaches of the peace, as well as against all public commotions or general insurrections; and to attain the object of this clause fully, the government must exercise the power of passing laws on these subjects, as well as of appointing magistrates with authority to execute them. And the courts will adopt these ideas in their expositions. I might proceed to the other clause, in the preamble, and it would appear by a consideration of all of them separately, as it does by taking them together, that if the spirit of this system is to be known from its declared end and design in the preamble, its spirit is to subvert and abolish all the powers of the state governments, and to embrace every object to which any government extends.

As it sets out in the preamble with this declared intention, so it proceeds in the different parts with the same idea. Any person, who will peruse the 8th section with attention, in which most of the powers are enumerated, will perceive that they either expressly or by implication extend to almost every thing about which any legislative power can be employed. But if this equitable mode of construction is applied to this part of the constitution; nothing can stand before it.

This will certainly give the first clause in that article a construction which I confess I think is the most natural and grammatical one, to authorise the Congress to do any thing which in their judgment will tend to provide for the general welfare, and this amounts to the same thing as general and unlimited powers of legislation in all cases.

[*To be continued.*]

NO. XII (PART II)

[February 14, 1788]

This same manner of explaining the constitution, will fix a meaning, and a very important one too, to the 12th clause of the same section, which authorises the Congress to make all laws which shall be proper and necessary for carrying into effect the foregoing powers, &c. A voluminous writer in favor of this system, has taken great pains to convince the public, that this clause means nothing; for that the same powers expressed in this, are implied in other parts of the constitution. Perhaps it is so, but still this will undoubtedly be an excellent auxilliary to assist the courts to discover the spirit and reason of the constitution, and when applied to any and every of the other clauses granting power, will operate powerfully in extracting the spirit from them.

I might instance a number of clauses in the constitution, which, if explained in an *equitable* manner, would extend the powers of the government to every case, and reduce the state legislatures to nothing; but, I should draw out my remarks to an undue length, and I presume enough has been said to shew, that the courts have sufficient ground in the exercise of this power, to determine, that the legislature have no bounds set to them by this constitution, by any supposed right the legislatures of the respective states may have, to regulate any of their local concerns.

I proceed, 2nd, To inquire, in what manner this power will increase the jurisdiction of the courts.

I would here observe, that the judicial power extends, expressly, to all civil cases that may arise save such as arise between citizens of the same state, with this exception to those of that description, that the judicial of the United States have cognizance of cases between citizens of the same state, claiming lands under grants of different states. Nothing more, therefore, is necessary to give the courts of law, under this constitution, complete jurisdiction of all civil causes, but to comprehend cases between citizens of the same state not included in the foregoing exception.

I presume there will be no difficulty in accomplishing this. Nothing more is necessary than to set forth, in the process, that the party who brings the suit is a citizen of a different state from the one against whom the suit is brought, & there can be little doubt but that the court will take cognizance of the matter, & if they do, who is to restrain them? Indeed, I will freely confess, that it is my decided opinion, that the courts ought to take cognizance of such causes, under the powers of the constitution. For one of the great ends of the constitution is, "to establish justice." This supposes that this cannot be done under the existing governments of the states; and there is certainly as good reason why individuals, living in the same state, should have justice, as those who live in different states. Moreover, the constitution expressly declares, that "the citizens of each state shall be entitled to all the privileges and immunities of citizens in the several states." It will therefore be no fiction, for a citizen of one state to set forth, in a suit, that he is a citizen of another; for he that is entitled to all the privileges and immunities of a country, is a citizen of that country. And in truth, the citizen of one state will, under this constitution, be a citizen of every state.

But supposing that the party, who alledges that he is a citizen of another state, has recourse to fiction in bringing in his suit, it is well known, that the courts have high authority to plead, to justify them in suffering actions to be brought before them by such fictions. In my last number I stated, that the court of exchequer tried all causes in virtue of such a fiction. The court of king's bench in England, extended their jurisdiction in the same way. Originally, this court held pleas in civil cases, only of tresspasses and other injuries alledged to be committed *vi et armis*. They might likewise, says Blackstone, upon the division of the *aula regia*, have originally held pleas of any other civil action whatsoever (except in real actions which are now very seldom in use) provided the defendant was an officer of the court, or in the custody of the marshall or prison-keeper of this court, for breach of the peace, &c. In process of time, by a fiction, this court began to hold pleas of any personal action whatsoever, it being surmised, that the defendant has been arrested for a supposed trespass that "he has never committed, and being thus in the custody of the marshall of the court, the plaintiff is at liberty to proceed against him for any other personal injury: which surmise of being in the marshall's custody, the defendant is not at liberty to dispute." By a much less fiction, may the pleas of the courts of the United States extend to cases between citizens of the same state. I shall add no more on this head, but proceed briefly to remark, in what way this power will diminish and destroy both the legislative and judicial authority of the states.

It is obvious that these courts will have authority to decide upon the validity of the laws of any of the states, in all cases where they come in question before them. Where the constitution gives the general government exclusive jurisdiction, they will adjudge all laws made by the states, in such cases, void *ab initio*. Where the constitution gives them concurrent jurisdiction, the laws of the United States must prevail, because they are the supreme law. In such cases, therefore, the laws of the state legislatures must be repealed, restricted, or so construed, as to give full effect to the laws of the union on the same subject. From these remarks it is easy to see, that in proportion as the general government acquires power and jurisdiction, by the liberal construction which the judges may give the constitution, will those of the states lose its rights, until they become so trifling and unimportant, as not to be worth having. I am much mistaken, if this svstem will not operate to effect this with as much celerity, as those who have the administration of it will think prudent to suffer it. The remaining objections to the judicial power shall be considered in a future paper.

BRUTUS, NO. XV.

[*Continued*]

[March 20, 1788]

I said in my last number, that the supreme court under this constitution would be exalted above all other power in the government, and subject to no controul. The business of this paper will be to illustrate this, and to shew the danger that will result from it. I question whether the world ever saw, in any period of it, a court of justice invested with such immense powers, and yet placed in a situation so little responsible. Certain it is, that in England, and in the several states, where we have been taught to believe, the courts of law are put upon the most prudent establishment, they are on a very different footing.

The judges in England, it is true, hold their offices during their good behaviour, but then their determinations are subject to correction by the house of lords; and their power is by no means so extensive as that of the proposed supreme court of the union. —I believe they in no instance assume the authority to set aside an act of parliament under the idea that it is inconsisent with their constitution. They consider themselves bound to decide according to the existing laws of the land, and never undertake to controul them by adjudging that they are inconsistent with the constitution—much less are they vested with the power of giv[ing] an *equitable* construction to the constitution.

The judges in England are under the controul of the legislature, for they are bound to determine according to the laws passed by them. But the judges under this constitution will controul the legislature, for the supreme court are authorised in the last report [*sic*], to determine what is the extent of the powers of the Congress; they are to give the constitution an explanation, and there is no power above them to sit aside their judgment. The framers of this constitution appear to have followed that of the British, in rendering the judges independent, by granting them their offices during good behaviour, without following the constitution of England, in instituting a tribunal in which their errors may be corrected; and without adverting to this, that the judicial under this system have a power which is above the legislative, and which indeed transcends any power before given to a judicial by any free government under heaven.

I do not object to the judges holding their commissions during good behaviour. I suppose it a proper provision provided they were made properly responsible. But I say, this system has followed the English government in this, while it has departed from almost every other principle of their jurisprudence, under the idea, of rendering the

judges independent; which in the British constitution,
means no more than that they hold their places during
good behaviour, and have fixed salaries, they have made
the judges *independent*, in the fullest sense of the word.
There is no power above them, to controul any of their
decisions. There is no authority that can remove them, and
they cannot be controuled by the laws of the legislature. In
short, they are independent of the people, of the legislature, and of every power under heaven. Men placed in this
situation will generally soon feel themselves independent
of heaven itself. Before I proceed to illustrate the truth
of these assertions, I beg liberty to make one remark
——Though in my opinion the judges ought to hold their
offices during good behaviour, yet I think it is clear, that the
reasons in favour of this establishment of the judges in
England, do by no means apply to this country.

The great reason assigned, why the judges in Britain
ought to be commissioned during good behaviour, is this,
that they may be placed in a situation, not to be influenced
by the crown, to give such decisions, as would tend to
increase its powers and prerogatives. While the judges
held their places at the will and pleasure of the king, on
whom they depended not only for their offices, but also for
their salaries, they were subject to every undue influence.
If the crown wished to carry a favorite point, to accomplish which the aid of the courts of law was necessary, the
pleasure of the king would be signified to the judges. And
it required the spirit of a martyr, for the judges to determine contrary to the king's will.— They were absolutely
dependent upon him both for their offices and livings. The
king, holding his office during life, and transmitting it to
his posterity as an inheritance, has much stronger inducements to increase the prerogatives of his office than those
who hold their offices for stated periods, or even for life.
Hence the English nation gained a great point, in favour of

liberty. When they obtained the appointment of the judges, during good behaviour, they got from the crown a concession, which deprived it of one of the most powerful engines with which it might enlarge the boundaries of the royal prerogative and encroach on the liberties of the people. But these reasons do not apply to this country, we have no hereditary monarch; those who appoint the judges do not hold their offices for life, nor do they descend to their children. The same arguments, therefore, which will conclude in favor of the tenor [*sic*] of the judge's offices for good behaviour, lose a considerable part of their weight when applied to the state and condition of America. But much less can it be shewn, that the nature of our government requires that the courts should be placed beyond all account more independent, so much so as to be above controul.

I have said that the judges under this system will be *independent* in the strict sense of the word: To prove this I will shew—That there is no power above them that can controul their decisions, or correct their errors. There is no authority that can remove them from office for any errors or want of capacity, or lower their salaries, and in many cases their power is superior to that of the legislature.

1st. There is no power above them that can correct their errors or controul their decisions—The adjudications of this court are final and irreversible, for there is no court above them to which appeals can lie, either in error or on the merits. —In this respect it differs from the courts in England, for there the house of lords is the highest court, to whom appeals, in error, are carried from the highest of the courts of law.

2nd. They cannot be removed from office or suffer a dimunition of their salaries, for any error in judgement or want of capacity.

It is expressly declared by the constitution,—"That they

shall at stated times receive a compensation for their services which shall not be diminished during their continuance in office."

The only clause in the constitution which provides for
the removal of the judges from offices, is that which declares that "the president, vice-president, and all civil
officers of the United States, shall be removed from office,
on impeachment for, and conviction of treason, bribery, or
other high crimes and misdemeanors." By this paragraph,
civil officers, in which the judges are included, are removable only for crimes. Treason and bribery are named, and
the rest are included under the general terms of high crimes
and the misdeameanors. — Errors in judgment, or want of
capacity to discharge the duties of the office, can never be
supposed to be included in these words, *high crimes and
misdemeanors*. A man may mistake a case in giving judgment, or manifest that he is incompetent to the discharge of
the duties of a judge, and yet give no evidence of corruption
or want of integrity. To support the charge, it will be necessary to give in evidence some facts that will shew, that the
the judges committed the error from wicked and corrupt
motives.

3rd. The power of this court is in many cases superior to
that of the legislature. I have shewed, in a former paper,
that this court will be authorised to decide upon the meaning of the constitution, and that, not only according to the
natural and obvious meaning of the words, but also according to the spirit and intention of it. In the exercise of
this power they will not be subordinant to, but above the
legislature. For all the departments of this government
will receive their powers, so far as they are expressed in
the constitution, from the people immediately, who are the
source of power. The legislature can only exercise such
powers as are given them by the constitution, they cannot
assume any of the rights annexed to the judicial, for this

plain reason, that the same authority which vested the legislature with their powers, vested the judicial with theirs—both are derived from the same source, both therefore are equally valid, and the judicial hold their powers independently of the legislature, as the legislature do of the judicial. —The supreme court then have a right, independent of the legislature, to give a construction to the constitution and every part of it, and there is no power provided in this system to correct their construction or do it away. If, therefore, the legislature pass any laws, inconsistent with the sense the judges put upon the constitution, they will declare it void; and therefore in this respect their power is superior to that of the legislature. In England the judges are not only subject to have their decisions set aside by the house of lards, for error, but in cases where they give an explanation to the laws or constitution of the country, contrary to the sense of the parliament, though the parliament will not set aside the judgement of the court, yet, they have authority, by a new law, to explain a former one, and by this means to prevent a reception of such decisions. But no such power is in the legislature. The judges are supreme—and no law, explanatory of the constitution, will be binding on them.

From the preceding remarks, which have been made on the judicial powers proposed in this system, the policy of it may be fully developed.

I have, in the course of my observation on this constitution, affirmed and endeavored to shew, that it was calculated to abolish entirely the state governments, and to melt down the states into one entire government, for every purpose as well internal and local, as external and national. In this opinion the opposers of the system have generally agreed—and this has been uniformly denied by its advocates in public. Some individuals indeed, among them, will confess, that it has this tendency, and scruple not to say, it is what they wish; and I will venture to predict, without the spirit of prophecy, that if it is adopted without amendments, or some such precautions as will ensure amendments immediately after its adoption, that the same gentlemen who have employed their talents and abilities with such success to influence the public mind to adopt this plan, will employ the same to persuade the people, that it will be for their good to abolish the state governments as useless and burdensome.

Perhaps nothing could have been better conceived to facilitate the abolition of the state governments than the constitution of the judicial. They will be able to extend the limits of the general government gradually, and by insensible degrees, and to accomodate themselves to the temper of the people. Their decisions on the meaning of the constitution will commonly take place in cases which arise between individuals, with which the public will not be generally acquainted; one adjudication will form a precedent to the next, and this to a following one. These cases will immediately affect individuals only; so that a series of determinations will probably take place before even the people will be informed of them. In the meantime all the art and address of those who wish for the change will be employed to make converts to their opinion. The people will be told, that their state officers, and state legislatures are a burden and expence without affording any solid advantage, for that all the laws passed by them, might be equally well made by the general legislature. If to those who will be interested in the change, be added, those who will be under their influence, and such who will submit to almost any change of government, which they can be persuaded to believe will ease them of taxes, it is easy to see, the party who will favor the abolition of the state governments would be far from being inconsiderable. ——In this situation, the general legislature, might pass one law after another, extending the general and abridging the state jurisdictions, and to sanction their proceedings would have a course of decisions of the judicial to whom the constitution has committed the power of explaining the constitution. —If the states remonstrated, the constitutional mode of deciding upon the validity of the law, is with the supreme court, and neither people, nor state legislatures, nor the general legislature can remove them or reverse their decrees.

Had the construction of the constitution been left with the legislature, they would have explained it at their peril; if they exceed their powers, or sought to find, in the spirit of the constitution, more than was expressed in the letter, the people from whom they derived their power could remove them, and do themselves right; and indeed I can see no other remedy that the people can have against their rulers for encroachemets of this nature. A constitution is a compact of a people with their rulers; if the rulers break the compact, the people have a right and ought to remove them, and do themselves justice; but in order to enable them to do this with the greater facility, those whom the people chuse at stated periods, should have the power in the last resort to determine the sense of the compact; if they determine contrary to the understanding of the people, an appeal will lie to the people at the period when the rulers are to be elected, and they will have it in their power to remedy the evil; but when this power is lodged in the hands of men independent of the people, and of their representatives, and who are not, constitutionally, accountable for their opinions, no way is left to controul them but *with a high hand and an outstretched arm.*

15. A Manifesto of a Number of Gentlemen from Albany County

This statement, published in *The New York Journal* during the campaign for the election of delegates to the state convention, provides an insight into the nature and methods of party organization during the period. It not only summarizes the case against the Constitution in a lengthy catalogue of objections, it also presents a slate of candidates, thus making it possible for Antifederalist voters to make their votes effective by centering them on this slate rather than dispersing them among miscellaneous individuals not backed by a central committee. It is significant that the entire slate—and no one else—was elected to the convention from Albany County. The list of objections included most of those common throughout the states, as well as a few that were somewhat less common. Among the latter were the objections to the election of the Senate by the state legislatures rather than by the people, and the prohibition to the states of the right to coin money. A comparison of this catalogue of the Albany Gentlemen with the list of amendments proposed by New York and other states is useful, serving somewhat the same purpose as a comparison between a modern party's platform and the legislative record of its members.

Reprinted from *The New York Journal and Weekly Register* [New York City] April 26, 1788.

ALBANY, APRIL 10, 1788

On the last Tuesday of April inst. delegates are to be chosen, by the people, to determine the important question, whether the proposed new constitution shall be adopted or rejected—A determination of the utmost consequence to the citizens of the state and to posterity. From an apprehension that the constitution, if adopted in its present form, would deprive the people of their dearest rights and liberties, a number of gentlemen, from different parts of this county, met for the purpose of nominating and recommending delegates for convention, and unanimously resolved on the following gentlemen:

Robert Yates, John Lansing, jun., Henry Oothoudt, Peter Vrooman, Dirck Swart, Israel Thompson, Anthony Ten Eyck.

As we have been informed, that the advocates for the new constitution, have lately travelled through the several districts in the county, and propagated an opinion, that it is a good system of government; we beg leave to state, in as few words as possible, some of the many objections against it.——

The convention, who were appointed for the sole and express purpose of revising and amending the confederation, have taken upon themselves the power of making a new one.

They have not formed a *federal* but a *consolidated* government, repugnant to the principles of a republican government; not founded on the preservation but the destruction of the state governments.

The great and extensive powers granted to the new government over the lives, liberties, and property of every citizen.

These powers in many instances not defined or sufficiently explained, and capable of being interpreted to answer the most ambitious and arbitrary purposes.

The small number of members who are to compose the general legislature, which is to pass laws to govern so large and extensive a continent, inhabited by people of different laws, customs, and opinions, and many of them residing upwards of 400 miles from the seat of government.

The members of the senate are not to be chosen by the people, but appointed by the legislature of each state for the term of six years. This would destroy their responsibility, and induce them to act like the masters and not the servants of the people.

The power to alter and regulate the time, place, and manner of holding elections, so as to keep them subjected to their influence.

The power to lay poll taxes, duties, imposts, excises, and other taxes.

The power to appoint Continental officers to levy and collect those taxes.

Their laws are to be *the supreme law of the land,* and the judges in every state are to be bound thereby, notwithstanding the *constitution or laws* of any state to the contrary.—A sweeping clause, which subjects every thing to the controul of the new government.

Slaves are taken into the computation in apportioning the number of representatives, whereby 50,000 slaves, give an equal representation with 30,000 freemen.

The provision that the net produce of all duties and imposts, *laid by the legislature of any state,* on imports or exports, shall be for the use of the treasury of the United States.

The provision that none of the states shall coin money or emit bills of credit.

The power to raise, support, and maintain a standing army *in time of peace.* The bane of a republican government; by a standing army most of the once free nations of the globe have been reduced to bondage; and by this Britain attempted to inforce her arbitrary measures.

The power to call forth the militia to any part of the continent, without any limitation of time or place, under the command of the president, or such continental officers as shall be appointed over them.

Men conscienciously scrupulous of bearing arms, made liable to perform military duty.

The power of the new government to establish the salaries for their own services.

The power with respect to the payment of the salaries to *inferior court judges in the several states;* and which salaries the new constitution declares are not to be diminished.

Their power relative to the migration or importation of foreigners.

The not securing the rights of conscience in matters of religion, of granting the liberty of worshipping God agreeable to the mode thereby dictated; whereas the experience of all ages proves that the benevolence and humility inculcated in the gospel, are no restraint on the love of domination.

The vast executive power vested in one man (not elected by the people) who, though called President, will have powers equal if not superior to many European kings.

His legislative power of negativing all laws, resolutions and votes, thereby to prevent their passing unless agreed to by two thirds of both houses of the legislature.

His long continuance in office, and even at the end of four years capable of being again chosen, and continued for life.

The great powers granted to the grand continental supreme court, extending to all cases in law and equity, and the allowing that court original jurisdiction in certain cases.

The granting of appeals to that court on both law and fact. A powerful engine in the hands of the rich, to oppress and ruin the poor.

The power to establish inferior courts in every state.

No provision being made to prevent placemen and pensioners.

Nor for the liberty of the press, that grand palladium of liberty and scourge of tyrants.

The tryal by jury, that sacred bulwark of liberty, is not provided for in civil cases.

The power of appointing as many continental officers as they shall think proper in every state, and thereby extending their influence over every part of the United States.

The great additional expences of the new government, and the burdensome and heavy taxes which will thereby be occasioned.

The guaranteeing to the several states, not the substance, but a republican form of government, and the states left at the mercy of the general government, to allow them such a form as they shall deem proper.

They have declared, that if the conventions of nine states ratify the constitution, it shall be established between the states so ratifying the same; by which means, if all the states should not adopt it, they have laid a foundation to defeat the confederation and dissolve the union of the states. A clause dictated by the same genius of aristocracy, which prompted the convention to enjoin secrecy on their members, to keep their doors shut, their journals locked up, and none of the members to take any extracts.

By the articles of confederation each state retains what is not expressly granted in Congress; but in the new constitution, there is no provision or bill of rights, to secure any of the fundamental rights and liberties of the people.

Notwithstanding so many and such powerful objections to this constitution, some of its zealous advocates, have industriously attempted to persuade the people to adopt it. Is it for the sake of poor and comon people, that the rich and well born are so indefatigable? or is it because they and their friends and connections expect to possess some of the many lucrative offices under the new government?

They have asserted, that the present confederation is defective and will tend to anarchy and confusion.

That the expenses of the new government will be less.

That the value of produce will be raised.

That the concurrence of nine states will bind the whole.

That the constitution may hereafter be amended.

As to the first, it is the weakest of all weak reasons, to adopt a bad constitution because the present one is defective.—A person of a sickly habit or constitution might as well put an end to his existence, for fear that his sickness or infirmity would be the cause of his death.——As to the second, a man must be very credulous and ignorant indeed, who can suppose that the new government will not be more expensive.——Will not the raising and supporting an army and navy, in time of peace, create additional expence? Can the multitude and variety of the salaries of the continental supreme court judges, the continental inferior court judges in the different states, and other civil officers in the judicial department, be paid without great additional expence? Can a federal town for the seat of the national government, be built without additional expence? Will not the furniture necessary for the continental president, vice-president, secretaries, treasurers, comptrollers, ministers, etc. etc. to grace their tables, and adorn the rooms of their stately palaces, be costly and expensive? Can all these things, with many others, be accomplished without great additional expence, and without laying heavy and burthensome taxes on the people? As well might the Israelites of old, have made brick without straw. With respect to the regulation of trade, this may be vested in Congress under the present confederation, without changing the fundamental principles of the general as well as all the state governments; nor is it probable, that if the new constitution should be adopted, the value of produce would be thereby increased—as well might it be said, that our soil will be better and our lands fruitful.

The assertion, that the adoption of the constitution by nine states will bind every state, is not true. This falsehood is contradicted by the express words of the last clause; and the threats given out that the dissenting states will be compelled to adopt it, is the language of tyrants, and an insult on the understandings of a free people.

With regard to amendments, some of the strongest and most zealous advocates for the new constitution, at first, and for a long time, affect to hold it up as a good system of government; but after various and repeated journies into the country (having discovered that the people were generally opposed to the constitution, and that they can and will judge on a matter of such consequence to themselves and their posterity) these same zealous advocates have since changed their ground, and altered their plan of operations: They now acknowledge it to be defective but endeavour to prevail on the people, first to adopt it, and afterwards (like Massachusetts) trust to a recommendation for future amendments. Would it be prudent or safe for the people to surrender their dearest rights and liberties, to the discretionary disposal of their future rulers? First to make a surrender and afterwards ask for terms of capitulation.

The free men of America have fought and bled to oppose the oppression and usurpation of Great-Britain; and shall they now resign these rights and privileges, to a government which, if possible, may be still more arbitrary and despotic? Sacred as well as profane history afford abundant examples to prove that the most strenuous assertors of liberty, in all ages, after having successfully triumphed over tyranny, have themselves become tyrants, when intrusted by the people with unlimited and uncontroulable powers.

No amendments can be obtained without the consent of three fourths of the states; is it probable that such consent will ever be obtained, to amendments which will tend to abridge the powers of the new government? is it not rather more probable, that if any amendments are made, they will rather enlarge those powers? will not those in power have influence sufficient at all times, to prevent more than one-fourth of the states to consent to future amendments? From this source then, amendments are not to be expected, nor is it to be presumed, that if the people once resign such great and extensive powers, they will ever be enabled to wrest them from a national government having the command of the purse as well as the sword.

The 5th article of the constitution points out a mode to obtain amendments, after it is adopted, which is to call a convention for the purpose; and we conceive that a convention may be called to amend the constitution, before it is adopted with so many material and radical defects.

These, among many others, are the reasons that have induced us to oppose the new constitution in its present form. A constitution destructive of the fundamental principles of the general as well as all the state governments; dangerous to the rights and liberties of the people, and which, if adopted without previous amendments, will, in our opinion, terminate in slavery.

If therefore you entertain the like sentiments, relative to

this constitution, we beg leave to request your vote and interest in favor of the above delegates, whose opinions, we have reason to conclude, agree with ours on this important subject.

We are, Gentlemen,
your must humble servants.

By order of the
Committee,
JER. VAN RENSSELAER, *Chairman.*
MAT. VISSCHER, *Clerk*

The subscribers being of opinion, that the reasons above mentioned, are conclusive against adopting the new constitution without previous amendments, recommend the above named gentlemen, as candidates for members of convention, and the following, for members of senate and assembly: to wit, Peter Van Ness, for senator; John Lansing, jun., Jeremiah Van Rensselaer, Cornelius Van Dyck, John Duncan, John Thompson, Henry K. Van Rensselaer, and John Younglove, for assemblymen.

Jacob C. Ten Eyck,
John R. Bleecker,
Gerrit Lansing, jun.
Cornelius K. Van Den Berg,
Abraham Yates, jun.
Gysbert Fonda,
Cornelius Wendell,
Volkert A. Douw,
Abraham Cuyler,
Henry Ten Eyck,
Henry Wendell,
Peter W. Douw,
Wm. Mancius,

Robert Lansing,
John Price,
Arie Lagrange,
Henry Lansing,
Jacob G. Lansing,
John W. Wendell,
Abm. Bloodgood,
Gysbert Marselus,
Peter W. Yates
Dirck B. Van Schoonhoven,
Jacob Roseboom,
Richard Bush,
Peter Sharp

6. *Debates in The New York Convention*

When the New York convention opened on June 17, 1788, the Antifederalist delegates constituted a large majority, perhaps as much as two-thirds. That delegation was largely controlled by Governor George Clinton, the most powerful figure in state politics. New York's eventual ratification of the Constitution by the very close vote of 30–27 was due partly to the fact that while the convention was sitting, news arrived of the ratification by New Hampshire, the ninth state, and also by Virginia. With the inauguration of the new government thus assured, and with the alleged possibility of a secession from the state by New York City in order to join the union, enough Antifederalists switched positions to secure New York's ratification. Their opposition was also tempered by Federalist agreement to seek amendments once the Constitution had been put into operation. The speeches reprinted here include the very thoughtful observations on the nature of representation by Melancton Smith, a critique of the Senate by Gilbert Livingston, and a despairing last word against "this Goliath, this uncircumcised Philistine," this government "founded in sin, and reared in iniquity," by Thomas Tredwell. In the end, Smith and Livingston voted for the Constitution, and Tredwell against.

Melancton Smith, merchant and lawyer had been an outstanding leader in New York politics for a number of years. During the Revolution, he had held a number of responsible positions in Dutchess County, and he was a member of the Continental Congress from 1785 to 1788. *Gilbert Livingston*, a

Elliot, *Debates*, II, 222–230, 243–251, 286–289, 396–406.

grandson of the first master of Livingston Manor, belonged to an eminent New York family and had been active in state politics for a number of years. A lawyer, he served in the legislature from 1775 to 1778. *Thomas Tredwell*, likewise a lawyer, had also served in the state legislature, from 1774 to 1783.

[MELANCTON SMITH]

The Hon. Mr. SMITH said, he conceived that the Constitution ought to be considered by paragraphs. An honorable gentleman yesterday had opened the debate with some general observations; another honorable gentleman had just answered him by general observations. He wished the Constitution to be examined by paragraphs. In going through it, he should offer his objections to such parts of it as he thought defective.

The first section of the first article was then read, and passed by without remark.

The second section being read,

Mr. SMITH again rose. He most heartily concurred in sentiment with the honorable gentleman who opened the debate, yesterday, that the discussion of the important question now before them ought to be entered on with a spirit of patriotism; with minds open to conviction; with a determination to form opinions only on the merits of the question, from those evidences which should appear in the course of the investigation.

How far the general observations made by the honorable gentleman accorded with these principles, he left to the house to determine.

It was not, he said, his intention to follow that gentle-man through all his remarks. He should only observe that what had been advanced did not appear to apply to the subject under consideration.

He was as strongly impressed with the necessity of a

union as any one could be. He would seek it with as much ardor. In the discussion of this question, he was disposed to make every reasonable concession, and, indeed, to sacrifice every thing for a union, except the liberties of his country, than which he could contemplate no greater misfortune. But he hoped we were not reduced to the necessity of sacrificing, or even endangering, our liberties, to preserve the Union. If that was the case, the alternative was dreadful. But he would not now say that the adoption of the Constitution would endanger our liberties; because that was the point to be debated, and the premises should be laid down previously to the drawing of any conclusion. He wished that all observations might be confined to this point, and that declamations and appeals to the passions might be omitted.

Why, said he, are we told of our weakness? of the defenceless condition of the southern parts of our state? of the exposed situation of our capital? of Long Island, surrounded by water, and exposed to the incursions of our neighbors in Connecticut? of Vermont having separated from us, and assumed the powers of a distinct government? and of the north-west parts of our state being in the hands of a foreign enemy? Why are we to be alarmed with apprehensions that the Eastern States are inimical, and disinclined to form alliances with us? He was sorry to find that such suspicions were entertained. He believed that no such disposition existed in the Eastern States. Surely it could not be supposed that those states would make war upon us for exercising the rights of freemen, deliberating and judging for ourselves, on a subject the most interesting that ever came before any assembly. If a war with our neighbors was to be the result of not acceding, there was no use in debating here; we had better receive their dictates, if we were unable to resist them. The defects of the old Confederation needed as little proof as the necessity of a union. But there was no proof in all this that the proposed Constitution was a good one. Defective as the old Confederation is, he said, no one could deny but it was possible we might have a worse government. But the question was not whether the present Confederation be a bad one, but whether the proposed Constitution be a good one.

It had been observed, that no example of federal republics had succeeded. It was true that the ancient confederated republics were all destroyed; so were those which were not confederated; and all ancient governments, of every form, had shared the same fate. Holland had, no doubt, experienced many evils from the defects in her government; but, with all these defects, she yet existed: she had, under her confederacy, made a principal figure among the nations of Europe, and he believed few countries had experienced a greater share of internal peace and prosperity. The Germanic confederacy was not the most pertinent example to produce on this occasion. Among a number of absolute princes, who consider their subjects as their property, whose will is law, and to whose ambition there are no bounds, it was no difficult task to discover other causes from which the convulsions in that country rose, than the defects of their confederation. Whether a confederacy of states, under any form, be a practicable government, was a question to be discussed in the course of investigating the Constitution.

He was pleased that, thus early in debate, the honorable gentleman had himself shown that the intent of the Constitution was not a confederacy, but a reduction of all the states into a consolidated government. He hoped the gentleman would be complaisant enough to exchange names with those who disliked the Constitution, as it appeared from his own concessions, that they were federalists, and those who advocated it were anti-federalists. He begged leave, however, to remind the gentleman, that Montesquieu, with all the examples of modern and ancient republics in view, gives it as his opinion, that a confederated republic has all the internal advantages of a republic, with the external force of a monarchical government. He was happy to find an officer of such high rank recommending to the other officers of government, and to those who are members of the legislature, to be unbiased by any motives of interest or state importance. Fortunately for himslf, he was out of the verge of temptation of this kind, not having the honor to hold any office under the state. But, then, he was exposed, in common with other gentlemen of the Convention, to another temptation, against which he thought it necessary that we should be equally guarded. If, said he, this Constitution is adopted, there will be a number of honorable and lucrative offices to be filled; and we ought to be cautious lest an expectancy of some of them should influence us to adopt without due consideration.

We may wander, said he, in the fields of fancy without end, and gather flowers as we go. It may be entertaining, but it is of little service to the discovery of truth. We may, on one side, compare the scheme advocated by our opponents to *golden images, with feet part of iron and part of clay;* and on the other, *to a beast dreadful and terrible, and strong exceedngly, having great iron teeth,—which devours, breaks in pieces, and stamps the residue with his feet;* and after all, said he, we shall find that both these allusions are taken from the same *vision;* and their true meaning must be discovered by sober reasoning.

He would agree with the honorable gentlemen that perfection in any system of government was not to be looked for. If that was the object, the debates on the one before them might soon be closed. But he would observe, that this observation applied, with equal force, against changing any system, especially against material and radical changes. Fickleness and inconstancy, he said, were characteristic of a free people; and, in framing a constitution for them, it was, perhaps, the most difficult thing to correct this spirit, and guard against the evil effects of it. He was persuaded it could not be altogether prevented without destroying their freedom. It would be like, attempting to correct a small indisposition in the habit of the body, fixing the patient in a confirmed consumption. This fickle and inconstant spirit was the more dangerous in bringing about changes in the government. The instance that had been adduced by the gentleman from sacred history, was an example in point to prove this. The nation of Israel, having received a form of civil government from Heaven, enjoyed it for a considerable period; but, at length, laboring under pressures which were brought upon them by their own misconduct and imprudence, instead of imputing their misfortunes to their true causes, and making a proper improvement of their calamities, by a correction of their errors, they imputed them to a defect in their constitution; they rejected their divine Ruler, and asked Samuel to make them a king to judge them, like other nations. Samuel was grieved at their folly; but still, by the command of God, he hearkened to their voice, though not until he had solemnly declared unto them the manner in which the king should rein over them. "This (says Samuel) shall be the manner of the king that shall reign over you. He will take your sons, and appoint them for himself, for his chariots, and for his horsemen, and some shall run before his chariots; and he will appoint him captains over thousands, and captains over fifties, and will set them to ear his ground, and to reap his harvest, and to make his instruments of war, and instruments of his chariots. And he will take your daughters to be confectionaries, and to be cooks, and to be bakers. And he will take your fields, and your vineyards, and your olive-yards, even the best of them, and give them to his servants. And he will take the tenth of your seed, and of your vineyards, and give to his officers and to his servants, and he will take your men-servants, and your maid-servants, and your goodliest young men, and your asses, and put them to his work. He will take the tenth of your sheep; and ye shall be his serv-ants. And ye shall cry out in that day, because of your king which ye have chosen you; and the Lord will not hear you in that day!" How far this was applicable to the subject, he would not now say, it could be better judged of when they had gone through it. On the whole, he wished to take up this matter with candor and deliberation.

He would now proceed to state his objections to the clause just read, (section 2, of article 1, clause 3.) His ob-jections were comprised under three heads: 1st, the rule of apportionment is unjust; 2d, there is no precise number fixed on, below which the house shall not be reduced; 3d, it is inadequate. In the first place, the rule of apportion-ment of the representatives is to be according to the whole number of the white inhabitants, with three fifths of all others; that is, in plain English, each state is to send rep-resentatives in proportion to the number of freemen, and three fifths of the slaves it contains. He could not see any rule by which slaves were to be included in the ratio of representation. The principle of a representation being that every free agent should be concerned in governing himself, it was absurd in giving that power to a man who could not exercise it. Slaves have no will of their own. The very operation of it was to give certain privileges to those people who were so wicked as to keep slaves. He knew it would be admitted that this rule of apportionment was founded on unjust principles, but that it was the result of accommodation; which, he supposed, we should be under the necessity of admitting, if we meant to be in union with the Southern States, though utterly repugnant to his feelings. In the second place, the number was not fixed by the Constitution, but left at the discretion of the legislature; perhaps he was mistaken; it was his wish to be informed. He understood, from the Constitution, that sixty-five members were to compose the House of Representatives for three years; that, after that time, the census was to be taken, and the numbers to be ascertained by the legislature, on the following principles: 1st, they shall be apportioned to the respective states according to numbers; 2d, each state shall have one, at least; 3d, they shall never exceed one to every thirty thousand. If this was the case, the first Congress that met might reduce the number below what it now is—a power inconsistent with every principle of a free government, to leave it to the discretion of the rulers to determine the number of representatives of the people. There was no kind of security except in the integrity of the men who were intrusted; and if you have no other security, it is idle to contend about constitutions. In the third place, supposing Congress should declare that there should be one representative for every thirty thousand of the people, in his opinion, it would be incompetent to the great purposes of representation. It was, he said, the fundamental principle of a free government, that the people should make the laws by which they were to be governed. He who is controlled by another is a slave; and that government which is directed by the will of any one, or a few, or any number less than is the will of the community, is a government for slaves.

The new point was, How was the will of the community to be expressed? It was not possible for them to come together; the multitude would be too great: in order, therefore, to provide against this inconvenience, the scheme of representation had been adopted, by which the people deputed others to represent them. Individuals entering into society became one body, and that body ought to be animated by one mind; and he conceived that every form of government should have that complexion. It was true, notwithstanding all the experience we had from others, it had appeared that the experiment of representation had been fairly tried; there was something like it in the ancient republics, in which, being of small extent, the people could easily meet together, though, instead of deliberating, they only considered of those things which were submitted to them by their magistrates. In Great Britain, representation had been carried much further than in any government we knew of, except our own; but in that country it now had only a name. America was the only country in which the first fair opportunity had been offered. When we were colonies, our representation was better than any that was then known: since the revolution; we had advanced still nearer to perfection. He considered it as an object, of all others the most important, to have it fixed on its true principle; yet he was convinced that it was impracticable to have such a representation in a consolidated government. However, said he, we may approach a great way towards perfection by increasing the representation and limiting the powers of Congress. He considered that the great interests and liberties of the people could only be secured by the state governments. He admitted that, if the new government was only confined to great national objects, it would be less exceptionable; but it extended to every thing dear to human nature. That this was the case, would be proved without any long chain of reasoning; for that power which had both the purse and the sword had the government of the whole country, and might extend its powers to any and to every object. He had already observed that, by the true doctrine of representation, this principle was established—that the representative must be chosen by the free will of the majority of his constituents. It therefore followed that the representative should be chosen from small districts. This being admitted, he would ask, Could 65 men for 3,000,000, or 1 for 30,000, be chosen in this manner? Would they be possessed of the requisite information to make happy the great number of souls that were spread over this extensive country? There was another objection to the clause: if great affairs of government were trusted to few men, they would be more liable to corruption. Corruption, he knew, was unfashionable amongst us, but he supposed that Americans were like other men; and though they had hitherto displayed great virtues, still they were men; and therefore such steps should be taken as to prevent the possibility of corruption. We were now in that stage of society in which we could deliberate with freedom; how long it might continue, God only knew! Twenty years hence, perhaps, these maxims might become unfashionable. We already hear, said he, in all parts of the country, gentlemen ridiculing that spirit of patriotism, and love of liberty, which carried us through all our difficulties in times of danger. When patriotism was already nearly hooted out of society, ought we not to take some precautions against the progress of corruption?

He had one more observation to make, to show that the representation was insufficient. Government, he said, must rest, for its execution, on the good opinion of the people; for, if it was made [in] heaven, and had not the confidence of the people, it could not be executed; that this was proved by the example given by the gentleman of the Jewish theocracy. It must have a good setting out, or the instant it takes place, there is an end of liberty. He believed that the inefficacy of the old Confederation had arisen from that want of confidence; and this caused, in a great degree, by the continual declamation of gentlemen of importance against it from one end of the continent to the other, who had frequently compared it to a rope of sand. It had pervaded every class of citizens; and their misfortunes, the consequences of idleness and extravagance, were attributed to the defects of that system. At the close of the war, our country had been left in distress; and it was impossible that any government on earth could immediately retrieve it; it must be time and industry alone that could effect it. He said, he would pursue these observations no further at present,—and concluded with making the following motion:—

"*Resolved,* That it is proper that the number of representatives be fixed at the rate of one for every twenty thousand inhabitants, to be ascertained on the principles mentioned in the 2d section of the 1st article of the Constitution, until they amount to three hundred; after which they shall be apportioned among the states, in proportion to the number of inhabitants of the states respectively; and that, before the first enumeration shall be made, the several states shall be entitled to choose double the number of representatives, for that purpose mentioned in the Constitution."

[Deletion of a speaker other than Smith]

Mr. M. SMITH. I had the honor, yesterday, of submitting an amendment to the clause under consideration, with some observations in support of it. I hope I shall be indulged in making some additional remarks in reply to what has been offered by the honorable gentleman from New York.

He has taken up much time in endeavoring to prove that the great defect in the old Confederation was, that it operated upon states instead of individuals. It is needless to dispute concerning points on which we do not disagree. It is admitted that the powers of the general government ought to operate upon individuals to a certain degree. How far the powers should extend, and in what cases to individuals, is the question.

As the different parts of the system will come into view in the course of our investigation, an opportunity will be afforded to consider this question. I wish, at present, to confine myself to the subject immediately under the consideration of the committee. I shall make no reply to the arguments offered by the honorable gentleman to justify the rule of apportionment fixed by this clause; for, though I am confident they might be easily refuted, yet I am persuaded we must yield this point, in accommodation to the Southern States. The amendment therefore proposes no alteration to the clause in this respect.

The honorable gentleman says, that the clause, by obvious construction, fixes the representation. I wish not to torture words or sentences. I perceive no such obvious construction.

I see clearly that, on one hand, the representatives cannot exceed one for thirty thousand inhabitants; and, on the other, that whatever larger number of inhabitants may be taken for the rule of apportionment, each state shall be entitled to send one representative. Every thing else appears to me in the discretion of the legislature. If there be any other limitation, it is certainly implied. Matters of moment should not be left to doubtful construction. It is urged that the number of representatives will be fixed at one for thirty thousand, because it will be the interest of the larger states to do it. I cannot discern the force of this argument. To me it appears clear, that the relative weight of influence of the different states will be the same, with the number of representatives at sixty-five as at six hundred, and that of the individual members greater; for each member's share of power will decrease as the number of the House of Representatives increases. If, therefore, this maxim be true, that men are unwilling to relinquish powers which they once possess, we are not to expect the House of Representatives will be inclined to enlarge the numbers. The same motive will operate to influence the President and Senate to oppose the increase of the number of representatives; for, in proportion as the House of Representatives is augmented, they will feel their own power diminished. It is, therefore, of the highest importance that a suitable number of representatives should be established by the Constitution.

It has been observed, by an honorable member, that the Eastern States insisted upon a small representation, on the principles of economy. This argument must have no weight in the mind of a considerate person. The difference of expense, between supporting a House of Representatives sufficiently numerous, and the present proposed one, would be twenty or thirty thousand dollars per annum. The man who would seriously object to this expense, to secure his liberties, does not deserve to enjoy them. Besides, by increasing the number of representatives, we open a door for the admission of the substantial yeomanry of our country, who, being possessed of the habits of economy, will be cautious of imprudent expenditures, by which means a greater saving will be made of public money than is sufficient to support them. A reduction of the numbers of the state legislatures might also be made, by which means there might be a saving of expense much more than sufficient for the purpose of supporting the general legislature; for as, under this system, all the powers of legislation, relating to our general concerns, are vested in the general government, the powers of the state legislatures will be so curtailed as to render it less necessary to have them so numerous as they now are.

But an honorable gentleman has observed, that it is a problem that cannot be solved, what the proper number is which ought to compose the House of Representatives, and calls upon me to fix the number. I admit that this is a question that will not admit of a solution with mathematical certainty; few political questions will; yet we may determine with certainty that certain numbers are too small or too large. We may be sure that ten is too small, and a thousand too large a number. Every one will allow that the first number is too small to possess the sentiments, be influenced by the interests of the people, or secure against corruption; a thousand would be too numerous to be capable of deliberating.

To determine whether the number of representatives proposed by this Constitution is sufficient, it is proper to examine the qualifications which this house ought to possess, in order to exercise their power discreetly for the happiness of the people. The idea that naturally suggests itself to our minds, when we speak of representatives, is, that they resemble those they represent. They should be a true picture of the people, possess a knowledge of their circumstances and their wants, sympathize in all their distresses, and be disposed to seek their true interests. The knowledge necessary for the representative of a free people not only comprehends extensive political and commercial information, such as is acquired by men of refined education, who have leisure to attain to high degrees of improvement, but it should also comprehend that kind of acquaintance with the common concerns and occupations of the people, which men of the middling class of life are, in general, more competent to than those of a superior class. To understand the true commercial interests of a country, not only requires just ideas of the general commerce of the world, but also, and principally, a knowledge of the productions of your own country, and their value, what your soil is capable of producing, the nature of your manufactures, and the capacity of the country to increase both. To exercise the power of laying taxes, duties, and excises, with discretion, requires something more than an acquaintance with the abstruse parts of the system of finance. It calls for a knowledge of the circumstances and ability of the people in general—a discernment how the burdens imposed will bear upon the different classes.

From these observations results this conclusion—that the number of representatives should be so large, as that, while it embraces the men of the first class, it should admit those of the middling class of life. I am convinced that this government is so constituted that the representatives will generally be composed of the first class in the community, which I shall distinguish by the name of the *natural aristocracy* of the country. I do not mean to give offence by using this term. I am sensible this idea is treated by many gentlemen as chimerical. I shall be asked what is meant by the *natural aristocracy*, and told that no such distinction of classes of men exists among us. It is true, it is our singular felicity that we have no legal or hereditary distinctions of this kind; but still there are real differences. Every society naturally divides itself into classes. The Author of nature has bestowed on some greater capacities than others; birth, education, talents, and wealth, create distinctions among men as visible, and of as much influence, as titles, stars, and garters. In every society, men of this class will command a superior degree of respect; and if the government is so constituted as to admit but few to exercise the powers of it, it will, according to the natural course of things, be in their hands. Men in the middling class, who are qualified as representatives, will not be so anxious to be chosen as those of the first. When the number is so small, the office will be highly elevated and distinguished; the style in which the members live will probably be high; circumstances of this kind will render the place of a representative not a desirable one to sensible, substantial men, who have been used to walk in the plain and frugal paths of life.

Besides, the influence of the great will generally enable them to succeed in elections. It will be difficult to combine a district of country containing thirty or forty thousand inhabitants,—frame your election laws as you please,—in any other character, unless it be in one of conspicuous military, popular, civil, or legal talents. The great easily form associations; the poor and middling class form them with difficulty. If the elections be by plurality,—as probably will be the case in this state,—it is almost certain none but the great will be chosen, for they easily unite their interests: the common people will divide, and their divisions will be promoted by the others. There will be scarcely a chance of their uniting in any other but some great man, unless in some popular demagogue, who will probably be destitute of principle. A substantial yeoman, of sense and discernment, will hardly ever be chosen. From these remarks, it appears that the government will fall into the hands of the few and the great. This will be a government of oppression. I do not mean to declaim against the great, and charge them indiscriminately with want of principle and honesty. The same passions and prejudices govern all men. The circumstances in which men are placed in a great measure give a cast to the human character. Those in middling circumstances have less temptation; they are inclined by habit, and the company with whom they associate, to set bounds to their passions and appetites. If this is not sufficient, the want of means to gratify them will be a restraint: they are obliged to employ their time in their respective callings; hence the substantial yeomanry of the country are more temperate, of better morals, and less ambition, than the great. The latter do not feel for the poor and middling class; the reasons are obvious—they are not obliged to use the same pains and labor to procure property as the other. They feel not the inconveniences arising from the payment of small sums.

The great consider themselves above the common people, entitled to more respect, do not associate with them; they fancy themselves to have a right of preëminence in every thing. In short, they possess the same feelings, and are under the influence of the same motives, as an hereditary nobility. I know the idea that such a distinction exists in this country is ridiculed by some; but I am not the less apprehensive of danger from their influence on this account. Such distinctions exist all the world over, have been taken notice of by all writers on free government, and are founded in the nature of things. It has been the principal care of free governments to guard against the encroachments of the great. Common observation and experience prove the existence of such distinctions. Will any one say that there does not exist in this country the pride of family, of wealth, of talents, and that they do not command influence and respect among the common people? Congress, in their address to the inhabitants of the province of Quebec, in 1775, state this distinction in the following forcible words, quoted from the Marquis Beccaria: "In every human society there is an essay continually tending to confer on one part the height of power and happiness, and to reduce the other to the extreme of weakness and misery. The intent of good laws is to oppose this effort, and to diffuse their influence universally and equally." We ought to guard against the government being placed in the hands of this class. They cannot have that sympathy with their constituents which is necessary to connect them closely to their interests. Being in the habit of profuse living, they will be profuse in the public expenses. They find no difficulty in paying their taxes, and therefore do not feel public burdens. Besides, if they govern, they will enjoy the emoluments of the government. The middling class, from their frugal habits, and feeling themselves the public burdens, will be careful how they increase them.

But I may be asked, Would you exclude the first class in the community from any share in legislation? I answer, By no means. They would be factious, discontented, and constantly disturbing the government. It would also be unjust. They have their liberties to protect, as well as others, and the largest share of property. But my idea is, that the Constitution should be so framed as to admit this class, together with a sufficient number of the middling class to control them. You will then combine the abilities and honesty of the community, a proper degree of information, and a disposition to pursue the public good. A representative body, composed principally of respectable yeomanry, is the best possible security to liberty. When the interest of this part of the community is pursued, the public good is pursued, because the body of every nation consists of this class, and because the interest of both the rich and the poor are involved in that of the middling class. No burden can be laid on the poor but what will sensibly affect the middling class. Any law rendering property insecure would be injurious to them. When, therefore, this class in society pursue their own interest, they promote that of the public, for it is involved in it.

In so small a number of representatives, there is great danger from corruption and combination. A great politician has said that every man has his price. I hope this is not true in all its extent; but I ask the gentleman to inform me what government there is in which it has not been practised. Notwithstanding all that has been said of the defects in the constitution of the ancient confederacies in the Grecian republics, their destruction is to be imputed more to this cause than to any imperfection in their forms of government. This was the deadly poison that effected their dissolution. This is an extensive country, increasing in population and growing in consequence. Very many lucrative offices will be in the grant of the government, which will be objects of avarice and ambition. How easy will it be to gain over a sufficient number, in the bestowment of offices, to promote the views and the purposes of those who grant them! Foreign corruption is also to be guarded against. A system of corruption is known to be the system of government in Europe. It is practised without blushing; and we may lay it to our account, it will be attempted amongst us. The most effectual as well as natural security against this is a strong democratic branch in the legislature, frequently chosen, including in it a number of the substantial, sensible yeomanry of the country. Does the House of Representatives answer this description? I confess, to me they hardly wear the complexion of a democratic branch; they appear the mere shadow of representation. The whole number, in both houses, amounts to ninety-one; of these forty-six make a quorum; and twenty-four of those, being secured, may carry any point. Can the liberties of three millions of people be securely trusted in the hands of twenty-four men? Is it prudent to commit to so small a number the decision of the great questions which will come before them? Reason revolts at the idea.

The honorable gentleman from New York has said, that sixty-five members in the House of Representatives are sufficient for the present situation of the country; and, taking it for granted that they will increase as one for thirty thousand, in twenty-five years they will amount to two hundred. It is admitted, by this observation, that the number fixed in the Constitution is not sufficient without it is augmented. It is not declared that an increase shall be made, but is left at the discretion of the legislature, by the gentleman's own concession; therefore the Constitution is imperfect. We certainly ought to fix, in the Constitution, those things which are essential to liberty. If any thing falls under this description, it is the number of the legislature. To say, as this gentleman does, that our security is to depend upon the spirit of the people, who will be watchful of their liberties, and not suffer them to be infringed is absurd. It would equally prove that we might adopt any form of government. I believe, were we to create a despot, he would not immediately dare to act the tyrant; but it would not be long before he would destroy the spirit of the people, or the people would destroy him. If our people have a high sense of liberty, the government should be congenial to this spirit, calculated to cherish the love of liberty, while yet it had sufficient force to restrain licentiousness. Government operates upon the spirit of the people, as well as the spirit of the people operates upon it; and if they are not conformable to each other, the one or the other will prevail. In a less time than twenty-five years, the government will receive its tone. What the spirit of the country may be at the end of that period, it is impossible to foretell. Our duty is to frame a government friendly to liberty and the rights of mankind, which will tend to cherish and cultivate a love of liberty among our citizens. If this government becomes oppressive, it will be by degrees: it will aim at its end by disseminating sentiments of government opposite to republicanism, and proceed from step to step in depriving the people of a share in the government. A recollection of the change that has taken place in the minds of many in this country in the course of a few years, ought to put us on our guard. Many, who are ardent advocates for the new system, reprobate republican principles as chimerical, and such as ought to be expelled from society. Who would have thought, ten years ago, that the very men, who risked their lives and fortunes in support of republican principles, would now treat them as the fictions of fancy? A few years ago, we fought for liberty; we framed a general government on free principles; we placed the state legislatures, in whom the people have a full and a fair representation, between Congress and the people. We were then, it is true, too cautious, and too much restricted the powers of the general government. But now it is proposed to go into the contrary, and a more dangerous extreme—to remove all barriers, to give the new government free access to our pockets, and ample command of our persons, and that without providing for a genuine and fair representation of the people. No one can say what the progress of the change of sentiment may be in twenty-five years. The same men who now cry up the necessity of an energetic government, to induce a compliance with this system, may, in much less time, reprobate this in as severe terms as they now do the Confederation, and may as strongly urge the necessity of going as far beyond this as this is beyond the Confederation. Men of this class are increasing: they have influence, talents, and industry. It is time to form a barrier against them. And while we are willing to establish a government adequate to the purposes of the Union, let us be careful to establish it on the broad basis of equal liberty.

[GILBERT LIVINGSTON]

Tuesday, *June* 24th, 1788.—Convention assembled; and being resolved into a committee, the 1st paragraph of the 3d section of the 1st article was read; when Mr. G. LIVING-STON rose, and addressed the chair.

He, in the first place, considered the importance of the *Senate* as a branch of the legislature, in three points of view:—

First, they would possess legislative powers coëxtensive with those of the House of Representatives except with respect to originating revenue laws; which, however, they would have power to reject or amend, as in the case of other bills. Secondly, they would have an importance, even exceeding that of the representative house, as they would be composed of a smaller number, and possess more firmness and system. Thirdly, their consequence and dignity would still further transcend those of the other branch, from their longer continuance in office. These powers, Mr. Livingston contended, rendered the Senate a dangerous body.

He went on, in the second place, to enumerate and animadvert on the powers with which they were clothed in their judicial capacity, and in their capacity of council to the President, and in the forming of treaties. In the last place, as if too much power could not be given to this body, they were made, he said, a council of appointment, by whom ambassadors and other officers of state were to be appointed. These are the powers, continued he, which are vested in this small body of twenty-six men; in some cases, to be exercised by a bare quorum, which is fourteen; a majority of which number, again, is eight. What are the checks provided to balance this great mass of power? Our present Congress cannot serve longer than three years in six: they are at any time subject to recall. These and other checks were considered as necessary at a period which I choose to honor with the name of *virtuous*. Sir, I venerate the spirit with which every thing was done at the trying time in which the Confederation was formed. America had then a sufficiency of this virtue to resolve to resist perhaps the first nation in the universe, even unto bloodshed. What was her aim? Equal liberty and safety. What ideas had she of this equal liberty? Read them in her Articles of Confederation. True it is, sir, there are some powers wanted to make this glorious compact complete. But, sir, let us be cautious that we do not err more on the other hand, by giving power too profusely, when, perhaps, it will be too late to recall it. Consider, sir, the great influence which this body, armed at all points, will have. What will be the effect of this? Probably a security of their reëlection, as long as they please. Indeed, in my view, it will amount nearly to an appointment for life. What will be their situation in a federal town? Hallowed ground! Nothing so unclean as state laws to enter there, surrounded, as they will be, by an impenetrable wall of adamant and gold, the wealth of the whole country flowing into it. [Here a member, who did not fully understand, called out to know what WALL the gentleman meant; on which he turned, and replied, "A wall of gold—of adamant, which will flow in from all parts of the continent." At which flowing metaphor, a great laugh in the house.] The gentleman continued: Their attention to their various business will probably require their constant attendance. In this Eden will they reside with their families, distant from the observation of the people. In such a situation, men are apt to forget their dependence, lose their sympathy, and contract selfish habits. Factions are apt to be formed, if the body becomes permanent. The senators will associate only with men of their own class, and thus become strangers to the condition of the common people. They should not only return, and be obliged to live with the people, but return to their former rank of citizenship, both to revive their sense of dependence, and to gain a knowledge of the country. This will afford opportunity to bring forward the genius and information of the states, and will be a stimulus to acquire political abilities. It will be the means of diffusing a more general knowledge of the measures and spirit of the administration. These things will confirm the people's confidence in government. When they see those who have been high in office residing among them as private citizens, they will feel more forcibly that the government is of their own choice. The members of this branch having the idea impressed on their minds, that they are soon to return to the level whence the suffrages of the people raised them,—this good effect will follow: they will consider their interests as the same with those of their constituents, and that they legislate for themselves as well as others. They will not conceive themselves made to receive, enjoy, and rule, nor the people solely to earn, pay, and submit.

Mr. Chairman, I have endeavored, with as much perspicuity and candor as I am master of, shortly to state my objections to this clause. I would wish the committee to believe that they are not raised for the sake of opposition, but that I am very sincere in my sentiments in this important investigation. The Senate, as they are now constituted, have little or no check on them. Indeed, sir, too much is put into their hands. When we come to that part of the system which points out their powers, it will be the proper time to consider this subject more particularly.

I think, sir, we must relinquish the idea of safety under this government, if the time for services is not further limited, and the power of recall given to the state legislatures. I am strengthened in my opinion by an observation made yesterday, by an honorable member from New York, to this effect—"that there should be no fear of corruption of the members in the House of Representatives; especially as they are, in two years, to return to the body of the people." I therefore move that the committee adopt the following resolution, as an amendment to this clause:—

"*Resolved*, That no person shall be eligible as a senator for more than six years in any term of twelve years, and that it shall be in the power of the legislatures of the several states to recall their senators, or either of them, and to elect others in their stead, to serve for the remainder of the time for which such senator or senators, so recalled, were appointed."

[THOMAS TREDWELL]

Mr. TREDWELL. Sir, little accustomed to speak in public, and always inclined, in such an assembly as this, to be a hearer rather than a speaker, on a less important occasion than the present I should have contented myself with a silent vote; but when I consider the nature of this dispute, that it is a contest, not between little states and great states, (as we have been told,) between little folks and great folks, between patriotism and ambition, between freedom and power; not so much between the navigating and non-navigating states, as between navigating and non-navigating individuals, (for not one of the amendments we contend for has the least reference to the clashing interests of states;) when I consider, likewise, that a people jealous of their liberties, and strongly attached to freedom, have reposed so entire a confidence in this assembly, that upon our determination depends their future enjoyment of those invaluable rights and privileges, which they have so lately and so gallantly defended at every risk and expense, both of life and property,—it appears to me so interesting and important, that I cannot be totally silent on the occasion, lest lisping babes should be taught to curse my name, as a betrayer of their freedom and happiness.

The gentleman who first opened this debate did (with an emphasis which I believe convinced every one present of the propriety of the advice) urge the necessity of proceeding, in our deliberations on this important subject, coolly and dispassionately. With how much candor this advice was given, appears from the subsequent parts of a long speech, and from several subsequent speeches almost totally addressed to our fears. The people of New Jersey and Connecticut are so exceedingly exasperated against us, that, totally regardless of their own preservation, they will take the two rivers of Connecticut and Delaware by their extremities, and, by dragging them over our country, will, by a sweeping deluge, wash us all into the Hudson, leaving neither house nor inhabitant behind them. But if this event should not happen, doubtless the Vermontese, with the British and tories our natural enemies, would , by bringing down upon us the great Lake Ontario, sweep hills and mountains, houses and inhabitants, in one deluge, into the Atlantic. These, indeed, would be terrible calamities; but terrible as they are, they are not to be compared with the horrors and desolation of tyranny. The arbitrary courts of Philip in the Netherlands, in which life and property were daily confiscated without a jury, occasioned as much misery and a more rapid depopulation of the province, before the people took up arms in their own defence, than all the armies of that haughty monarch were able to effect afterwards; and it is doubtful in my mind, whether governments, by abusing their powers, have not occasioned as much misery and distress, and nearly as great devastations of the human species, as all the wars which have happened since Milton's battle of the angels to the present day. The end or design of government is, or ought to be, the safety, peace, and welfare of the governed. Unwise, therefore, and absurd in the highest degree, would be the conduct of that people, who, in forming a government, should give to their rulers power to desroy them and their property, and thereby defeat the very purpose of their institutions; or, in other words, should give unlimited power to their rulers, and not retain in their own hands the means of their own preservation. The first governments in the world were parental, the powers of which were restrained by the laws of nature; and doubtless the early succeeding governments were formed on the same plan, which, we may suppose, answered tolerably well in the first ages of the world, while the moral sense was strong, and the laws of nature well understood, there being then no lawyers to explain them away. But in after times, when kings became great, and courts crowded, it was discovered that governments should have a right to tyrannize, and a power to oppress; and at the present day, when the *juris periti* are become so skilful in their profession, and quibbling is reduced to a science, it is become extremely difficult to form a constitution which will secure liberty and happiness to the people, or laws under which property is safe. Hence, in modern times, the design of the people, in forming an original constitution of government, is not so much to give powers to their rulers, as to guard against the abuse of them; but, in a federal one, it is different.

Sir, I introduce these observations to combat certain principles which have been daily and confidently advanced by the favorers of the present Constitution, and which appear to me totally indefensible. The first and grand leading, or rather misleading, principle in this debate, and on which the advocates for this system of unrestricted powers must chiefly depend for its support, is that, in forming a constitution, whatever powers are not expressly granted or given the government, are reserved to the people, or that rulers cannot exercise any powers but those expressly given to them by the Constitution. Let me ask the gentlemen who advanced this principle, whether the commission of a Roman dictator, which was in these few words—to take care that the state received no harm—does not come up fully to their ideas of an energetic government; or whether an invitation from the people to one or more to come and rule over them, would not clothe the rulers with sufficient powers. If so, the principle they advance is a false one. Besides, the absurdity of this principle will evidently appear, when we consider the great variety of objects to which the powers of the government must necessarily extend, and that an express enumeration of them all would probably fill as many volumes as Pool's Synopsis of the Critics. But we may reason with sufficient certainty on the subject, from the sense of all the public bodies in the United States, who had occasion to form new constitutions. They have uniformly acted upon a direct and contrary principle, not only in forming the state constitutions and the old Confederation, but also in forming this very constitution, for we do not find in every state constitution express resolutions made in favor of the people; and it is clear that the late Convention at Philadelphia, whatever might have been the sentiments of some of its members, did not adopt the principle, for they have made certain reservations and restrictions, which, upon that principle, would have been totally useless and unnecessary; and can it be supposed that that wise body, whose only apology for the great ambiguity of many parts of that performance, and the total omission of some things which many esteem essential to the security of liberty, was a great desire of brevity, should so far sacrifice that great and important object, as to insert a number of provisions which they esteemed totally useless? Why is it said that the privilege of the writ of *habeas corpus* shall not be suspended, unless, in cases of rebellion or invasion, the public safety may require it? What clause in the Constitution, except this very clause itself, gives the general government a power to deprive us of that great privilege, so sacredly secured to us by our state constitutions? Why is it provided that no bill of attainder shall be passed, or that no title of nobility shall be granted? Are there any clauses in the Constitution extending the powers of the general government to these objects? Some gentlemen say that these, though not necessary, were inserted for greater caution. I could have wished, sir, that a greater caution had been used to secure to us the freedom of election, a sufficient and responsible representation, the freedom of the press, and the trial by jury both in civil and criminal cases.

These, sir, are the rocks on which the Constitution should have rested; no other foundation can any man lay, which will secure the sacred temple of freedom against the power of the great, the undermining arts of ambition, and

the blasts of profane scoffers—for such there will be in
every age—who will tell us that all religion is in vain; that
is, that our political creeds, which have been handed down
to us by our forefathers as sacredly as our Bibles, and for
which more of them have suffered martyrdom than for the
creed of the apostles, are all nonsense; who will tell us
that paper constitutions are mere paper, and that parchment is but parchment, that jealousy of our rulers is a sin,
&c. I could have wished also that sufficient caution had
been used to secure to us our religious liberties, and to
have prevented the general government from tyrannizing
over our consciences by a religious establishment—a tyranny of all others most dreadful, and which will assuredly
be exercised whenever it shall be thought necessary for
the promotion and support of their political measures. It is
ardently to be wished, sir, that these and other invaluable
rights of freemen had been as cautiously secured as some
of the paltry local interests of some of the individual states.
But it appears to me, that, in forming this Constitution, we
have run into the same error which the lawyers and Phar-
isees of old were charged with; that is, while we have
secured the tithes of mint, anise, and cumin, we have
neglected the weightier matters of the law, judgment,
mercy, and faith. Have we not neglected to secure to ourselves the weighty matters of judgment or justice, by empowering the general government to establish one supreme, and as many inferior, courts as they please, whose
proceedings they have a right to fix and regulate as they
shall think fit, so that we are ignorant whether they shall
be according to the common, civil, the Jewish, or Turkish
law? What better provisions have we made for mercy,
when a man, for ignorantly passing a counterfeit continental note, or bill of credit, is liable to be dragged to a distant
county, two or three hundred miles from home, deprived
of the support and assistance of friends, to be tried by a

strange jury, ignorant of his character, ignorant of the character of the witnesses, unable to contradict any false testimony brought against him by their own knowledge of facts, and with whom the prisoner being unacquainted, he must be deprived totally of the benefit of his challenge? and besides all that, he may be exposed to lose his life, merely for want of property to carry his witnesses to such a distance; and after all this solemn farce and mockery of a trial by jury, if they should acquit him, it will require more ingenuity than I am master of, to show that he does not hold his life at the will and pleasure of the Supreme Court, to which an appeal lies, and consequently depend on the tender mercies, perhaps, of the wicked, (for judges may be wicked;) and what those tender mercies are, I need not tell you. You may read them in the history of the Star Chamber Court in England, and in the courts of Philip, and in your Bible.

This brings me to the third and last weighty matter mentioned in the text—to wit, faith. The word *faith* may, with great propriety, be applied to the articles of our political creed, which, it is absolutely necessary, should be kept pure and uncorrupted, if we mean to preserve the liberties of our country and the inestimable blessings of a free government. And, sir, I cannot but be seriously alarmed on this head, as has frequently been the case during the present discussion,—gentlemen of the first rank and abilities openly opposing some of the most essential principles of freedom, and endeavoring, by the most ingenious sophistry, and the still more powerful weapons of ridicule, to shake or corrupt our faith therein. Have we not been told that, if government is but properly organized, and the powers were suitably distributed among the several members, it is unnecessary to provide any other security against the abuse of its power? that power thus distributed needs no restriction? Is this a whig principle? Does not every constitution on the continent contradict this position? Why are we told that all restrictions of power are found to be inconvenient? that we ought to put unlimited confidence in our rulers? that it is not our duty to be jealous of men in power? Have we not had an idea thrown out of establishing an aristocracy in our own country,—a government than which none is more dreadful and oppressive?

What the design of the preacher on this occasion is, I will not attempt to determine; far be it from me to judge men's hearts: but thus much I can say, from the best authority, they are deceitful above all things, and desperately wicked. But whatever be the design of the preachers, the tendency of their doctrines is clear; they tend to corrupt our political faith, to take us off our guard, and lull to sleep that jealousy which, we are told by all writers,—and it is proved by all experience,—is essentially necessary for the preservation of freedom. But notwithstanding the strongest assertions that there are no wolves in our country, if we see their footsteps in every public path, we should be very credulous and unwise to trust our flocks abroad, and to believe that those who advised us to do it were very anxious for their preservation.

In this Constitution, sir, we have departed widely from the principles and political faith of '76, when the spirit of liberty ran high, and danger put a curb on ambition. Here we find no security for the rights of individuals, no security for the existence of our state governments; here is no bill of rights, no proper restriction of power; our lives, our property, and our consciences, are left wholly at the mercy of the legislature, and the powers of the judiciary may be extended to any degree short of almighty. Sir, in this Constitution we have not only neglected,—we have done worse,—we have openly violated, our faith,—that is, our public faith.

The seventh article, which is in these words, "The rati-

fications of the Conventions of nine states shall be sufficient for the establishment of this Constitution between
the states so ratifying the same," is so flagrant a violation of
the public faith of these states, so solemnly pledged to
each other in the Confederation, as makes me tremble to
reflect upon; for, however lightly some may think of *paper*
and *parchment* constitutions, they are recorded, sir, in that
high court of appeals, the Judge of which will do right, and
I am confident that no such violation of public faith ever
did, or ever will, go unpunished.

The plan of the *federal city*, sir, departs from every
principle of freedom, as far as the distance of the two polar
stars from each other; for, subjecting the inhabitants of that
district to the exclusive legislation of Congress, in whose
appointment they have no share or vote, is laying a foundation on which may be erected as complete a tyranny as
can be found in the Eastern world. Nor do I see how this
evil can possibly be prevented, without razing the foundation of this happy place, where men are to live, without
labor, upon the fruit of the labors of others; this political
hive, where all the drones in the society are to be collected to feed on the honey of the land. How dangerous
this city may be, and what its operation on the general liberties of this country, time alone must discover; but I pray
God, it may not prove to this western world what the city
of Rome, enjoying a similar constitution, did to the eastern.

There is another clause in this Constitution, which,
though there is no prospect of getting it amended, I think
ought not to be passed over in silence, lest such a silence
should be construed into a tacit approbation of it. I mean
the clause which restricts the general government from
putting a stop, for a number of years, to a commerce which
is a stain to the commerce of any civilized nation, and has
already blackened half the plains of America with a race of
wretches made so by our cruel policy and avarice, and

which appears to me to be already repugnant to every principle of humanity, morality, religion, and good policy. There are other objections to this Constitution, which are weighty and unanswerable; but they have been so clearly stated, and so fully debated, in the course of this discussion, that it would be an unjustifiable intrusion on the patience of the house to repeat them. I shall therefore content myself with a few observations on the general plan and tendency. We are told that this is a federal government. I think, sir, there is as much propriety in the name, as in that which its advocates assume, and no more; it is, in my idea, as complete a consolidation as the government of this state, in which legislative powers, to a certain extent, are exercised by the several towns and corporations. The sole difference between a state government under this Constitution, and a corporation under a state government, is, that a state being more extensive than a town, its powers are likewise proportionably extended, but neither of them enjoys the least share of sovereignty; for, let me ask, what is a state government? What sovereignty, what power is left to it, when the control of every source of revenue, and the total command of the militia, are given to the general government? That power which can command both the property and the persons of the community, is the sovereign, and the sole sovereign. The idea of two distinct sovereigns in the same country, separately *possessed* of sovereign and supreme power, in the same matters at the same time, is as supreme an absurdity, as that two distinct separate circles can be bounded exactly by the same circumference. This, sir, is demonstration; and from it I draw one corollary, which, I think clearly follows, although it is in favor of the Constitution, to wit—that at least that clause in which Congress guaranties to the several states a republican *form* of government, speaks honestly; that is, that no more is intended by it than is expressed; and I think it is

clear that, whilst the mere form is secured, the substance—to wit, the whole power and sovereignty of our
state governments, and with them the liberties of the
country—is swallowed up by the general government; for
it is well worth observing, that, while our state governments are held up to us as the great and sufficient security
of our rights and privileges, it is carefully provided that
they shall be disarmed of all power, and made totally dependent on the bounty of Congress for their support, and
consequently for their existence,—so that we have scarce a
single right secured under either.

Is this, sir, a government for freemen? Are we thus to be
duped out of our liberties? I hope, sir, our affairs have not
yet arrived to that long-wished-for pitch of confusion. That
we are under the necessity of accepting such a system of
government as this.

I cannot, sir, express my feelings on a late occasion,
when I consider with what unspeakable indignation the
spirit of a Montgomery, a Herkimer, a Paris, &c., must
have fired at the insults offered to their memories on this
floor, and that not by a stranger, but by a brother, when
their names, which will ever be dear to freemen, were
profanely called upon as an inducement for us to surrender
up those rights and privileges, in the defence of which
they so gallantly fought, and so gloriously died. We are
called upon at this time (I think it is an early day) to make
an unconditional surrender of those rights which ought to
be dearer to us than our lives.

But I hope, sir, that the memory of these patriot heroes
will teach us a duty on this occasion. If we follow their
example, we are sure not to err. We ought, sir, to consider—and it is a most solemn consideration—that we may
now give away, by a vote, what it may cost the dying
groans of thousands to recover; that we may now surrender, with a little ink, what it may cost seas of blood to

regain; the dagger of Ambition is now pointed at the fair bosom of Liberty, and, to deepen and complete the tragedy, we, her sons, are called upon to give the fatal thrust. Shall we not recoil at such a deed, and all cry out with one voice, "Hands off!" What distraction has seized us? Is she not our mother, and if the frenzy of any should persist in the parricidal attempt, shall we not instantly interpose, and receive the fatal point into our own bosom? A moment's hesitation would ever prove us to be bastards, not sons. The liberties of the country are a deposit, a trust, in the hands of individuals; they are an entailed estate, which the possessors have no right to dispose of; they belong to our children, and to them we are bound to transmit them as a representative body. The trust becomes tenfold more sacred in our hands, especially as it was committed to us with the fullest confidence in our sentiments, integrity, and firmness. If we should betray that trust on this occasion, I fear (think there is reason to fear) that it will teach a lesson dangerous to liberty—to wit, that no confidence is to be placed in men.

But why, sir, must we be guilty of this breach of trust? Why surrender up the dear-bought liberties of our country? Because we are told, in very positive terms, that nothing short of this will satisfy, or can be accepted by, our future rulers? Is it possible that we can be at a loss for an answer to such declarations as these? Can we not, ought we not, to speak like freemen on this occasion, (this perhaps may be the last time when we shall dare to do it,) and declare, in as positive terms, that we cannot, we will not, give up our liberties; that, if we cannot be admitted into the Union as freemen, we will not come in as slaves? This I fully believe to be the language of my constituents; this is the language of my conscience; and, though I may not dare longer to make it the language of my tongue, yet I trust it will ever be the language of my heart. If we act with coolness, firmness, and decision, on this occasion, I have the fullest confidence that the God who has so lately delivered us out of the paw of the lion and the bear, will also deliver us from this Goliath, this uncircumcised Philistine. This government is founded in sin, and reared up in iniquity; the foundations are laid in a most sinful breach of public trust, and the top-stone is a most iniquitous breach of public faith; and I fear, if it goes into operation, we shall be justly punished with the total extinction of our civil liberties. We are invited, in this instance, to become partakers in other men's sins; if we do, we must likewise be content to take our share in the punishment.

We are told, sir, that a government is like a mad horse, which, notwithstanding all the curb you can put upon him, will sometimes run away with his rider. The idea is undoubtedly a just one. Would he not, therefore, justly be deemed a mad man, and deserve to have his neck broken, who should trust himself on this horse without any bridle at all? We are threatened, sir, if we do not come into the Union, with the resentment of our neighboring states. I do not apprehend we have much to fear from this quarter, for our neighbors must have the good sense to discover that not one of our objections is founded on motives of particular state interest. They must see likewise, from the debates, that every selfish idea that has been thrown out has come from those who very improperly call themselves the *federal* side of the house. A union with our sister states I as ardently desire as any man, and that upon the most generous principles; but a union under such a system as this, I think, is not a desirable thing. The design of a union is safety, but a union upon the proposed plan is certain destruction to liberty. In one sense, indeed, it may bring us to a state of safety, for it may reduce us to such a condition that we may be very sure that nothing worse can happen to us, and consequently we shall have nothing to fear.

This, sir, is a dreadful kind of safety; but I confess it is the only kind of safety I can see in this union. There are no advantages that can possibly arise from a union which can compensate for the loss of freedom, nor can any evils be apprehended from a disunion which are as much to be dreaded as tyranny.

17. *Debates in The North Carolina Convention*

North Carolina had two conventions to consider ratification of the Constitution. The first, from which the selections reprinted here are taken, met from July 21 to August 4, 1788, and rejected the Constitution by a vote of 184–184. A second convention, meeting November 16–23, 1789, ratified by a vote of 136–168. In the first convention, the Antifederalists were so sure of their majority that their leader, Willie Jones, after the convention had been organized, moved that "the question upon the Constitution should be immediately put."[1] Not all of his supporters agreed with such peremptory proceedings, however, and the Federalists were accordingly given a chance to expound their views. Nevertheless, the great Antifederalist predominance may have made them less interested in debate than they would have been otherwise, for their speeches tend to be brief and not particularly distinguished. Opinion from one of the two states that refused to ratify the Constitution should nevertheless be included in this collection. Few of the North Carolina Antifederalists were men of distinction, and about most of them little or nothing is known.

Samuel Spencer had been a member of the colonial and provincial legislatures, had been a state judge since 1777, and was awarded a doctor of laws degree from Princeton in 1784. *William Lancaster* was a Baptist minister.

Elliot, *Debates*, IV, 116–119, 152–155, 212–215.

[1] Elliot, *Debates*, IV, 4.

[SAMUEL SPENCER]

The 2d clause of the 2d section read [regarding the power of appointment exercised with the Senate]

Mr. SPENCER. Mr. Chairman, I rise to declare my disapprobation of this, likewise. It is an essential article in our Constitution, that the legislative, the executive, and the supreme judicial powers, of government, ought to be forever separate and distinct from each other. The Senate, in the proposed government of the United States, are possessed of the legislative authority in conjunction with the House of Representatives. They are likewise possessed of the sole power of trying all impeachments, which, not being restrained to the officers of the United States, may be intended to include all the officers of the several states in the Union. And by this clause they possess the chief of the executive power; they are, in effect, to form treaties, which are to be the law of the land; and they have obviously, in effect, the appointment of all the officers of the United States. The President may nominate, but they have a negative upon his nomination, till he has exhausted the number of those he wishes to be appointed. He will be obliged, finally, to acquiesce in the appointment of those whom the Senate shall nominate, or else no appointment will take place. Hence it is easy to perceive that the President, in order to do any business, or to answer any purpose in this department of his office, and to keep himself out of perpetual hot water, will be under a necessity to form a connection with that powerful body, and be contented to put himself at the head of the leading members who compose it. I do not expect, at this day, that the outline and organization of this proposed government will be materially altered. But I cannot but be of opinion that the government would have been infinitely better and more secure, if the President had been provided with a standing council, composed of one member from each of the states, the duration of whose office might have been the same as that of the President's office, or for any other period that might have been thought more proper; for it can hardly be supposed, if two senators can be sent from each state, who are fit to give counsel to the President, that one such cannot be found in each state qualified for that purpose. Upon this plan, one half the expense of the Senate, as a standing council to the President in the recess of Congress, would evidently be saved; each state would have equal weight in this council, as it has now in the Senate. And what renders this plan the more eligible is, that two very important consequences would result from it, which cannot result from the present plan. The first is, that the whole executive department, being separate and distinct from that of the legislative and judicial, would be amenable to the justice of the land: the President and his council, or either or any of them, might be impeached, tried, and condemned, for any misdemeanor in office. Whereas, on the present plan proposed, the Senate, who are to advise the President, and who, in effect, are possessed of the chief executive powers, let their conduct be what it will, are not amenable to the public justice of their country: if they may be impeached, there is no tribunal invested with jurisdiction to try them. It is true that the proposed Constitution provides that, when the President is tried, the chief justice shall preside. But I take this to be very little more than a farce. What can the Senate try him for? For doing that which they have advised him to do, and which, without their advice, he would not have done. Except what he may do in a military capacity—when, I presume, he will be entitled to be tried by a court martial of general officers— he can do nothing in the executive department without the advice of the Senate, unless it be to grant pardons, and adjourn the two Houses of Congress to some day to which they cannot agree to adjourn themselves—probably to some term that may be convenient to the leading members of the Senate.

I cannot conceive, therefore, that the President can ever be tried by the Senate with any effect, or to any purpose for any misdemeanor in his office, unless it should extend to high treason, or unless they should wish to fix the odium of any measure on him, in order to exculpate themselves; the latter of which I cannot suppose will ever happen.

Another important consequence of the plan I wish had taken place is that, the office of the President being thereby unconnected with that of the legislative, as well as the judicial, he would have that independence which is necessary to form the intended check upon the acts passed by the legislature before they obtain the sanction of laws. But, on the present plan, from the necessary connection of the President's office with that of the Senate, I have little ground to hope that his firmness will long prevail against the overbearing power and influence of the Senate, so far as to answer the purpose of any considerable check upon the acts they may think proper to pass in conjunction with the House of Representatives; for he will soon find that, unless he inclines to compound with them, they can easily hinder and control him in the principal articles of his office. But, if nothing else could be said in favor of the plan of a standing council to the President, independent of the Senate, the dividing the power of the latter would be sufficient to recommend it; it being of the utmost importance towards the security of the government, and the liberties of the citizens under it. For I think it must be obvious to every unprejudiced mind, that the combining in the Senate the power of legislation, with a controlling share in the appointment of all the officers of the United States, (except those chosen by the people,) and the power of trying all impeachments that may be found against such officers, invests the Senate at once with such an enormity of power, and with such an overbearing and uncontrollable influence, as is incompatible with every idea of safety to the liberties of a free country, and is calculated to swallow up all other powers, and to render that body a despotic aristocracy. . . .

Mr. SPENCER. Mr. Chairman, I hope to be excused for making some observations on what was said yesterday, by gentlemen, in favor of these two clauses [*regarding a Bill of Rights*]. The motion which was made that the committee should rise, precluded me from speaking then. The gentlemen have showed much moderation and candor in conducting this business; but I still think that my observations are well founded, and that some amendments are necessary. The gentleman said, all matters not given up by this form of government were retained by the respective states. I know that it ought to be so; it is the general doctrine, but it is necessary that it should be expressly declared in the Constitution, and not left to mere construction and opinion. I am authorized to say it was heretofore thought necessary. The Confederation says, expressly, that all that was not given up by the United States was retained by the respective states. If such a clause had been inserted in this Constitution, it would have superseded the necessity of a bill of rights. But that not being the case, it was necessary that a bill of rights, or something of that kind, should be a part of the Constitution. It was observed that, as the Constitution is to be a delegation of power from the several states to the United States, a bill of rights was unnecessary. But it will be noticed that this is a different case.

The states do not act in their political capacities, but the government is proposed for individuals. The very caption of the Constitution shows that this is the case. The expression, "We, the people of the United States," shows that this government is intended for individuals; there ought, therefore, to be a bill of rights. I am ready to acknowledge that the Congress ought to have the power of executing its laws. Heretofore, because all the laws of the Confederation were binding on the states in their political capacities, courts had nothing to do with them; but now the thing is entirely different. The laws of Congress will be binding on individuals, and those things which concern individuals will be brought properly before the courts. In the next place, all the officers are to take an oath to carry into execution this general government, and are bound to support every act of the government, of whatever nature it may be. This is a fourth reason for securing the rights of individuals. It was also observed that the federal judiciary and the courts of the states, under the federal authority, would have concurrent jurisdiction with respect to any subject that might arise under the Constitution. I am ready to say that I most heartily wish that, whenever this government takes place, the two jurisdictions and the two governments—that is, the general and the several state governments—may go hand in hand, and that there may be no interference, but that every thing may be rightly conducted. But I will never concede that it is proper to divide the business between the two different courts. I have no doubt that there is wisdom enough in this state to decide the business, without the necessity of federal assistance to do our business. The worthy gentleman from Edenton dwelt a considerable time on the observations on a bill of rights, contending that they were proper only in monarchies, which were founded on different principles from those of our government; and, therefore, though they might be necessary for others, yet they were not necessary for us. I still think that a bill of rights is necessary. This necessity arises from the nature of human societies. When individuals enter into society, they give up some rights to secure the rest. There are certain human rights that ought not to be given up, and which ought in some manner to be secured. With respect to these great essential rights. no latitude ought to be left. They are the most inestimable gifts of the great Creator, and therefore ought not to be destroyed, but ought to be secured. They ought to be secured to individuals in consideration of the other rights which they give up to support society.

The trial by jury has been also spoken of. Every person who is acquainted with the nature of liberty need not be informed of the importance of this trial. Juries are called the bulwarks of our rights and liberty; and no country can ever be enslaved as long as those cases which affect their lives and property are to be decided, in a great measure, by the consent of twelve honest, disinterested men, taken from the respectable body of yeomanry. It is highly improper that any clause which regards the security of the trial by jury should be any way doubtful. In the clause that has been read, it is ascertained that criminal cases are to be tried by jury in the states where they are committed. It has been objected to that clause, that it is not sufficiently explicit. I think that it is not. It was observed that one may be taken to a great distance. One reason of the resistance to the British government was, because they required that we should be carried to the country of Great Britain, to be tried by juries of that country. But we insisted on being tried by juries of the vicinage, in our own country. I think it therefore proper that something explicit should be said with respect to the vicinage.

With regard to that part, that the Supreme Court shall have appellate jurisdiction both as to law and fact, it has been observed that, though the federal court might decide without a jury, yet the court below, which tried it, might have a jury. I ask the gentleman what benefit would be received in the suit by having a jury trial in the court below, when the verdict is set aside in the Supreme Court. It was intended by this clause that the trial by jury should be suppressed in the superior and inferior courts. It has been said, in defence of the omission concerning the trial by jury in civil cases, that one general regulation could not be made; that in several cases the constitution of several states did not require a trial by jury,—for instance, in cases of equity and admiralty,—whereas in others it did, and that, therefore, it was proper to leave this subject at large. I am sure that, for the security of liberty, they ought to have been at the pains of drawing some line. I think that the respectable body who formed the Constitution should have gone so far as to put matters on such a footing as that there should be no danger. They might have provided that all those cases which are now triable by a jury should be tried in each state by a jury, according to the mode usually practised in such state. This would have been easily done, if they had been at the trouble of writing five or six lines. Had it been done, we should have been entitled to say that our rights and liberties were not endangered. If we adopt this clause as it is, I think, notwithstanding what gentlemen have said, that there will be danger. There ought to be some amendments to it, to put this matter on a sure footing. There does not appear to me to be any kind of necessity that the federal court should have jurisdiction in the body of the country. I am ready to give up that, in the cases expressly enumerated, an appellate jurisdiction (except in one or two instances) might be given. I wish them also to have jurisdiction in maritime affairs, and to try offences committed on the high seas. But in the body of a state, the jurisdiction of the courts in that state might extend to carrying into execution the laws of Congress. It must be unnecessary for the federal courts to do it, and would create trouble and expense which might be avoided. In all cases where appeals are proper, I will agree that it is necessary there should be one Supreme Court. Were those things properly regulated, so that the Supreme Court might not be oppressive, I should have no objection to it.

[WILLIAM LANCASTER]

Mr. LANCASTER. Mr. Chairman, it is of the utmost importance to decide this great question with candor and deliberation. Every part of this Constitution has been elucidated. It hath been asserted, by several worthy gentlemen, that it is the most excellent Constitution that ever was formed. I could wish to be of that opinion if it were so. The powers vested therein were very extensive. I am apprehensive that the power of taxation is unlimited. It expressly says that Congress shall have the power to lay taxes, &c. It is obvious to me that the power is unbounded, and I am apprehensive that they may lay taxes too heavily on our lands, in order to render them more productive. The amount of the taxes may be more than our lands will sell for. It is obvious that the lands in the Northern States, which gentlemen suppose to be more populous than this country, are more valuable and better cultivated than ours; yet their lands will be taxed no higher than our lands. A rich man there, from report, does not possess so large a body of land as a poor man to the southward. If so, a common poor man here will have much more to pay for poor land, than the rich man there for land of the best quality. This power, being necessarily unequal and oppressive, ought not to be given up. I shall endeavor to be as concise as possible. We find that the ratification of nine states shall be sufficient for its establishment between the states so ratifying the same. This, as has been already taken notice of, is a violation of the Confederation. We find that, by that system, no alteration was to take place, except it was ratified by every state in the Union. Now, by comparing this last article of the Constitution to that part of the Confederation, we find a most flagrant violation. The Articles of Confederation were sent out with all solemnity on so solemn an occasion, and were to be always binding on the states; but, to our astonishment, we see that nine states may do away the force of the whole. I think, without exaggeration, that it will be looked upon, by foreign nations, as a serious and alarming change.

How do we know that, if we propose amendments, they shall be obtained after actual ratification? May not these amendments be proposed with equal propriety, and more safety, as the condition of our adoption? If they violate the 13th article of the Confederation in this manner, may they not, with equal propriety, refuse to adopt amendments, although agreed to and wished for by two thirds of the states? This violation of the old system is a precedent for such proceedings as these. That would be a violation destructive to our felicity. We are now determing a question deeply affecting the happiness of millions yet unborn. It is the policy of freemen to guard their privileges. Let us, then, as far as we can, exclude the possibility of tyranny. The President is chosen for four years; the senators for six years. Where is our remedy for the most flagrant abuses? It is thought that North Carolina is to have an opportunity of choosing one third of their senatorial members, and all their representatives, once in two years. This would be the case as to senators, if they should be of the first class; but, at any rate, it is to be after six years. But if they deviate from their duty, they cannot be excluded and changed the first year, as the members of Congress can now by the Confederation. How can it be said to be safe to trust so much power in the hands of such men, who are not responsible or amenable for misconduct?

As it has been the policy of every state in the Union to guard elections, we ought to be more punctual in this case.

The members of Congress now may be recalled. But in this Constitution they cannot be recalled. The continuance of the President and Senate is too long. It will be objected, by some gentlemen, that, if they are good, why not continue them? But I would ask, How are we to find out whether they be good or bad? The individuals who assented to any bad law are not easily discriminated from others. They will, if individually inquired of, deny that they gave it their approbation; and it is in their power to conceal their transactions as long as they please.

There is also the President's conditional negative on the laws. After a bill is presented to him, and he disapproves of it, it is to be sent back to that house where it originated, for their consideration. Let us consider the effects of this for a few moments. Suppose it originates in the Senate, and passes there by a large majority; suppose it passes in the House of Representatives unanimously; it must be transmitted to the President. If he objects, it is sent back to the Senate; if two thirds do not agree to it in the Senate, what is the consequence? Does the House of Representatives ever hear of it afterwards? No, it drops, because it must be passed by two thirds of both houses; and as only a majority of the Senate agreed to it, it cannot become a law. This is giving a power to the President to overrule fifteen members of the Senate and every member of the House of Representatives. These are my objections. I look upon it to be unsafe to drag each other from the most remote parts in the state to the Supreme Federal Court, which has appellate jurisdiction of causes arising under the Constitution, and of controversies between citizens of different states. I grant, if it be a contract between a citizen of Virginia and a citizen of North Carolina, the suit must be brought here; but may they not appeal to the Supreme Court, which has cognizance of law and fact? They may be carried to Philadelphia. They ought to have limited the sum on which appeals should lie. They may appeal on a suit for only ten pounds. Such a trifling sum as this would be paid by a man who thought he did not owe it, rather than go such a distance. It would be prudence in him so to do. This would be very oppressive.

I doubt my own judgment; experience has taught me to be diffident; but I hope to be excused and put right if I be mistaken.

The power of raising armies is also very exceptionable. I am not well acquainted with the government of other countries, but a man of any information knows that the king of Great Britain cannot raise and support armies. He may call for and raise men, but he has no money to support them. But Congress is to have power to raise and support armies. Forty thousand men from North Carolina could not be refused without violating the Constitution. I wish amendments to these parts. I agree it is not our business to inquire whether the continent be invaded or not. The general legislature ought to superintend the care of this. Treaties are to be the supreme law of the land. This has been sufficiently discussed: it must be amended some way or other. If the Constitution be adopted, it ought to be the supreme law of the land, and a perpetual rule for the governors and governed. But if treaties are to be the supreme law of the land, it may repeal the laws of different states, and render nugatory our bill of rights.

As to a religious test, had the article which excludes it provided none but what had been in the states heretofore, I would not have objected to it. It would secure religion. Religious liberty ought to be provided for. I acquiesce with the gentleman, who spoke, on this point, my sentiments better than I could have done myself. For my part, in reviewing the qualifications necessary for a President, I did not suppose that the pope could occupy the President's chair. But let us remember that we form a government for millions not yet in existence. I have not the art of divination. In the course of four or five hundred years, I do not know how it will work. This is most certain, that Papists may occupy that chair, and Mahometans may take it. I see nothing against it. There is a disqualification, I believe, in every state in the Union—it ought to be so in this system. It is said that all power not given is retained. I find they thought proper to insert negative clauses in the Constitution, restraining the general government from the exercise of certain powers. These were unnecessary if the doctrine be true, that every thing not given is retained. From the insertion of these we may conclude the doctrine to be fallacious. Mr. Lancaster then observed, that he would disapprove of the Constitution as it then stood. His own feelings, and his duty to his constituents, induced him to do so. Some people, he said, thought a delegate might act independently 'of the people. He thought otherwise, and that every delegate was bound by their instructions, and if he did any thing repugnant to their wishes, he betrayed his trust. He thought himself bound by the voice of the people, whatever other gentlemen might think. He would cheerfully agree to adopt, if he thought it would be of general utility; but as he thought it would have a contrary effect, and as he believed a great majority of the people were against it, he would oppose its adoption.

18. *Bills of Rights and Amendments Proposed by Massachusetts, and Virginia,*

In the campaign over ratification of the Constitution, as in many American political campaigns since 1787–1788, it was the practice of both sides to engage in a considerable amount of mutual hyperbole. This results in a problem of interpretation for the political analyst: to separate the froth of debate from its substance. There is no certain way of doing this, but a study of the amendments proposed by the state conventions in which the vote was close does provide some insight into the real core of Antifederalist opposition, and also into that process of compromise that has been essential to the operation of republican government in this country. Throughout the debate, as the reader will have observed in the preceding documents, the Antifederalists frequently called for a new convention, or for ratification conditional upon the prior adoption of various amendments. The Federalists, aware of the great difficulties the Philadelphia convention had experienced in achieving agreement upon its compromise proposal, feared that any subsequent attempt prior to ratification would not be as successful. In some of the states, they offered as a substitute a gentlemen's agreement to work for amendments after ratification according to the procedures provided in the Constitution.

Massachusetts was the first state in which this arrangement between the two sides was made, and the list of proposed amendments is relatively modest in number. The idea caught on, and was elaborated upon in states that acted later. The Virginia list is a very ambitious one, and it was apparently very closely followed in New York and North Carolina, the latter state first rejecting the Constitution unless amendments were adopted prior to its own ratification. (It later ratified, in December of 1789, without amendments.) A look at the four lists will quickly reveal what ideas were common to Antifederalists in these quite different states. All were concerned with making explicit that the powers not delegated to the national government were reserved to the states (but not, it should be noted, alternatively to "the people," as the Tenth Amendment was to state). All were concerned that the ratio of representatives to population should not be less than one per thirty thousand until the House of Representatives reached a membership of two hundred. All were concerned with the application of Congress's power to regulate the time, manner, and place of election; all wanted to limit Congress's power of direct taxation to cases in which a state failed or refused to meet its fair requisition as determined by the census. All were concerned with at least some of the provisions associated with a Bill of Rights, and all but Massachusetts prefaced its list with a model of such a bill, which was strongly influenced by Virginia's Revolutionary Declaration of Rights, and which was reflected in the federal Bill of Rights subsequently adopted. There were also other similarities, and there were some differences which indicated particular interests or opinions. A few of these are worthy of comment.

Virginia, New York, and North Carolina all sought to inhibit the power of Congress to act in certain areas by requiring extraordinary majority rather than simple majority votes. This obviously reflected the very prevalent fear and distrust of Congress held by the Antifederalists, and their unwillingness to submit to simple majority rule exercised by national representatives. New York proposed more restrictive qualifications for membership in the House of Representatives and the Senate: Only native-born citizens, or those who had been naturalized on or before July 4, 1776, or who had held commission under the United States during the war and who had subsequently been naturalized, were to be eligible. The same requirements would have been applied to the President and Vice-President, and both these officers and members of Congress would be required to be freeholders. These requirements were, of course, much less equalitarian or democratic than those provided for in the original constitution, especially as applied to the House of Representatives. New York also proposed an interesting check on the Supreme Court: Persons aggrieved by its decision in areas of original jurisdiction might appeal to a commission of "Men learned in the Law" to be appointed by the President by and with the advice and consent of the Senate. New York, together with Virginia and North Carolina, proposed some tribunal other than the Senate for the trial of impeachments, thus repairing what was thought to be a violation of the principle of separation of powers. These states also proposed compulsory rotation in office for the President, and New York did so for the Senate as well. All four states sought to limit the jurisdiction of the inferior federal courts which the Constitution authorized Congress to establish.

Taken together, the amendments proposed from all the states added up to a strong desire to limit the power of the national government, and to impose additional checks upon its exercise. Some, such as those relating to taxation, would have had serious ramifications had they been adopted, and would probably have weakened the union very severely, and perhaps have crippled its power to govern effectively. Those which were actually adopted as part of the Bill of Rights, on the other hand, have proved their value as guarantees of individual liberty without permanently impairing the power of the national government to pursue the other goals listed in the Preamble to the Constitution. Because of the great amount of duplication in the Virginia, New York, and North Carolina lists, only that of Virginia, together with that of Massachusetts, has been published here.

AMENDMENTS PROPOSED
BY THE MASSACHUSETTS STATE CONVENTION.

Commonwealth of Massachusetts.

In Convention of the delegates of the PEOPLE of the Com-

The Convention having impartially discussed, & fully considered The Constitution for the United States of America, reported to Congress by the Convention of Delegates from the United States of America, & submitted to us by a resolution of the General Court of the said Commonwealth, passed the twenty fifth day of October last past, & acknowledging with grateful hearts, the goodness of the Supreme Ruler of the Universe in affording the People of the United States in the course of his providence an opportunity deliberately & peaceably without fraud or surprize of entering into an explicit & solemn Compact with each other by assenting to & ratifying a New Constitution in order to form a more perfect Union, establish Justice, insure Domestic tranquillity, provide for the common defence, promote the general welfare & secure the blessings of Liberty to themselves & their posterity; Do in the name & in behalf of the People of the Commonwealth of Massachusetts assent to & ratify the said Constitution for the United States of America.

And as it is the opinion of this Convention that certain amendments & alterations in the said Constitution would remove the fears & quiet the apprehensions of many of the good people of this Commonwealth & more effectually guard against an undue administration of the Federal Government, The Convention do therefore recommend that the following alterations & provisions be introduced into the said Constitution.

First, That it be explicitly declared that all Powers not expressly delegated by the aforesaid Constitution are reserved to the several States to be by them exercised.

Secondly, That there shall be one representative to every thirty thousand persons according to the Census men-

Reprinted from *Documentary History of the Constitution*, in *Bulletin of the Bureau of Rolls and Library*, Department of State, Washington, D. C. No. 5 (May 1894) Appendix, pp. 93–96.

tioned in the Constitution until the whole number of the Representatives amounts to Two hundred.

Thirdly, That Congress do not exercise the powers vested in them by the fourth Section of the first article, but in cases when a State shall neglect or refuse to make the regulations therein mentioned or shall make regulations subversive of the rights of the People to a free & equal representation in Congress agreeably to the Constitution.

Fourthly, That Congress do not lay direct Taxes but when the Monies arising from the Impost & Excise are insufficient for the publick exigencies nor then until Congress shall have first made a requisition upon the States to assess levy & pay their respective proportions of such Requisition agreeably to the Census fixed in the said Constitution; in such way & manner as the Legislature of the States shall think best, & in such case if any State shall neglect or refuse to pay its proportion pursuant to such requisition then Congress may assess & levy such State's proportion together with interest thereon at the rate of Six per cent per annum from the time of payment prescribed in such requisition.

Fifthly, That Congress erect no Company of Merchants with exclusive advantages of commerce.

Sixthly, That no person shall be tried for any Crime by which he may incur an infamous punishment or loss of life until he be first indicted by a Grand Jury, except in such cases as may arise in the Government & regulation of the Land & Naval forces.

Seventhly, The Supreme Judicial Federal Court shall have no jurisdiction of Causes between Citizens of different States unless the matter in dispute whether it concerns the realty or personalty be of the value of three thousand dollars at the least nor shall the Federal Judicial Powers extend to any actions between Citizens of different States where the matter in dispute whether it concerns the Realty or personalty is not of the value of Fifteen hundred dollars at the least.

Eighthly, In civil actions between Citizens of different States every issue of fact arising in Actions at common law shall be tried by a Jury if the parties or either of them request it.

Ninthly, Congress shall at no time consent that any person holding an office of trust or profit under the United States shall accept of a title of Nobility or any other title or office from any King, prince or Foreign State.

And the Convention do in the name & in behalf of the People of this Commonwealth enjoin it upon their Representatives in Congress at all times until the alterations & provisions aforesaid have been considered agreeably to the Fifth article of the said Constitution to exert all their influence & use all reasonable & legal methods to obtain a ratification of the said alterations & provisions in such manner as is provided in the said Article.

And that the United States in Congress Assembled may have due notice of the Assent & Ratification of the said Constitution by this Convention it is, Resolved, that the Assent & Ratification aforesaid be engrossed on Parchment together with the recommendation & injunction aforesaid & with this resolution & that His Excellence John Hancock Esqr President & the Honble William Cushing Esqr Vice President, of this Convention transmit the same, countersigned by the Secretary of the Convention under their hands & seals to the United States in Congress Assembled.

JOHN HANCOCK President

W^M CUSHING Vice President

GEORGE RICHARDS MINOT, Secretary.

Pursuant to the Resolution aforesaid We the President & Vice President abovenamed Do hereby transmit to the

United States in Congress Assembled, the same Resolution
with the above Assent and Ratification of the Constitution
aforesaid for the United States, And the recommendation
& injunction above specified.

In Witness whereof We have hereunto set our hands &
Seals at Boston in the Commonwealth aforesaid this
Seventh day of February Anno Domini, one thousand
Seven Hundred & Eighty eight, and in the Twelfth year of
the Independence of the United States of America.

JOHN HANCOCK PRESIDENT   [*seal.*]

W^M CUSHING VICE PRESIDENT [*seal*]

DECLARATION OF RIGHTS AND AMENDMENTS
PROPOSED BY THE VIRGINIA CONVENTION.

Friday, *June* 27, 1788.

Another engrossed form of the ratification, agreed to on
Wednesday last, containing the proposed Constitution of
government, as recommended by the federal Convention
on the seventeenth day of September, one thousand seven
hundred and eighty-seven, being prepared by the secretary, was read and signed by the president, in behalf of the
Convention.

On motion, *Ordered,* That the said ratification be
deposited by the secretary of this Convention in the archives of the General Assembly of this state.

Mr. WYTHE reported, from the committee appointed,
such *amendments* to the proposed Constitution of government for the United States as were by them deemed necessary to be recommended to the consideration of the
Congress which shall first assemble under the said Constitution, to be acted upon according to the mode prescribed

---

Elliot, *Debates,* III, 657–663.

in the 5th article thereof; and he read the same in his place, and afterwards delivered them in at the clerk's table, where the same were again read, and are as follows:—

"That there be a declaration or bill of rights asserting, and securing from encroachment, the essential and unalienable rights of the people, in some such manner as the following:—

"1st. That there are certain natural rights, of which men, when they form a social compact, cannot deprive or divest their posterity; among which are the enjoyment of life and liberty, with the means of acquiring, possessing, and protecting property, and pursuing and obtaining happiness and safety.

"2d. That all power is naturally invested in, and consequently derived from, the people; that magistrates therefore are their *trustees* and *agents*, at all times amenable to them.

"3d. That government ought to be instituted for the common benefit, protection, and security of the people; and that the doctrine of non-resistance against arbitrary power and oppression is absurd, slavish, and destructive to the good and happiness of mankind.

"4th. That no man or set of men are entitled to separate or exclusive public emoluments or privileges from the community, but in consideration of public services, which not being descendible, neither ought the offices of magistrate, legislator, or judge, or any other public office, to be hereditary.

"5th. That the legislative, executive, and judicial powers of government should be separate and distinct; and, that the members of the two first may be restrained from oppression by feeling and participating the public burdens, they should, at fixed periods, be reduced to a private station, return into the mass of the people, and the vacancies be supplied by certain and regular elections, in which all or any part of the former members to be eligible or ineligible, as the rules of the Constitution of government, and the laws, shall direct.

"6th. That the elections of representatives in the legislature ought to be free and frequent, and all men having sufficient evidence of permanent common interest with, and attachment to, the community, ought to have the right of suffrage; and no aid, charge, tax, or fee, can be set, rated or levied, upon the people without their own consent, or that of their representatives, so elected; nor can they be bound by any law to which they have not, in like manner, assented, for the public good.

"7th. That all power of suspending laws, or the execution of laws, by any authority, without the consent of the representatives of the people in the legislature, is injurious to their rights, and ought not to be exercised.

"8th. That, in all criminal and capital prosecutions, a man hath a right to demand the cause and nature of his accusation, to be confronted with the accusers and witnesses, to call for evidence, and be allowed counsel in his favor, and to a fair and speedy trial by an impartial jury of his vicinage, without whose unanimous consent he cannot be found guilty, (except in the government of the land and naval forces;) nor can he be compelled to give evidence against himself.

"9th. That no freeman ought to be taken, imprisoned, or disseized of his freehold, liberties, privileges, or franchises, or outlawed, or exiled, or in any manner destroyed or deprived of his life, liberty, or property, but by the law of the land.

"10th. That every freeman restrained of his liberty is entitled to a remedy, to inquire into the lawfulness thereof, and to remove the same, if unlawful, and that such remedy ought not to be denied nor delayed.

"11th. That, in controversies respecting property, and in suits between man and man, the ancient trial by jury is one of the greatest securities to the rights of the people, and to remain sacred and inviolable.

"12th. That every freeman ought to find a certain remedy, by recourse to the laws, for all injuries and wrongs he may receive in his person, property, or character. He ought to obtain right and justice freely, without sale, completely and without denial, promptly and without delay; and that all establishments or regulations contravening these rights are oppressive and unjust.

"13th. That excessive bail ought not to be required, nor excessive fines imposed, nor cruel and unusual punishments inflicted.

"14th. That every freeman has a right to be secure from all unreasonable searches and seizures of his person, his papers, and property; all warrants, therefore, to search suspected places, or seize any freeman, his papers, or property, without information on oath (or affirmation of a person religiously scrupulous of taking an oath) of legal and sufficient cause, are grievous and oppressive; and all general warrants to search suspected places, or to apprehend any suspected person, without specially naming or describing the place or person, are dangerous, and ought not to be granted.

"15th. That the people have a right peaceably to assemble together to consult for the common good, or to instruct their representatives; and that every freeman has a right to petition or apply to the legislature for redress of grievances.

"16th. That the people have a right to freedom of speech, and of writing and publishing their sentiments; that the freedom of the press is one of the greatest bulwarks of liberty, and ought not to be violated.

"17th. That the people have a right to keep and bear

arms; that a well-regulated militia, composed of the body of the people trained to arms, is the proper, natural, and safe defence of a free state; that standing armies, in time of peace, are dangerous to liberty, and therefore ought to be avoided, as far as the circumstances and protection of the community will admit; and that, in all cases, the military should be under strict subordination to, and governed by, the civil power.

"18th. That no soldier in time of peace ought to be quartered in any house without the consent of the owner, and in time of war in such manner only as the law directs.

"19th. That any person religiously scrupulous of bearing arms ought to be exempted, upon payment of an equivalent to employ another to bear arms in his stead.

"20th. That religion, or the duty which we owe to our Creator, and the manner of discharging it, can be directed only by reason and conviction, not by force or violence; and therefore all men have an equal, natural, and unalienable right to the free exercise of religion, according to the dictates of conscience, and that no particular religious sect or society ought to be favored or established, by law, in preference to others."

AMENDMENTS TO THE CONSTITUTION

"1st. That each state in the Union shall respectively retain every power, jurisdiction, and right, which is not by this Constitution delegated to the Congress of the United States, or to the departments of the federal government.

"2nd. That there shall be one representative for every thirty thousand according to the enumeration or census mentioned in the Constitution, until the whole number of representatives amounts to two hundred: after which, that number shall be continued or increased, as Congress shall direct, upon the principles fixed in the Constitution, by apportioning the representatives of each state to some greater number of people, from time to time, as population increases.

"3d. When the Congress shall lay direct taxes or excises, they shall immediately inform the executive power of each state, of the quota of such state, according to the census herein directed, which is proposed to be thereby raised; and if the legislature of any state shall pass a law which shall be effectual for raising such quota at the time required by Congress, the taxes and excises laid by Congress shall not be collected in such state.

"4th. That the members of the Senate and House of Representatives shall be ineligible to and incapable of holding, any civil office under the authority of the United States during the time for which they shall respectively be elected.

"5th. That the journals of the proceedings of the Senate and House of Representatives shall be published at least once in every year, except such parts thereof, relating to treaties, alliances, or military operations, as, in their judgment, require secrecy.

"6th. That a regular statement and account of the receipts and expenditures of public money shall be published at least once a year.

"7th. That no commercial treaty shall be ratified without the concurrence of two thirds of the whole number of the members of the Senate; and no treaty ceding, contracting, restraining, or suspending, the territorial rights or claims of the United States, or any of them, or their, or any of their rights or claims to fishing in the American seas, or navigating the American rivers, shall be made, but in cases of the most urgent and extreme necessity; nor shall any such treaty be ratified without the concurrence of three fourths of the whole number of the members of both houses respectively.

"8th. That no navigation law, or law regulating commerce, shall be passed without the consent of two thirds of the members present, in both houses.

"9th. That no standing army, or regular troops, shall be raised, or kept up, in time of peace, without the consent of two thirds of the members present, in both houses.

"10th. That no soldier shall be enlisted for any longer term than four years, except in time of war, and then for no longer term than the continuance of the war.

"11th. That each state respectively shall have the power to provide for organizing, arming, and disciplining its own militia, whensoever Congress shall omit or neglect to provide for the same. That the militia shall not be subject to martial law, except when in actual service, in time of war, invasion, or rebellion; and when not in the actual service of the United States, shall be subject only to such fines, penalties, and punishments, as shall be directed or inflicted by the laws of its own state.

"12th. That the exclusive power of legislation given to Congress over the federal town and its adjacent district, and other places, purchased or to be purchased by Congress of any of the states, shall extend only to such regulations as respect the police and good government thereof.

"13th. That no person shall be capable of being President of the United States for more than eight years in any term of sixteen years.

"14th. That the judicial power of the United States shall be vested in one Supreme Court, and in such courts of admiralty as Congress may from time to time ordain and establish in any of the different states. The judicial power shall extend to all cases in law and equity arising under treaties made, or which shall be made, under the authority of the United States; to all cases affecting ambassadors, other foreign ministers, and consuls; to all cases of admiralty and maritime jurisdiction; to controversies to which

the United States shall be a party; to controversies between two or more states, and between parties claiming
lands under the grants of different states. In all cases affecting ambassadors, other foreign ministers, and consuls,
and those in which a state shall be a party, the Supreme
Court shall have original jurisdiction; in all other cases
before mentioned, the Supreme Court shall have appellate
jurisdiction, as to matters of law only, except in cases of
equity, and of admiralty, and maritime jurisdiction, in
which the Supreme Court shall have appellate jurisdiction
both as to law and fact, with such exceptions and under
such regulations as the Congress shall make: but the judicial power of the United States shall extend to no case
where the cause of action shall have originated before the
ratification of the Constitution, except in disputes between
states about their territory, disputes between persons
claiming lands under the grants of different states, and
suits for debts due to the United States.

"15th. That, in criminal prosecutions, no man shall be
restrained in the exercise of the usual and accustomed
right of challenging or excepting to the jury.

"16th. That Congress shall not alter, modify, or interfere in the times, places, or manner of holding elections for
senators and representatives, or either of them, except
when the legislature of any state shall neglect, refuse, or
be disabled, by invasion or rebellion, to prescribe the same.

"17th. That those clauses which declare that Congress
shall not exercise certain powers, be not interpreted, in
any manner whatsoever, to extend the powers of Congress;
but that they be construed either as making exceptions to
the specified powers where this shall be the case, or otherwise, as inserted merely for greater caution.

"18th. That the laws ascertaining the compensation of
senators and representatives for their services, be post-
poned, in their operation, until after the election of repre-

sentatives immediately succeeding the passing thereof; that excepted which shall first be passed on the subject.

"19th. That some tribunal other than the Senate be provided for trying impeachments of senators.

"20th. That the salary of a judge shall not be increased or diminished during his continuance in office, otherwise than by general regulations of salary, which may take place on a revision of the subject at stated periods of not less than seven years, to commence from the time such salaries shall be first ascertained by Congress."

And the Convention do, in the name and behalf of the people of this commonwealth, enjoin it upon their representatives in Congress to exert all their influence, and use all reasonable and legal methods, to obtain a ratification of the foregoing alterations and provisions, in the manner provided by the 5th article of the said Constitution; and, in all congressional laws to be passed in the mean time, to conform to the spirit of these amendments, as far as the said Constitution will admit.

And so much of the said amendments as is contained in the first twenty articles, constituting the bill of rights, being read again, *Resolved*, That this Convention doth concur therein.

The other amendments to the said proposed Constitution, contained in twenty-one articles, being then again read, a motion was made, and the question being put,—to amend the same by striking out the third article, containing these words,—

"When Congress shall lay direct taxes or excises, they shall immediately inform the executive power of each state of the quota of such state, according to the census herein directed, which is proposed to be thereby raised; and if the legislature of any state shall pass a law which shall be effectual for raising such quota at the time required by

Congress, the taxes and excises laid by Congress shall not be collected in such state."—

It passed in the negative—ayes, 65; noes, 85.

On motion of Mr. George Nicholas, seconded by Mr. Benjamin Harrison, the ayes and noes on the said question were taken, as followeth:—

AYES.

George Parker,
George Nicholas,
Wilson Nicholas,
Zachariah Johnson,
Archibald Stuart,
William Dark,
Adam Stephen,
Martin M'Ferran,
J. Taylor of Caroline,
David Stuart,
Charles Simms,
John Prunty,
Abel Seymour,
Governor Randolph,
John Marshall,
Nathaniel Burwell,
Robert Andrews,
James Johnson,
Rice Bullock,
Burdet Ashton,
William Thornton,
Henry Towles,
Archibald Woods,
James Madison,
J. Gordon, of Orange,
William Ronald,
Thomas Walke,
Anthony Walke,
Benjamin Wilson,

John Wilson,
William Peachy,
Andrew Moore,
Thomas Lewis,
Humphrey Marshall,
Martin Pickett,
Humphrey Brooke,
John S. Woodcock,
Alexander White,
Warner Lewis,
Thomas Smith,
John Stewart,
Daniel Fisher,
Alexander Woodrow,
George Jackson,
Levin Powell,
Wm. Overton Callis,
Ralph Wormley, Jun.,
Francis Corbin,
William M'Clerry,
James Webb,
James Taylor, of Norfolk
John Stringer,
Littleton Eyre,
Walter Jones,
Thomas Gaskins,
Gabriel Jones,
Jacob Rinker,
John Williams,

Benjamin Blunt,
Samuel Kello,
John Allen,
Cole Digges,

Bushrod Washington,
George Wythe,
Thomas Matthews.

NOES.

E. Pendleton *President*,
William Clayton,
Burwell Bassett,
Matthew Walton,
John Steele,
Robert Williams,
John Wilson,
Thomas Turpin,
Patrick Henry,
Edmund Ruffin,
Theodorick Bland,
William Grayson,
Cuthbert Bullitt,
Walter Tomlin,
William M'Kee,
Thomas Carter,
Henry Dickenson,
James Monroe,
James Dawson,
George Mason,
Andrew Buchanan,
John Hartwell Cocke,
John Howell Briggs,
Thomas Edmonds,
Richard Carey,
Samuel Edminson,
James Montgomery,
Edmund Custis,
John Pride,
William Cabell,
Samuel Jordan Cabell,
John Trigg,

Charles Clay,
William Fleming,
Henry Lee, of Bourbon,
John Jones,
Binns Jones,
Charles Patteson,
David Bell,
Robert Alexander,
Edmund Winston,
Thomas Read,
Paul Carrington,
Benjamin Harrison,
John Tyler,
David Patteson,
Stephen Pankey, Jun.,
Joseph Michaux,
French Strother,
Joseph Jones,
Miles King,
Joseph Haden,
John Early,
Thomas Arthurs,
John Guerrant,
William Sampson,
Isaac Coles,
George Carrington,
Parke Goodali,
John Carter Littlepage,
Thomas Cooper,
William Fleete,
Thomas Roane,
Holt Richeson,

Benjamin Temple,	Green Clay,
J. Gordon, of Lancaster,	Samuel Hopkins,
Stephens T. Mason,	Richard Kennon,
William White,	Thomas Allen,
Jonathan Patteson,	Alexander Robertson,
John Logan	Walter Crocket,
Henry Pawling,	Abraham Trigg,
John Miller,	Solomon Shepherd.

And then, the main question being put, that this Convention doth concur with the committee in the said amendments,—

It was resolved in the affirmative.

On motion, *Ordered*, That the foregoing amendments be fairly engrossed upon parchment, signed by the president of this Convention, and by him transmitted, together with the ratification of the federal Constitution, to the United States in Congress assembled.

On motion, *Ordered*, That a fair, engrossed copy of the ratification of the federal Constitution, with the subsequent amendments this day agreed to, signed by the president, and attested by the secretary of this Convention, be transmitted by the president, in the name of the Convention, to the executive or legislature of each state in the Union.

Ordered, That the secretary do cause the journal of the proceedings of this Convention to be fairly entered into a well-bound book, and, after being signed by the president, and attested by the secretary, that he deposit the same in the archives of the privy council, or council of state.

On motion, *Ordered*, That the printer to this Convention do strike, forthwith, fifty copies of the ratification and subsequent amendments of the federal Constitution, for the use of each county in the commonwealth.

On motion, *Ordered*, That the public auditor be requested to adjust the accounts of the printer to the Convention for his services, and of the workmen who made some temporary repairs and alterations in the new academy, for the accommodation of the Convention, and to grant his warrant on the treasurer for the sum due the respective claimants.

On motion, *Resolved, unanimously,* That *the thanks* of the Convention be presented to *the president,* for his able, upright, and impartial discharge of the duties of that office.

Whereupon *the president* made his acknowledgment to the Convention for so distinguished a mark of its approbation.

And then the Convention adjourned, *"sine die."*

Signed, EDMUND PENDLETON, *President.*

Attest, JOHN BECKLEY, *Secretary.*

INDEX *

Abraham, 148–149
Adams, John, cxiii, 1, 5–8, 107, 278
*Address and Reasons of Dissent
. . . of the Convention of
Pennsylvania . . .* , lin, liin.,
27–60, 71
Admiralty and maritime jurisdiction, 50
"Agrippa," Letters of, xlviii, lxvin.,
lxxixn., cxiiin., 131–160, 301
"Albany Manifesto," 359–367
Alexander the Great, 148–149
Algerines, 279, 280
Allegheny Mountains, legality of
sale of, 274
Ambassadors, 12, 192, 231, 267,
306, 343, 392, 433–434
Amendments, 421–423
manner of making, 244–246
power to make, 365–367
proposed by Massachusetts,
423–427
proposed by Virginia, 427–439
(*See also* Conventions, States)
American Mercury, The, 161n.
American Revolution, the, xxxiii-
xxxiv, 4, 118, 237

causes of, xxiii, xxvi, 134
controversy preceding, xxvi
problems before and during,
296–297
American Whig, 305
(*See also* Whigs, *An Old Whig*)
An Address of Thanks . . . , 1n.
*"An Officer of the Late Continental
Army,"* xlixn.
An Old Whig, xl
(*See also* American Whig,
Whigs)
Anarchy, dangers of, 70–76,
213–214
Anglo-American liberalism, cvii
Anti-intellectualism, l
Appellate jurisdiction, 14, 164,
167, 232
Aristocracy
"artificial," cxiii, 17
dangers of an, xlix, lii, lxi, 2–7,
12–13, 127–129, 197, 315–316,
385–387, 399
definition of, xxv
and democracy, xcvii, 69–87,
216–217, 316
despotic, 8, 218

---

*This index was prepared by Elizabeth Sullivan of New York.

441

THE AMERICAN HERITAGE SERIES

TOPICAL VOLUMES